Handcraft
ILLUSTRATED

~ 1997 ~

Copyright 1997 © by *Handcraft Illustrated*
All rights reserved
including the right of reproduction
in whole or in part in any form

Published by
Boston Common Press Limited Partnership
17 Station Street
Brookline Village, Massachusetts 02147

ISBN: 0-9640179-8-9
ISSN: Pending

To get home delivery of future issues of *Handcraft Illustrated* magazine call 1-800-526-8447 or write to the above address.

$29.95

NUMBER FIFTEEN   WINTER 1997

Handcraft
ILUSTRATED

30 Projects for Winter Weekends

PLUS:
Annual Mail-Order Directory

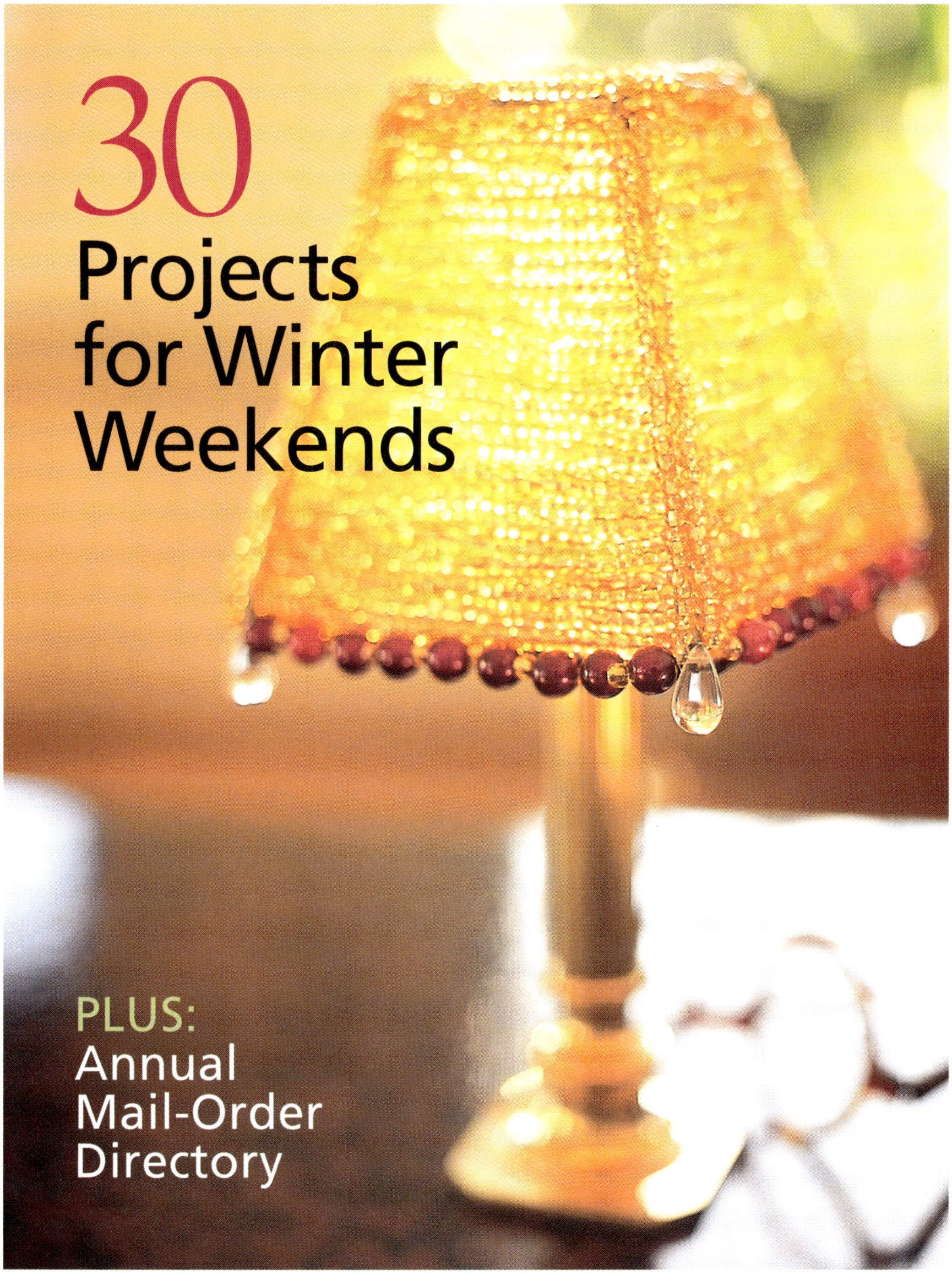

Heirloom Beaded Lampshade
Make Your Own Shade for a Fraction of the Retail Cost

Embossed Velvet Pillow
Emboss Your Own Velvet Using Coils of Armature Wire

Bathroom Shag Rug
Transform Cut Rags into a Soft Throw Rug

Arts & Crafts-Style Tiled Table
Turn an Oak Table into a Period Look-Alike

Alice-in-Wonderland Cookies
The Look of Hand-Painted Ceramic with Paste Food Coloring

ALSO
Fast Sweater Pillows
Faux Marquetry Frame
Quick-Sew Buffet Tray
Faux Suede and Crocodile Backpacks

NUMBER FIFTEEN WINTER 1997

Contents

Embossed velvet pillow, page 17

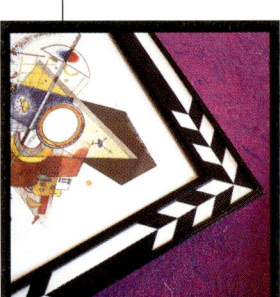

Faux marquetry frame, page 18

Alice-in-Wonderland cookies, page 30

COVER PHOTOGRAPH:
Carl Tremblay

STYLING:
Ritch Holben

Paint a festive plaid cachepot. *See* page 12.

FEATURE STORIES

8
ROSE BLOSSOM GARLAND
Fashion a sweeping floral garland using handmade crepe paper roses accented with velvet foliage.

10
BATHROOM SHAG RUG
Use a basic knitting stitch and strips of fabric to create a cozy bathroom throw rug.

12
PAINTED PLAID CACHEPOT
Transform a plain tin container into a decorative planter using bold shades of paint. Finishing accents such as dots and squiggles complete the festive look.

14
ARTS & CRAFTS–STYLE TILED TABLETOP
Build this period look-alike by setting assorted tiles inside an oak framework.

17
EMBOSSED VELVET PILLOW
Use coils of armature wire to imprint a pattern on squares of velvet, then add a pillow form to create a soft throw cushion.

18
FAUX EBONY AND IVORY MARQUETRY FRAME
Transform an unfinished wooden frame into an old-world masterpiece using cut paper and a simple decoupage technique.

20
LAVENDER BOLSTER PILLOW
Make your own bath pillow using a dinner napkin, rolled batting, and dried lavender.

22
BATH SUNDRIES
Mix up your own body lotion, massage oil, and bath salts with our master recipes, then "flavor" each recipe with essential oil.

25
BEADED CANDLESHADE
Forget those beaded shades in retail stores. Build your own version for a fraction of the cost using a wire shade and glass beads.

26
HOME SWEET HOME SIGN
Create an antique wall plaque using self-adhesive wooden letters and a crackled paint finish.

28
FRENCH BUFFET TRAY
Sew together a pair of colorful napkins to make a softly sculptured tableware and napkin dish.

30
ALICE-IN-WONDERLAND FANTASY COOKIES
Re-create the look of hand-painted ceramic ornaments by decorating sugar cookies with paste food coloring.

32
FAUX SUEDE AND CROCODILE BACKPACKS
Select an unusual fabric such as Ultrasuede or vinyl, then sew a backpack in one of two sizes using our five-piece pattern.

36
APPLIQUÉ BLANKET TURNOVER
Dress up an ordinary blanket with this appliquéd wool turnover.

38
FOOLPROOF HAND-PAINTED WALLS
Create a template for freehand painting by hanging a sheer lace panel from the ceiling, then casting a patterned shadow onto your walls.

39
ANNUAL MAIL-ORDER DIRECTORY
Having trouble locating materials in your local craft or fabric store? Give our yearly list of mail-order catalogs a try.

IN EVERY ISSUE
NOTES FROM READERS   2
QUICK TIPS   4
GREAT MARRIAGES   6
THE PERFECT GIFT   7
PATTERNS   44
SOURCES & RESOURCES   48
QUICK PROJECTS   49
SWEATER PILLOWS   BACK COVER

Handcraft ILLUSTRATED

EDITOR
Carol Endler Sterbenz

EXECUTIVE EDITOR
Barbara Bourassa

ART DIRECTOR
Amy Klee

SENIOR EDITOR
Michio Ryan

MANAGING EDITOR
Keith Powers

DIRECTIONS EDITOR
Candie Frankel

COPY EDITOR
Gary Pfitzer

EDITORIAL ASSISTANT
Elizabeth Cameron

PUBLISHER AND FOUNDER
Christopher Kimball

EDITORIAL CONSULTANT
John Kelsey

MARKETING DIRECTOR
Adrienne Kimball

VICE PRESIDENT CIRCULATION
Carolyn Adams

CIRCULATION MANAGER
David Mack

FULFILLMENT MANAGER
Larisa Greiner

NEWSSTAND MANAGER
Jonathan Venier

VICE PRESIDENT PRODUCTION AND TECHNOLOGY
James McCormack

EDITORIAL PRODUCTION MANAGER
Sheila Datz

ADVERTISING PRODUCTION MANAGER
Pamela Slattery

SYSTEMS ADMINISTRATOR
Paul Mulvaney

PRODUCTION ARTIST
Kevin Moeller

EDITORIAL PRODUCTION ASSISTANT
Robert Parsons

ADVERTISING PRODUCTION ASSISTANT
Daniel Frey

VICE PRESIDENT
Jeffrey Feingold

CONTROLLER
Lisa A. Carullo

ACCOUNTING ASSISTANT
Mandy Shito

OFFICE MANAGER
Tonya Estey

Handcraft Illustrated (ISSN 1072-0529) is published quarterly by Boston Common Press Limited Partners, 17 Station Street, P.O. Box 509, Brookline, MA 02147-0509. Copyright 1997 Boston Common Press Limited Partners. Second-class postage paid at Boston, MA, and additional mailing offices, USPS #011-895. For list rental information, please contact Direct Media, 200 Pemberwick Road, Greenwich, CT 06830; (203) 532-1000. Editorial office: 17 Station Street, P.O. Box 509, Brookline, MA 02147-0509; (617) 232-1000, FAX (617) 232-1572, e-mail: hndcftill-@aol.com. Editorial contributions should be sent or e-mailed to: Editor, Handcraft Illustrated. We cannot assume responsibility for manuscripts submitted to us. Submissions will be returned only if accompanied by a large, self-addressed stamped envelope. Subscription rates: $24.95 for one year; $45 for two years; $65 for three years. (Canada: add $3 per year; all other countries add $12 per year.) Postmaster: Send all new orders, subscription inquiries, and change of address notices to Handcraft Illustrated, P.O. Box 7448, Red Oak, IA 51591-0448. Single copies: $4 in U.S.; $4.95 in Canada and other countries. Back issues available for $5 each. PRINTED IN THE U.S.A.

Rather than put ™ in every occurrence of trademarked names, we state that we are using the names only and in an editorial fashion and to the benefit of the trademark owner, with no intention of infringement of the trademark.

Note to Readers: Every effort has been made to present the information in this publication in a clear, complete, and accurate manner. It is important that all instructions are followed carefully, as failure to do so could result in injury. Boston Common Press Limited Partners, the editors, and the authors disclaim any and all liability resulting therefrom.

From the Editor

PARIS, FRANCE: IT IS EARLY SATURDAY morning. By nightfall on this day, three relative strangers will forever be related by one handmade object. (I've changed certain names in this story to protect their privacy.)

Madame Claire Bobigny:
It is 4:30 in the morning. Madame Bobigny is descending the three flights of wooden stairs that lead from her apartment to the ground level pâtisserie she owns with her husband. Under her arm, she carries a small handmade fireplace screen. Once inside her shop, she turns on the lights, illuminating dark counters and empty glass shelves. She sets the screen down on a side counter. The screen, cut from a piece of wood in the shape of an urn, has been decoupaged with flowers in grand profusion. Madame has made many screens like this one over the years, which she sells to a local merchant specializing in home decoration. At first, the work was undertaken as a matter of economics, but now she is inspired by the process of making a few of these little works of art each year. The merchant who buys her work has agreed to pick up the screen on his way to Rue de Grenelle, the street on which his cluttered yet orderly shop is located.

Monsieur Jean-Luc George:
Monsieur George drives his car along the Périphérique, taking Porte St. Cloud onto the Left Bank, mindless of the clatter of the poorly fitted door of his little Citroën, a reliable relic bought in the fifties. After a few quick turns, he pushes down the clutch, grinds the gear shift into neutral, and jerks the car to a stop in front of a pâtisserie. The shop's gleaming window is filled with rows of tiny pastries nested in crenellated paper caps. Leaving the motor running, he disappears through the front door, only to return a few minutes later with the colorful fireplace screen, which he places in the back seat of his car. Annoyed at having made himself come into town on a Saturday, he speeds off to his shop on Rue de Grenelle and the neglected paperwork on his desk.

Monsieur George enters the shop, absentmindedly leaving the door slightly open. The open door reveals a shop filled with a jumble of needlepoint pillows, sagging carpets on hooks, decorative *boutis* (quilts), and statues of monkeys that have been transformed into lamps. His trip to the trade show last month has yielded much of this merchandise, mostly new, but he is fortunate now to have a fine piece of work from a local artist. He pushes the fireplace screen to a prominent place in the front window, then walks to his desk to begin working.

Although it is a bulky purchase...the fireplace screen is something I cannot leave behind.

Madame Carol Endler Sterbenz:
I am sitting at a small kitchen table in my daughter's apartment in Paris, where she is spending her junior year of college. I slide a little pile of postcards toward me and write on one: "Paris at last...I have eased into life in a city rich in fundamentals: good food, wine, friends, and shopping." It is the day before my scheduled departure, and I have met with a friend who has handed me a list of the holy grail of shops for great home decorations and art.

With a low sun washing copper light over the buildings, I make my way to "Pour la Maison," a shop I have passed several times without particular interest. But today I see an exceptional fireplace screen in the front window, and a *fermé* sign on the door. I lean forward with cupped hands to get a better look, and the door moves open. When I call out, a scowling man appears from behind a curtain in the back. After a brief but ultimately companionable exchange, I leave with the fireplace screen (and the details of its history described above). Although it is a bulky purchase that I will have to carry onto the plane, the fireplace screen is something I simply can not leave behind.

While we may view the series of events that brought the screen into my hands as unremarkable, if taken together, they continue a thread of connections that began in the past, and will extend, ultimately, to many, many others, including you, our readers. It is connections like this that remind me of the reassuring serendipity of life.

Carol Endler Sterbenz

P.S. Look for the screen in an upcoming issue of *Handcraft Illustrated*.

Notes from Readers

Learn how to force lily of the valley, recycle your greeting cards, paint a porch, or transfer photos to Christmas ornaments.

Forcing Lily of the Valley

I've seen lily of the valley growing in the gardens in the spring and love the look of this delicate perennial. Can you teach me how to force them indoors during the winter?
SANDRA INMAN
BOSTON, MA

A native of the northern temperate regions, the dainty, fragrant, white lily of the valley, *Convallaria majalis*, has long been a favorite garden plant. Forcing lily of the valley in pots is not difficult, and the resulting flowers are quite beautiful and long-lasting. After blooming, the plants can be planted outside in a shady spot, where they will return year after year in cool climates.

Lily of the valley can be forced into bloom at any time of year provided treated crowns, or pips, are available. Pips can be mail-ordered from White Flower Farm from December through April (write or call the company at P.O. Box 50, Litchfield, CT 06759; 203-496-1661). When ordering, allow for shipping time plus three weeks for flowering. Upon arrival, the pips should be planted immediately or put in a cool, dark place. This is important, as the buds will begin to emerge before the leaves if light is admitted.

To get started, you will need a decorative 4-inch terra-cotta pot, approximately 2 cups of potting soil (or 2½ cups of seed-starting mix), about ½ cup of sand, ½ cup of finely milled peat moss, three lily of the valley pips, ½ teaspoon of grass seed, and a pair of scissors.

Start by mixing the potting soil with the sand. Remove the pips from the packaging and separate them; the roots will be long and possibly tangled. Trim the roots so they fit into the pot without bending them up—they should be about the same height as the pot. Arrange the pips in a triangle in the pot with the roots facing down and the shoots facing up. Place the potting soil and sand mixture around the pips, keeping them in position as you add soil. Leave the tips of the shoots just above the soil line. Sprinkle the grass seed evenly on top of the soil, then cover it with a thin layer of peat moss. Gently tamp the pot, and water evenly so that water begins to seep out the bottom of the pot. Place the pot in a fairly warm area (65 to 75 degrees) and out of the direct sunlight. As the shoots emerge, gradually move the pot to a sunny window. Check the water daily, keeping the soil moist. You will need to water every few days when the shoots are small and daily as the leaves and buds emerge.

Belt Buckle Backs for Polymer Clay Designs

I need help finding a belt buckle back to which I can attach a polymer clay design. I have combed local fabric stores and many catalogs and can't locate such an item anywhere. Also, I understand there is a National Polymer Clay Guild. Could you give me the address?
BETTY RICHARDSON
ST. LOUIS, MO

Try a leather shop for belt buckle backs. Tandy Leather, with over 275 locations nationwide, carries such a variety of buckle backs, including one flat version that might work with your designs. Write or call the company and ask for a catalog: Tandy Leather, 141 Concord Plaza Shopping Center, Lindbergh at Baptist Church Road, St. Louis, MO 63128; 800-552-9319.

The National Polymer Clay Guild is also a great place to turn to for an answer to your question. The Guild, located at 1350 Beverly Road, Suite 115-345, McLean, VA 22101, studies and promotes the use of polymer clay as a medium. In addition to publicizing polymer clay work to the public, the Guild offers its members a newsletter, publications, a loan-by-mail library, a slide bank, an annual retreat, and regular meetings. Individual memberships cost $20; phone the Guild at 202-895-5212.

You can even turn to the Internet for answers regarding polymer clay or for lists of suppliers and information. We dialed the newsgroup "rec.crafts.polymerclay" and found it's a great way to seek out answers to design problems or ask other artists for advice.

Crackle Finish and Spray-on Shellac

In your Spring 1996 issue, you answered a reader's questions about crackle finish. Can you provide a mail-order source for LeFranc and Bourgeous Crackle Picture Varnish and Bulls Eye spray-on shellac?
JAN AMMANN
VIA THE INTERNET

Bulls Eye Spray Shellac, which is neater and faster than brush-on shellac, can be purchased from Dick Blick Art Materials. A 12-ounce spray can costs $5.20. Write or call the company at P.O. Box 1267, Galesburg, IL 61402-1267; 800-447-8192. Pearl Paint Company, Inc. carries LeFranc and Bourgeous Crackle Picture Varnish; 75 milliliters is priced at $6.13. To order, call the company at 800-221-6845, ext. 2297, or write: 308 Canal Street, New York, NY 10013-2572.

Dip Your Own Candles

I would like to find wax and dyes for use in hand-dipping candles, as well as instructions on dipping.
JOAN MILLER
BARRINGTON, RI

Craft King, Inc. sells a variety of candle-making supplies, including scents, colors, molds, wax, kits, and books. Call 800-769-9494 or write the company at P.O. Box 90637, Lakeland, FL 33804. Barker Candle Supplies also carries a wide variety of molds, waxes, wicking, scents, and colors. The catalog, which includes instructions and a listing of books, costs $2. Call 800-543-0601 or write: 15106 10th Avenue SW, Seattle, WA 98166.

Chipboard for Box Making

I make fabric-covered boxes as a cottage business and need a source for process board. I use a type of mat board that is available locally and have been unable to find regular cardboard measuring 1/12-inch thick. Can you help?
PATRICIA LAUNMAN
HARLINGTON HEIGHTS, IL

Chipboard is a smooth, noncorrugated cardboard that comes in different thicknesses. The term "ply" is often used to describe thickness; for example, one-ply chipboard is a little thicker than a cereal box. We recommend two- or three-ply chipboard for box making. Consider your glue, however, before purchasing your chipboard. If your preferred glue contains a lot of moisture, it may cause the chipboard to warp. One glue we like, called Yes Stikflat, has less moisture and works well with chipboard. Otherwise, museum board can withstand more moisture and makes a good substitute.

Pearl Paint Company, Inc. carries chipboard in different sizes and thicknesses. Call 800-221-6845 or write: 308 Canal Street, New York, NY 10013-2572. Yes Stikflat glue can be ordered from New York Central Art Supply, Inc., 62 Third Avenue, New York, NY 10003; 800-950-6111.

Locating Decorative Decals

I hope you can provide me with a source for old-fashioned decoupage labels (the type you dip in water and slide onto furniture). My mother used to use them, and they looked hand-painted. I would also like a mail-order source for cutout decoupage pictures.
DEBORAH WHEATLEY
FREDERICKSBURG, VA

What you are describing is a decal, or a piece of plastic on paper that peels away from a backing when soaked. We've seen little packs of them in flea markets but have not been able to find a mail-order source at this time.

You might want to try rub-on transfers, available from Sunshine

Discount Crafts. Rub-on transfers can be applied to wood, metal, paper, glass, ceramics, plastic, candles, and more. Sunshine also offers a variety of decoupage cutouts for $3.79 per 21-inch-by-32 ¾-inch sheet and books starting at $3.99. Call or write the company at 800-729-2878; P.O. Box 301, Largo, FL 34649-0301.

Glue Glitter for Crafts
Recently I saw your magazine at a friend's home and spotted an item I'd like to find called glue glitter. Can you help?

PENNY DEROSE
GRAYSLAKE, IL

We found a variety of glue glitter products while searching through our mail-order catalogs. Dick Blick Art Materials carries Glitter Magic, available in a 1-ounce tube for $1.50. Call 800-447-8192 or write the company at P.O. Box 1267, Galesburg, IL 61402-1267. You can also try Crayola Washable Glitter Glue Pens, priced at $3.49 per set of three colors, but not for use on fabrics. They can be ordered from Sax Arts & Crafts, P.O. Box 510710, New Berlin, WI 53151-0710; 800-558-6696. Or try metallic Glitz Glitter Glue, designed for highlighting or drawing details, but not on fabric. Call Stampendous! at 800-869-0474 for a referral to the retail store nearest you.

Clear Glycerin Soap
I read in your Spring 1996 issue about a supplier of bulk soap in 1- and 5-pound blocks. I am looking for soap in these size increments, but I need clear glycerin soap. It is beautiful when melted and reformed with delicate tints and natural items such as flowers and herbs inside. Remelting individual bars gets to be quite costly, and the premade blocks are usually already colored.

KIMBERLY STERLING-ADAMS
BETHEL, CT

In truth, all soaps are glycerin soaps, according to Karon Adams, owner of Sugar Plum Sundries in Stone Mountain, Georgia. Most commercial companies remove the glycerin and sell it as a separate product. Adding an extra large amount of glycerin is what makes "glycerin soap." On a molecular level, soap forms in a crystalline structure, says Adams. It is difficult for a home soap maker to make a clear soap because the molecules have to be coaxed into what is called a colloid, or the rearrangement of the molecules so you can see between them.

For the lowest retail price, Adams suggests purchasing clear soaps at a local department store. For more information, contact Karon Adams at 404-297-0158 or write to Sugar Plum Sundries at 5152 Fair Forest Drive, Stone Mountain, GA 30088.

Recycling Greeting Cards
I save all my holiday greeting cards and would love to recycle them for use next year. Do you have any ideas?

LAURA CAHNERS
SAN JOSE, CA

Here are a handful of ideas for your old greeting and Christmas cards. Cards can be used in a collage to create a scene, which could be very creative for kids as well as adults. Use them to decorate an old shoebox for storage or to decoupage a wastebasket. You could even tear off the front of the card, fold it into a box, and make a tree ornament out of it. Card tops can also be made into gift tags (*see* Quick Tips, Christmas 1996).

We know a lot of people who also like to save wrapping paper. One quick gift using giftwrap is decorated soap. All you need is household wax, flat bars of soap, and a stove. Wet the soap very slightly in order to "glue" your cutout onto the soap, then dip the top of the soap into melted wax to "laminate" the design. Don't dip the entire soap, or you won't be able to use the soap after the wax has dried.

In Search of Needlepoint Lace
Six years ago I went to Venice, Italy. On an island called Burano, I saw a woman making a lace that was described as a "lace only the old women are making." Apparently, the process for making this beautiful lace exists only in these women's heads. I was able to watch a few minutes, but was hurried off by the tour director. The woman had a pillow on her lap with a paper design attached. Using white thread and what appeared to be a sewing needle, she followed the design with what looked like a very simple stitch. When it was done, it was said she would tear off the paper and have a piece of lace. I don't remember the name or exactly how it is done. Can you help me find out how to do this beautiful art?

T. LINDA MERRILL
HOPKINTON, MA

It sounds like you are referring to the art of needlepoint lace, which was developed in Italy and practiced mainly around Venice, Genoa, Milan, and Burano. According to *Lace and Lace Making* by Alice-May Bullock (Larousse & Company, Inc., 1981), the art died out in the 1860s but was revived in 1872 when someone discovered a very old woman who remembered the art. She taught a younger woman, who then became the teacher of the first eight pupils at the New Burano School of Lace.

For further information and history, check out *The Story of Lace and Embroidery* by David E. Schwab (Fairchild Publications, Inc., 1951) or *Lace and Lace-Making* by Marian Powys (Charles T. Branford Company, 1953). To learn more about making needlepoint lace, look for *The Gentle Arts* (Exeter Books, 1986). It contains directions and illustrations on making needlepoint lace as well as other kinds of lace.

Mail-Order Pinecones
I'm looking for a source of pinecones to use in my craft and Christmas projects. Can you help?

KENT A. STAFF
SCAPPOOSE, OR

Creative Craft House sells such pinecone varieties as Black Spruce, Douglas Fir, Sequoia, Hemlock, Pinion, and more. The company also sells other natural products for use in crafts. Call the company at 520-754-3300 or write: P.O. Box 2567, Bullhead City, AZ 86430. A catalog can be purchased for $2, which is refundable with your first purchase.

Painting a Porch
I would like to try my hand at painting a design on the floor of my screened-in porch. I'm not certain whether to use stain or some other form of paint. What can you recommend? Also, I'd like to sponge paint the ceiling, but I'm not certain if the weather would play havoc with the painted surface.

SHEILA COBB
ZIONSVILLE, IN

For a high-traffic porch floor, you need a paint that wears well. For greatest durability, we recommend exterior deck enamel, the type of paint used on boats. If you can't find the color you want, try purchasing a light-colored shade of deck base and tint it with additives, such as Tints-All Paint Pigments. If you just want a decorative border and the design won't be walked on that much, you can use solid deck stains, which can be found in many attractive colors.

As for the ceiling, if the wood and paint are in good condition, any exterior paint can be used. Sponging is fine as long as compatible paints are used (e.g., acrylic with acrylic). You don't need a sealer unless the sponged finish is directly exposed to weather. In more humid climates, you may add fungicide additives (found in paint stores) to the paint in order to keep mold from growing. A few drops per gallon should suffice.

Custom Photo Ornaments
Our historical society would like to find a company that puts pictures on ornaments. We own over five hundred old pictures of our village and would like to put them on ornaments, then sell them to our residents. Any ideas?

BEATRICE G. BENNETT
WALTON, NY

Your best bet is to check with a local silk-screen printing company. Keep in mind that you'll probably have to silk-screen a large quantity of one picture in order to keep your costs down. Ask your local company for details. As for the ornaments themselves, it's probably too difficult to put the pictures on a round ball, so consider a flat ornament instead. ◆

ATTENTION READERS

Need advice on a craft or home decorating project?
Drop us a line, and we'll find the answer. Although we can't respond to every letter we receive, we will try to publish those letters with the widest appeal. Please include your name, address, and a daytime telephone number with your question. Write to:

Notes from Readers
Handcraft Illustrated
17 Station Street
P.O. Box 509
Brookline Village, MA
02147-0509

Quick Tips

NO-SLIP DRAFTING TABLE
To keep tools from sliding off her slanted drafting table, Roxanne Beard of Ashland, Ohio, laid strips of rubbery shelf-lining material along the edges.

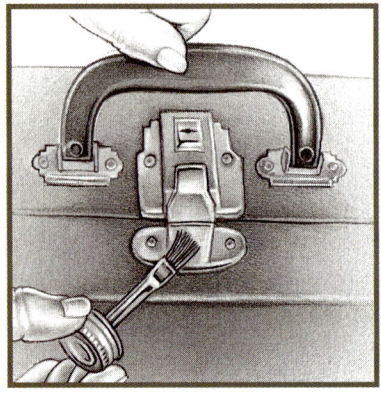

MASKING HARDWARE
When Dolores Prichard of Greeley, Colorado, paints trunks, she first coats the hardware with rubber cement. The cement creates a protective mask that is easily peeled off once the paint is dry.

FAUX FINISH PAINTING MITTS
If sponges tend to slip out of your grasp during sponging or faux finishing projects, try making your own sponging mitt. (This mitt sells for $11 in a hardware store. You can make your own for under $2.)

1. Trace the sponge outline on the palm side of a canvas glove.

2. Apply washable fabric glue to the sponge and the glove.

3. Press the sponge onto the glove. Let the glue dry for 24 hours.

4. To keep your hand dry during painting, wear a latex glove as a liner.

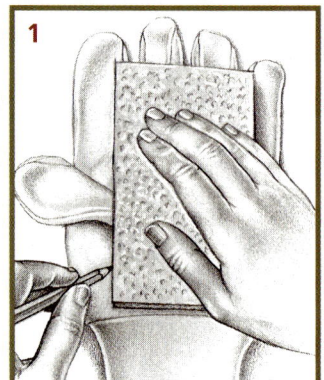 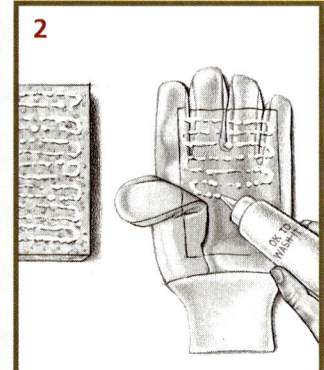
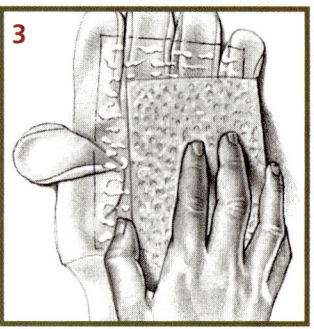 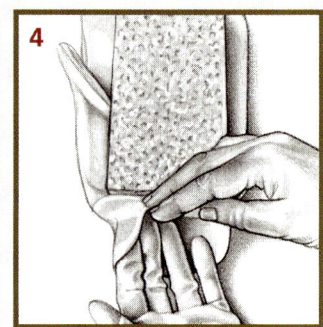

ATTENTION READERS
See Your Tip in Print
Do you have a craft, sewing, or decorating technique you'd like to share with other readers? We'll give you a one-year complimentary subscription for each Quick Tip that we publish. Send your tip to:

Quick Tips
Handcraft Illustrated
17 Station Street
P.O. Box 509
Brookline Village, MA
02147-0509

Please include your name, address, and daytime phone number.

ILLUSTRATION:
Harry Davis

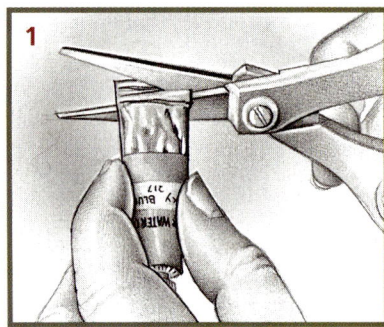 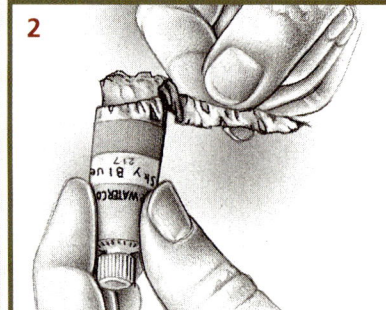

WATERCOLOR TIPS
To salvage dried-out tube watercolors, Pauline Robinson of Franklin, Massachusetts, uses a 7-day vitamin dispenser.

1. Cut the watercolor tube across the bottom.

2. Peel off and discard the tube foil.

3. Put the hardened pigments into individual dispenser wells.

4. Add a few drops of water to soften the pigment for painting.

4 HANDCRAFT ILLUSTRATED • WINTER 1997

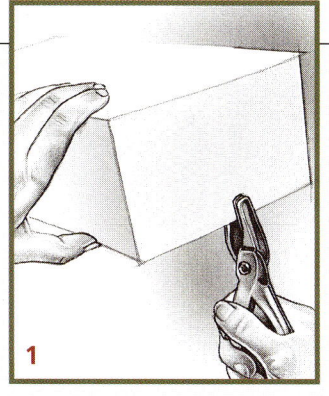 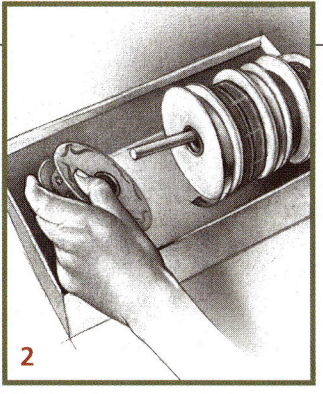 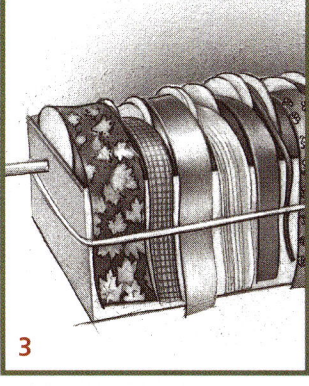

RIBBON DISPENSER

The ribbon storage tip in our *Fall 1996* issue reminded Beth Pitcher of Takoma Park, Maryland, of her shoebox method.

1. Cut or punch a hole at each end of a shoebox just below the center top edge.

2. Cut a dowel to match the box size, then run it from hole to hole to hold the ribbon spools.

3. Secure the ribbon ends under a jumbo rubber band.

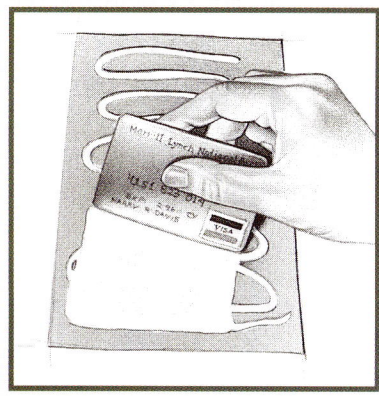

FAST GLUE SPREADER

To spread glue evenly over a large surface, use an expired credit card as a squeegee. Thanks to Martha Ann Henry from Severn, Maryland, for this tip.

 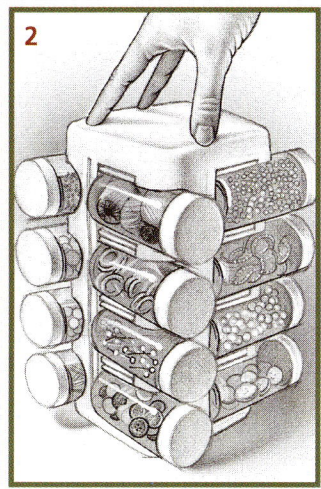

SMALL ITEMS STORAGE

Two readers write that small glass jars provide visible, accessible storage for frequently used notions.

Sandie Wrightson of Alva, Florida, uses baby food jars mounted up off her work surface (illustration 1). Use screws to attach the caps of baby food jars to a shelf underside. Fill the jars, then twist each one into a cap.

Karyn DeLuca of Cortlandt Manor, New York, turned a revolving spice rack into a notions display (illustration 2). Beads, snaps, pin backs, and similar findings are easy to locate and use.

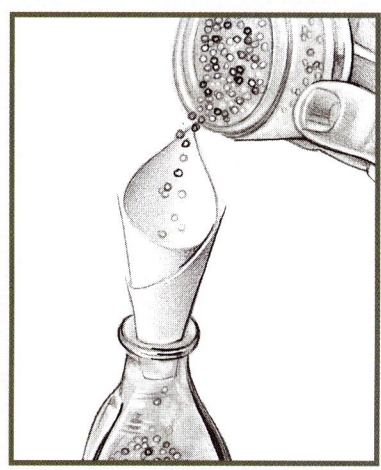

PERFECT PAPER FUNNEL

Roll a Post-it Note to make a paper cone funnel that won't pop open. This tip comes from Susan Dunham of Plattsburgh, New York.

COFFEE FILTER ROSES

Nancy Rhodes of Redding, California, dyes and shapes these dainty roses in one easy operation.

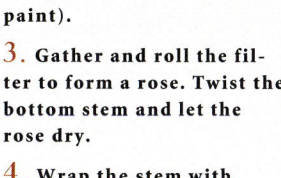 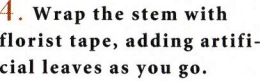 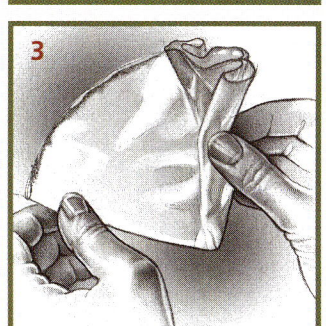 

1. Spray-mist a basket-style coffee filter, then fold it into quarters.

2. Dip the curved edge into strong raspberry or cranberry tea (or diluted red paint).

3. Gather and roll the filter to form a rose. Twist the bottom stem and let the rose dry.

4. Wrap the stem with florist tape, adding artificial leaves as you go.

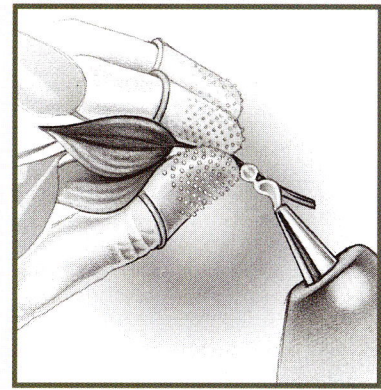

NO HOT-GLUE BURNS

To prevent fingertip burns when using her hot-glue gun, Annabelle Frausto of San Antonio, Texas, wears rubber fingers. Traditionally used in office work for gripping and sorting papers, rubber fingers are sold in stationery stores.

Great Marriages

Create new interest at your windows by layering two sheer curtains.

SHEER DELIGHT

COLOR PHOTOGRAPHY:
Carl Tremblay

STYLING:
Ritch Holben

Traditionally, sheer curtains are used to filter light without shutting it out completely. Patterned sheers also filter light, but add texture and character. Although it's possible to purchase intricately detailed sheers, you can create the same effect by pairing two less expensive designs. The resulting combination offers more depth and dynamic than one layer of fabric alone, and when lit with natural sunlight, throws a dramatic new pattern across your floor, rugs, and furniture.

The goal is to find any two sheers that play well together without losing their own personality. We paired a feminine floral silk sheer, for instance, with a bold masculine plaid. The resulting combination is fresh and enchanting.

For variation, try playing with scale, mixing a small polka dot pattern with a large arabesque design. Mix metallics to create a new color, like a platinum-colored open weave grid over a bronze leafy lace, or try a vertical stripe over a horizontal pattern.

The same principle can be applied to other home decorations, such as layering two sheer tablecloths together, pairing two sheer bed curtains, or draping two sheer remnants around a lampshade. ◆

The Perfect Gift

Create one-of-a-kind packaging for tiny gifts using eggshells and nail polish.

EGG BOXES

Nothing says "precious" better than an egg. These tiny, colorful gift boxes, made from real eggs, are the perfect way to package that heirloom locket, ring, or pair of earrings. Use them for a special occasion, to hold Easter candies, for a bridesmaid present, or to send a special note.

To make an egg box, score a large white egg lightly along the desired break line using an X-Acto knife. Make a jagged line for authenticity. Then tap the scored line very gently with the handle of the knife until it gives way. Use the X-Acto knife again to cut the egg's membrane, holding the egg over a bowl to catch the contents as they spill out. Gently rinse each half of the shell, then let the eggshell halves dry thoroughly (preferably overnight).

To color and strengthen the eggs, we used nail polish. Choose two complementary or contrasting colors and paint the egg halves with a quick, dappling technique. You can paint the inside of the shell as well or leave it plain. Hinge the halves with a small piece of ribbon glued to both halves. To hold the egg box closed, glue a 12-inch piece of ribbon or metallic cording to the outside of the egg at the hinge point. ◆

COLOR PHOTOGRAPHY:
Carl Tremblay

STYLING:
Ritch Holben

HOME DECORATING

Rose Blossom Garland

Fashion a sweeping floral garland using handmade crepe paper roses accented with velvet foliage.

🌹 BY CAROL ENDLER STERBENZ

The large crepe paper roses on this garland measure about 3½ inches across while the medium roses measure about 1¾ inches.

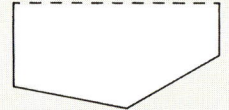

PATTERNS
See page 45 for pattern pieces.

COLOR PHOTOGRAPHY:
Carl Tremblay

ILLUSTRATION:
Michael Gellatly

STYLING:
Ritch Holben

MATERIALS
- 7½" x 20" crepe paper in the following colors:*
  White
  Pale Pink
  Pink or Rose
  Mauve
- Matte fabric rose leaves
- Silk roses and buds up to 1" across*
- Leafy garland vine
- 18-gauge cloth-covered stem wire
- 30-gauge spool wire
- ½"-wide olive green florist tape

*See note at beginning of instructions for amounts.

You'll also need:
large and small petal patterns (see page 45); pliers with wire cutters; ¼"- and ⅜"-diameter dowels; access to photocopier; ruler; and scissors.

CREPE PAPER IS THE PERFECT medium for making lifelike roses. Its sheerness simulates the look of real rose petals, and the crinkly quality of the paper makes it easy to stretch and shape into three-dimensional forms. Crepe paper roses can be used in a variety of ways; I used mine to create a vinelike garland, mixing in store-bought silk roses and buds and velvet foliage in order to achieve a subtle blend of textures.

To make my roses more lifelike, I layered three shades of paper for each petal. This mixing and matching of colors varies the intensity of the cumulative color. A petal formed from three pink crepe layers, for example, will be more intense than one formed from two pink layers and one white one. The darker, more intense shades make up the rose's inner petals while the lighter ones are used for the outer petals, which fade first on a live rose. This is particularly effective for the fully formed blossom because when the petal's edge is curled over, the rim color is different from that on the back of the petal.

After all the petals have been cut from crepe paper, each edge is rolled around a dowel to give the petals a soft curl. The curl appears in different places on the petal, depending on where the petal appears within the rose. The innermost petals are curled along their entire top edge, for example, then crimped to create a tighter feel. The middle petals have a curl on each side and a more pointed tip, while the outermost petals are curled along the entire top edge. To further shape the petals, I gently stretched the center area to form a bowl-shaped dome.

When attaching the handmade roses to the garland, arrange them around the core randomly. I recommend wiring them to one side of the garland and bending the heads in various directions for a more natural look.

INSTRUCTIONS

Note: To determine the necessary number of roses, measure the leafy garland vine. The suggested quantity is five roses (mixed sizes) for every 15 inches of garland, though you can vary this number to suit your purpose. Three packages of crepe paper, when layered, will yield approximately twelve large roses and six medium roses. You will need additional packages to vary the color palette.

Making the Large Roses

1. *Cut layered petals.* Photocopy and cut out large and small petal patterns (see page 45). Using your own color combinations, cut and layer three 20"-square sheets of paper so grain runs in same direction. Keeping layers together, cut four 2½" squares, three to five 3½" squares, and one 6" square. Still keeping layers intact, fold each 2½" square in half along grain line, hold small petal pattern against fold, and cut edges to match pattern (*see* illustration A, below). Repeat with large petal pattern to cut large petals from 3½" squares. Unfold petals, but do not separate layers.

2. *Curl petals.* Lay petals in row, smaller petals at left, with rose outer color face up. Pick up first small petal, set ¼" dowel on top edge, and roll toward you for two to three revolutions (illustration B). To crimp and set curl, push crepe at each end toward middle (illustration C). Remove dowel and return petal to lineup. Curl second petal in same way. Curl and crimp third petal diagonally along sides, so curls meet in point at top edge (illustration D). Repeat diagonal curling until last two petals, changing to ⅜" dowel to curl large petals. On last two petals, curl and crimp diagonal and top edges to form one continuous rounded edge (illustration E).

3. *Shape petals.* Turn petals over. Using thumb, gently stretch and push out middle of each petal to form bowl-shaped dome (illustration F). For innermost petals (first three in lineup), form bowl closer to top edge. For outermost petals (last three in lineup), form bowl closer to lower edge and swell generously.

4. *Make rose core.* Cut 18" length from stem wire, then fold in half. Roll 6" square of crepe paper into tube, rumpling paper to increase bulk. Center tube within wire fold, fold both tube ends up, and twist wire (illustration G). To form core, fold tube ends back down around twisted wire (illustration H). To secure, wrap base with 30-gauge wire, clip wire from spool, and twist ends together (illustration I).

5. *Add petals to rose.* Press first (smallest) petal from lineup against core, opposite crevice. Cup second petal around core, then third petal to fill open space (illustration J). Bind these three petals to core with 30-gauge wire, as in step 4. Continue adding petals from lineup, staggering them around core. Set last two to three petals slightly higher on core so edges cup outward. To secure petals, bind base of rose tightly with 30-gauge wire. Then wrap florist tape firmly around base and down stem. Bind in leaf stem as you tape (illustration K).

Making the Medium Roses
Note: For a smaller, partially open bloom, layer two sheets of crepe paper instead of three sheets.

Cut, curl, shape, and add petals. Cut one 5" square and three to five small petals from 2½" squares (*see* "Making the Large Roses," step 1). Use ¼" dowel to curl petals diagonally along sides, then shape bowls (*see* steps 2 and 3). Make core from 5" square and add petals as with large rose (*see* steps 4 and 5). Shape outermost petals to fall away from core.

Assembling the Garland
Join roses to garland. Lay garland vine flat. Arrange roses along length, interspersing large and medium blooms with small silk roses and buds. For naturalistic trailing effect, place some small blooms and buds near ends of garland. Once arrangement is set, weave stems into vine so all blooms "grow" in same direction. Bind with florist tape. Bend rose heads in various directions for naturalistic look. ◆

> **DESIGNER'S TIP**
> Because these crepe paper roses can be made larger than life, they work well as decorative backdrops for wedding celebrations or parties. They also work on valances, mantels, or as curtain tiebacks, for which the visual prominence of an oversized bloom is not out of place. But they are less suitable where they will be inspected at close range. In a bouquet on a dinner table, for example, they would seem unnaturally large and unreal.

Making the Roses

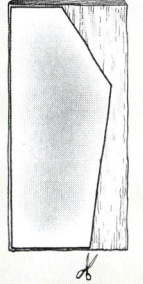

A. Cut each petal from a triple layer of crepe paper, folded vertically along the grain.

B. Roll the top edge of the petal around a dowel.

C. Crimp the rolled section to set the curl.

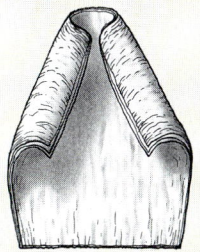

D. On the rose's middle petals, make diagonal curls ending at the top center.

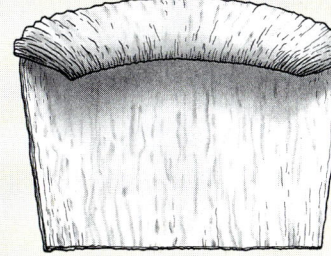

E. On the rose's outermost petals, curl the entire top edge.

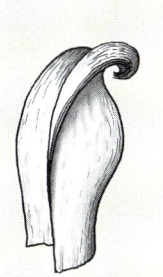

F. Gently stretch the crepe through the middle to give each petal additional shape.

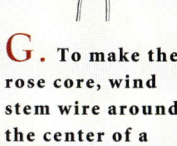

G. To make the rose core, wind stem wire around the center of a crepe paper tube.

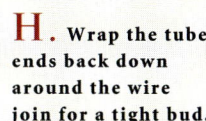

H. Wrap the tube ends back down around the wire join for a tight bud.

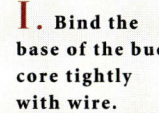

I. Bind the base of the bud core tightly with wire.

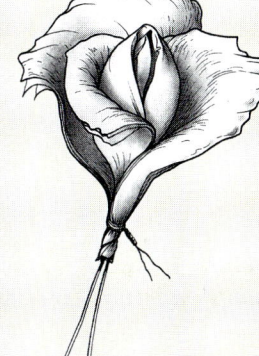

J. Bind the pre-shaped petals around the core in the order indicated.

K. When all of the petals are attached, bind in a leaf stem with florist tape.

HOME DECORATING

Bathroom Shag Rug
Use a basic knitting stitch and strips of fabric to create a cozy bathroom throw rug.

BY SUZANN THOMPSON

This bathroom rag rug uses knit fabric purchased by the yard. You can substitute a variety of other fabrics, such as old T-shirts, denim (cut the strips on the bias), tights, or fleece.

COLOR PHOTOGRAPHY:
Carl Tremblay

SILHOUETTE PHOTOGRAPHY:
Daniel van Ackere

ILLUSTRATION:
Mary Newell DePalma

STYLING:
Ritch Holben

IF YOU CAN CAST ON, KNIT, AND BIND off, you can make a rag rug for any room. I created this rug by knitting a web into which strips of knit fabric are trapped. The center portion of the rug uses alternating strips of cream and mossy green fabric while the outer border uses a shade of melon.

The first step of this project, cutting the strips of fabric, is somewhat time-consuming. To save time, I recommend using a rotary cutter. Before you cut all the strips, cut a test strip lengthwise and another one crosswise across the fabric's grain, then examine them for curling and decide which orientation you prefer. The flat, no-curl strips for my rug were cut along the crosswise grain. If you want a strip with curl, stretch the knit prior to cutting, then cut the strips along the lengthwise grain.

The knitting portion of this project is very fast and easy. The first row, and all the odd-numbered rows, require standard knitting. For the alternating shag rows, however, you'll need to hang a strip of fabric between your needles, then knit over it to secure it in place. The shag is basically folded around every other stitch.

Suzann Thompson is a writer and designer living in the United Kingdom.

INSTRUCTIONS
Cutting the Shag Strips
Using rotary cutter, cut two 1" x 3" test strips from knit fabric, one along lengthwise grain and one along crosswise grain. Select the look you prefer, then cut remainder of fabric accordingly. First cut 1"-wide strips, then cut those strips into 3"-long sections. Keep colors separate.

Knitting the Rug
Note: Refer to illustration A, next page, for schematic of color changes.

On size 8 needles, cast on 89 sts.
Row 1: Knit.
Row 2 (shag st row): K 1, end with yarn in back (illustration B). * Lay melon fabric strip between needles so it hangs evenly in front and back (illustration C), k 1. Lift back of strip through needles to front (illustration D), k 1, end with yard in back (illustration E). * Repeat from * to * to end of row. Repeat rows 1 and 2, end row 18.
Row 19: Knit.
Row 20: K 1, k 11 melon shag sts, * k 2 moss green shag sts, k 2 cream shag sts, * repeat from * to * for 66 sts, k 11 melon shag sts.
Row 21: Knit.
Row 22: K 1, k 11 melon shag sts, * k 2 cream shag sts, k 2 moss green shag sts, * repeat from * to * for 66 sts, knit 11 melon shag sts. Repeat rows 19 through 22 for 25" (measure on wrong side), end even-numbered row.
Next row: Knit.
Next row: Same as row 2. Repeat these two rows for 18 rows total. Bind off. ◆

> **KEY**
>
> **SHAG GAUGE:**
> 16 sts = 4"
> 23 rows = 4"
>
> **ABBREVIATIONS:**
> k = knit
> st = stitch
> sts = stitches

> **MATERIALS**
> *Yields one 22" x 31" rug*
>
> - Six 4-ounce skeins worsted weight yarn
> - 60"-wide single jersey-knit fabric:
>   2¼ yards melon
>   1½ yards cream
>   1½ yards moss green
>
> *You'll also need:*
> size 8 knitting needles; rotary cutter; and tape measure.

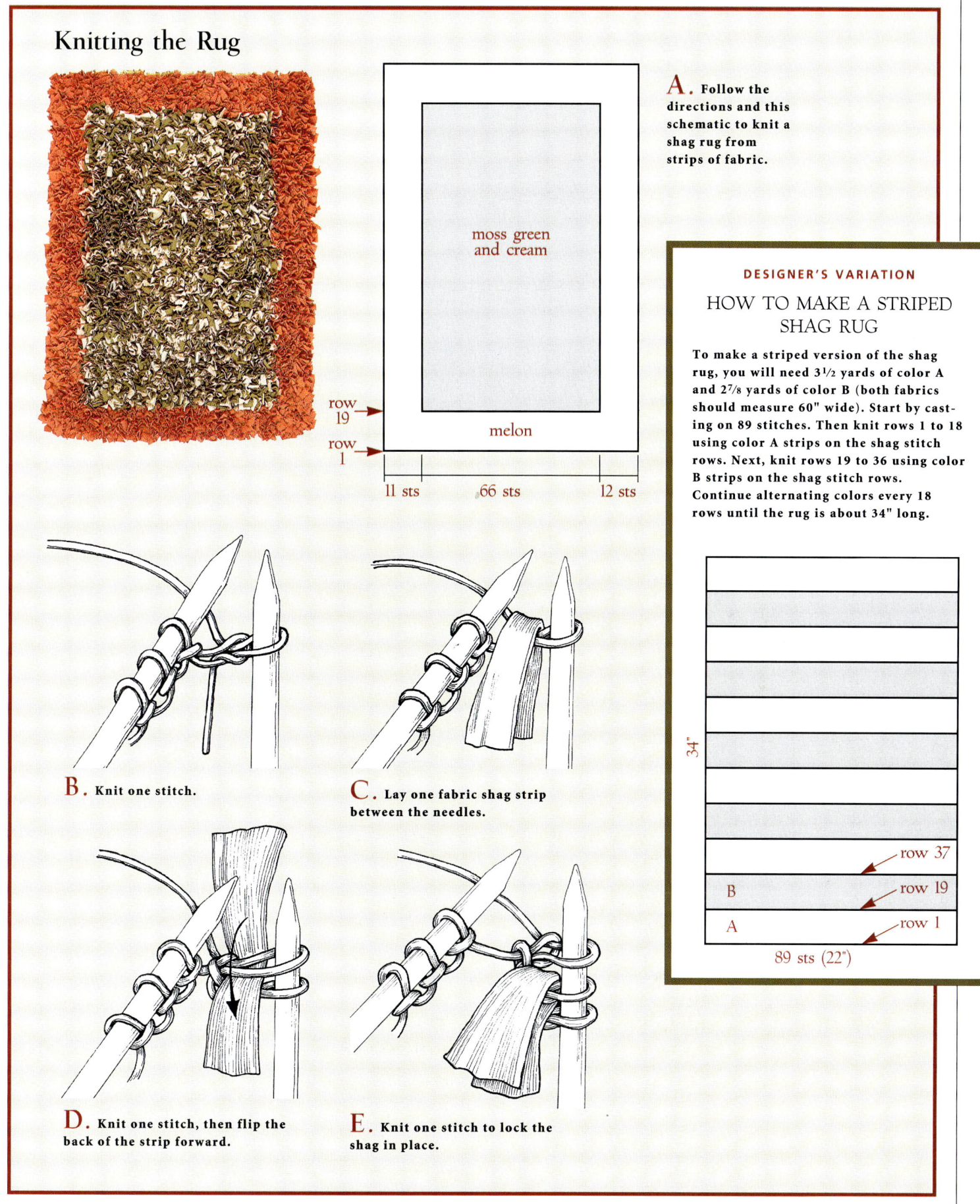

PAINTING

Painted Plaid Cachepot

Transform a plain tin container into a decorative planter using bold shades of paint. Finishing accents such as dots and squiggles complete the festive look.

🌶 BY MICHIO RYAN

The 6¼-inch-square by 5¾-inch-high size of this container makes it perfect for small-scale foliage such as wheatgrass.

COLOR PHOTOGRAPHY:
Carl Tremblay

ILLUSTRATION:
Nenad Jakesevic

STYLING:
Ritch Holben

THE BEAUTY OF THIS TINWARE cachepot revolves around contrast. I wanted to decorate this container using a set of vibrant colors that would not only complement and highlight each other but also offset the foliage of the wheatgrass inside.

To accomplish these goals, my loose plaid pattern uses periwinkle, red-orange, fuchsia, and foliage green on top of a canary yellow basecoat. For a whimsical finishing touch, I added dots of paint along the rim and through the stripes, as well as crisscrossing squiggly lines and a gold border to echo but not compete with the delicate scale of the flora.

My soldered tin cachepot, which measures 6¼ inches square by 5¾ inches high, is ideal in both size and style for this type of decoration. The cachepot has straight sides, which makes the continuation of the stripes from one side to the next quite simple. (This is trickier to do with a flared container.) The container's scalloped rim and soldered feet dress up an otherwise boxy shape.

I started by painting the container with enamel paint in canary yellow. For the stripes I chose Plaid's FolkArt Acrylic Colors, which I found offer better coverage than other brands.

Before applying any stripes, I needed to rough out the plaid pattern using strips of tape. I recommend painter's tape because it won't affect the underlying paint.

After you've painted the plaid pattern, seal the container with one coat of shellac. This way, if you make a mistake while painting the finishing accents, the protective coat of shellac will let you wipe off the wet paint with a damp sponge and start over. After the cachepot is finished, it should be covered with two thin coats of shellac to both level the sheen of the surface and further protect the paint.

INSTRUCTIONS

1. *Paint basecoat.* Make 50-50 solution of vinegar and water. Rub entire container with soft cloth dipped in solution to remove oily residue. Dry container thoroughly. Using flat brush, coat container with primer following manufacturer's instructions. Let dry 1 hour. Mask ball feet with tape. Spray container (inside and out) with three to four very light coats latex enamel, letting dry 10 minutes between coats. Let container dry 24 to 36 hours before proceeding. Remove tape from feet.

2. *Mask container for left diagonal stripes.* Set container on level surface. To mark 45-degree diagonal stripes, stand triangle on edge, flat against outer wall of container, with angle slanting toward upper left. Press painter's tape to surface along triangle edge (*see* illustration A, next page). Repeat to add second piece of tape, allowing random-width space between tape strips for painted stripe. Press on six additional diagonal tapes around container, taping around corners onto adjacent sides. To vary pattern, add more tape to make some masked areas wider (illustration B). Confirm angles with triangle. When complete, you should have eight unmasked stripe areas.

3. *Paint left diagonal stripes.* Using ½" flat brushes, apply Light Periwinkle and Red-Orange paints alternately to eight unmasked stripe areas. To discourage bleeding, run bristles flush against tape edge (illustration C). Remove tape while paint is still wet. Let dry 10 minutes, then apply additional coats freehand as needed to fill gaps or eliminate streaking. Let dry at least 1 hour, but preferably overnight.

4. *Mask and paint right diagonal stripes.*

PAINTING

MATERIALS

- 6¼"-square x 5¾"-high tin cachepot
- Krylon Living Color latex enamel, Canary #7221
- 2 ounces Plaid FolkArt acrylic paints in the following colors: Fresh Foliage #954, Fuchsia #635, Light Periwinkle #640, Red-Orange #629, Warm White #649
- 2 ounces Plaid FolkArt Pure Pigment Color, Rose Crimson #557
- 2 ounces Accent Crown Jewels paint, Imperial Antique Gold #2538
- 1.1 ounce Tulip Colorpoint Paintstitching, Pearl #WH21
- Krylon sandable primer, White #1315
- Clear spray shellac

You'll also need:
1"-wide painter's tape; 45-degree triangle; scissors; two ½"-wide flat sabeline brushes; #3 round sabeline brush; 3 fine-tipped plastic paint syringes; newsprint; white vinegar; 1-cup bowl; measuring cup; soft cloths; paint palette or moist paper towel; and cellulose sponge.

Using triangle method from step 2, apply tape strips to container in right-facing diagonal position, varying width of strips and spacing, to create eight new areas for stripes. Paint unmasked stripe areas as in step 3, alternating between Fresh Foliage and Fuchsia. Paint directly over previously painted stripes (illustration D). Remove tape and apply additional coats as in step 3. Let dry at least 1 hour, but preferably overnight.

5. *Paint stripe intersections.* To create plaid effect, paint rectangular stripe intersections freehand using round brush; refer to chart, above, for colors. At each intersection, press wet brush in center of rectangle to shed excess paint, define corners and edges using tip of brush, then fill in remainder of rectangle (illustration E). Let paint dry at least 1 hour, but preferably overnight.

6. *Add finishing accents.* Seal painted surface with shellac following manufacturer's instructions. Let dry 20 minutes. Transfer Rose Crimson, Warm White, and Light Periwinkle paint to individual paint syringes. Using syringes, paint the following: (1) a series of small white dots ¼" in from left edge of three blue stripes, (2) a series of small crimson dots through center of three right-facing yellow stripes, (3) a squiggly crimson line through center of four right-facing yellow stripes, and (4) a squiggly white line through center of three left-facing yellow stripes (illustration F). Let painted dots and lines dry 20 minutes. Using round brush and working freehand, apply ⅛"-wide band of Imperial Antique Gold paint to lower edge and scalloped rim of container. Let dry 20 minutes. Apply tiny dots of Pearl paint along lower edge and scalloped rim to camouflage irregularities. Turn container upside down and paint five gold stripes on each ball foot. Then squeeze dots of blue paint onto white areas in between. Let dry 1 hour. Seal container with two coats shellac. ◆

INTERSECTION COLORS

At the intersection of the two stripes, cover the resulting rectangle with the intended color. At the intersection of the Fresh Foliage and Light Periwinkle stripes, for instance, paint the "overlap" rectangle in Fuchsia.

STRIPE COLOR	FRESH FOLIAGE	FUCHSIA
LT. PERIWINKLE	Fuchsia	Red-Orange
RED-ORANGE	Lt. Periwinkle	Fresh Foliage

1. Create the left diagonal stripes using Light Periwinkle and Red-Orange.

2. Then create the right diagonal stripes using Fresh Foliage and Fuchsia.

3. Paint the intersections of each stripe using the colors outlined in the chart, above.

4. To finish, add the dots and squiggly lines using a new set of colors.

PAINTING THE CACHEPOT

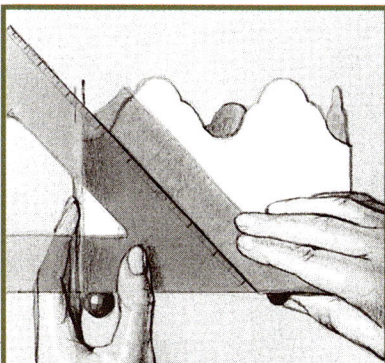

A. Press painter's tape against the cachepot, using a triangle as a guide.

B. Vary the spacing as you continue the tape around the corners.

C. Paint the exposed areas between the strips of tape.

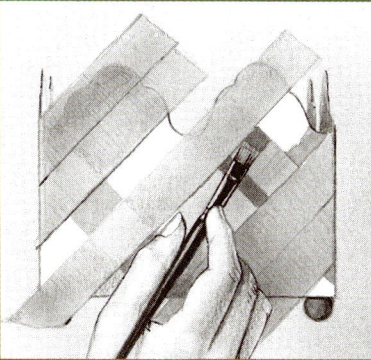

D. Repeat the previous steps to paint stripes in the opposite direction.

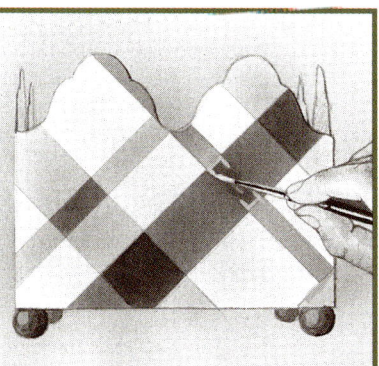

E. For a plaid effect, paint each stripe intersection a contrasting color.

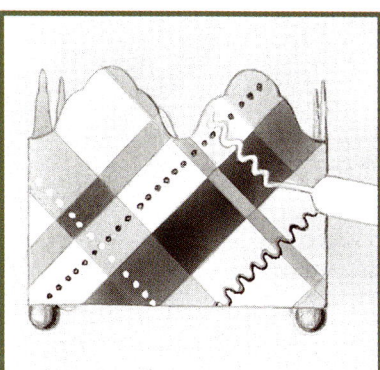

F. Use a paint syringe to apply very fine squiggly lines and small dots.

WINTER 1997 • HANDCRAFT ILLUSTRATED   13

MASTER PROJECT

Arts and Crafts–Style Tiled Tabletop
Build this period look-alike by setting assorted tiles inside an oak framework.

≈ BY MICHIO RYAN

The mottled shades of green on these handmade tiles evoke the style of the Arts and Crafts movement. Handmade tiles, however, can be expensive. If your budget is tight, substitute commercial wall or floor tiles for this project.

COLOR PHOTOGRAPHY:
Carl Tremblay

ILLUSTRATION:
Michael Gellatly

STYLING:
Ritch Holben

SILHOUETTE PHOTOGRAPHY:
Daniel van Ackere

CREATING THIS TILED TABLETOP involves two main tasks: adding edges to an existing tabletop to create a recessed area for tiles, then insetting assorted 4-inch tiles in a pleasing pattern. To suggest a table in the style of the Arts and Crafts movement, I used an oak table that I purchased at Ikea and chose handmade tiles in mottled shades of green.

Because I didn't want the tiles to extend all the way to the table's edges, I created a recessed well by adding four oak slats around the edges. The slats protect the exposed edges of the tile, and their depth is equal to the thickness of the tile, making a smooth overall surface. For a finished look, I added four flanges to the underside edge of the tabletop. This small overhang completely camouflages the old tabletop.

I glued the oak slats into place with panel adhesive instead of wood glue, then anchored them with screws. Although such expediencies might make an experienced woodworker groan, these techniques yield a table that looks nicely carpentered although, in fact, it has no joints and requires minimal woodworking skills.

A few notes of caution before you get started. The slats and flanges must be cut with precision to guarantee that they fit together accurately. If you are not entirely confident of your woodworking skills, I recommend working with an experienced woodworker for this part of the project. In some wood crafts, errors can add personality and quirkiness, but this tabletop is not as forgiving.

Choosing Your Table and Tiles
If you don't have a woodshop, this project will require some back-and-forth shopping. A person with a workshop can buy the tiles and wood in one trip, then return to the workshop and trim the wood down to size. A person without a workshop, however, will need to buy the tiles, lay them out on the table, then figure out the dimensions for the rest of the project and materials. The slats and flanges can be cut to size at the lumberyard when they are purchased. Make sure you choose a lumberyard that's equipped to make rip and plane cuts on your purchases.

The tabletop and tiles you select will together dictate the layout proportions, which in turn affect the width and length of the slats that must be cut. The thickness of the tiles will also mandate adjustments in the thickness of the slats.

Although the tiles are probably the most expensive component of the project, they are also the most aesthetically important. I used handmade wall tiles with a matte glaze, combining several different green hues to re-create the Arts and Crafts style. Choose the color you want first, then work around whatever size tile it happens to come in. While 4 inches by 4 inches is a somewhat standard size, the tiles I selected ranged from

14 HANDCRAFT ILLUSTRATED • WINTER 1997

MATERIALS

- Low square table (Formica, veneered, or plywood top, ¾" thick or less)
- 4" x 4" x ⅜" handmade tiles, related hues (*see* step 1 for quantity)
- 4 oak slats (*see* step 3 for size)
- 4 oak flanges (*see* step 3 for size)
- Eight 1" x 8" pan-head wood screws
- Eight 1" fender washers to fit screws
- 1" finishing nails
- 1 tube panel adhesive (to fit caulking gun)
- 1 tube tub-and-tile adhesive caulk
- Gray floor grout (*see* step 8)
- 1 pint clear satin polyurethane varnish

You'll also need:
drill with bits: ⅛", 3/16", and 1" Speedbor; hammer; table saw or miter box and backsaw; sanding block; 60- and 180-grit sandpaper; steel tape measure; caulking gun; rubber mallet; 4 wood blocks; paper; pencil; calculator; grease pencil; chalk; grid ruler; 2"-wide foam brush; measuring cup; 1-gallon plastic pail; rubber spatula; rubber gloves; cellulose sponge; terry cloth rag; painter's tape; and scraps of chipboard.

3½ inches to 3¾ inches across. In addition, the handmade tiles are not inexpensive: I needed twenty-five tiles, priced at $3.22 each, making a total tile cost of just over $80.

Other options exist, albeit with conditions. Wall tiles, for instance, tend to be very thin—about ¼ inch (the handmade ones are ⅜ inch thick), which makes the oak slats higher than the surface of the tiles. I don't recommend planing the slat to the depth of a ¼-inch tile, as it could warp. If cost is an issue, commercial wall or floor tiles can be used, but do select the thickest tiles you can find. Note, also, that commercial tiles usually must be purchased by the carton, which may mean buying more tiles than required for the table.

The table you tile should be of a plain, square design. The tabletop must be absolutely flat, made out of a single piece rather than joined together from several pieces. A drop-leaf top, for instance, is not suitable. End tables, patio tables, or low coffee or accent tables are suitable, as are other small tables with a low center of gravity. This latter point is important because the weight of the tiles will make a tall table very top-heavy. The table I chose, Ikea's "Jussi" table, is 17¾ inches high with a 24¼-inch-square tabletop.

You can also use a yard sale or junkyard find, even if the tabletop is not acceptable as is. An old table with stable legs and a laminated Formica top is suitable: Merely sand the tabletop with coarse 60-grit sandpaper to provide a good bonding surface for the tile adhesive. If the top is structurally unsound, you can replace it with plywood. Have a lumberyard cut a piece of ¾-inch outdoor grade (AXC) or marine grade plywood (BC grade) to the dimensions of the old tabletop, then attach the new top using screws.

INSTRUCTIONS

1. *Determine tile count.* Measure square tabletop, then refer to chart, at right, to determine tile count. Purchase tiles.

2. *Design tile layout.* If tile count is odd number, center one tile on tabletop; if tile count is even number, center four tiles on tabletop (*see* illustration A, below). Arrange remaining tiles in grid, leaving an even border 1¼" to 3" wide around perimeter. Rearrange tiles as desired for pleasing color arrangement, then make spacing between tiles uniform (¼" to ⅜" wide). Using grease pencil and grid ruler, draft four slat overlap guidelines on tabletop, making spacing between tile edge and guideline match spacing between tiles (illustration B). Make sketch of tabletop with dimensions. Remove tiles from grid row by row and stack in order for duplicating layout later.

3. *Cut boards for slats and flanges. Note:* If you have access to a wood workshop, rip and plane the slats and flanges yourself. Otherwise, have a lumberyard or woodworking shop make the cuts. A rip is a lengthwise cut. Plane to thickness indicates a lengthwise cut that shortens the board depth, but not its width.

Referring to sketch and illustration G, and working with the three equations below, calculate dimensions for slats and flanges:
- slat width = flange width + slat overlap + ⅛" to ¼" ease
- slat width = 2½" to 4"
- slat overlap > flange width + ease

Once you have determined compatible sizes, rip 1 x 4 or 1 x 6 oak boards for slats and flanges. Buy enough running feet for each to equal table perimeter plus four times slat width. Finally, plane board for slats to ⅜" thickness (or to match tile depth).

4. *Saw and join slats and flanges.* Using table saw, or miter box and backsaw, cut two short slats to span tabletop between parallel slat overlap guidelines. Set on opposite edges along guideline, extending off tabletop. Next, cut two longer slats to fit remaining edges, butting corners (illustration C). Lay slats face down on flat surface, butt ends, and tape together. Cut four flanges to align with outside edge, mitering corners precisely at 45 degrees (illustration D). Tape flanges to slats. Using ⅛" bit, drill starter holes 5" to 6" apart clear through flanges and ⅛" into slats. Drive finishing nail

TILE COUNT

TABLETOP SIZE	NUMBER OF TILES NEEDED
11½" to 15" square	4
15½" to 19" square	9
19¾" to 24" square	16
24" to 28" square	25

DESIGNER'S TIP

For variation on this tile design, showcase antique or paving tiles by insetting them into a field of plain, modern tiles.

Laying Out the Tiles

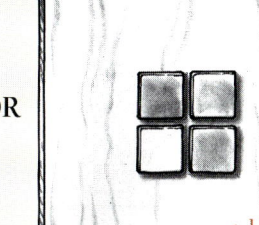

tabletop   tabletop

A. For odd numbers of tiles, center one tile on the tabletop. If the tile count is an even number, start with four tiles.

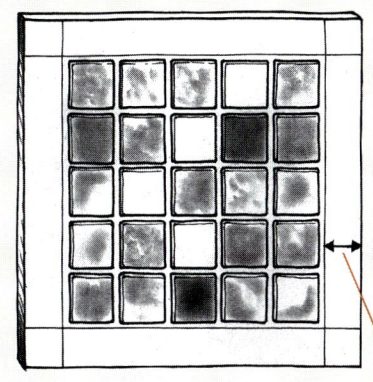
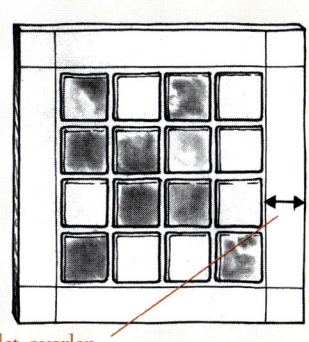

slat overlap

B. Lay out the remaining tiles, then draft four guidelines for the slat overlap.

MASTER PROJECT

FOR FURTHER READING
Professional Tiling: How to Install, Repair, or Replace Ceramic Tile by Edwin and Selma Field, Macmillan, 1993.

into each hole, stopping when about ¼" of nailhead remains visible. Remove all tape, apply wood glue to flanges and slats, and nail together (illustration E). Reassemble face down and tape together.

5. *Fit slats/flanges to tabletop.* Rest table upside down on wood blocks, then mark slat overlap guidelines on underside with chalk. Using 1" bit, drill eight ⅛"-deep depressions centered within overlap area and corresponding to ends of short and long slats. Then drill clear through with 3/16" bit. Set table face down on slat/flange square. To prevent shifting, shim cracks between flange and table edge with chipboard (illustration F). Insert ⅛" bit into each hole and drill into slat for ⅛". Number table edges and corresponding slat/flange pieces with chalk. Remove table and stand upright. Remove tape.

6. *Join slats/flanges to tabletop.* Using caulking gun, gently extrude panel adhesive onto back of first slat, then spread and smooth with chipboard spatula. Position slat on edge of table and press gently to set adhesive. Fit washers into each cavity and drive in screws from underside; do not screw tight. Repeat to glue and screw three remaining slats. Check corners for squareness, tapping gently with rubber mallet to adjust fit, then drive in screws completely (illustration G). Let set ½ hour. Sand lightly with 180-grit sandpaper. Following manufacturer's instructions, apply two to three coats varnish to all oak pieces and table underside. Let dry overnight.

7. *Adhere tiles to tabletop.* Roughen recessed area of tabletop with 60-grit sandpaper to improve adhesion (this is particularly important when adhering tiles to Formica tops). Using caulking gun, apply tub-and-tile adhesive in tight zigzag pattern over entire area. Unstack tiles and set into adhesive in predetermined order (illustration H). Let cure at least 2 hours, but preferably overnight.

8. *Apply grout.* Wear rubber gloves. In pail, mix enough grout for tabletop in accordance with manufacturer's instructions. Grout should be stiff, not watery. Using spatula or finger, trowel grout into crevices between tiles. Let set 15 minutes, then wipe tiles with damp sponge to remove small particles. Smooth grout lines with sponge, let cure 1 hour, then resmooth with gloved fingertip. Avoid rubbing oak, as abrasive particles in grout could mar polyurethane finish (full polyurethane curing takes 4 weeks). Let set overnight; then polish tiles with terry cloth rag. ◆

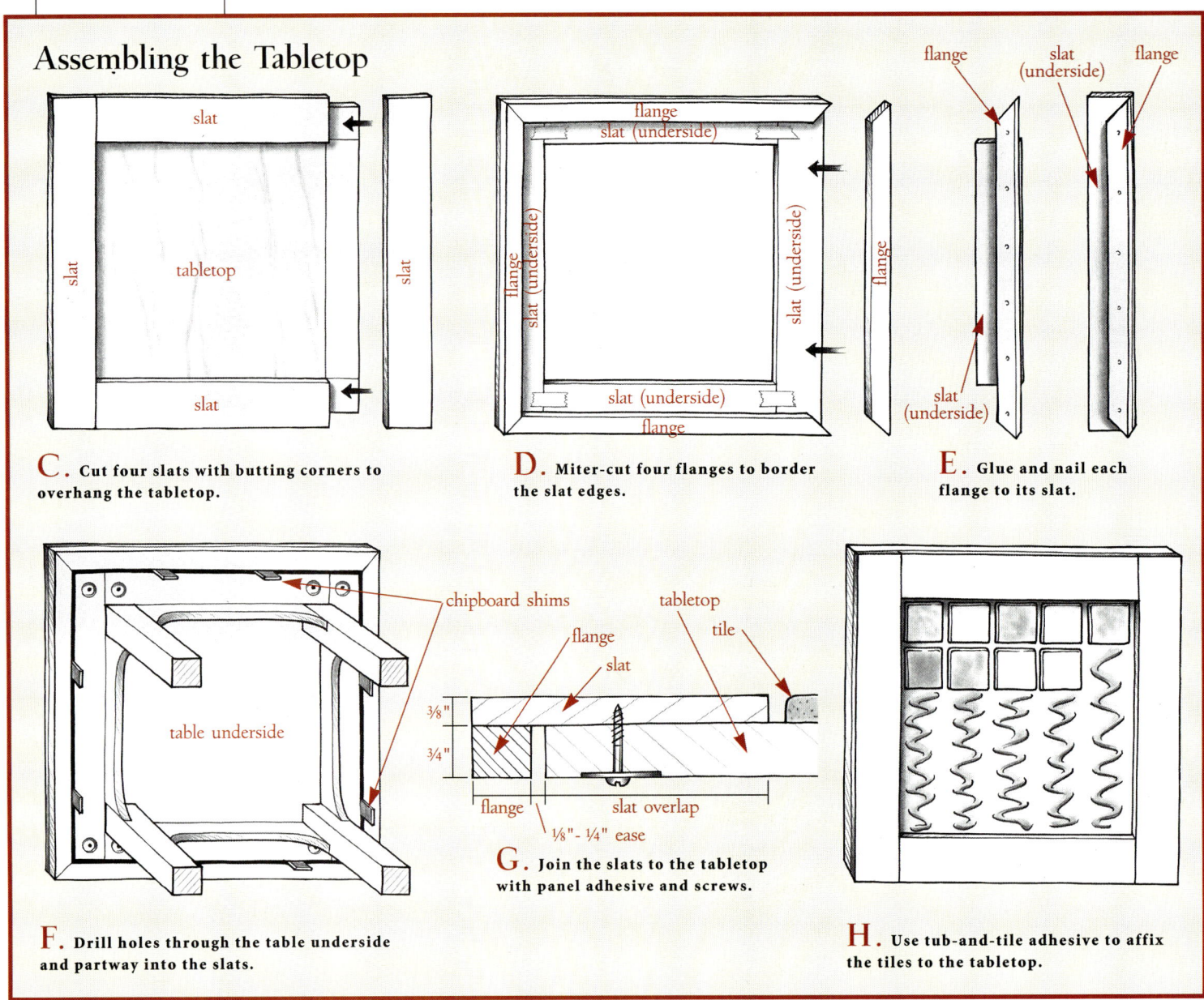

Assembling the Tabletop

C. Cut four slats with butting corners to overhang the tabletop.

D. Miter-cut four flanges to border the slat edges.

E. Glue and nail each flange to its slat.

F. Drill holes through the table underside and partway into the slats.

G. Join the slats to the tabletop with panel adhesive and screws.

H. Use tub-and-tile adhesive to affix the tiles to the tabletop.

Embossed Velvet Pillow

Use coils of armature wire to imprint a pattern on a square of velvet, then add a pillow form to create a soft throw cushion.

BY ELIZABETH CAMERON

WHEN I FIRST ENCOUNTERED embossed velvet at the fabric store, I was enchanted by the shimmering patterns, but the price tag—$50 per yard—sent me home empty-handed. After several days of experimenting, however, I successfully developed my own basic embossing technique. Now, I can emboss velvet at the kitchen table and turn it into a pillow for about $10.

Velvet's luxury is derived from its nap, the short pieces of fiber that rise above the woven backing of the fabric, alternately absorbing and reflecting light. If you're familiar with velvet, you know that brushing the nap in different directions can create instant designs. These pillows beat velvet at its own game. By crushing the nap in very specific places using coils of armature wire, then setting the impressions with spray starch and an iron, you can create a stunning, controlled effect.

The embossing technique works with most types of velvet, but this project shines when done on rayon velvet. The synthetic fibers virtually glow when crushed. This technique should not be used on velvet with a stretchy backing, however, as the pattern will get pulled out when the fabric is stretched.

This embossing technique will work with most any fairly flat, heat-resistant shape. For variation, consider embossing triangles cut from mat board or metal house numbers. These pillows should be dry cleaned only.

MATERIALS

- 5/8 yard 45"-wide rayon or silk velvet (or rayon/silk blend)
- 18"-square pillow form
- Thread to match fabric

You'll also need: 8' 1/8"-inch armature wire; spray starch; 2-quart pot; iron; rotary cutter; wire cutters; sewing machine; scissors; hand-sewing needle; ruler; and 8"-square cotton fabric.

DESIGNER'S TIP

Some canned spray starch leaves a flaky residue. In my tests, however, I circumvented this problem (and saved money) by mixing my own spray starch. To do this, mix liquid starch and water in a 1:1 ratio, then put the mixture in a spray bottle.

INSTRUCTIONS

1. *Make wire spirals.* Cut 45", 30", and 18" lengths from wire. Bend into flat coils approximately 5", 4", and 3" in diameter, respectively (*see* illustration A, below).

2. *Emboss velvet.* Using rotary cutter, cut two 18" squares from velvet. Heat iron to hottest (linen) setting. Do not use steam. Set pot face down on ironing board, then set coil on pot bottom (illustration B). Lay velvet over coil, right side down. Apply spray starch liberally (illustration C). Lay cotton fabric on velvet and press with hot iron 10 seconds (illustration D). Carefully lift and reposition iron until entire coil area has been pressed. Repeat entire process with different-sized coils to create random design over both velvet squares.

3. *Assemble pillow.* Place velvet squares right sides together, edges matching. Stitch all around, leaving 9" opening along one edge for turning. Clip corners with scissors, turn right side out, and insert pillow form. Slip-stitch opening closed. ◆

COLOR PHOTOGRAPHY: **Carl Tremblay**

ILLUSTRATION: **Nenad Jakesevic**

STYLING: **Ritch Holben**

EMBOSSING THE VELVET

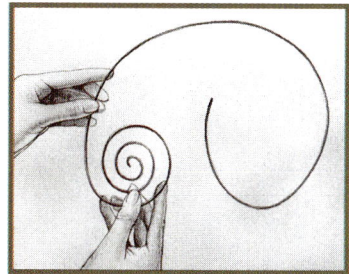

A. Bend the armature wire into flat coils.

B. Place the coil on an overturned pot.

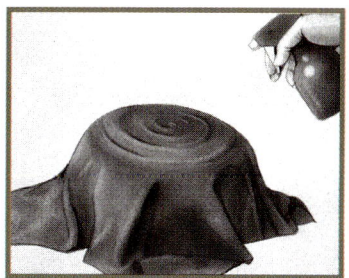

C. Lay the velvet down on the coil and apply starch.

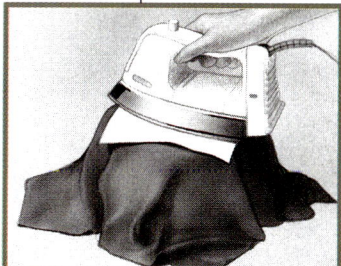

D. Press the velvet with a hot iron to emboss the coil design.

Faux Ebony and Ivory Marquetry Frame

Transform an unfinished wooden frame into an old-world masterpiece using cut paper and a simple decoupage technique.

BY LILY FRANKLIN

For a variation on this two-tone graphic design, cut the triangles, parallelograms, and trapezoids from several different colors of paper.

COLOR PHOTOGRAPHY:
Carl Tremblay

ILLUSTRATION:
Judy Love

STYLING:
Ritch Holben

IN DESIGNING THIS MARQUETRY frame, I set out to simulate the look of inlaid ebony and ivory using everyday materials. After some experimentation, I ended up painting a wooden frame black, then decoupaging pieces of ivory-colored paper in a repeating pattern. The resulting design is boldly graphic, with a classic contrast.

To start off, I added narrow three-dimensional rims along the inside and outside edges of my flat frame. These rims, cut from basswood strips, create a natural enclosure for the inlaid paper. After I glued the basswood rims in place, I sanded and painted the frame.

I found that several paper characteristics are key to simulating inlaid ivory. First and foremost, the paper must be thick enough to remain opaque after it is decoupaged in place. If the paper is so thin that it becomes translucent during decoupage, the black paint will show through and the inlay will appear gray and dull. To test a paper's opacity, wet it and press it against a dark background. It should remain a strong off-white color, be stiff for easy handling, and be free from warping. A second characteristic is surface texture: Your paper should be smooth, without any pebbly or laid textures to mar the illusion of inlaid ivory.

Most of the graphic pattern on the frame is created with one basic shape: the parallelogram. To make identical parallelograms, I employed a simple geometric formula. The width of the parallelogram is exactly one-half of the width of the area to be inlaid. The corners are filled in with triangles, which are parallelograms trimmed to fit. All the pieces can be cut from a single 8½-inch-by-11-inch sheet of paper.

Lily Franklin is a designer living in Albuquerque, New Mexico.

INSTRUCTIONS

1. *Mark frame for basswood rims.* Remove backing and glass from frame and set aside. Using grid ruler and pencil, draft guidelines on face of frame ¼" from each outer edge and ⅜" from each inner edge (*see* illustration A, next page). Measure and jot down perpendicular distance between two lines x and diagonal distance between lines at corner y.

2. *Miter-cut and glue basswood rims.* Align basswood on outer edge of ¼" line so ends extend beyond frame miter (illustration B). At each end, press X-Acto knife blade into stick at 45-degree angle, using frame miter as guide. Then transfer stick to cutting mat and cut clear through. Repeat to miter-cut eight strips total, one for each inner and outer edge of frame. Apply wood glue to bottom of each stick and to marked areas on frame, then glue sticks to frame to create raised rims along inner and outer edges of frame. When all sticks are glued in place, double-check that corners are square. Wipe oozing glue with damp sponge. Weight evenly with heavy books and let dry at least 1 hour, but preferably overnight.

3. *Paint frame.* Protect work surface with newsprint. Prop frame on small blocks to prevent sticking, then brush light coat sanding sealer over front and back of frame. Clean brush with soap and water. Let frame dry 1 hour. Sand lightly with 220-grit sandpaper wrapped around small wood block, then wipe off dust using damp paper towel. Brush on black paint and let dry 20 minutes. Apply second coat. Clean brush with soap and water. Let frame dry 24 hours.

4. *Cut parchment parallelograms.* Divide x measurement from step 1 in half.

MATERIALS

- 11" x 14" unfinished wood frame
- Eight 3/16" x 3/16" x 24" basswood sticks
- 8½" x 11" sheet ivory parchment paper
- 2 ounces black craft flat acrylic paint
- Mod Podge, gloss-lustré finish
- Sanding sealer
- Acrylic sealer
- Wood glue

You'll also need:
X-Acto knife; steel ruler; steel triangle; clear plastic grid ruler; self-healing cutting mat; pencil; 220-grit sandpaper; 400-grit wet-dry emery paper; small wood blocks; newsprint; soft ½"-wide flat brush; paper towels; sponge; soap; and heavy books.

Measuring from left edge of parchment, mark off this amount evenly spaced across top and bottom edge. Lay steel ruler across parchment to connect marks, then cut parchment with X-Acto knife, stopping just short of edges (illustration C). Divide *y* measurement from step 1 in half. Measuring from top left corner of parchment, mark off this amount evenly spaced across top edge and down left edge. Lay steel ruler across paper diagonally to connect marks, and cut with X-Acto knife from edge to edge until you have about forty parallelograms (illustration D, #1). Align steel triangle on excess strips to cut four right-angle triangles (illustration D, #2). Set aside remaining trapezoidal strips.

5. *Glue parallelograms to frame.* Test-fit pieces on frame, placing one triangle at corner and four parallelograms along each side between basswood rims (illustration E). Remove pieces from frame and set on newsprint. Brush moderately thick coat of Mod Podge across triangle and onto newsprint to fully coat edges. Beginning at frame corner, press triangle into position and smooth to remove air bubbles. Working out from corner, glue on four parallelograms one by one. Repeat to decorate all four corners. To fill each middle area, cut four trapezoidal strips from excess paper in step 4. To cut correct length, position one strip on frame so angled end touches point of parallelogram (illustration F). Make tick mark at other end. Then cut angle using scrap parallelogram as guide. Double-check strip length, then glue in place.

6. *Coat frame with Mod Podge.* Brush light coat of Mod Podge over face of frame and let dry 20 minutes. Sand lightly with 400-grit wet-dry emery paper. To build finish, repeat at least four more times or until surface is even. Let dry overnight. To eliminate tackiness, apply acrylic sealer (illustration G). ◆

Making the Frame

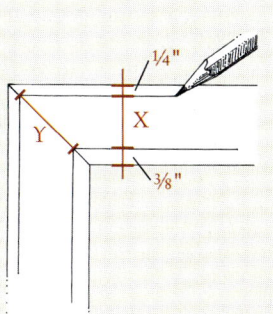

A. Draft guidelines along the frame's inner and outer edges. Measure and record *x* and *y*.

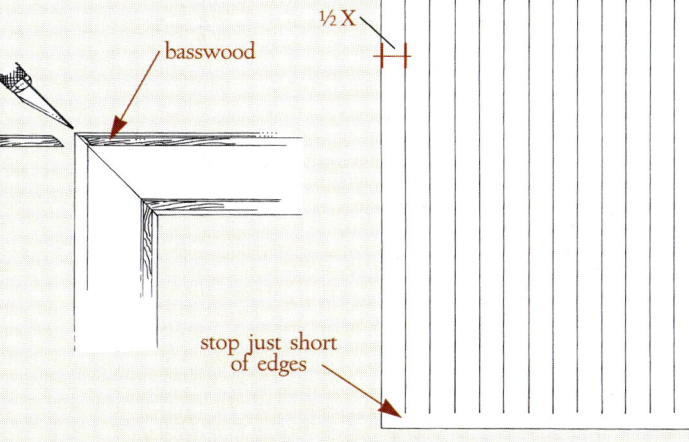

B. Miter the corners of eight basswood sticks, then glue them in place.

C. Use the *x* measure to cut vertical strips on the sheet of parchment.

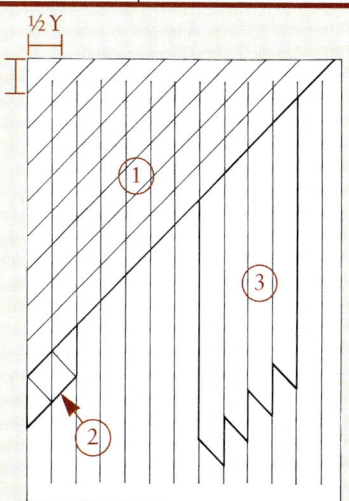

D. Use the *y* measure to make diagonal cuts for (1) parallelograms, (2) triangles, and (3) trapezoids.

E. Starting at each corner, glue one triangle and four parallelograms in place.

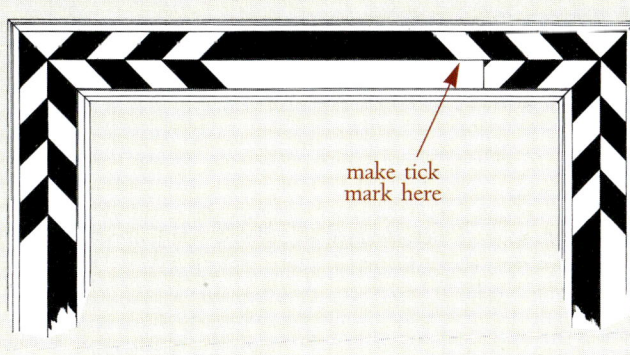

F. Mark and angle-cut a long trapezoid to span each middle section.

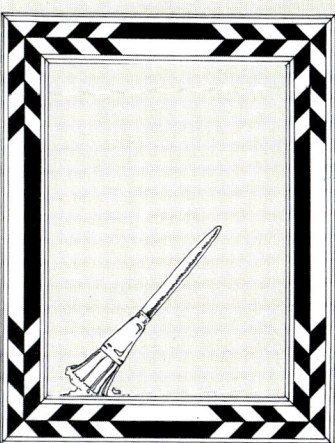

G. Coat the frame face with four layers of Mod Podge, then apply acrylic sealer.

LOW-SEW

Lavender Bath Bolster
Make your own soothing bath pillow using a napkin, rolled batting, and dried lavender.

BY FRANCOISE HARDY

For added convenience, attach the lavender pillow to the bathtub using suction cups. Look for cups with a small hook, then hand-stitch two tiny ribbon hanging loops to the pillow.

COLOR PHOTOGRAPHY:
Carl Tremblay

ILLUSTRATION:
Judy Love

STYLING:
Ritch Holben

THIS BEAUTIFUL BOLSTER IS THE perfect accessory for any bathtub. The steam from a warm bath will release the relaxing scent of lavender, while the pillow fits perfectly between you and the tub's edge.

Instead of purchasing fabric, I used a blue and white jacquard dinner napkin for the pillowcase. This outer case covers the inner pillow form, which is constructed by sprinkling dried lavender on batting, rolling the batting like a jelly roll, and fitting the roll inside a muslin cover.

I chose Mountain Mist batting. It's soft, but completely synthetic, meaning it will dry quickly should it get splashed with bathwater.

I chose lavender for my pillow because it's known for relaxing the mind and invigorating the body, but you can substitute any favorite dried herb, such as peppermint or chamomile.

Francoise Hardy is a Boston-based artisan and craftsperson.

INSTRUCTIONS

1. *Sew bolster case with eyelet trim.* Fold napkin in half, wrong side out, and stitch edge opposite fold (*see* illustration A, next page). Press seam open; turn tube right side out. Cut eyelet trim in half. At each end of tube, pin trim to edge, wrong sides together. Fold and overlap one cut end to conceal raw edges. Stitch 1⅞" from edge all around (illustration B).

2. *Sew muslin cover for bolster form.* Using rotary cutter, cut 21" x 24½" rectangle from muslin. Fold rectangle in half crosswise and stitch 21" edge opposite fold. Press seam to one side, then fold and press each end 1" to inside. Stitch ¾" from each fold all around to form casing at each end. To make opening in casings, pick out a few stitches along seam with seam ripper. Cut string in half and use grip bodkin to draw 27" length of string through each casing. Tie string ends together (illustration C).

3. *Make rolled bolster form.* Unfold packaged batting into 30" x 45" rectangle (double thickness), then cut two 13" x 45" strips. Sprinkle lavender evenly over surface of both pieces. Beginning at short edge, roll one batting strip into "jelly roll" about 4" in diameter, then butt in second strip and continue rolling until diameter is 7" (illustration D). Insert log into muslin cover, pull drawstrings closed and tie off each end, tuck loose strings inside bolster form, then insert into bolster case (illustration E).

4. *Finish bolster.* Gather fabric at each end of bolster and secure with rubber band. Cut cord in half, knot ends to prevent raveling, and tie around gathered bolster ends (illustration F). Seal cord ends with fray preventer and let dry. ◆

MATERIALS
- 1.5 ounces dried lavender
- 23"-square napkin
- 1⅜ yards 2"-wide white eyelet trim
- 40 inches ⁵⁄₁₆"-diameter white decorative cord
- ⅝ yard 45"-wide muslin
- Crib-size (45" x 60") Mountain Mist Fatt Batt
- White sewing thread
- 54" cotton string
- 2 rubber bands or hair elastics
- Fray preventer

You'll also need:
sewing machine; iron; sewing shears; rotary cutter; straight pins; grip bodkin; and seam ripper.

Making the Scented Bolster

A. Sew two edges of a 23"-square napkin together to make a case.

B. Turn the case right side out and line each inside edge with eyelet trim.

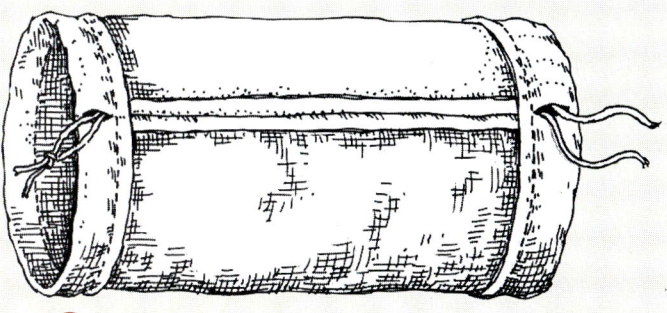

C. Sew a drawstring cover from muslin for the bolster form.

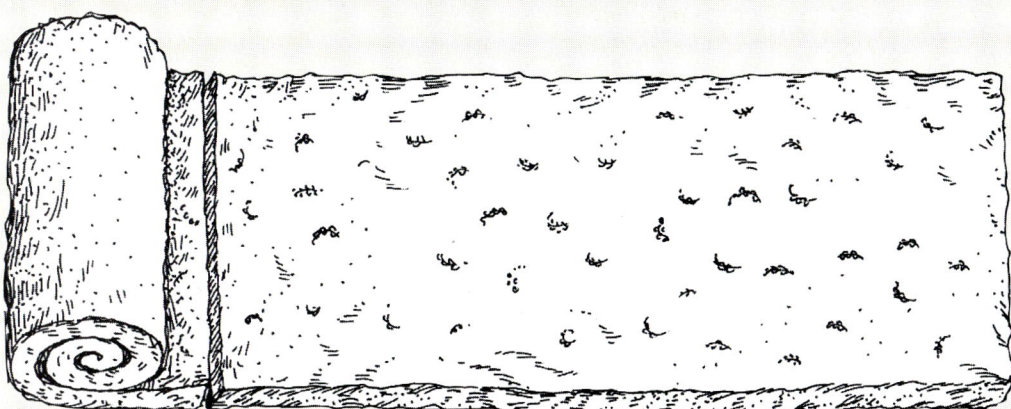

D. Sprinkle dried lavender across the batting, then roll it up.

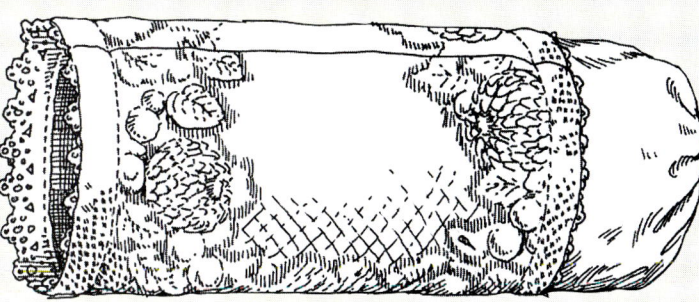

E. Place the roll inside the muslin cover, then insert the form into the case.

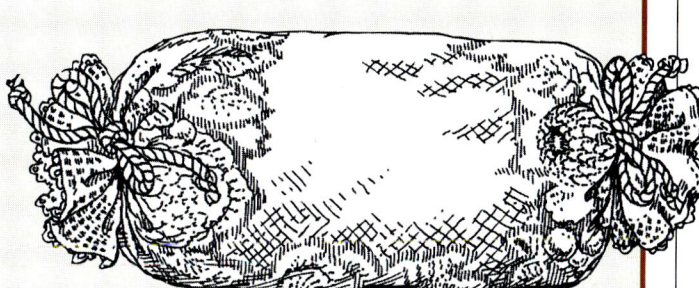

F. Tie the loose ends with decorative cord.

MORE HERBAL BATH OPTIONS

Looking for another way to enjoy herbs in your bath? Consider making an herb bag. All you need is a small square of muslin or old T-shirt, about 7 inches by 7 inches in size. Place the herbs (*see* recipes, next paragraph) in the center of the square, then pull up the sides and tie the bag closed with a piece of decorative ribbon. Hang the bag under the faucet as the tub fills and/or use it to scrub your skin while you're bathing.

For a skin-softening bath, combine 3 tablespoons of dried chamomile, 3 tablespoons of dried calendula, 2 tablespoons of dried comfrey, and 1 tablespoon of dried sandalwood chips. For a romantic bath, combine ½ cup of dried rosebuds with five whole dried cloves.

GIFTS

Aromatherapeutic Bath Sundries

Mix up your own body lotion, massage oil, and bath salts with our master recipes, then "customize" each recipe with your favorite essential oil.

🌹 BY AMY JENNER

Homemade massage oil, body lotion, and bath salts make a uniquely personal gift. To further personalize the items, name each one for the recipient.

COLOR PHOTOGRAPHY:
Carl Tremblay

ILLUSTRATION:
Nenad Jakesevic

STYLING:
Ritch Holben

IF YOU'VE EVER CONSIDERED MAKING bath products for your own use or to give as gifts, this article is for you. Following are three master recipes for body lotion, massage oil, and bath salts. To personalize these mixtures or to create a particular mood, you can add one or more essential oils (see "Adding Scent to Your Bath Products" and "Blending Essential Oils," right and next page). While such oils can be used to ease ailments ranging from skin problems to the common cold, my aromatherapeutic recipes are designed to lift the spirit.

The body lotion, which is mild enough for the face or the body, is mixed in a blender or food processor. One note of caution, however, if your machine has plastic parts: Some essential oils (such as lavender) can "craze" plastic; they chemically interact with it and cause hairline cracks to appear over time. Crazing can weaken and eventually break plastic. To prevent essential oils from coming into contact with the plastic, remove the top of your processor or blender and drop the oil directly onto the other ingredients rather than dribbling it down the sides. When you are through, wash the plastic parts right away. Transfer the lotion to small, fancy glass (not plastic) jars as soon as possible and let it thicken as it cools.

The massage oil is made by blending almond or pecan oil with vitamin E oil. The bath salts recipe calls for borax, French white clay, and sea salt. All of the above ingredients can be found at health foods stores, as can essential oils. The amount of essential oil added to each mixture will vary, depending on the one you select. A light, volatile oil such as lavender, for example, requires a greater quantity than a heavier oil such as patchouli. Whatever the scent, always make it stronger than you think you like, because some of it will dissipate.

Amy Jenner makes body lotion, massage oil, bath salts, and soap at Stoney Hill Soap Works in Groton, Massachusetts, with the help of husband Dana and three-year-old twins Blaise and Olin.

INSTRUCTIONS
Massage Oil
1. *Mix ingredients.* Measure 1 cup almond or pecan oil. If coloring oil,

---

ADDING SCENT TO YOUR BATH PRODUCTS

The following essential oils are commonly used in single form:

- **Jasmine:** Reduces anxiety, depression, and nervous fatigue; relaxes, elevates the spirit, balances mood.
- **Lavender:** Calming; balances emotions, lowers blood pressure, soothes the skin.
- **Lemon:** Cooling, refreshing; assists in communication and decision making.
- **Orange:** Warm and light; prevents overseriousness, awakens creativity.
- **Patchouli:** Reduces mental fatigue and lethargy, calms the nerves, stimulates sexual desire.
- **Rose:** Eases anxiety, promotes feelings of love and happiness.
- **Rosemary:** Lifts the spirits, invigorates, brings mental clarity, opens the heart.
- **Sandalwood:** Soothes emotions, relaxes, subdues irritability.

MATERIALS

Master Recipe: Massage Oil
Yields 1 cup

- 1 cup almond or pecan oil
- 1/8 to 1/4 teaspoon pure vitamin E oil
- 1/4 to 1/2 teaspoon essential oil(s), plus more as desired to prolong scent (see "Adding Scent to Your Bath Products" and "Blending Essential Oils")
- Concentrated candle dye (optional)
- Dried herbs or flowers (such as lavender sprigs or rose petals)
- 8-ounce bottle with cork stopper

You'll also need:
measuring cup with spout; measuring spoons; microwave oven; sharp knife; chopstick; and Pyrex custard cup.

Master Recipe: Body Lotion
Yields 2 cups

- 1 cup aloe vera gel
- 1 teaspoon lanolin
- 1 teaspoon pure vitamin E oil
- 1/3 cup coconut oil
- 1/2 to 3/4 ounce beeswax (small ice cube–size piece)
- 3/4 cup almond or pecan oil(s)
- Up to 1 1/2 teaspoons essential oil(s), plus more as desired to prolong scent (see "Adding Scent to Your Bath Products" and "Blending Essential Oils")
- Four 4-ounce wide-mouthed glass jars with corks or screw caps

You'll also need:
microwave oven or double boiler; blender or food processor; kitchen scale; 1- and 2-cup Pyrex measuring cups; measuring spoons; rubber spatula; and chopstick.

Master Recipe: Bath Salts
Yields about 2 cups

- 2 cups borax
- 1/8 cup French white clay
- 1/8 cup sea salt (coarse or fine)
- 2 1/4 to 3 tablespoons essential oil(s) (see "Adding Scent to Your Bath Products" and "Blending Essential Oils")
- Paste food color (optional)
- Two 8-ounce wide-mouthed jars with cork or glass stoppers

You'll also need:
1- to 2-quart mixing bowl; whisk; measuring cup; measuring spoons; serving spoon; and toothpick.

ES...

For t... ...g blends, prepare the recipe using 1 drop as one part. For large quantities, use 1 teaspoon as one part.

LOVER'S BLEND
- 10 parts rose oil
- 10 parts palma rosa oil
- 8 parts lemon oil
- 2 parts ylang-ylang oil
- 2 parts Peru balsam oil

STRESS-BUSTER BLEND
- 20 parts lemon oil
- 7 parts neroli oil
- 3 parts chamomile oil
- 3 parts lavender oil

ENERGIZING BLEND
- 10 parts basil oil
- 8 parts coriander oil
- 8 parts rosemary oil
- 5 parts ginger oil
- 5 parts peppermint oil
- 4 parts ylang-ylang oil

---

pour off about 1/8 cup into custard cup. Shave three to four slivers candle dye into custard cup oil, microwave on high 10 seconds, and stir with chopstick. Repeat until dye is melted and color is evenly distributed, then return mixture to oil in measuring cup. Add vitamin E oil and essential oil(s), pour entire contents into bottle, and insert cork stopper.

2. *Mix and bottle oil.* Mix oils by gently turning bottle over and back a few times (*see* illustration A, below). Test scent by rubbing oil into skin. Add more essential oil(s) as desired to prolong scent. For visual interest, drop in dried herbs or flowers.

Body Lotion
1. *Mix ingredients.* Place aloe vera gel, lanolin, and vitamin E oil into blender or food processor. Place coconut oil and beeswax in 2-cup Pyrex measuring cup, microwave on high 30 seconds, and stir with chopstick. Repeat heating in 10-second blocks until fully melted. Stir in almond or pecan oil, reheating if necessary. Run blender or food processor at low to medium speed, then pour in melted oils in thin stream as if making mayonnaise (illustration B). As oil is blended in, cream will turn white and blender's motor will start to grind. As soon as melted oils are added and you've achieved mayonnaiselike consistency, stop motor, add essential oil(s) and pulse-blend. Do not overblend. Transfer cream to glass jars while still warm, as it thickens quickly.

Bath Salts
1. *Combine ingredients.* Whisk dry ingredients together in bowl. Make well in center and add 1 1/2 tablespoons of the essential oil(s) and, if coloring salts, dab of paste food color on end of toothpick. Whisk to break up clumps and distribute color evenly (illustration C).

2. *Transfer salts to jars.* Test scent. If necessary, add up to 1/2 tablespoon more of the essential oil(s). Once desired scent is

---

MIXING THE INGREDIENTS

A. Massage Oil: Turn the bottle over and back a few times to combine the massage oil ingredients.

B. Body Lotion: Combine the ingredients for this milky white lotion in a blender or food processor.

C. Bath Salts: Whisk the wet and dry ingredients together to make scented colored bath salts.

MAKING THE LABELS

MATERIALS

- Cream rough-laid letter paper
- Waxed beige cord
- 1/2"-wide rayon ribbon or seam binding
- Red sealing wax (no wick)
- Gold embossing powder
- Rubber cement

You'll also need: computer with laser printer; ordinary paper for test prints; scissors; deckle-edged scissors; newsprint; seal stamp or signet ring; miniature rubber stamp and stamp pad; toaster or toaster oven; candle; matches; cutting surface; sharp knife; tongs; tweezers; scrap paper; and vegetable oil.

D. Slip cord around the bottle neck, catching a ribbon at the back.

E. Wrap and tie the cord to secure the ribbon.

F. Trim the ribbon ends, then top with a wax seal.

achieved, add one-half again as much essential oil(s) as scent will dissipate over time. Leave salts uncovered overnight to dry. Spoon into wide-mouthed jars. To use, add a few tablespoons to bath just as tub fills.

Making Your Own Labels

If you plan to give the bath lotion, oil, or salts as a gift, consider these finishing touches: homemade labels, ribbon, and sealing wax.

To create labels of my own, I chose old-fashioned typefaces, printed them on laid paper, embossed the center with a gold motif, and cut a deckled edge around the border. To dress up the bottles further, I corked them and wrapped waxed cord around their necks, then affixed a ribbon onto the front of each one with sealing wax.

Instead of handwriting the labels, I used the word processing program on my computer. Because every computer has different fonts and typefaces available, your labels may vary slightly from mine. Once you've picked a font, you may need to experiment a bit with the type size to achieve the right look for each bottle. Remember to leave enough white space in the center of the label for the embossed design.

Your label paper should fit in the printer tray, which means it should measure 8½ inches by 11 inches and have a weight classification of less than 24 pounds. I used a miniature rubber stamp for my embossed design and cut the edges of the label with deckle-edged scissors to create a rippled edge.

INSTRUCTIONS

1. *Create label outline.* To gauge label size, cut rectangle from scrap paper, hold it against bottle, and trim to size. Using word processing software, create double-bordered box about 1/4" smaller than sample label.

2. *Type and print label.* Type name of item (e.g., Sarah's Soothing Bath Salts), scent (if desired), and volume on three separate lines inside box. Center all lines, then select font and point size for each line of type. Vertical spacing can be adjusted by inserting blank lines of very small point size. Add space between first and second lines for embossing (*see* sample label, left). Test-print on ordinary paper, then print on letter paper. Cut out 1/4" beyond box using deckle-edged scissors. Repeat to create additional labels.

3. *Emboss label.* Stamp image on label between first and second lines. Immediately sprinkle embossing powder on top, then shake off excess. Hold label face up over heated toaster 10 seconds or until fused embossing forms.

4. *Attach label to bottle and seal.* Lay label face down on newsprint and brush rubber cement across back. Wait 1 minute until cement is tacky, but no longer wet, then press into position. Fill bottle and replace cork or cap. Loop cord around neck, catching ribbon at back (illustration D), then draw both ribbon ends over top of bottle and down front. Wind cord around neck, tie off (illustration E), and cut excess, then trim ribbon ends. Apply thin coat vegetable oil to seal stamp or ring. Hold wax over candle flame 10 seconds, then cut 1/8"-thick "coin" from softened wax. Using tweezers, position coin on ribbons above label, then impress with seal stamp or ring (illustration F). ◆

DESIGNER'S TIPS

- The nature of the contents will, in part, determine the shape of your bottle. Massage oil should be packaged in a narrow-necked bottle. The body lotion, on the other hand, will not flow easily, if at all, meaning it should be packaged in a wide-mouthed jar.

- Purchasing individual vials of essential oil can become expensive. Instead, consider purchasing preblended combinations. Aura Cacia, for instance, offers blends with names such as Tranquility, Heart Song, and Euphoria.

Heirloom Beaded Lampshade

Forget those beaded shades in retail stores. Build your own version for a fraction of the cost using a wire shade and glass beads.

🌹 BY ELIZABETH CAMERON

MATERIALS
- 2" x 4" x 4" wire candleshade frame
- Eleven 2/3-ounce vials 5mm gold seed beads
- Thirty-six 8mm magenta Miracle beads
- 4 Czech teardrops
- 2 spools 24-gauge wire

You'll also need: beading pliers and wire cutters.

On the shade shown here, the beaded wire strands are pulled fairly taut. For a Victorian look, use a scalloped shade and "drape" the beaded wires downward.

DESIGNER'S TIP
Once you start winding the beaded wire to the shade, you'll discover that finding the right tension for the wire is critical. If you pull the wire too tight, it will slip upward. If you let it hang too loose, it will sag.

COLOR PHOTOGRAPHY: **Carl Tremblay**

ILLUSTRATION: **Judy Love**

STYLING AND SHADE DESIGN: **Ritch Holben**

BEADED LAMPSHADES HAVE always been out of my budget: This 2-inch-by-4-inch-by-4-inch lampshade, for example, might sell for $250 in a retail store. You can make your own version for under $50, however, with just three basic materials: a wire shade frame, 24-gauge wire, and an assortment of glass beads.

When I went shopping for beads, I discovered why beaded lampshades are so expensive. The first beads I chose would have cost $150. So I compromised, opting for less expensive 5mm beads on the shade's body and more expensive beads for the bottom edge and corners.

INSTRUCTIONS

1. *String beads on wire.* Cut an arm's length of wire, then string with gold seed beads. When done, loop both ends of wire. Repeat to string all gold seed beads.

2. *Wind beaded wire around frame.* Wrap end of beaded wire strand to spoke at upper rim of shade, then begin winding beaded wire around shade frame (see illustration A, right). At each spoke, spread beads to expose wire, then wrap once around spoke to secure to frame. Repeat process to cover entire shade (illustration B), ending strands at spoke and adding new beaded wire strands as necessary. To end off, twist wire tightly around spoke and clip excess.

3. *Add beads to bottom rim.* Start new wire at one lower corner of shade. String on teardrop at corner, then string on enough beads to cover bottom spoke (illustration C). String on alternating gold seed beads with magenta Miracle beads. At corner spoke, wrap wire once to secure as in step 2, then repeat along remaining three edges.

4. *Cover side spokes.* Using strung seed beads, secure wire at lower corner (near teardrop), then pull wire taut to upper corner (illustration D). Secure at upper corner by wrapping once, then reverse direction and pull taut to starting point. Wrap several times to secure, then trim excess. Repeat to cover remaining side spokes. To further secure beads along side spokes, wrap small piece of wire about halfway up side spoke. Twist to secure, hide twisted wire on inside of shade, then trim excess. ◆

Beads courtesy Beadworks, Boston, Massachusetts.

Beading the Lampshade

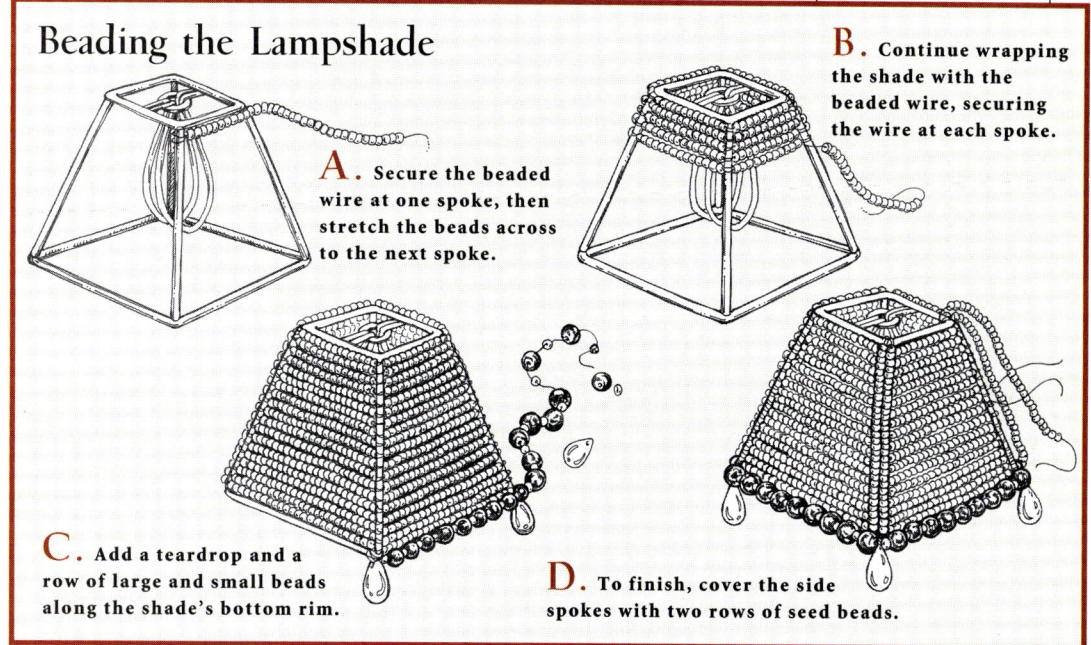

A. Secure the beaded wire at one spoke, then stretch the beads across to the next spoke.

B. Continue wrapping the shade with the beaded wire, securing the wire at each spoke.

C. Add a teardrop and a row of large and small beads along the shade's bottom rim.

D. To finish, cover the side spokes with two rows of seed beads.

PAINTING

Home Sweet Home Sign
Create an antique wall plaque using self-adhesive wooden letters and a crackled paint finish.

BY LILY FRANKLIN

The sign can be propped on a ledge or mantel or hung on a wall using a pair of 3-inch eyehooks. If you plan to hang the sign, position the eyehooks 3 inches from each end of the sign.

PATTERNS
See page 45 for pattern pieces and enlargement instructions.

COLOR PHOTOGRAPHY:
Carl Tremblay

ILLUSTRATION:
Mary DePalma

STYLING:
Ritch Holben

SILHOUETTE PHOTO:
Daniel van Ackere

MATERIALS
- 1½" self-adhesive wooden letters (Walnut Hollow Farm #14300 series), 1 package each H, O, M, S, W, T (each package contains two letters) and 2 packages E
- 1 package Walnut Hollow Farm self-adhesive small wooden hearts
- 2' of 1 x 10 clear pine board (board should measure 24" x ¾" x 9½")
- 6' x ⅜" x ¼" beaded glass molding
- ½" brads
- Plaid acrylic paint, 2 ounces each in the following colors: Apple Barrel gloss enamel Black #20662, Apple Barrel Twill #20780, FolkArt Ivory White #427, FolkArt Parchment #450, FolkArt Rusty Nail #914
- 2 ounces Accent Crown Jewels acrylic paint Imperial Antique Gold #2528
- 2 ounces Plaid FolkArt crackle medium
- Matte acrylic spray
- Wood glue

You'll also need:
pattern for sign arc (*see* page 45); access to photocopier with enlarger; transfer paper (do not use carbon paper); pencil; grid ruler; miter box; backsaw with closely spaced teeth; 180-grit sandpaper; sanding block; tack hammer; four paintbrushes in the following sizes: #3 round, ¼" flat, ½" flat, and 1" flat; paper towels; spray mister; small cup; and cellulose sponge.

ALTHOUGH THIS ANTIQUE SIGN may look like it was carved by hand, the raised lettering was created using self-adhesive wooden letters, and the edges with glass molding. To give the sign its crackled, aged look, I applied a variety of paint colors and a crackle medium.

To create the sign's lettering, I selected Walnut Hollow Farm's self-adhesive basswood letters. The letters are very easy to use: Simply peel off the protective backing, then press in place. The letters come in two sizes and two font styles; I chose the 1½-inch Times Roman letters for a more classic look and a size appropriate to my 9½-inch-by-24-inch sign.

I considered using a ready-made sign board, which comes with routed edges, but such boards are expensive and come in limited sizes. Instead I used a plain pine plank. You can substitute other soft, light-colored woods such as poplar, basswood, or alder, but in most regions pine will be the least expensive choice.

To define the edges of the sign and frame the raised letters, I added molding around the edges of the board. I used ⅜-inch-wide-by-¼-inch-high glass molding, a type of molding used next to window mullions to hold in a pane of glass. I recommend a small, delicate molding such as glass molding, as a larger molding will overwhelm the size of the pine plank. If you can't find glass molding, you can substitute ¼-inch half-round molding or the like.

Creating an Antique Finish
Creating the aged finish on this sign involves three different stages: painting and crackling the undercoats, gilding and aging the letters, and applying a final wash of diluted ivory-colored paint. Although it may seem complicated at first, it actually goes very quickly, allowing for drying time in between certain steps. I started by painting the entire sign

with Ivory White, then created smudgy, irregular patches using Twill (grayish beige) paint. Once these layers had dried, I applied crackle medium over the open areas of the sign, followed by a coat of Parchment-colored paint. Any areas coated with the crackle medium will be completely crackled in about 20 minutes. If you haven't used crackle medium before, I recommend testing it on scrap wood in order to gauge its effect.

Next, I painted the letters using Black paint. After those layers of paint had dried, I applied crackle medium to the letters, then brushed on Imperial Antique Gold. As soon as the gold surface began to crackle, I dabbed it with a damp piece of paper towel to expose about half of the black undercoat. I repeated this sequence on the molding, then finished the Home Sweet Home sign with an overall wash using diluted ivory paint.

Lily Franklin is a designer living in Albuquerque, New Mexico.

INSTRUCTIONS
Constructing the Sign

1. *Join molding strips to board.* Lightly sand surface and edges of board, removing dust with damp paper towel. Lay board flat. Using grid ruler and pencil, draft line ⅛" in from each edge to make rectangle. From molding, cut two 23¾" strips and two 9¼" strips, mitering ends 45 degrees picture frame–style. Test-fit strips along guidelines allowing ⅛" rim all around. Hammer three brads partway into each shorter strip and five brads into each longer strip. Apply glue to board along line, then on each strip bottom. Reposition strips on board and tap down brads flush with molding surface (*see illustration A, right*).

2. *Affix letters and heart to board.* Photocopy arc pattern on page 45, enlarging it 200 percent, or until arc measures 21½" across. Center pattern on board and slip transfer paper under. Trace center line, arc guideline, and heart outline (do not trace letters). Remove pattern. Referring to pattern and starting at center of board, arrange letters on guideline in each direction to spell HOME SWEET HOME (illustration B). Starting at center, peel off backing and press each letter into position. Work carefully because letters cannot be repositioned once they are adhered. Adhere heart within outline. Sand lightly to remove any visible tracing lines.

Painting the Sign

1. *Paint undercoats.* Using 1" flat brush for large areas and ½" brush around letters, apply Ivory White paint to entire board, including edges. Brush with grain, using round brush or cotton swab to absorb and smooth out drops of paint that collect in crevices. To prevent paint buildup on letter surface, wipe with slightly damp sponge. Let dry 1 hour. Brush Twill paint onto open areas of sign in smudgy, irregular patches (illustration C). Let dry at least 1 hour, but preferably overnight. Clean brushes using soap and water.

2. *Paint crackle finish.* Using ½" flat brush, apply crackle medium randomly over open areas of sign, including between words. Vary application so some areas receive thicker coat than others. Let dry to touch, 10 to 15 minutes. Using 1" flat brush for large areas and ½" brush around letters, apply Parchment paint to entire surface, brushing with woodgrain. Smooth out drops of paint that collect in crevices as in step 1. Set aside board; do not attempt touch-ups. Areas coated with crackle medium will begin crackling right away and be completed in about 20 minutes (illustration D). Let dry overnight. Clean brushes using soap and water.

3. *Paint and "gild" letters and molding.* Using ¼" flat brush, paint surface of letters with two coats Black and surface of heart with two coats Rusty Nail. Using round brush, paint molding black. Let dry 20 minutes. Using ¼" flat brush and working one word at a time, apply thin layer of crackle medium to letters. When medium is dry to touch, 10 minutes or less, brush on Imperial Antique Gold. As soon as gold surface begins to crackle, dab it with small piece of moistened paper towel to lift and remove gold flecks and expose about 50 percent of black undercoat. Apply crackle medium, then gold paint, to beaded section of molding in same way. Rub towel along length of strips to break up gold into streaks. Finally, use round brush to paint ⅛" gold border around edge of heart. Let dry at least 1 hour, but preferably overnight. Clean brushes using soap and water.

4. *Apply ivory wash.* Following manufacturer's instructions, spray sign with two coats acrylic sealer. Let dry minimum 3 hours, but preferably overnight. To make wash, squeeze about 1 tablespoon Ivory White paint in small cup, then dilute with one or two drops of water. Using round brush, work wash into crevices and up sides of letters. Blot up excess with damp paper towel and wipe wash that seeps onto surface of letters immediately with damp sponge. Brush wash onto molding, then immediately sponge off beaded portion. Finally, use 1" flat brush to apply wash to all remaining flat areas. Blot with paper towel to soften and blend smooth and crackled sections. Let dry 1 hour. Clean brushes using soap and water. ◆

Making the Sign

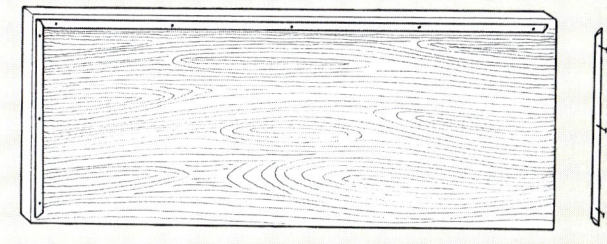

A. Miter-cut strips of molding and adhere them to the edges of the pine plank.

B. Arrange the self-stick wooden letters on a curved guideline, working from the center outward.

C. Paint the entire surface, then add random splotches of a second color.

D. Use crackle medium and another paint layer to "weather" the surface.

LOW-SEW

French Buffet Tray

Sew together a pair of colorful napkins to make a softly sculptured tableware and napkin dish.

BY JOANNE S. BEMBRY

MATERIALS

- 2 complementary cotton napkins, 20" to 21" square
- 2 yards ½"-wide single-fold bias tape
- Thread to match fabrics and bias tape
- ¾ yard fusible fleece
- 1-ply chipboard, as large as the napkin
- High-tack white glue
- Fray preventer

You'll also need:
Sewing machine; iron; scissors; pins; utility knife; self-healing cutting mat; steel ruler; triangle; pencil; fine-tip marker; and stiff, flat 1"-wide brush.

This 14-inch-square buffet tray uses two napkins with the same pattern, but different color schemes. For variation, match the colors and vary the pattern.

DESIGNER'S TIP
For variation on this tray, consider making smaller-size trays using Christmas prints and filling them with wrapped homemade bread.

COLOR PHOTOGRAPHY:
Carl Tremblay

ILLUSTRATION:
Judy Love

STYLING:
Ritch Holben

Looking to add some new color, or a little organization, to your sideboard or buffet? Consider this fabric-covered tray, which is assembled using a pair of cotton napkins, bias tape, and chipboard. The tray can be used to organize such items as dishes, silverware, napkins, or condiments.

The tray's beauty lies in the choice of "fabric"—in this case, two 20- to 21-inch-square napkins in complementary colors. Cotton napkins are available in a wide range of prints—from the charming French-style napkins I chose to more elegant, formal designs. You can also use a pair of your own mismatched napkins or a tag sale find.

I opted for 4-inch high sides on my tray in order to highlight the napkin's border pattern. You can vary this height as necessary to accommodate the edge of your napkins, but keep the edge deep enough so items don't slide off the tray.

Joanne Bembry is a designer and writer living in Jasper, Florida.

INSTRUCTIONS

1. *Make chipboard inserts.* Steam-press napkins until smooth. Measure each napkin horizontally and vertically to find shortest dimension. Subtract 8" from shortest dimension to obtain measurement Y. On chipboard, using pencil, steel ruler, and triangle, draft one Y x Y square for tray base. Then draft four 3¼" x Y rectangles for tray sides. Cut out all five pieces using utility knife and steel ruler.

2. *Glue chipboard to exterior napkin.* Lay napkin for tray exterior wrong side up. Center chipboard base on it, then position four chipboard sides around it, ⅜" from base and at least ⅜" from napkin edges (*see* illustration A, next page). Working one piece at a time, brush chipboard with glue. (If necessary, make glue more spreadable by diluting sparingly with water.) Turn chipboard glue side down and press gently in place. When all five pieces are glued, turn napkin face up and press with palms to adhere. Let dry 20 minutes.

3. *Fuse fleece to interior napkin.* Lay fusible fleece on flat work surface. Using fine-tip marker, steel ruler, and triangle, draft square measuring Y + 8", then cut out. Draft 4" square in each corner (illustration B), then cut out marked corners. Lay napkin for tray interior wrong side up and center fleece on it. Trim fleece edges ¼" inside napkin edges (illustration C). Fuse fleece to napkin following manufacturer's directions.

4. *Attach ties.* Press bias tape in half lengthwise and stitch edges together. Cut into eight 9" pieces. Machine-baste ties to exterior napkin edge alongside chipboard sides (illustration D).

5. *Assemble tray.* Pin both napkins together, wrong sides facing and edges matching (illustration E). Position exterior napkin on top. Using zipper foot, stitch all four edges together. If edges don't match exactly, ease to fit. Stitch four straight lines from edge to edge in channels created between base and sides (illustration F). For even stitching, position tray so base is to left of needle. Treat cut ends of ties with fray preventer to discourage raveling, then let ties dry 24 hours. To assemble tray, raise sides and tie so corners flare out handkerchief style (illustration G). ◆

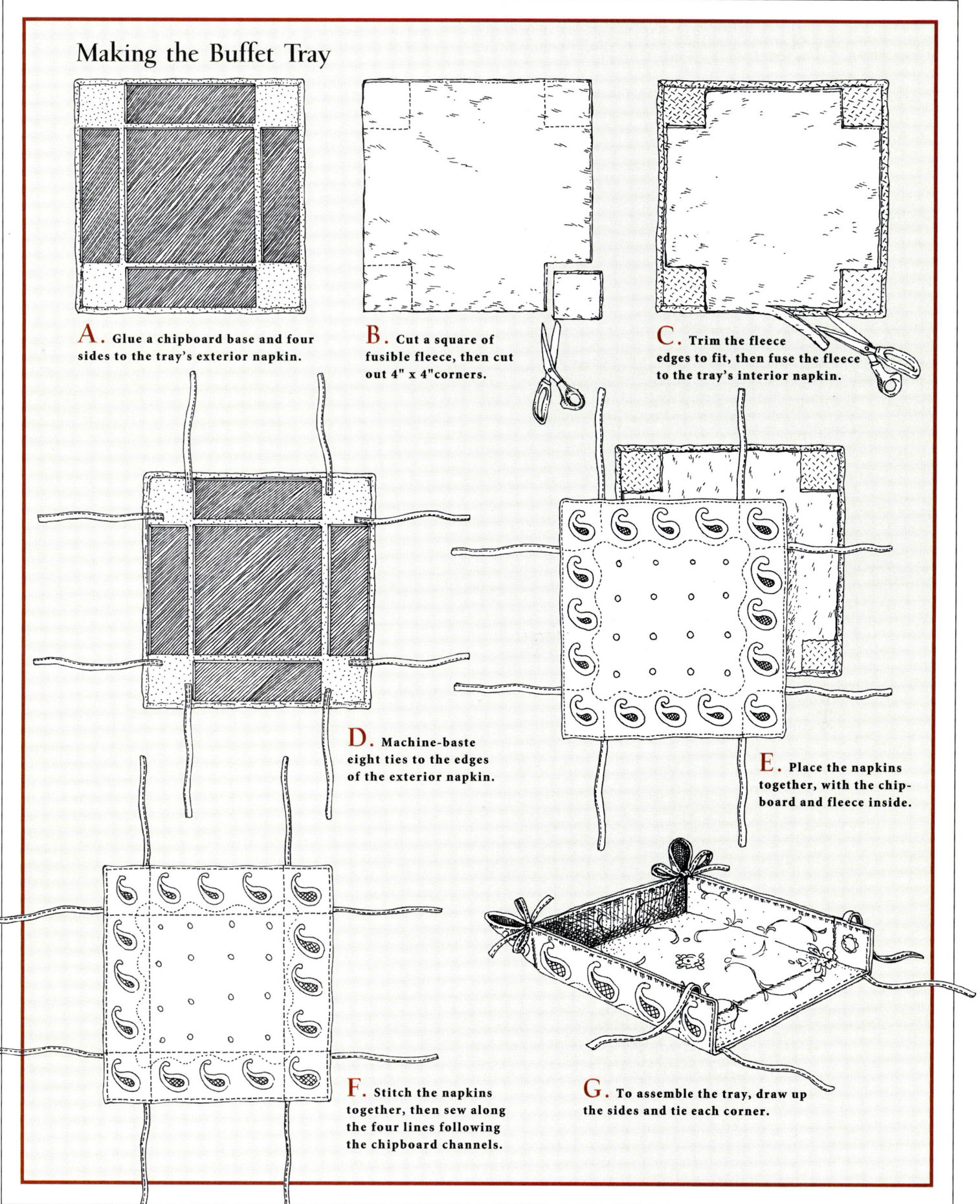

DECORATIVE FOOD

Alice-in-Wonderland Fantasy Cookies

Re-create the look of hand-painted ceramic ornaments by decorating sugar cookies with paste food coloring.

🍪 BY LILY FRANKLIN

These cookies can be used as ornaments. Create a hanging loop from 28-gauge wire, tie the ends together, and position the knot under the cookie before baking.

COLOR PHOTOGRAPHY:
Carl Tremblay

ILLUSTRATION:
Nenad Jakesevic

STYLING:
Ritch Holben

SILHOUETTE PHOTO:
Daniel van Ackere

THE CARTOONISH SHAPES AND whimsical palette of these cookies are inspired by an Alice-in-Wonderland fantasy tea party. Although they resemble hand-painted ceramic ornaments, the cookies are actually tinted with paste food coloring, making them completely edible.

While the cookie shapes are beautiful on their own, their true uniqueness comes in the piped icing designs. For this task, I needed several colors of icing, which presented two problems: which type of icing to use and how to create an interesting palette of colors.

After testing several ready-made icings, I ended up making my own icing from scratch. The ready-made icings in squeeze tubes were convenient to use, but the available colors were either too ordinary or too bright. I also had difficulty getting these icings to flow easily and smoothly. My icing extrudes easily but is stiff enough not to run off the edges of the cookies. The icing levels to a smooth, satiny surface in a few minutes, hardens to the touch in 15 to 20 minutes, and is completely hard in an hour.

Making my own icing also meant I needed an easy way to color it. I tested ordinary food coloring and found the results not special enough. I ended up combining several shades of Chefmaster paste food coloring and Chefmaster Neon Brite airbrush colors, both of which are used by professional chefs and cake decorators. (Paste food coloring is available at cake-decorating supply stores or through mail order; *see* Sources & Resources, page 48.) Both types of food coloring come in a wide range of colors and can be combined to create new colors. Mixing 2 drops of Brite Purple airbrush color with 3 drops of Royal Blue paste food color, for instance, creates a beautiful shade of periwinkle.

After a certain amount of testing, I discovered that fine-tipped plastic squeeze bottles are the best means of decorating the cookies. For the finishing details, I added a variety of decorative items such as polka dots of icing, pre-made florets, and dragées.

Lily Franklin is a designer living in Albuquerque, New Mexico.

INSTRUCTIONS

1. *Make cookie templates.* Photocopy teapot, teacup, and cake patterns (*see* page 44). Trim each pattern ½" beyond edges, then glue to cardboard. Cut along pattern outlines.

2. *Mix cookie dough.* In large bowl, sift flour, salt, and baking powder. Use electric mixer to cream butter and granulated sugar until fluffy, then beat in egg. Add dry ingredients in ½-cup increments and mix at low speed until combined. Mix in brandy and vanilla. Shape dough into two portions, wrap in plastic, and refrigerate 30 minutes.

3. *Cut and bake cookies.* Lightly grease cookie sheets. Roll out dough on lightly floured surface to ⅛" thickness. Lay templates on dough, then run paring knife along template to cut cookie. If dough tends to distort, press knife blade straight down into dough instead of slicing through it. Use floured metal spatula to transfer cut shapes to cookie sheet. Repeat to cut five of each design, gathering up dough scraps and rerolling as needed. Refrigerate cookies 15 minutes while preheating oven to 325 degrees. Bake cookies 8 to 10 minutes or until golden brown.

4. *Mix icing.* Beat egg whites, confectioners' sugar, vanilla, and cream of tartar

DECORATIVE FOOD

MATERIALS
Yields 15 cookies

Cookie Dough
- 2 cups all-purpose flour, plus extra for surfaces
- 1/4 teaspoon salt
- 1/2 teaspoon baking powder
- 1/2 cup unsalted butter, softened, plus extra for greasing pans
- 1 cup granulated sugar
- 1 large egg, lightly beaten
- 1 tablespoon brandy
- 1/2 teaspoon vanilla extract

Icing
- 2 large egg whites
- 2 cups confectioners' sugar
- 1 teaspoon vanilla extract
- 1/4 teaspoon cream of tartar
- 1-ounce Chefmaster paste food colors:
  Egg Shade
  Deep Pink
  Sunset Orange
  Royal Blue
- 2-ounce Chefmaster Neon Brite airbrush colors:
  Brite Green
  Brite Purple
- 55 gumpaste florets
- 4-ounce bottle silver dragées

You'll also need:
cookie patterns (*see* page 44); six 2-ounce plastic squeeze bottles, each with coupler and size 2 round cake-decorating tip; five small containers with lids (e.g., baby food jars); electric mixer; sifter; large mixing bowl; measuring cup; measuring spoons; metal spatula; plastic wrap; rolling pin; cookie sheets; wire racks; paring knife; medium-size bowl; teaspoon; toothpicks; access to photocopier with enlarger; thin cardboard; scissors; glue; and ruler.

until peaks begin to form. Consistency should be smooth.

5. *Color icing and fill squeeze bottles.* Fill one 2-ounce plastic squeeze bottle with icing, screw on coupler with round tip, and set upside down in medium-size bowl. Divide remaining icing evenly among five jars, then cap to prevent hardening. Following color recipes below, add food colors 1 drop or grain at a time, stirring thoroughly with teaspoon after each addition. Because colors are concentrated and difficult to measure, modify recipes as needed to create desired shades. Airbrush colors can be dispensed by drop from their containers. For paste colors, use toothpick to transfer amount equal to one grain of long-grain rice. As each icing color is mixed, transfer to plastic squeeze bottle and set upside down in bowl next to white icing.

- *Chartreuse:* 6 drops Brite Green, 1/2 grain Deep Pink
- *Peach:* 1 grain each Egg Shade, Deep Pink, and Sunset Orange
- *Periwinkle:* 3 grains Royal Blue, 2 drops Brite Purple
- *Plum:* 3 drops Brite Purple
- *Yellow:* 1 grain Egg Shade

6. *Apply icing outlines to cookies.* Following directions below and referring to boldface lines on cookie templates, pipe icing outlines onto cookies. To start icing flow, shake bottles down sharply once or twice and keep bottles not in use upside down in bowl. For smooth lines, hold tip of squeeze bottle at 45-degree angle 1/8" above surface; do not scrape tip against cookie. Let outlines harden 10 to 15 minutes.

Teapot: Outline spout with chartreuse, handle with peach, lid rim with periwinkle, and base with plum. Draw eighteen-square checkerboard on bottom half of pot with white (*see* illustration A, below).

Teacup: Outline cup, rim, and stripes on bottom half of cup with white. To fill in thick white stripes, pipe closely spaced parallel bands, which will sink and fuse together to make solid color blocks. Outline handle with yellow and saucer rim with plum.

Cake: Outline cake with white and platter rim with plum. Draw ten-square checkerboard on pedestal with yellow.

7. *Apply ground colors and decorations.* Following directions below and referring to cookie templates, pipe icing to outline each solid area, then fill in areas with closely spaced parallel bands.

Teapot: Fill spout with peach, handle and lid with chartreuse, and lid knob with plum. Fill every other square in checkerboard with periwinkle (illustration B), then fill remaining squares with white. Fill in top half of pot with yellow, then press three florets and seven dragées into yellow section while icing is still wet (illustration C). Let icing harden 20 minutes. Pipe yellow dots onto spout and plum dots onto handle.

Teacup: Fill in lower half of cup and saucer base with periwinkle, saucer with yellow, cup interior with peach, and handle with plum. To create yellow dots on plum handle, touch yellow tip to surface while still wet and lift off. Fill top half of cup with chartreuse. Press three florets and six dragées into chartreuse section while icing is still wet. Let icing harden 20 minutes.

Cake: Fill every other square in checkerboard with periwinkle, then fill remaining squares with yellow. To create yellow dot on each periwinkle square, touch yellow tip to surface while still wet and lift off. Fill pedestal rim with white, remaining platter area with chartreuse, and cake with peach. Press four dragées into chartreuse platter rim and five florets and eleven dragées into peach section while icing is still wet. Let icing harden 20 minutes. Pipe chartreuse dots onto pedestal rim. ◆

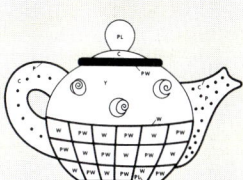

PATTERNS
See **page 44** for pattern pieces.

DECORATING THE COOKIES

A. Pipe the design outline, then let the icing harden for 10 to 15 minutes.

B. Ice the areas within the outlines to make solid blocks of color.

C. Press florets and dragées into the icing while it is still wet.

LOW-SEW

Faux Suede and Crocodile Backpacks

Select an unusual fabric such as Ultrasuede or vinyl, then sew a backpack in one of two sizes using our five-piece pattern.

🌰 BY MICHIO RYAN

The larger version of the backpack measures approximately 10" high when complete, while the smaller bag measures about 6" high.

COLOR PHOTOGRAPHY:
Carl Tremblay

ILLUSTRATION:
Michael Gellatly

CUTTING LAYOUTS:
Roberta Frauwirth

STYLING:
Ritch Holben

SILHOUETTE PHOTOGRAPHY:
Daniel van Ackere

THESE LEATHER-LOOK BACKPACKS are both easy to sew and fully functional. I selected a camel-colored Ultrasuede to give the larger bag an understated and classic design; the smaller one is sewn from faux crocodile vinyl for a flashier look.

These backpacks are not very expensive to make. Although the fabric starts at about forty dollars per yard, each backpack requires less than a yard of fabric. Ultrasuede, a brand name for imitation suede, is very easy to work with. It is supple and soft like suede, yet sturdy enough to hold both the backpack's shape and its contents. Furthermore, it is easily washable, wears well, is available in a wide range of colors, and features no nap, meaning it can be cut in any direction.

The faux crocodile vinyl looks quite different from Ultrasuede but behaves similarly and can be handled in much the same way. Vinyls come in a range of colors, including metallic, iridescent, and neon, as well as embossed patterns. Unlike conventional vinyl-coated fabrics, such as those used for upholstery, these newer versions are much thinner and easy to sew. In addition, vinyls with an embossed pattern tend to mask any sewing imperfections.

The five pattern pieces on page 46 include the main panels as well as the add-on elements, which comprise a front pocket with flap, an oval bottom, and a top flap that closes over the bag's drawstring pull. Strips for the straps and the handle are cut without patterns using a rotary cutter.

To add some contrast to the large pack, I lined the front pocket and top flaps with a leopard print. For variation, consider a small floral or striped pattern or a different texture such as grosgrain. Be sure to select a fabric with about the same thickness as the Ultrasuede so the two sides are consistent. (To strengthen the bottom and flap pieces, I used interfacing between the two layers. I interfaced the entire small backpack for the same reason.) Because the smaller bag already has a busy surface texture, I didn't need a contrasting lining and used the same vinyl material.

I chose Velcro to fasten the flaps, primarily because snaps would have to be precisely aligned for proper closure. The top flap conceals a drawstring closure. I recommend using a boot or shoe lace for the string, as it is easy to thread through the sleeve. For a finishing touch, I attached metallic beads to the two ends of the laces, giving the otherwise sleek and plain design a little flash.

One note regarding the two bags: The instructions for the two versions are slightly different to account for differences between the Ultrasuede and vinyl.

Large Backpack
INSTRUCTIONS

Note: To prevent pin holes from marring the Ultrasuede fabric, insert pins in the seam allowances only. For smooth sewing, use a #11 leather needle and set the stitch length at 8 to 10 stitches per inch. To ease sewing over bulky layers, use a walking or roller foot. Practice stitching on a scrap of Ultrasuede fabric before stitching your project.

1. *Cut out pattern pieces.* Photocopy five pattern pieces, enlarging 286 percent or so front/back panel measures 9¼" by 15¾" (see page 46). Referring to cutting layout (see page 34), use rotary cutter to cut two 2¾" x 31½" straps and one 2¼" x 10" handle parallel to selvage and one 1¾" x

Making the Pouch and Straps

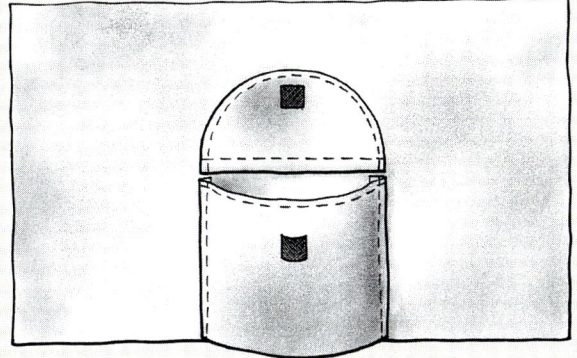

A. Stitch the pocket and its flap to the backpack front.

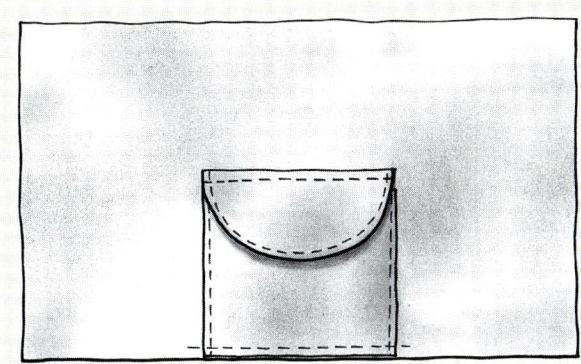

B. Pleat the pocket sides to take up the fullness. Topstitch the flap so it lies flat.

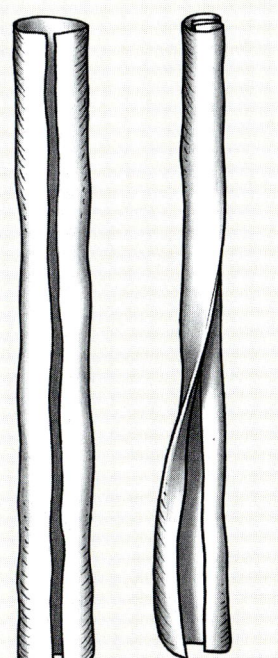

C. Fold the handle in fourths and topstitch the edge.

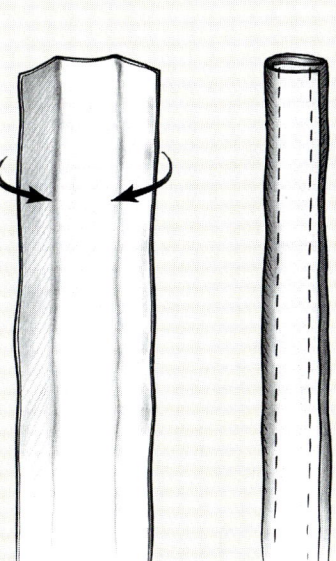

D. Fold the straps in thirds and topstitch both edges.

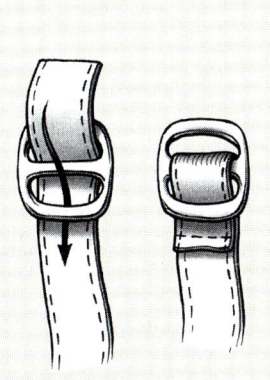

E. Wrap the strap end around the slide's middle bar and stitch securely.

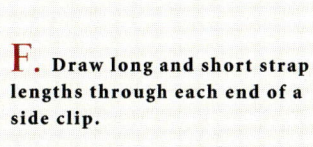

F. Draw long and short strap lengths through each end of a side clip.

29¾" casing perpendicular to selvage. Then cut two bottoms and one each of front, back, top flap, pocket flap, and pocket. From interfacing, cut one each of bottom, top flap, and pocket flap. Fuse interfacing pieces to corresponding fabric pieces using pressing cloth and following manufacturer's instructions. From leopard print, cut one top flap and one pocket flap.

2. *Assemble flaps.* Cut Velcro tape into 1" and 1½" lengths. Separate into loop and hook tapes. Referring to pattern pieces for placement, zigzag 1½" loop tape to front panel, then topstitch edges. Repeat to stitch 1" loop tape to pocket. Position 1½" hook tape on leopard print top flap and topstitch edges. Stitch 1" hook tape to leopard print pocket flap. Pin solid and leopard print flaps right sides together in pairs and stitch ¼" from curved edges. For each, notch seam allowance, turn right side out, and press lightly, then topstitch ¼" from edge.

3. *Join front pocket and flap.* Press long top edge of pocket ⅜" to wrong side, then topstitch. Press two side edges ⅜" to wrong side. Position pocket on front panel, bottom edges aligned, then topstitch side edges, as marked on pattern. Excess fabric will puff out. Set pocket flap face down on front panel, raw edge butting pocket top, and stitch ⅜" from edge (*see* illustration A, above). To shape pocket, tuck and pleat excess fabric evenly at each side, then machine-baste lower edge. Trim flap allowance ⅛" from stitching, fold down flap to conceal cut edge, and topstitch ¼" from fold (illustration B).

4. *Assemble handle and straps.* Fold long edges of handle to center, fold in half lengthwise, then topstitch open edge through all layers (illustration C). Set handle aside. For each strap, press long edges ⅞" toward wrong side to make 1"-wide triple layer; topstitch 3/16" from folded edges (illustration D). Cut off 4½" length and set aside. Slip end of long piece around middle bar of slide and stitch

LOW-SEW

MATERIALS

Large Backpack
- ⅞ yard 54"-wide Ultrasuede fabric
- 8" x 12" remnant leopard-print Ultrasuede fabric
- ½ yard 21"-wide fusible interfacing
- Two 1"-wide side-release clips
- Two 1" single-bar slides
- 1" x 2½" Velcro strip
- 36" dress shoe or boot lace
- Two ½"-diameter beads
- Sewing thread to match fabric

Small Backpack
- ⅞ yard 54"-wide fabric-backed vinyl
- 1½ yards 21"-wide fusible interfacing
- Two ¾" side-release clips
- Two ¾" single-bar slides
- ¾" x 1¾" Velcro strip
- 30" dress shoe or boot lace
- 4 pony beads
- Sewing thread to match fabric

You'll also need:
pattern pieces (*see* page 46); access to photocopier with enlarger; sewing machine; #11 leather sewing machine needle; walking or roller foot; sharp scissors; rotary cutter; ruler; iron; bodkin; pins; and pressing cloth.

PATTERNS
See page 46 for pattern pieces and enlargement instructions.

down (illustration E). Draw free end through male end of side clip and back through slide. Draw 4½" piece through female end of side clip (illustration F).

5. *Attach straps and top flap.* Lay back panel face up. Bend handle into loop and pin to top edge between dots (*see* pattern). Pin long strap ends at each side of handle, then pin short doubled straps to lower edge. Machine-baste through all layers (illustration G). Place top flap face down on back between Xs (*see* pattern) with edges aligned, then machine-baste (illustration H).

6. *Assemble backpack.* Stack front and back panels right sides together and stitch side edges (illustration I). Press seams open, then to one side, and topstitch. Stack two bottoms, concealing interfacing, and pin to lower edge of joined panels, matching dots. Machine-stitch all around, easing to fit. Then topstitch to reinforce seam. Press short ends of casing strip ⅜" to wrong side, then topstitch. Pin strip around top edge, right sides together, leaving ¾" gap above Velcro. Machine-stitch through all layers ⅜" from edge (illustration J). To form casing, fold strip and seam allowance to inside, then topstitch edge of backpack all around through all layers (illustration K). Use bodkin to draw shoelace drawstring through casing. Trim lace ends with beads.

Small Backpack
INSTRUCTIONS

Note: To prevent pin holes from marring the vinyl fabric, insert pins in the seam allowances only. For smooth sewing, use a #11 leather needle and set the stitch length at 8 to 10 stitches per inch. To ease sewing over bulky layers, use a walking or roller foot. Practice stitching on a scrap of vinyl before stitching your project. Do not use iron on vinyls; instead, finger-press where needed.

1. *Cut out pattern pieces.* Photocopy five pattern pieces, enlarging 200 percent, or so front/back panel measures 6½" x 11". Cut vinyl in half lengthwise to yield two 27"-wide pieces. (Set aside one piece for a future project.) Fuse interfacing in sections to remaining piece using pressing cloth and following manufacturer's instructions. Referring to cutting layout below, use rotary cutter to cut two 2" x 31½" straps and one 2¼" x 10" handle parallel to selvage and one 1¾" x 21" casing perpendicular to selvage. Using rotary cutter or scissors and observing pattern grain lines, cut two bottoms, two top flaps, two pocket flaps, and one each of front, back, and pocket.

2. *Assemble flaps.* Cut Velcro tape into ¾" and 1" lengths. Separate into loop and hook tapes. Referring to pattern pieces for placement, zigzag 1" loop tape to front panel, then topstitch edges. Repeat to stitch ¾" loop tape to pocket. Position 1" hook tape on top flap and topstitch edges. Stitch ¾" hook tape to pocket flap. Pin flaps right sides together in pairs and stitch ¼" from curved edges. Notch seam allowance, turn right side out, finger-press, and topstitch ¼" from edge.

3. *Join front pocket and flap.* Same as large backpack, step 3. Remember to finger-press instead of using iron.

4. *Assemble handle and straps.* Make handle same as large backpack handle, step 4. For each strap, finger-press long edges ⅝" toward wrong side to make ¾"-wide triple layer, then topstitch ³⁄₁₆" from folded edges (illustration D). Continue as for large backpack, step 4.

5. *Attach straps and top flap.* Same as for large backpack, step 5. Trim handle to shorten loop as desired (for example, if pack is for a child).

6. *Assemble backpack.* Same as for large backpack, step 6. ◆

CUTTING LAYOUT

LARGE BACKPACK

Also cut one bottom, one pocket flap, and on top flap from fusible interfacing.

LARGE BACKPACK LINING

SMALL BACKPACK

Fuse interfacing to vinyl, then cut all pieces as shown.

Attaching the Straps

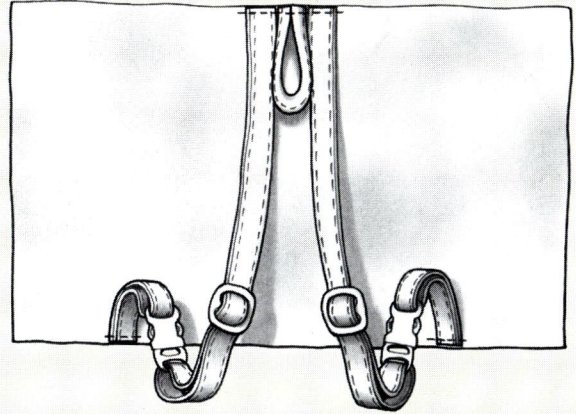

G. Baste the handle and straps to the backpack back.

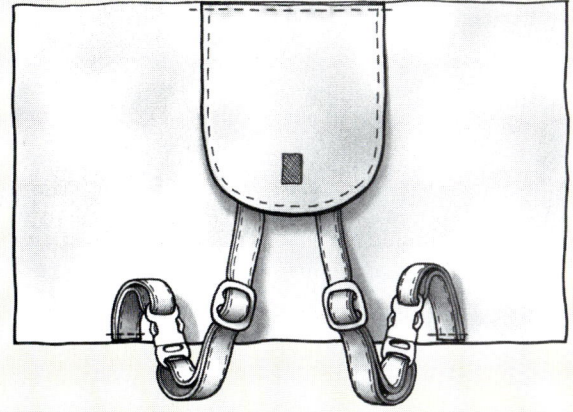

H. Baste the top flap to the back over the handle and straps.

Assembling the Backpack

I. Stitch the front and back together at the sides.

J. Sew in the bottoms, then sew the casing strip around the top edge.

K. To form the casing, fold the strip to the inside and topstitch. Add a shoe or boot lace drawstring.

DESIGNER'S TIP

These bags are machine-washable, but it is advisable to wash them in a lingerie bag or by hand. Otherwise, the straps might get caught in the machine or wrapped up in your clothes.

LOW-SEW

Appliqué Blanket Turnover
Dress up an ordinary blanket with this appliquéd wool turnover.

BY MICHIO RYAN

To dress up this blanket, we appliquéd leaves to a brown wool turnover. The same appliqué technique can be used to create decorative pillows and throws.

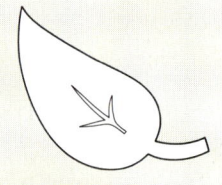

PATTERNS
See **page 47** for pattern pieces and enlargement instructions.

COLOR PHOTOGRAPHY:
Carl Tremblay

ILLUSTRATION:
Mary Newell DePalma

Looking for a beautiful and unique gift? Consider adding an appliquéd turnover to a solid-colored blanket.

To get started, I purchased an ordinary cream-colored blanket. I cut six leaves from camel-colored wool, then appliquéd them to a section of brown wool. The brown wool is folded in half, then sewn onto the top of the blanket, thereby extending its length by 30 inches. When the blanket is placed on the bed, the brown-colored section is turned over to reveal the appliquéd design (see illustration E, next page).

My blanket fits a queen-size bed; as such, the turnover requires 2½ yards of 60-inch-wide fabric. This measurement will vary, however, if you purchase a twin- or full-size blanket (see instructions, step 1, for determining yardage.) The leaf appliqués can be cut from ⅜ yard of contrasting wool, or from remnants if you have them.

To appliqué the leaves with an "invisible" zigzag stitch, thread the upper half of your sewing machine with very fine (size .004) nylon monofilament thread and load the bobbin with cotton sewing thread. Cotton thread is needed in the bobbin to counteract the upper thread's springiness as the stitches are formed and locked. Don't use nylon monofilament thread in the bobbin, as the stitches will form large loops that tangle together and jam the machine.

INSTRUCTIONS

1. *Cut brown wool for turnover.* Measure blanket width along binding edge. Purchase brown wool yardage at least ⅛ yard longer than width of blanket. Using rotary cutter, trim selvages from brown wool; trim and square ends so piece matches blanket width. Trim binding from one end of blanket (see illustration A, next page).

2. *Cut out leaf appliqués.* Photocopy six leaf patterns, enlarging 200 percent, or so leaf #1 measures 10" x 9". Cut out patterns with scissors, then cut vein outlines. Pin patterns to camel-colored wool. Cut leaf outlines with rotary cutter. Snip into inside angles and cut leaf veins with sewing shears.

3. *Appliqué leaves to turnover.* Fold brown wool yardage in half, right side out. Lay flat with fold at bottom (illustration B). Rub glue stick onto back of each wool leaf, then arrange leaves in lower right corner, as shown or as desired, and press in place. Unfold turnover carefully without dislodging leaves. Thread upper machine with monofilament thread and

MATERIALS

- Off-white woven acrylic or wool blanket
- 60"-wide dark brown wool (see step 1 for yardage)
- ⅜ yard 60"-wide camel- or tan-colored wool
- 4 ounces off-white worsted wool yarn
- 4 ounces camel worsted wool yarn
- Dark brown cotton sewing thread
- Clear nylon monofilament thread

You'll also need:
leaf patterns (see page 47); sewing machine; rotary cutter; sewing shears; dressmaker's measuring tape; tapestry needle; straight pins; light and dark fabric marking pencils; fabric glue stick; clear grid ruler; scissors; and access to photocopier with enlarger.

Sewing the Blanket

A. Cut a turnover from the wool to match the blanket width.

B. Fold the turnover in half to arrange the leaves, then unfold it to appliqué them.

C. Topstitch the turnover to the blanket edge.

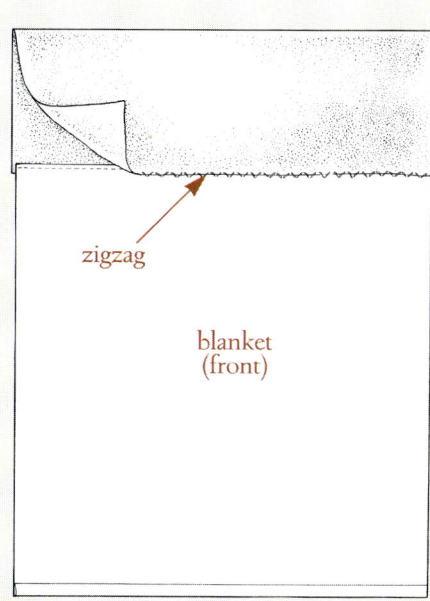

D. Fold the turnover to the other side and zigzag the free edge.

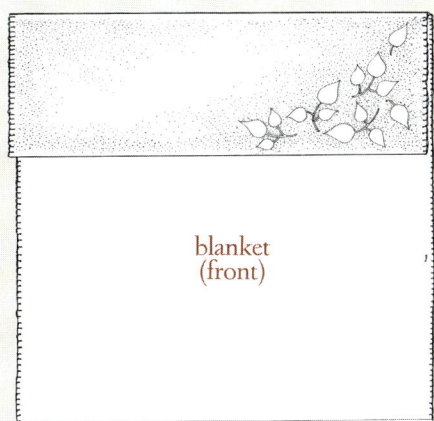

E. Blanket-stitch the side edges. To use the blanket, fold the turnover toward the front.

DESIGNER'S TIP

To further decorate the appliquéd leaves, add decorative stitching, such as a satin, blanket, or herringbone stitch, along the edges. For further variation, outline the leaves just inside the edges with a backstitch, chain stitch, or stem stitch.

---

bobbin with cotton thread. Set sewing machine for narrow (1/8"-wide) zigzag stitch. Practice sewing on scrap of wool to test thread tension; for smoother stitching, loosen upper thread. Appliqué leaves to turnover by zigzagging over all raw edges.

4. *Join turnover to blanket.* Lay turnover flat, right side up, with leaves at lower left (illustration C). Lay blanket flat so back faces up, then slip cut edge of blanket under lower edge of turnover, overlapping for 2". Pin in place, then topstitch turnover edge to blanket. Turn blanket over. Fold down turnover so edge conceals brown straight stitching on blanket. Zigzag turnover edge to blanket, stitching through all three layers (illustration D).

5. *Blanket-stitch edges.* Lay grid ruler along unbound edge of blanket, measuring 5/8" in from edge. Using contrasting fabric marking pencil, mark dot along ruler edge every 5/8". Thread tapestry needle with 36" length of camel yarn. Following dots, work blanket stitch (see below) along edge. Join in new yarn when needed; change to off-white yarn when stitching reaches brown turnover. Repeat to trim opposite side (illustration E). To use blanket, place on bed, then turn down brown section to reveal design. ◆

Blanket Stitch

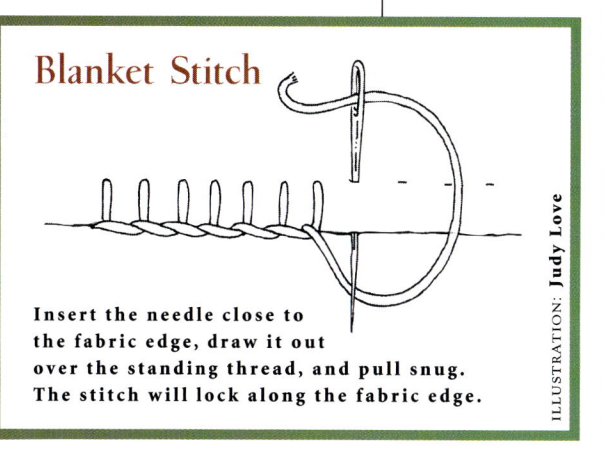

Insert the needle close to the fabric edge, draw it out over the standing thread, and pull snug. The stitch will lock along the fabric edge.

ILLUSTRATION: Judy Love

FAUX FINISHES

Foolproof Hand-Painted Walls

Create a template for freehand painting by hanging a sheer lace panel, then casting a patterned shadow onto your walls.

BY CAROL ENDLER STERBENZ

MATERIALS
- 1 pint off-white latex paint
- 3 yards patterned lace (or 108"-long lace curtain panel)

You'll also need: small, medium, and large (e.g., up to ½" diameter) round artist's acrylic/oil brushes; 100-watt clip-on lamp; extension cord; 2 ladders; 1½"-wide painter's tape; 1-quart plastic container; disposable gloves; paint-stirring stick; tape measure; pencil; and paper.

DESIGNER'S TIP
The pattern can only be projected onto one wall at a time, yet it's important to create the same size pattern on each wall. For a larger overall image, hang the panel further from the wall and/or move the lamp back. The image will blur as it grows larger; for this reason, experiment with different positions for size but keep the image clear enough that you can follow it with a paintbrush.

COLOR PHOTOGRAPHY:
Carl Tremblay

ILLUSTRATION:
Michael Gellatly

STYLING:
Ritch Holben

This faux wallpaper was created by painting an off-white design and freehand curlicues on top of a coffee-colored background.

IN DESIGNING THIS WALL FINISH, I wanted to create a hand-painted effect but was reluctant to start freehand painting without some guarantee of the results. To make the method virtually foolproof, I hung a patterned sheer curtain from the ceiling. Then I fixed a lamp behind the panel, which projected a patterned shadow onto the wall. To paint the design, I simply followed the shadows with a paintbrush, then added a few freehand curlicues.

To create depth and variation in the design, I used different strengths of paint. I painted the basic design using a thicker coat of paint, while I added the flourishes using a very light wash. One word of caution: This painting is very free-form. Circulating air will move the lace panel, for instance, which can change the position of the shadow. Don't expect a printed wallpaper look with a regular repeat pattern, but rather a dynamic and irregular design that resembles wallpaper.

INSTRUCTIONS
Note: To begin, paint the wall with one or two coats of the background color. Let it dry overnight before proceeding. If the ceiling is freshly painted, wait a minimum of 1 week before applying tape to it.

1. *Cast design on wall.* Darken windows or work in evening. Working with partner and standing on separate ladders, suspend lace or curtain panel from ceiling to floor, parallel to wall and about 30" away from it. Tape top of panel to ceiling from both sides with double band of painter's tape (see illustration A, below). Clip lamp to ladder halfway between ceiling and floor, then position so bulb is about 30" in front of lace. To cast shadow, turn on lamp and turn off all other light sources (illustration B). Adjust ladder position for desired size or clarity, then measure and record wall-to-lace and lace-to-lamp distances in order to duplicate setup on remaining walls.

2. *Paint design.* Pour paint into plastic container. If right-handed, paint from right to left; if left-handed, paint from left to right. Decide whether to paint shadowed or lit motifs. Paint largest motifs first, choosing brush size that outlines and fills motif with fewest strokes. To load brush, dip bristles in paint, then slap them back and forth against inside wall of bucket to shed excess from outer bristles (prevents drips). To prevent wavering strokes, hold brush handle between middle and tip of handle, rather than at ferrule. Starting at broadest part of design, press brush firmly against wall and draw bristles along in smooth, confident motion. To taper end of stroke, lessen pressure as you lift brush off. Switch to smaller brush for more delicate areas.

3. *Repeat motif on remaining walls.* Take down lace panel. Using recorded measurements, repeat step 1 setup for next side of room. Tape panel to ceiling and paint new area as in step 2. Repeat around room.

4. *Add freehand flourishes.* After entire room has been painted, use small round brush to paint freehand curlicues and tendrils. For a wispy look, dilute paint slightly with water. ◆

PAINTING THE WALL

A. Suspend the lace from the ceiling with a double band of painter's tape.

B. Shine a lamp through the lace to cast a patterned shadow on the wall.

Mail-Order Directory

Annual Mail-Order Supplier Directory

ART SUPPLIES

ART SUPPLY WAREHOUSE EXPRESS
5325 Departure Drive
Raleigh, NC 27604
800-995-6778
Offers: Wide range of artist's supplies, including paints, brushes, pencils, pastels, mat cutters, and frames. **Free catalog.**

DANIEL SMITH
4150 First Avenue South
P.O. Box 84268
Seattle, WA 98124-5568
800-426-6740
Offers: Artist's materials from paints, brushes, paper, and canvas to frames, metallic leafing supplies, and books. **Catalog $5 (includes $5 certificate; free supplemental catalogs).**

DICK BLICK ART MATERIALS
P.O. Box 1267
Galesburg, IL 61402-1267
800-447-8192
Offers: Large selection of artist's supplies, including paints, brushes, paper and boards, screen-printing materials, printmaking tools, craft supplies, ceramic tools, and computer software. **Free catalog.**

ATTENTION READERS

Do you know of a superior mail-order supplier or catalog that's not listed here? Send us a copy of the catalog or the supplier's name and address and we'll include them in our 1998 directory. Mail information to:

ANNUAL MAIL-ORDER DIRECTORY
Handcraft Illustrated
17 Station Street
P.O. Box 509
Brookline Village, MA
02147-0509
e-mail: hncftill@aol.com

FIDELITY GRAPHIC ARTS
5601 International Parkway
P.O. Box 155
Minneapolis, MN 55440-0155
800-326-7555
Offers: Tools and supplies for architects, engineers, contractors, designers (including computer-aided design), and desktop publishers. **Free catalog.**

FLAX ART AND DESIGN
240 Valley Drive
Brisbane, CA 94005
800-547-7778
Offers: Tools and supplies for artists as well as gifts for art enthusiasts. **Free catalog.**

GRAPHIK DIMENSIONS LTD.
2103 Brentwood Street
High Point, NC 27263
800-221-0262
Offers: Supplies and materials for do-it-yourself framing. **Free catalog.**

JERRY'S ARTARAMA
5325 Departure Drive
Raleigh, NC 27604
800-827-8478
Offers: Full line of art supplies and furniture as well as gifts and books for the art enthusiast. **Free catalog.**

OTT'S DISCOUNT ART SUPPLY
102 Hungate Drive
Greenville, NC 27858
800-356-3289
Offers: Discount art supplies from paints, brushes, calligraphy supplies, and palettes to drawing materials, canvas, markers, and varnish. **Free catalog.**

PEARL PAINT COMPANY, INC.
308 Canal Street
New York, NY 10013-2572
800-221-6845
Offers: Wide selection of art and craft supplies, including paints, mediums, canvas, framing materials, books, drawing materials, paper, gold leaf, and accessories. **Catalog $1 (free supplemental catalogs).**

PIERCE TOOLS
1610 Parkdale Drive
Grants Pass, OR 97527
541-476-1778
Offers: Tools for the ceramist, doll maker, sculptor, and potter. **Free catalog.**

SAX ARTS AND CRAFTS
P.O. Box 510710
New Berlin, WI 53151-0710
800-323-0388
Offers: A full supply of art supplies, tools, and materials as well as books and gifts for the art enthusiast. **Catalog $5 (can be applied toward first purchase).**

TEXAS ART SUPPLY
2001 Montrose Boulevard
Houston, TX 77006-1299
800-888-9278
Offers: Large selection of art supplies. **Catalog $3 ($1 for CD-ROM version).**

TORRINGTON BRUSH WORKS, INC.
63 Avenue "A"
P.O. Box 56
Torrington, CT 06790
800-262-7874 (CT)
800-525-1416 (FL)
Offers: Wide selection of brushes and accessories from china bristle and nylon paintbrushes to dusters, foam brushes, artist brushes, mops, and tube brushes. **Free catalog.**

GENERAL CRAFT SUPPLIES

AMERICAN ART CLAY COMPANY, INC.
4717 West 16th Street
Indianapolis, IN 46222
800-374-1600
Offers: Craft supplies, toys, books, and accessories relating to products such as Fimo polymer clay, Friendly Plastic modeling material, and more. **Free catalog.**

CIRCLECRAFT SUPPLY
P.O. Box 3000
Dover, FL 33527-3000
813-659-0992
Offers: Assorted craft supplies from beads, fabrics, jewelry findings to brushes, Styrofoam, and wood products, among others. **Free catalog.**

CRAFT CATALOG
P.O. Box 1069
Reynoldsburg, OH 43068
800-777-1442
Offers: Wide selection of craft supplies, including wood turnings, paint, jewelry findings, brushes, stencils, trims, and ribbons. **Free catalog.**

CRAFT KING
P.O. Box 90637
Lakeland, FL 33804
800-769-9494
Offers: Discount craft supplies covering a wide range of products, including beads, books, doll parts, floral supplies, paint, ribbon, and wood items. **Free catalog.**

EARTH GUILD
33 Haywood Street
Asheville, NC 28801
800-327-8448
Offers: Tools, materials, and books for handcrafts. Specific topics include basketry, dyeing, spinning, candle making, beading, and modeling clays. **Free catalog.**

ENTERPRISE ART
P.O. Box 2918
Largo, FL 33779
800-366-2218
Offers: Large assortment of beads, rhinestones, and findings as well as assorted craft supplies. **Free catalog.**

HANDCRAFT VARIETY SOURCE BOOK
National Artcraft Company
7996 Darrow Road
Twinsburg, OH 44087
800-793-0152 (orders only)
800-292-4916 (Fax)
216-963-6011
Offers: Wide variety of crafts components, including miniatures, buttons by the bag, picture frame supplies, tiles, and brushes. **Catalog $1.**

DIRECTORY

LARK BOOKS
50 College Street
Asheville, NC 28801-2896
800-284-3388
Offers: Books, kits, and gifts for craft enthusiasts. **Free catalog.**

MAPLEWOOD CRAFTS
Humboldt Industrial Park
1 Maplewood Drive
Hazleton, PA 18201-0676
800-899-0134
Offers: Wide range of seasonal craft kits as well as beading and needlecraft supplies, books, tools, plastic canvas, paint, dolls, and floral craft materials. **Free catalog.**

MUNRO CORPORATION
3954 West 12 Mile Road
Berkley, MI 48072
800-638-0543
Offers: Pottery and jewelry supplies; Fimo, Sculpey, and Cernit; and crystal beads as well as kits and books. **Catalog $5 (refundable with purchase).**

NASCO ARTS AND CRAFTS
P.O. Box 901
Fort Atkinson, WI 53538-0901
800-558-9595
Offers: Arts and crafts teaching aids, supplies, and equipment. Hundreds of products for art appreciation, drawing, painting, ceramics, printing, and more. **Free catalog.**

PARRISH'S CAKE DECORATING SUPPLIES/MAGIC LINE
225 West 146th Street
Gardena, CA 90248
310-324-2253
800-736-8443
Offers: Magic Modelling Foam for jewelry, barrettes, magnets, ornaments, picture frames, and miniatures. **Catalog $3.**

S&S WORLDWIDE
P.O. Box 515, 75 Mill Street
Colchester, CT 06415-0513
800-243-9232
860-537-3451
Offers: Extensive line of general crafts for children, including sand, clays, fabric paints, yarn, and needlework. **Free catalog.**

SUNSHINE DISCOUNT CRAFTS
P.O. Box 301
Largo, FL 33779
800-729-2878
Offers: Large assortment of craft supplies, including modeling clays and accessories, beads, dolls, miniatures, brushes, and wood items. **Free catalog.**

VANGUARD CRAFTS
P.O. Box 340170
1081 East 48th Street
Brooklyn, NY 11234
800-662-7238
718-377-5188
Offers: Wide variety of crafts supplies, including jewelry kits, fabric-decorating and candle-making supplies, baskets, and clays. Good selection of crafts for children. **Free catalog.**

SPECIALTY CRAFT SUPPLIES

ADVENTURES IN CRAFTS
P.O. Box 6058
Yorkville Station
New York, NY 10128
212-410-9793
Offers: Decoupage prints, tools, kits, and books as well as unfinished wood items. **Catalog $3.50.**

ALLEN'S BASKETWORKS
P.O. Box 82638
Portland, OR 97282
800-284-7333 (orders only)
503-238-6384
Offers: Basketry materials, including reed, rattan, cane, fiber rush, tools, patterns, and books. **Free catalog.**

ANYTHING IN STAINED GLASS
P.O. Box 444
1060 Rte. 47 South
Rio Grande, NJ 08242
800-462-1209
609-886-0416
Offers: Stained glass and supplies, including shears, band saws, foil, crystals, and jewels; kaleidoscope, lamp, and clock kits; and books and patterns. **Free catalog.**

BASIC CERAMIC SUPPLIES
National Artcraft Company
7996 Darrow Road
Twinsburg, OH 44087
800-793-0152 (orders only)
216-963-6011
Offers: Ceramic tools, kilns, glazes, paints, and more. **Catalog $1.**

CERAMIC SUPPLY OF NEW YORK AND NEW JERSEY
7 Rte. 46 West
Lodi, NJ 07644
800-723-7264
201-340-3005
Offers: Full line of glazes, colors, kilns, embossing tools, pens, brushes, respirators, books, videos, and more. **Free catalog.**

CRAFT EDUCATIONAL MARKETING SERVICES
P.O. Box 111422
Stamford, CT 16901-1422
203-325-3748
Offers: Original Santa patterns and related supplies, including Santa faces, heads, hair, and accessory kits. **Catalog $1.**

EASTERN ART GLASS
P.O. Box 341
Wyckoff, NJ 07481
800-872-3458
Offers: Glass- and mirror-etching and decorating supplies. **Free catalog.**

ELECTRICAL AND LIGHTING COMPONENTS CATALOG
National Artcraft Company
7996 Darrow Road
Twinsburg, OH 44087
800-793-0152 (orders only)
216-963-6011
Offers: Lamp and specialty wiring supplies. **Catalog $1.**

H.H. PERKINS COMPANY
10 South Bradley Road
Woodbridge, CT 06525
800-462-6660
203-389-9501
Offers: Basketry supplies, including plastic cane, fiber rush, ash splint, and Danish cord; Nantucket supplies; basket kits; and books. **Free catalog.**

THE LAMP SHOP
P.O. Box 3606
Concord, NH 03302-3606
603-224-1603
603-224-6677 (Fax)
Offers: Wide variety of lamp-making supplies, including wire, bases, paper, frames, ribbon, fabric, tools, and parts. **Catalog $2.**

MAINELY SHADES
100 Gray Road
Falmouth, ME 04105
800-624-6359
207-797-7568
Offers: Lampshade crafting materials, including frames, fabrics, papers, and paints; lamp bases and electrical supplies; pre-drafted arcs; and books. **Catalog $3.**

METALLIFEROUS
34 West 46th Street
New York, NY 10036
212-944-0909
Offers: Large selection of wire, flat metals, jewelry supplies, and enameling supplies. **Catalog $7.50.**

MUSIC AND CLOCK
National Artcraft Company
7996 Darrow Road
Twinsburg, OH 44087
800-793-0152 (orders only)
216-963-6011
Offers: Musical movements, timepieces, rotation assemblies, carousel kits, and specialty movements for greeting cards and clothing. **Catalog $1.**

SURMA
11 East 7th Street
New York, NY 10003
212-477-0729
Offers: Ukrainian Easter egg–decorating dyes, tools, kits, and supplies. **Free catalog.**

TANDY LEATHER COMPANY
127 Medallion Center
Northwest Highway at Abrams
Dallas, TX 75214
214-361-2718
Offers: Starter kits; belts and buckles; bead looms; Native American–style supplies; tools, dyes, conditioners, and stitching supplies; and books, patterns, and stamps. **Free catalog.**

TINKER BOB'S TINWARE
209 Summit Street
Norwich, CT 06360
860-886-7365
Offers: A complete selection of reproduction colonial tinware. **Catalog $3.**

BEADS and JEWELRY MAKING

BEADS GALORE INTERNATIONAL, INC.
2123 South Priest #201
Tempe, AZ 85282
602-921-3949
800-424-9577
Offers: Large selection of stone, glass, silver, and trade beads as well as findings, pendants, and earrings (minimum order $30). **Catalog $5 (refundable with first order).**

DIRECTORY

BEADWORKS
Riverside Plaza
149 Water Street
Norwalk, CT 06854
203-852-9108
800-232-3761
Offers: Large selection of beads and jewelry-making supplies. **Catalog $7.95 (with $5 gift certificate toward list order).**

BUCK'S COUNTY CLASSIC
73 Coventry Lane
Langhorne, PA 19047
800-942-4367
Offers: Jewelry kits, supplies, and tools as well as assorted beads. **Catalog $2.**

CENTRAL CASTING
1150 6th Street
Berkeley, CA 94710
800-745-1350
Offers: Wide assortment of cast, lead-free pewter pieces and parts (minimum order $150). **Free catalog.**

CONTEMPORARY BEADS & CASTINGS, INC.
114 Wilkins Avenue
Port Chester, NY 10573
914-939-6833
Offers: Pewter castings in a variety of finishes as well as polymer clay, ceramic, and glass beads (minimum order $150). **Catalog $6.**

CREATIVE BEGINNINGS
475 Morro Bay Boulevard
Morro Bay, CA 93442
800-367-1739
Offers: Wide assortment of silver- and brass-plated charms and ornaments for jewelry making or embellishing craft projects. Also offers findings, books, paints, and kits. **Free catalog.**

ORNAMENTAL RESOURCES
1427 Miner Street
P.O. Box 3010
Idaho Springs, CO 80452
800-876-6762
(orders and catalog)
303-567-2222
Offers: Wide variety of beads, findings, books, supplies, and tools (minimum order $25). **Catalog $15.**

SHIPWRECK BEADS
2727 Westmoor Court SW
Olympia, WA 98502
800-950-4232 (orders only)
360-754-2323
Offers: Imported Czech lamp, seed, and bugle beads; findings; cut crystal beads; and books. **Catalog $4.**

CANDLE MAKING

POURETTE CANDLE MAKING SUPPLIES
1418 NW 53rd
P.O. Box 17056
Seattle, WA 98115
800-888-9425
206-789-3188
Offers: A complete selection of candle-making supplies, including wax, molds, and wicks. **Free catalog.**

WALNUT HILL
Green Lane and Wilson Avenue
P.O. Box 599
Bristol, PA 19007
215-785-6511
800-NEEDWAX (633-3929)
Offers: Candle-making supplies and specialty waxes such as beeswax, batik wax, and freeze-dry wax (minimum order $75). **Free catalog.**

DECORATIVE BAKING and COOKING

A COOK'S WARES
211 37th Street
Beaver Falls, PA 15010-2103
412-846-9490
Offers: Gourmet cooking and baking supplies, books, equipment, and ingredients. **Catalog $2.**

GRAPEVINE TRADING COMPANY
59 Maxwell Court
Santa Rosa, CA 95401
800-469-6478
707-576-3950
Offers: Dried berries and fruits as well as crystallized edible flowers. **Free catalog.**

KING ARTHUR FLOUR BAKER'S CATALOGUE
P.O. Box 876
Norwich, VT 05055-0876
800-827-6836
Offers: Wide assortment of baking-related supplies and gifts, including breadmaking equipment and books, baker's appliances, grains and yeasts, cake and pastry supplies, and pasta equipment. **Free catalog.**

KITCHEN KRAFTS
P.O. Box 442
Waukon, IA 52172
800-776-0575
319-535-8000
Offers: Food-crafting supplies, equipment, books, and ingredients. **Free catalog.**

LITTLE FOX FACTORY
931 Marion Road
Bucyrus, OH 44820
419-562-5420
Offers: Handmade cookie cutters, suitable for quilt patterns and other crafts. Hundreds of shapes, including dinosaurs, states, and animals. **Free catalog with long, self-addressed stamped envelope.**

SUR LA TABLE
410 Terry Avenue North
Seattle, WA 98109-5229
800-243-0852
206-682-7175
Offers: Cooking equipment, housewares, and gifts, including cake-decorating supplies, Calphalon cookware, a large selection of copper cookware, and more. **Free catalog.**

SWEET CELEBRATIONS INC.
7009 Washington Avenue South
Edina, MN 55439
800-328-6722
Offers: Wide assortment of dessert supplies and accessories, including baking equipment, bridal figures, cake-decorating tools, and candy-making supplies. **Free catalog.**

WILLIAMS-SONOMA
P.O. Box 7456
San Francisco, CA 94120-7456
800-541-2233
Offers: Large selection of housewares and cookware, including glasses, dinnerware, cooking and baking equipment, flatware, appliances, linens, chef's clothing, and more. Also offers recipes, books, herbs, cleaning supplies, and gifts. **Free catalog.**

DOLL MAKING

BEAR CLAWSET
27 Palermo Walk
Long Beach, CA 90803
310-434-8077
Offers: Bear-making supplies and materials from fur, growlers, and joints to patterns and books. **Catalog $2.**

G. SCHOEPFER, INC.
460 Cook Hill Road
Cheshire, CT 06410
800-875-6939
Offers: A complete line of eyes for dolls. **Free catalog.**

SEW-SWEET DOLLS
Carolee Creations, Inc.
787 Industrial Drive
Elmhurst, IL 60126
708-530-7175
Offers: Patterns and materials for making dolls, including beginner patterns, jointed animals (mice, moose, rabbits, puppies, kittens), autograph hounds, hair looms, and instruction books. **Catalog $2.**

FLORAL SUPPLIES

BOUNTIFUL GARDENS
18001 Shafer Ranch Road
Willits, CA 95490-9626
707-459-6410
Offers: Organic seeds, tools, tips, and books. **Free catalog.**

DUTCH GARDENS
P.O. Box 200
Adelphia, NJ 07710-0200
800-818-3861
Offers: Bulbs, tubers, corms, and perennials shipped straight from Holland as well as gardening supplies. **Free catalog.**

GARDENER'S EDEN
P.O. Box 7307
San Francisco, CA 94120-7307
800-822-9600
Offers: A full supply of gardening tools and supplies as well as gifts for gardening enthusiasts. **Free catalog.**

GARDENER'S SUPPLY COMPANY
128 Intervale Road
Burlington, VT 05401-2804
800-444-6417
Offers: A full line of supplies, equipment, and tools for gardeners. **Free catalog.**

MAY SILK
16202 Distribution Way
Cerritos, CA 90703
800-282-7455
Offers: Silk flowers, plants, foliage, trees, arrangements, and accessories. **Free catalog.**

PAINTING, FAUX FINISHING, and STENCILS

ARTEX MANUFACTURING COMPANY
5894 Blackwelder Street

Culver City, CA 90232-7304
213-870-6000
Offers: Full line of Nova Color, an artist's acrylic paint suitable for use on canvas, paper, fabric, wood, plaster, masonry, and most nonslick, nonoily surfaces. **Free catalog.**

ARTIST'S CLUB
13118 NE 4th Ave.
Vancouver, WA 98684
800-845-6507
360-260-8900
Offers: Books, kits, projects, and supplies for tole and decorative painting. **Free catalog.**

BINDER'S DISCOUNT ART CENTER
P.O. Box 52815
Atlanta, GA 30355
800-877-3242
Offers: Artist's supplies and accessories, including oil and acrylic paints, easels, brushes, drawing materials, studio tools, adhesives, portfolios, modeling materials, and frames. **Free catalog.**

CRAFTS JUST FOR YOU!
2030 Clinton Avenue
Alameda, CA 94501
800-272-3848
Offers: A complete range of tole-painting items, including books, kits, paints, brushes, and accessories. **Free catalog.**

CUTBILL & COMPANY
274 Sherman Avenue North
Unit 207
Hamilton, Ontario
Canada L8L 6N6
800-960-3592
Offers: Block-printing supplies and materials, including kits, block-printing pads, and glazes. **Free catalog.**

GAIL GRISI STENCILING, INC.
P.O. Box 1263
Haddonfield, NJ 08033
800-338-1325
609-354-1757
Offers: Wide selection of precut stencils and stencil paints. **Catalog $3.75 (refundable with first order).**

JANOVIC/PLAZA'S INCOMPLETE CATALOGUE FOR DECORATIVE AND SCENIC PAINTERS
30-35 Thomson Avenue
Long Island City, NY 11101
800-772-4381 (outside NY)
718-392-3999
Offers: Brushes, tools, and materials for both home and commercial painting as well as many specialty items used in restoration and preservation work. **Catalog $6.95.**

NEW YORK CENTRAL ART SUPPLY, INC.
62 Third Avenue
New York, NY 10003
800-950-6111
212-475-2513 (Fax)
Offers: Paints, pastels, mediums, brushes, canvas, easels, and more. **Free catalog.**

THE OLD FASHIONED MILK PAINT COMPANY, INC.
436 Main Street
P.O. Box 222
Groton, MA 01450
508-448-6336
Offers: Collection of authentic reproduction paint supplies, including milk paint, antique crackle finish, and more. **Free catalog.**

POTTERY BARN
P.O. Box 7044
San Francisco, CA 94120-7044
800-922-5507
Offers: Small selection of faux finishing products, including woodwash and distressing kit, crackle glaze, stencil kits, colorwash kit, and related books. **Free catalog.**

STENCIL HOUSE OF NEW HAMPSHIRE INC.
P.O. Box 16109
Hooksett, NH 03106
800-622-9416
603-625-1716
Offers: Precut stencils, stencil paints, stencil brushes, and varnish. **Catalog $4 (refundable with first order).**

STU-ART
2045 Grand Avenue
Baldwin, NY 11510
800-645-2855
Offers: Artist's supplies, frames, mats, shrink-wrap material, and picture-saver panels. **Free catalog.**

STULB'S OLD VILLAGE PAINT
P.O. Box 1030
Fort Washington, PA 19034
800-498-7687
215-654-1770
Offers: A collection of authentic acrylic restoration paints, Colonial Williamsburg Simulated Buttermilk paint, paste stains, clear glaze products, and beeswax polish. **Free catalog.**

PAPER ARTS

BAUDVILLE
5380 52nd Street SE
Grand Rapids, MI 49512-9765
800-728-0888
Offers: Software, bordered paper, postcards, place cards, name badges, notecards, plaques, embossers, accessories, and specialty products. **Free catalog.**

THE BOOKBINDER'S WAREHOUSE
31 Division Street
Keyport, NJ 07735
908-264-0306
Offers: Full range of bookbinding supplies, including leather, vellum, parchment, paper, finishing tools, book cloth, instruction manuals for papermaking and marbling, and related supplies and equipment. **Free catalog.**

COLOPHON BOOK ARTS SUPPLY, INC.
3046 Hogum Bay Road NE
Lacey, WA 98516
360-459-2940
Offers: Supplies, equipment, and books related to marbling, making decorative papers, and bookbinding. **Free catalog.**

GOLD'S ARTWORKS INC.
2100 North Pine Street
Lumberton, NC 28358
800-356-2306
Offers: Papermaking supplies, including cotton pulp, molds and deckles, kits, and pigments. **Free catalog.**

LOOSE ENDS
P.O. Box 20310
Keizer, OR 97307
503-390-7457
Offers: Unusual natural fiber papers, ribbons, and botanicals, including seagrass, raffia, dried fruits, and fungi. **Catalog $5.**

LOTUS DESIGN
P.O. Box 1993
Union City, CA 94587
510-487-8357
800-487-5279
Offers: Handmade recycled papers and papermaking supplies. **Free catalog.**

ON PAPER
3342 Melrose Avenue NW
Roanoke, VA 24017
800-820-2299
Offers: A complete line of paper supplies, including designer paper, preprinted stationery and sets, novelty paper, colored paper, software, books, and office products. **Free catalog.**

POTPOURRI

A WORLD OF PLENTY
P.O. Box 1153
Hermantown, MN 55810-9724
218-729-6761
Offers: Potpourri and sachet ingredients, oils, herbs, teas, and tools. **Catalog $1.**

NATURE'S FINEST
P.O. Box 10311
Burke, VA 22009-0311
703-978-3925
Offers: Potpourri supplies, including large selection of oils, dry ingredients, mixes, and reviving solutions. **Free catalog.**

SAN FRANCISCO HERB COMPANY
250 14th Street
San Francisco, CA 94103
800-227-4530
Offers: Complete line of spices for cooking and crafting and potpourri recipes and ingredients. **Free catalog.**

TOM THUMB WORKSHOPS
14100 Lankford Highway
P.O. Box 357
Mappsville, VA 23407
800-526-6502
804-824-3507
Offers: Potpourri, herbs, spices, essential oils, dried and pressed flowers, skeletonized leaves, and crafts. **Free catalog.**

RUBBER STAMPS

DELAFIELD STAMP COMPANY
P.O. Box 56
Delafield, WI 53018
414-646-8599
Offers: More than eight hundred rubber stamp designs as well as ink pads, embossing supplies, heat guns, and inks. **Catalog $4.**

EMBOSSING ARTS COMPANY
P.O. Box 439
Tangent, OR 97389
541-928-9898
Offers: Rubber stamps, brass sten-

DIRECTORY

cils, and card-making and embossing supplies. **Catalog $3 (specify retail catalog). Refundable with first order.**

MAINE STREET STAMPS
P.O. Box 14
Kingfield, ME 04947
207-265-2500
Offers: Selection of rubber stamps, stamp pads, and embossing powder. **Catalog $2.**

STAMPER'S COMPANION
1173 West Country Creek Drive
South Jordan, UT 84095
800-727-2427
Offers: Azadi Earles stamps, inks, and other supplies. **Catalog $2.**

SEWING and FIBER ARTS

ATLANTA THREAD & SUPPLY COMPANY
695 Red Oak Road
Stockbridge, GA 30281
800-847-1001
Offers: Wide assortment of thread, notions, buttons, scissors, drapery hardware, press boards, and other related supplies and equipment. **Free catalog.**

CLOTILDE INC.
2 Sew Smart Way B8031
Stevens Point, WI 54481-8031
800-772-2891
Offers: Large selection of sewing supplies, notions, equipment, and tools, including sewing machine accessories, tables, books, patterns, and gifts. **Free catalog.**

DHARMA TRADING COMPANY
P.O. Box 150916
San Rafael, CA 94915
800-542-5227
415-456-7657
Offers: Procion dyes, resists, and silk and wool dyes; cotton, rayon, denim, and hemp; brushes and painting tools; silk steamers; and a large selection of clothing for adults and children, including sweats, leggings, T-shirts, dresses, hats, and underwear. **Free catalog.**

THE FABRIC CENTER
P.O. Box 8212
485 Electric Avenue
Fitchburg, MA 01420-8212
508-343-4402

Offers: Large selection of fabrics for home-decorating use, including lightweight fabrics for draperies and bedding, multipurpose fabrics suitable for almost any interior use, and heavyweight fabrics designed for upholstery applications. **Catalog $2.**

GLORIA E. CROUSE
4325 John Luhr Road NE
Olympia, WA 98516-2320
360-491-1980
Offers: Rug-hooking supplies, book, and video. **Free catalog with self-addressed stamped envelope.**

HALCYON YARN
12 School Street
Bath, ME 04530
800-341-0282
207-442-7909
Offers: Specialty yarns; videos (available for sale or rental), books, and software; sample boxes for knitters, rug hookers, and spinners; kits and patterns for children; and floor and table looms. **Free catalog/newsletter.**

HOME-SEW
P.O. Box 4099
Bethlehem, PA 18018
610-867-3833
Offers: Sewing and craft supplies, including thread, notions, glues, lace, ribbon, scissors, trims, and doilies. **Free catalog.**

KEEPSAKE QUILTING
Route 25B
P.O. Box 1618
Centre Harbor, NH 03226-1618
800-865-9458
Offers: Quilting and sewing supplies, including fabrics by the yard, patterns, books, and notions. **Free catalog.**

NANCY'S NOTIONS LTD.
P.O. Box 683
Beaver Dam, WI 53916-0683
800-833-0690
Offers: Wide assortment of sewing supplies and notions, including fabric, patterns, lace, thread, books, and videos. **Free catalog.**

NEWARK DRESSMAKER SUPPLY
6473 Ruch Road
P.O. Box 20730
Lehigh Valley, PA 18002-0730
610-837-7500
800-736-6783

Offers: Sewing, craft, and needlework supplies, including beads, bridal basics, fabric, jewelry findings, ribbon, and silk flowers. **Free catalog.**

OPPENHEIM'S
P.O. Box 29
120 East Main Street
North Manchester, IN 46962-0052
800-461-6728
219-982-6848
Offers: Pillow, rag rug, and quilt kits; country prints; mill remnants; and denim, chambray, flannel, and broadcloth. Swatches upon request with self-addressed stamped envelope. **Free catalog.**

OREGON TAILOR SUPPLY COMPANY
2123 SE Division Street
P.O. Box 42284
Portland, OR 97292
800-678-2457
503-232-6191
Offers: Sewing, dressmaking, and dry-cleaning supplies, including thread, buttons, zippers, shoulder pads, and pressing equipment. **Free catalog.**

SEW/FIT COMPANY
P.O. Box 397
Bedford Park, IL 60499
800-547-4739
708-458-5600
Offers: Sewing supplies and tools from books, cutting mats, needles, and thread to sewing machine feet and rotary cutters. **Free catalog.**

THAI SILKS!
252 State Street
Los Altos, CA 94022
800-722-7455
800-221-7455 (CA)
415-948-8611
Offers: Silk, velvet, organza, jacquard, taffeta, and many other imported silks; batik and hemp; and sarongs, tank tops, neckties, and handkerchiefs. **Free catalog.**

TINSEL TRADING COMPANY
47 West 38th Street
New York, NY 10018
212-730-1030
Offers: Metallic threads from the 1930s on original wooden spools; metallic and nonmetallic braids, tassels, cords, and fringes; and contemporary bullions, threads, and Lurex threads. **Free price list.**

SOAP MAKING

SUGAR PLUM SUNDRIES
5152 Fair Forest Drive
Stone Mountain, GA 30088
404-297-0158
Offers: Soap-making supplies, bath oils, and massage oils. **Free catalog.**

SUNFEATHER HERBAL SOAP COMPANY
1551 State Highway 72
Potsdam, NY 13676
800-771-7627 (orders only)
315-265-3648
Offers: Soap-making supplies, essential oils, powdered clay, pumice, molds, kits, soap-making video, and books. **Catalog $3.**

PATTERNS

Winter 1997 Patterns

Alice-in-Wonderland Fantasy Cookies

(*see* article, page 30)

NOTE: PHOTOCOPY ALL PIECES FOR THIS PROJECT AT 100%.

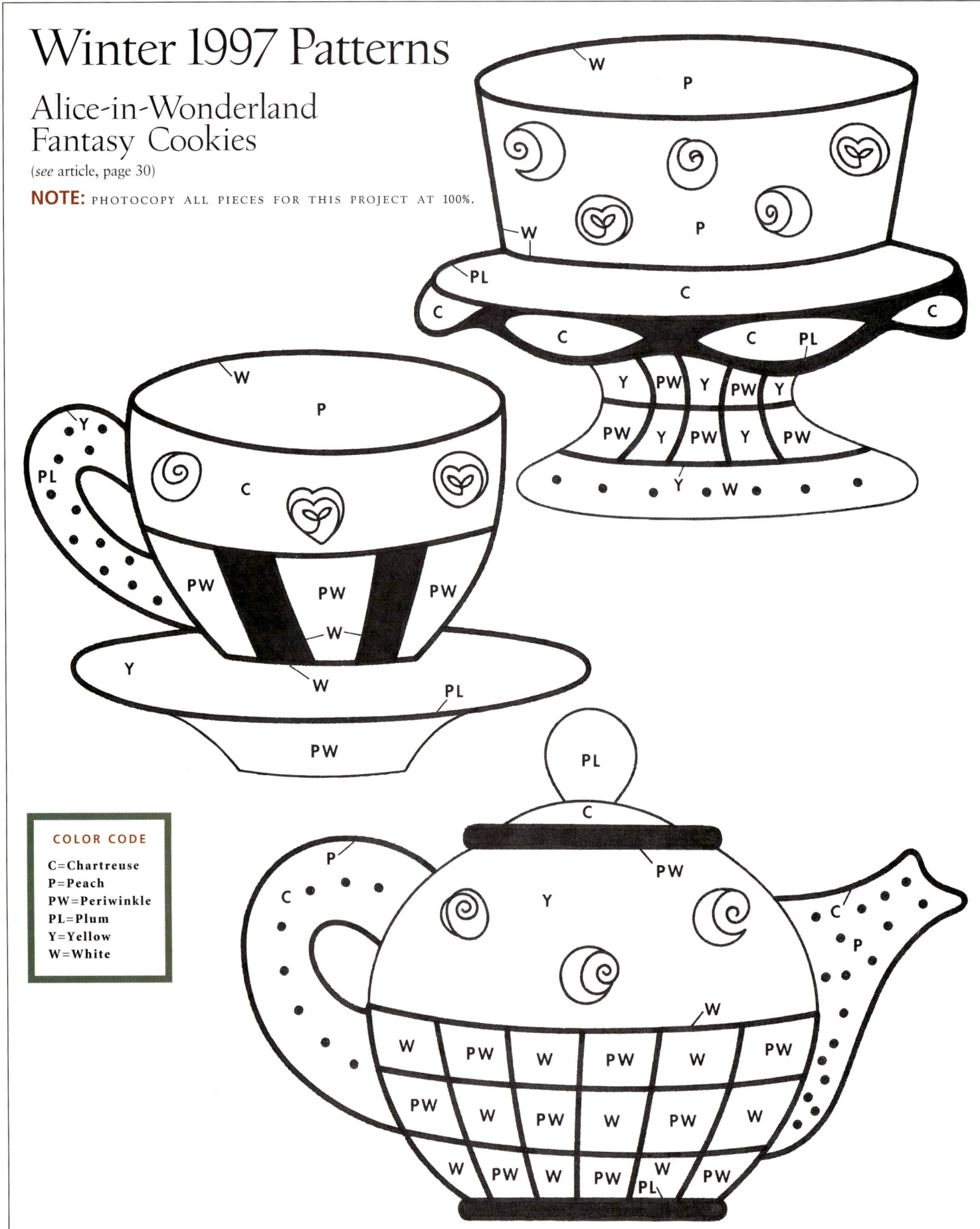

COLOR CODE

C = Chartreuse
P = Peach
PW = Periwinkle
PL = Plum
Y = Yellow
W = White

PATTERNS: **Roberta Frauwirth**

Home Sweet Home Sign

(*see* article, page 26)

NOTE: photocopy the sign template at 200%.

Rose Blossom Garland

(*see* article, page 8)

NOTE: photocopy all pieces for this project at 100%.

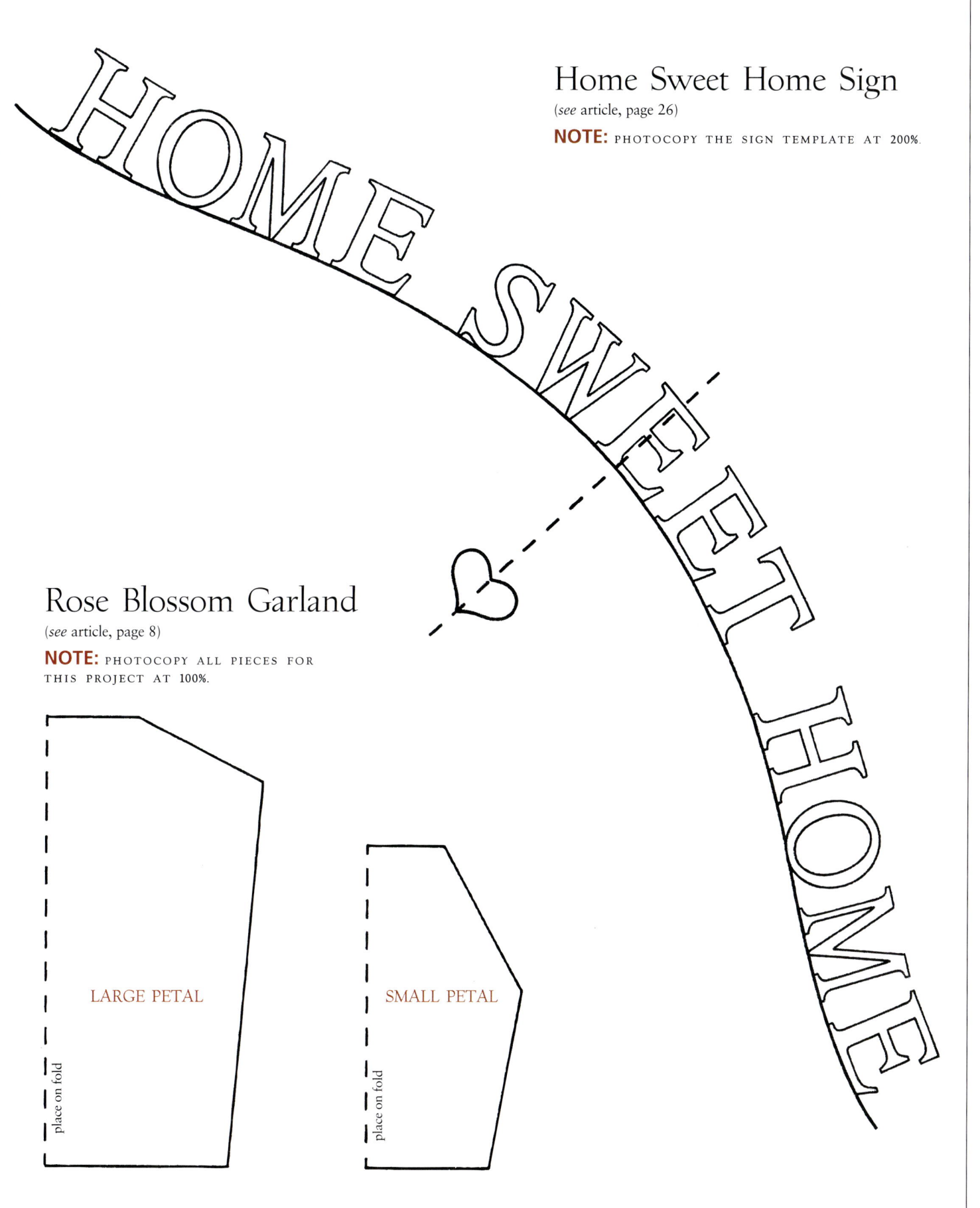

PATTERNS

Faux Suede and Crocodile Backpacks
(*see* article, page 32)

NOTE: FOR SMALL VERSION OF BACKPACK PHOTOCOPY ALL PIECES AT 200%.
FOR LARGE VERSION OF BACKPACK PHOTOCOPY ALL PIECES AT 286%.

Sources & Resources

The following are specific mail-order sources for particular items, arranged by article.

Most of the materials used in this issue are available at your local craft supply store, florist's, fabric shop, hardware store, or bead and jewelry supply. Generic craft supplies can be ordered from such catalogs as Craft King, Dick Blick Art Materials, Newark Dressmaker Supply, Pearl Paint Company, or Sunshine Discount Crafts. The following are specific sources for harder-to-find items, arranged by article. The suggested retail prices listed here were current at press time. Contact the suppliers directly to confirm prices and availability.

Great Marriages, page 6
Sheer curtains from $49 for 84" panel from Pottery Barn.

Rose Blossom Garland, page 8
Crepe paper from $1.36 per sheet from Texas Art Supply.

Bathroom Shag Rug, page 10
Worsted weight yarn from $5.75 per 4-ounce skein and knitting needles from $4.30 per pair from Halcyon Yarn. Single jersey-knit fabric for $5.95 per yard from North End Fabrics.

Painted Plaid Cachepot, page 12
Tin cachepot (#105) for $23.10 from Tinker Bob's Tinware. Paint syringes $1 each from Nasco Arts and Crafts. Tulip Colorpoint Paintstitching for $2.79 per bottle from Munro Corporation.

Tiled Tabletop, page 14
Table (#575.755.02) for $99 from IKEA.

Embossed Velvet Pillow, page 17
Armature wire for $5.50 for 20 feet from Nasco Arts and Crafts. Rayon velvet from $16.95 per yard from North End Fabrics.

Faux Ebony and Ivory Marquetry Frame, page 18
Basswood sticks for 38¢ each and parchment from $1.20 per sheet from Texas Art Supply. Unfinished wood frame from $9.90 from Pearl Paint's main store.

Lavender Bolster Pillow, page 20
Napkin for $32 per pair from Linens on the Hill. Dried lavender from 98¢ per ounce from A World of Plenty. Muslin from $1.98 per yard and eyelet trim from $1.50 per yard from North End Fabrics. Mountain Mist Fatt Batt batting from $12.10 from Atlanta Thread & Supply Co.

Bath Sundries, page 22
Aloe vera gel for $3.38 per ounce, lanolin for $4.03 for 2 ounces, vitamin E oil for $9.12 per ounce, coconut oil for $1.40 per ounce, beeswax for $3 for 4 ounces, almond oil for $2.39 per ounce, essential oils starting at $1.06 per 1/8 ounce, dried herbs from 98¢ per ounce, French white clay for $1.95 per ounce, all from A World of Plenty. Concentrated candle dye for $1.39 per square from Craft King. Paste food colors from $1.30 per ounce from Sweet Celebrations.

Beaded Lampshade, page 25
Wire shade $4.95 from The Lamp Shop. Seed beads from $3 per vial and specialty beads from 15¢ each from Beadworks. Wire for 74¢ for 24 yards from Craft King.

Home Sweet Home Sign, page 26
Self-adhesive wooden letters from $1.48 and hearts from $1.14 from Walnut Hollow Farm.

French Buffet Tray, page 28
Napkins for $16 each from Pierre Deux. Bias tape for $2.25 for 10 yards from Newark Dressmaker Supply. Fusible fleece for $3.75 per yard from Nancy's Notions. Chipboard for 98¢ a sheet from Texas Art Supply.

Alice-in-Wonderland Cookies, page 30
Chefmaster paste and air brush food colors from $2.85 for two ounces, two dozen gumpaste florets for $2.35, 4 ounces of silver dragées for $4.20, all from Sweet Celebrations.

Faux Suede and Crocodile Backpacks, page 32
Ultraseude from $35 per yard and fabric-backed vinyl from $14.95 per yard from North End Fabrics. Quick-release clips for $1 per pair from Frostline Kits. Fusible interfacing for $2.10 per yard and leather sewing machine needles from $3.99 for package of five from Nancy's Notions.

Appliqué Blanket, page 36
Wool from $16 per yard from North End Fabrics. Worsted wool yarn for $5.75 per 4-ounce skein from Halcyon Yarn. Nylon monofilament thread for $2.80 for 1,500 yards from Newark Dressmaker Supply.

Hand-Painted Walls, page 38
Curtain lace from $5.95 per yard from North End Fabrics.

Quick Projects, page 49
Armature wire for $5.50 for 20 feet and wire for 94¢ for 24 yards from Nasco Arts and Crafts.

The following companies are mentioned in the listing above. Contact each individually for a price list or catalog.

ATLANTA THREAD & SUPPLY CO.
695 Red Oak Road, Stockbridge, GA 30281; 800-847-1001

BEADWORKS
149 Water Street, Norwalk, CT 06854; 203-852-9108

CRAFT KING
P.O. Box 90637, Lakeland, FL 33804; 800-769-9494

DICK BLICK ART MATERIALS
P.O. Box 1267, Galesburg, IL 61402-1267; 800-447-8192

FROSTLINE KITS
2525 River Road, Grand Junction, CO 81505-2525; 800-548-7872

HALCYON YARN
12 School Street, Bath, ME 04530; 800-341-0282

IKEA
IKEA Catalog Department, 185 Discovery Street, Colmar, PA 18915; 800-434-4532

THE LAMP SHOP
P.O. Box 3606, Concord, NH 03302-3606; 603-224-1603

LINENS ON THE HILL
52 Charles Street, Boston, MA 02114; 617-227-1255

MUNRO CORPORATION
3954 West 12 Mile Road, Berkley, MI 48072; 800-638-0543

NANCY'S NOTIONS, LTD.
P.O. Box 683, Beaver Dam, WI 53916-9976; 800-833-0690

NASCO ARTS AND CRAFTS
901 Janesville Avenue, P.O. Box 901, Fort Atkinson, WI 53538-0901; 800-558-9595

NEWARK DRESSMAKER SUPPLY
6473 Ruch Road, P.O. Box 20730, Lehigh Valley, PA 18002-0730; 610-837-7500

NORTH END FABRICS
31 Harrison Avenue, Boston, MA 02111; 617-542-2763

PEARL PAINT COMPANY, INC.
308 Canal Street, New York, NY 10013-2572; 800-451-7327 (catalog) or 800-221-6845 x2297 (main store)

PIERRE DEUX
111 Newbury Street, Boston, MA 02116; 617-536-6364

POTTERY BARN
P.O. Box 7044, San Francisco, CA 94120-7044; 800-922-5507

SUNSHINE DISCOUNT CRAFTS
P.O. Box 301, Largo, FL 34649-0301; 800-729-2878

SWEET CELEBRATIONS
P.O. Box 39426, Edina, MN 55439-0426; 800-328-6722

TEXAS ART SUPPLY
2001 Montrose Boulevard, Houston, TX 77006-1299; 713-526-5221 or 800-888-9278

TINKER BOB'S TINWARE
209 Summit Street, Norwich, CT 06360; 860-886-7365

WALNUT HOLLOW FARM
Highway 23 North, Dodgeville, WI 53533; 608-935-5216

A WORLD OF PLENTY
P.O. Box 1153, Hermantown, Minnesota 55810; 218-729-6761 ◆

Quick Projects

Combine armature wire and crystals to make these unique decorative items.

ARMATURE WIRE ACCESSORIES

Armature wire may be the perfect craft material. Not only is it inexpensive and widely available, it's easy to bend and is tarnish-proof. To make the four items shown here, we simply bent and cut the wire, then added crystals. When working with armature wire, handle the wire with steady yet gentle pressure to avoid crimping. In addition to the wire, you will require wire cutters, pliers, fine-gauge silver or silver-colored wire, and assorted crystals.

For the candelabra (left), start by forming three J-shaped arms of the same size. On one arm, form a hanging loop. To create a candle holder, curl the opposite end of the arm around the candle three times, then cut it. Create a candle holder on the two remaining arms. Bind the three arms together at the hook and the base using fine-gauge wire, then conceal the binding with an S-shaped coil. Add crystals as desired.

For a votive candle, wrap the wire around the container, then twist the opposite end into a coil and attach a crystal. The same principle can be used to make a napkin ring or the candlestick decoration. ◆

COLOR PHOTOGRAPHY:
Carl Tremblay

STYLING:
Ritch Holben

Sweater Pillows

When old sweaters become torn or moth-eaten, recycle the usable sections by sewing colorblock pillow covers. Cut a piece of batting to match the pillow dimensions, then cut strips and rectangles from old sweaters. Vary the colors and knit patterns. Here, we've mixed cables, bouclés, and a stockinette stitch. Once the design is set, zigzag over the raw edges. Conceal the edges with velvet ribbons or wide bands of velvet, then topstitch them in place. To complete the covering, stitch each pillow front to a velvet backing.

COLOR PHOTOGRAPHY: **Carl Tremblay**   STYLING: **Ritch Holben**

NUMBER SIXTEEN SPRING 1997

Handcraft
ILLUSTRATED

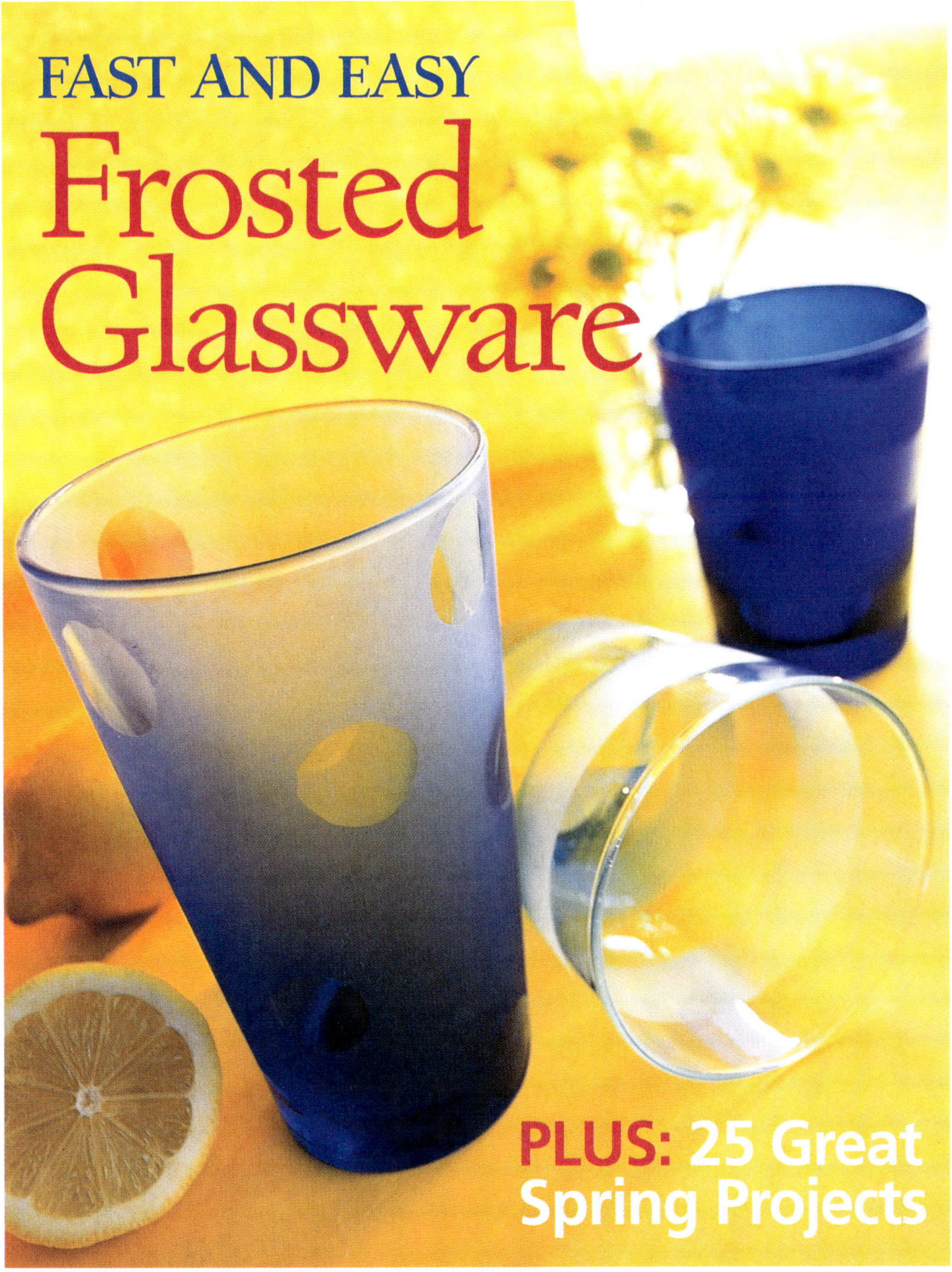

FAST AND EASY
Frosted Glassware

PLUS: 25 Great Spring Projects

Vintage Tablecloth
Re-create the '40s Look with Fruit Stencils and Retro Paint Colors

Hand-Painted Parrot Tulips
Hand-Color Silk Flowers Using Watercolor Paint

Parisian Fireplace Screen
Decoupage a Floral Bouquet on Foam Board

Rose Petal Jelly
Transform Garden Roses into Delicate Jelly

Quick-Sew Velvet Peaches
Lifelike Peaches with Stretch Cotton Velvet and Fabric Dye

1930s Farmhouse Table
Easy Antique Patina with Varnish, Paint, and Glaze

ALSO
Tufted Napkin Quilt
Broken China Stepping Stones
Cut-and-Punch Garden Lights
Quick Collage Cards
Chicken Wire Candlecage

NUMBER SIXTEEN   SPRING 1997

Contents

Parchment paper lanterns, page 12

Plaid silk footstool, page 18

Vintage tablecloth, page 28

COVER PHOTOGRAPH:
Carl Tremblay
STYLING:
Ritch Holben

Create your own Parrot tulips with watercolor paint. See page 12.

FEATURE STORIES

8
FROSTED GLASSWARE
Transform ordinary glasses, plates, or bowls into frosted giftware using rubber cement, masking tape, and etching cream.

10
VELVET PEACHES
These lifelike peaches resemble the real thing in shape, color, and texture. The trick: stretch cotton velvet.

12
GARDEN LANTERNS
Assemble these festive lights quickly and easily using parchment paper, glue, and specialty hole punchers.

14
1930S FARMHOUSE TABLE
Create this vintage patina, reminiscent of a farmhouse kitchen, using layers of varnish, paint, and glaze.

15
ANTIQUED COLLAGE CARDS
Antique a blank watercolor card with a wash of instant coffee, then decoupage a layered collage of giftwrap and flower blossoms.

16
TUFTED NAPKIN QUILT
Stitch up this eye-catching quilt in an afternoon's time using ordinary dinner napkins instead of fabric.

18
PLAID SILK FOOTSTOOL
Create a small-scale footstool using a square of plywood for the base, foam for loft, and curtain finials for legs.

21
LEAFY FERN PORCH RUG
Transform any natural fiber rug with a quick reverse-stenciling technique. The trick: Cut your leaves and stems from painter's tape.

22
DECORATIVE PAINTED PLATES
Forget special glass plates or freehand painting. You can make these decorative plates using decoupage and acrylic craft paint.

25
HAND-PAINTED PARROT TULIPS
Transform inexpensive silk flowers into prized Parrot tulips using watercolor paint.

26
CHICKEN WIRE CANDLECAGE
Create a simple onion-dome-like sculpture using ordinary chicken wire.

28
VINTAGE TABLECLOTH
Create your own collectible tablecloth using our fruit and foliage stencils and retro paint recipes.

32
ARTS AND CRAFTS BANDBOX
Transform a cardboard craft box into a period piece.

34
ROSE PETAL JELLY
Prepare this delicate, sweet condiment using roses from your garden.

36
DECORATIVE SAILBOAT
Create your own nautical accent using a balsa wood hull, dowel masts, muslin sails, and rigging made from string.

40
PARISIAN FIREPLACE SCREEN
Cut a silhouette of a floral bouquet from Gatorfoam board, then add your own colorful flowers using decoupage.

42
BROKEN CHINA STEPPING STONES
Assemble these waterproof garden accents easily and quickly using thrift store china, mortar, and tile grout.

IN EVERY ISSUE
NOTES FROM READERS	2
QUICK TIPS	4
QUICK HOME ACCENTS	6
THE PERFECT GIFT	7
PATTERNS	44
SOURCES & RESOURCES	48
QUICK PROJECTS	49
VINTAGE FRAME	BACK COVER

Handcraft ILLUSTRATED

From the Editor

EDITOR
Carol Endler Sterbenz
EXECUTIVE EDITOR
Barbara Bourassa
ART DIRECTOR
Amy Klee
SENIOR EDITOR
Michio Ryan
MANAGING EDITOR
Keith Powers
DIRECTIONS EDITOR
Candie Frankel
COPY EDITOR
Gary Pfitzer
EDITORIAL ASSISTANT
Melissa Nachatelo

PUBLISHER AND FOUNDER
Christopher Kimball
MARKETING DIRECTOR
Adrienne Kimball
CIRCULATION MANAGER
David Mack
FULFILLMENT MANAGER
Larisa Greiner
NEWSSTAND MANAGER
Jonathan Venier
MARKETING ASSISTANT
Connie Forbes

VICE PRESIDENT PRODUCTION AND TECHNOLOGY
James McCormack
EDITORIAL PRODUCTION MANAGER
Sheila Datz
SYSTEMS ADMINISTRATOR
Paul Mulvaney
PRODUCTION ARTIST
Kevin Moeller
EDITORIAL PRODUCTION ASSISTANT
Robert Parsons
PRODUCTION ASSISTANT
Daniel Frey

CONTROLLER
Lisa A. Carullo
ACCOUNTING ASSISTANT
Mandy Shito
OFFICE MANAGER
Tonya Estey

Handcraft Illustrated (ISSN 1072-0529) is published quarterly by Boston Common Press Limited Partners, 17 Station Street, Brookline, MA 02146. Copyright 1997 Boston Common Press Limited Partners. Second-class postage paid at Boston, MA, and additional mailing offices, USPS #011-895. For list rental information, please contact List Services Corporation, 6 Trowbridge Drive, P.O. Box 516, Bethel, CT 06801; (203) 743-2600; Fax (203) 743-0589. Editorial office: 17 Station Street, Brookline, MA 02146; (617) 232-1000, FAX (617) 232-1572, e-mail: hndcftill@aol.com. Editorial contributions should be sent or e-mailed to: Editor, Handcraft Illustrated. We cannot assume responsibility for manuscripts submitted to us. Submissions will be returned only if accompanied by a large, self-addressed stamped envelope. Subscription rates: $24.95 for one year; $45 for two years; $65 for three years. (Canada: add $6 per year; all other countries add $12 per year.) Postmaster: Send all new orders, subscription inquiries, and change of address notices to Handcraft Illustrated, P.O. Box 7450, Red Oak, IA 51591-0450. Single copies: $4 in U.S.; $4.95 in Canada and other countries. Back issues available for $5 each. PRINTED IN THE U.S.A.

Rather than put ™ in every occurrence of trademarked names, we state that we are using the names only and in an editorial fashion and to the benefit of the trademark owner, with no intention of infringement of the trademark.

Note to Readers: Every effort has been made to present the information in this publication in a clear, complete, and accurate manner. It is important that all instructions are followed carefully, as failure to do so could result in injury. Boston Common Press Limited Partners, the editors, and the authors disclaim any and all liability resulting therefrom.

I HAVE TRAVELED A LOT IN MY LIFE, AND I HAVE lived in several cities in the United States. At different times I have also lived in Europe. And although I have been charmed beyond words by the culture and geography of France, I cannot escape the gravitational pull of New York. Wherever I go, I always return to this city of seven million people and thirty thousand cabbies. It is where I was born. It is home. Not in the traditional sense, for I don't reside in New York anymore, not since I took up the nomadic life of Editor of Handcraft Illustrated. It is the home within, however, the internal guidance system that frames my choices and my expectations, both good and bad.

New York: noisy, defiant, gritty, energetic, vital, and necessary. I know its drawbacks; I have found myself repeating them with some urgency to my children, all of whom live there. But when I return to New York, I settle back into its rhythm, lightly and watchfully. I have compared it to other great cities, and it doesn't always fare well. But the equation is always balanced in its favor when I factor in the nonquantitative aspects of New York. I simply love the city.

My New York is a metaphor that stems from passion, not reason. Passion is my compass and timepiece, directing my steps on the streets I walk and the hours I walk them. As tourists make their pilgrimage to Rockefeller Center with its Atlas holding a 21-foot sphere or to the Museum of Modern Art, the Met, or the Hard Rock Cafe, I find myself heading over to Takashimaya and Bergdorf's to check out the windows and see what's new in home and fashion accessories. Or I taxi south to Hyman Hendler's, M&J Trimming, and Tinsel Trading, or to the visual cacophony of ABC Carpet. Then it's over to SoHo where nineteenth-century cast-iron architecture frames shops such as Wolfman Gold, Kate's Paperie, and Portico, and finally to the southern margin of SoHo, to the mecca of art supplies, Pearl Paint.

It was here, in Pearl Paint, that I found myself recently, along with my daughter, Genevieve. We were both on deadline. We only had a half hour to find materials for our projects before the store closed, so we decided to take a cab from her apartment instead of going by subway. The cab sped along FDR Drive, moving precariously from one lane to another, zigzagging onto the exit and screeching short behind a stopped bus.

A few minutes later, we were standing in front of Pearl, checking our formidable lists of craft materials to buy. Among other things, Genevieve was looking for glitter (look for the results in the Fall 1997 issue), and I was looking for etching cream. We could have rushed to separate floors of the store to make sure we got what we wanted, but we didn't. Instead we collaborated on each item, sharing the subtleties known to us from our experiences with craft supplies. Genevieve studied drama and philosophy at Wellesley College and now brought the same natural intelligent grace to her work as a visual manager for a large retail store in Manhattan. Only four years ago, our forays into city traffic were about gowns for dances and Christmas shopping. Now as I stood in the aisle with her, I quietly realized that Genevieve and I had approached this place from very different paths, and yet we had met where our passions converged, in the aisle of an art store in New York.

My New York is a metaphor that stems from passion, not reason. Passion is my compass and timepiece, directing my steps on the streets I walk and the hours I walk them.

Over the following days we worked together in the easy camaraderie and familiar clutter of glue and glitter projects (evidence of which would surface on brow and cheek for weeks thereafter); Genevieve's work was beautiful. And a thought that had been on the edge of my awareness slipped into place: Crafts had become an unexpected but welcomed conjunction to our relationship. In her own way and in her own time, Genevieve had developed an aesthetically distinct and true voice of her own.

Home is where the heart is, indeed. Once Isaac Stern described the violinist Jascha Heifetz as "the sound in every player's ear." New York is the sound in mine, and when I return there, a sympathetic vibration begins that is as recognizable as a family member's voice.

Carol Endler Sterbenz

Notes from Readers

Learn how to make potpourri using your own flowers, paint on wine glasses, preserve foliage with glycerin, and re-cover a lampshade.

Locating Projects for Decoupage
I'm looking for good quality items to decoupage, such as wood or metal trays, small wooden stools, or benches. Can you help?
COLLEEN CONRAD
BETHLEHEM, PA

Although yard sales can yield some great finds for decoupage, many mail-order catalogs carry trays and smaller unfinished wood items. S&S, for instance, offers lightweight wooden trays, trunk boxes, cabinets, canisters, planters and more. A set of three trays (small, medium, and large) retails for $8.89, although the company requires a minimum mail-order of $25. Call S&S at 800-243-9232 or write: P.O. Box 513, Colchester, CT 06415-0513. Craft King, Inc. also sells a variety of items for decoupage, including a small heart-shaped stool priced at $10.25. To order or receive a catalog, call 800-769-9494.

Backyard Flowers in Potpourri and Candles
I live on an island in the Central Pacific. We have many native flowers that I would like to make into potpourri. I'd also like information on how to get the natural scent of certain flowers into candles. Can you help?
NORMA HEATH
LELU, KOSRAE

Those are both great ideas! To get started with making potpourri, here's a quick primer. All potpourri is composed of three kinds of ingredients: fragrant materials (such as your flowers), fixative (bulky materials that bind the fragrance in the potpourri, such as oak moss), and decorative accents, such as pine cones, which give the mix color and texture. Start by drying the flowers you like, either by hanging them in a cool, dark place for several days or spreading them on cheesecloth stretched across an embroidery hoop. Then add in your fixative and decorative accents; if you're not sure what to use with your particular flowers, consult one of the many potpourri recipes available in books (see below). After the mixture is complete, place it in a heavy paper bag lined with waxed paper and leave it to cure for a week or two, shaking occasionally. If desired, add a few drops of an essential oil to enhance the scent of the mixture.

Making scented candles is also easy. If you've never made candles before, be sure to follow a set of precise directions. Once the wax and stearin are melted, add the flowers. Keep the temperature near 180 degrees F (75 degrees C) for 45 minutes, then remove the flower pieces. The candle will release the floral scent as it burns. For a stronger and longer lasting scent, mix a few drops of a matching scented oil into the melted wax. The Barker Company, a mail-order firm, offers a variety of candle-making supplies. To order the company's $2 catalog, call or write: 15106 10th Ave. S.W., Seattle, WA 98166; 800-543-0601.

For further information on transforming your backyard scents into indoor fragrances, *Natural Fragrances: Outdoor Scents for Indoor Uses*, by Gail Duff (Garden Way Publishing, 1989), offers many hints and recipes for potpourri, scented candles, and dried flowers.

Finding Glass Bottles
In your Spring 1996 issue, I came across the article, "Soothing Scented Waters." I loved the decorative bottles in the photo. Could you tell me where I can find these glass bottles?
LYLIAN CHEN
SANTA CLARA, CA

Sunshine Discount Crafts carries a large variety of glass decorative bottles starting at $1.47. Shapes vary, and sizes range from 2½" to 12". All bottles include a cork, but the company also sells natural cork stoppers for $1.59 each. To order a catalog, call 800-729-2878 or write: Sunshine Discount Crafts, P.O. Box 301, Largo, FL 33779-0301. For a colorful look, Gardener's Eden offers decorative bottles in a variety of shades. The bottles, which come in sets of three, four, six, or eight, are 3¼" to 6" high, resemble old pharmaceutical bottles, and do not include stoppers. Call 800-822-9600 for a catalog, or write: P.O. Box 7307, San Francisco, CA, 94120-7307. Thrift and antique stores are another good source for unique and beautiful bottles.

Painting on Wine Glasses
Recently, I visited a craft shop where a woman was "glass painting" flowers and greenery on stemmed wine glasses. Where can I find information and supplies needed to get started with this craft? Also, I understand that after applying the glass paint to the stemware, it needs to be fired. Can you have this done at a ceramic shop, or can you do it at home?
JOYCE MEIKI
OKLAHOMA CITY, OK

Glass painting supplies are not expensive and are easily found at local craft or artist supply stores. Designers we contacted suggest using an acrylic or porcelain paint labeled specifically for use on glass. One brand we like is Liquitex Glossies Acrylics, a nontoxic enamel designed for use on glass. Dick Blick Art Materials carries 24 different colors of the Glossies line priced at $3.60 each for a 2-ounce jar. Call 800-447-8192 to order a catalog.

Before you begin painting on glass, trace your design with a grease pencil for accuracy. Then use a brush with a fine, flexible point, such as a sable brush, to apply the paint. If you use an acrylic paint designed for glass use, the firing can be done in your own oven. If you select wine glasses, which thin out along the stem, make sure the pieces are durable and oven-safe to prevent cracking. Place the painted piece in a cold oven, and slowly raise the temperature to 325 degrees for 30 minutes. Remove the piece once cool. You can handwash or dishwash the finished product, but do not use an abrasive material to scrub the glass.

If you are interested in a networking source for information and ideas on glass painting, write or call the Society of Decorative Painters, 393 North McLean Blvd., Wichita, KS 67203-5968; 316-269-9300. The organization acts as a resource for painters of all mediums.

Preserving Branches with Glycerin
I've heard that you can retain the flexibility of birch branches by soaking them in glycerin. Exactly how is this done? What other plants is glycerin suitable for?
DOROTHY NELSEN
GARFIELD, AZ

Glycerin is a syrupy, colorless substance derived from certain fats such as palm oil. When placed in contact with a plant material, it replaces the plant's moisture. You can use glycerin to preserve foliage such as magnolia leaves, copper beech, and eucalyptus, and flowers like heather, hydrangea, Jerusalem sage, and Bells of Ireland. These plants will remain flexible, but may change color substantially. The best time to pick foliage, according to Malcolm Hillier, author of *Decorating with Dried Flowers* (Crown Publishers, Inc., 1987), is when the stems reach maturity in high summer or as leaves reach their changing colors in autumn.

To preserve birch, however, Hillier suggests winter as the best time to collect stems. Select the more flexible twigs, then cut stems of branches at a sharp angle. Remove the bottom few inches of leaves, then stand the stems in a bucket containing 4 inches of a 40 percent glycerin and 60 percent hot water solution. Leave the branches in a cool, dark place. When beads of glycerin form on the upper part of the plant, the preservation is complete, and the stems should be removed immediately (the process may take up to 3 weeks). You can also preserve single leaves by soaking them in a 50/50 solution of glycerin and hot water for about 6 days. After removing the leaves, wash with a mild detergent and water, then pat dry. The foliage should now retain its flexibility for up to a year.

If you cannot find glycerin at your local drugstore or with soap-making supplies, it can be mail-ordered from Dorothy Biddle Service for $11.95 per quart. Write or call the company at: HCO1 Box 900, Greeley, PA 18425; 717-226-3239.

Make-at-Home Wind Chimes
I would like to make wind chimes using air-dry clay, Fimo, and natural materials. I am wondering where I can find the "chimes" or "tubes" of various sizes and tones. Also, can you suggest a method of cording besides nylon?

CYNTHIA GREGORY
HAYWARD, CA

Wind chimes can be made from a variety of materials. First decide what kind of sound you want, and then choose the material accordingly. Metal tubing is the most common choice because it produces a smooth and fairly loud sound when struck lightly, as opposed to shells or clay. Brass is preferable over copper or aluminum tubing.

The holes made for cording the chimes should be kept small, so sound is not disrupted. Although you can use nylon for cording, a variety of other materials is available, such as woven stainless steel cable, wax-linen wire, or hemp cord. When choosing your cord, be sure to select a material sturdy enough to support the metal tubing or other chimes you've selected.

Silk and Velvet Ribbons
I'm looking for a source of high-quality silk and velvet ribbons. Can you help?

DEBORAH GOLDBERG
WILMINGTON, MA

Creative Craft House sells a variety of ribbons, including velvet, satin, waterproof vinyl, and others. Call 520-754-3300, or write to P.O. Box 2567, Bullhead City, AZ 86430. Catalogs cost $2 (refundable after first order). You can also try Craft King, Inc., which carries wired ribbon, double-faced satin ribbon, red velvet, burgundy wired velvet, burlap ribbon, and assorted wire-edged ribbons. The company is located at P.O. Box 90637, Lakeland, FL 33804; 800-769-9494. For those with Internet access, TFW, of Portland, OR, offers an on-line, full-color ribbon catalog at its new website: www.tfw.com.

To find a local supplier, check with your local florist for wholesale sources, as they use ribbon for corsages, boutonnieres, and arrangements.

Sources for Stencil Burners
I'd like to design my own stencils. I am searching for a tool called a stencil burner, which is used to cut or burn Mylar and/or acetate. I've had no luck in locating such a tool. Can you help me?

JENNIFER D. WALLACE
BIRMINGHAM, AL

We found two sources for stencil burners, which are faster than knives and which will cut through acetate, Mylar, polyester, and other materials. Sax Arts & Crafts offers a stencil burner with two tips (fine and blunt), which heats up in 45 seconds. The burner retails for $26.35. Contact the company at P.O. Box 510710, New Berlin, WI 53151-0710; 800-558-6696. Dick Blick Art Materials also sells a fine-tipped stencil burner for approximately $24. The company offers a blunt tip for an additional $2.95. Call 800-447-8192, or write to P.O. Box 1267, Galesburg, IL 61402-1267.

Trompe l'Oeil Painting Outdoors
Can you give me advice on painting trompe l'oeil ("fool the eye") scenes outdoors? I would like to paint both my metal garage door and one side of my wooden garage. Both structures have been painted with latex.

JO OSBORNE
GARLAND, TX

Because the metal door and the wood side are both painted with latex, you should use latex paint on top for the best adhesion. We recommend using fade-resistant exterior latex paints for your design, followed by an outdoor grade sealer (we like Diamond-IPNS Varathane Interior/Exterior grade) on top of the design to seal and stabilize it.

Dressing Up Lampshades
I would like to re-cover two old lampshades that feature scalloped edges, but I can't seem to find the directions I need to get started. What type of fabric and glue should I use?

MARY ROBINSON
YOUNGSTOWN, OH

Decorating an old lampshade with new fabric is a great way to revitalize a room. From the description of your frames, it sounds like you need information on traditional and/or Victorian lampshades. Mainely Shades, a lampshade materials distributor, offers how-to pamphlets that detail necessary materials, instructions on how to size a shade, and gluing methods. The company also offers instructional pamphlets and videos that include specifics on Victorian and traditional lampshades. To order a catalog, call 800-624-6359 or write the company at 100 Gray Road, Falmouth, ME 04105.

Coloring Paraffin Wax
I am working on a project with melted paraffin wax. To color the wax, I added broken crayons. My problem is this: I use a lot of gold and silver, and the large crayon boxes contain one small gold and silver crayon a piece. Can you suggest another gold or silver tint that would dissolve in paraffin, or do you know of a source for large gold or silver crayons?

JANE ROODBERG
CLOSTER, NJ

Instead of using crayons for color, try using dyes designed especially for coloring wax. Color chips can be purchased from Pourette Candle Making Supplies; a package of eight costs 85¢. Call the company at 206-789-3188, or write to P.O. Box 17056, Seattle, WA 98107.

As for crayons, Dick Blick Art Materials carries boxes of twelve crayons of one color, including silver and gold. Each box of twelve costs $2.10. Call the company at 800-447-8192, or write to P.O. Box 1267, Galesburg, IL 61402-1267.

Searching for Lye
I wanted to make soap using your article ("Secrets of Making Soap at Home," Christmas 1996), but I had trouble locating lye. Unfortunately, my hardware store does not carry it. Could you recommend another source?

SUSAN BARTHER
HARRICK, VERMONT

Lye, also called sodium hydroxide, is one of three main ingredients needed for soap making. Along with water and a fat/oil, such as vegetable shortening, this chemical triggers a reaction that produces soap and glycerin. Because lye is highly caustic when dissolved in water, it must be handled with extreme caution. If you cannot find lye in your hardware store or the household-cleaning section of your local grocery store, mail-order sources are your best option. The Sunfeather Herbal Soap Company carries a sodium hydroxide mix for $5.25 per pound plus shipping costs. To order, call 800-771-7627 or write to Sunfeather at 1551 State Highway 72, Potsdam, NY 13676. Sugar Plum Sundries also carries lye; ten pounds is priced at $29.95. For a free catalog, call or write the company at 5152 Fair Forest Drive, Stone Mountain, GA 30088; 404-297-0158.

Thanks To An Anonymous Reader
In the Winter 1997 issue, Deborah Wheatley asked us where she could find old-fashioned decoupage labels that are dipped in water for easy application. Thanks to a reader from Marfa, Texas, we located Decorcal, Inc., a producer of such hand-painted decals. Decorcal offers a free catalog of decoupage items and other products. Write or call the company at: 165 Marine St., Farmingdale, NY 11735; 516-752-0076.

Our Readers Write
It can be very expensive to purchase the materials used to make a quilt. A great way to find fabric is to check with your local wallpaper store, and ask if they save any discontinued sample books, some of which include fabric samples. The fabric swatches contained in these books are the perfect size (2" x 4" and sometimes larger) for quilt-making, and they provide a great variety of patterns and colors. Note: These sample pieces may not have been made colorfast, so test them first.

SHARON FRUTH
WILLIAMSVILLE, NY

ATTENTION READERS

Need Advice on a Craft or Home Decorating Project?
Drop us a line, and we'll find the answer. Although we can't respond to every letter we receive, we will try to publish those letters with the widest appeal. Please include your name, address, and a daytime telephone number with your question. Write to:

Notes from Readers
Handcraft Illustrated
17 Station Street
Brookline, MA
02146

Quick Tips

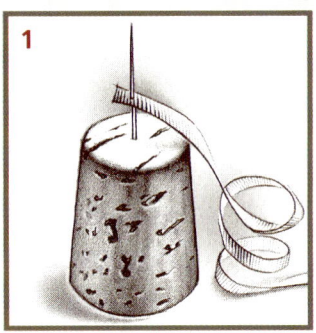
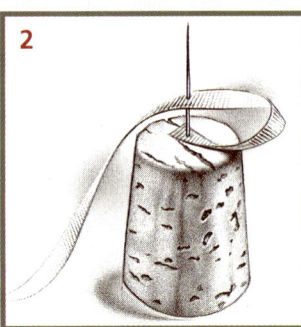

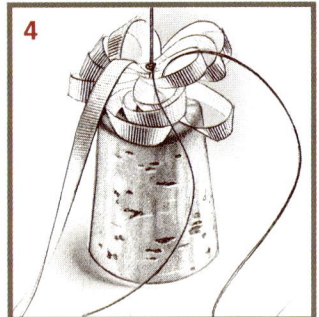

RIBBON FLOWERS
To make ribbon flowers, Ione M. Rodnick, of Crescent City, California, uses a needle held upright in a cork stopper.

1. Pierce one end of the ribbon.

2. Loop the ribbon, twist it once, and pierce it again.

3. Repeat the looping, twisting, and piercing motion to make additional petals. As you near the center of the flower, make the loops shorter.

4. Pull the rose up slightly on the needle, then tack the ribbon petals together at the middle with needle and thread.

5. Sew the flower to your project using French knots.

Calling All Crafters
Do you have a craft, sewing, or decorating technique that saves time or money? We'll give you a one-year complimentary subscription for each Quick Tip that we publish. Send your tip to:

Quick Tips
Handcraft Illustrated
17 Station Street
Brookline, MA
02146

Please include your name, address, and daytime phone number with all correspondence.

ILLUSTRATION:
Harry Davis

PLASTIC TEMPLATES
Plastic liners, such as those used in bacon packaging, make excellent tracing templates, writes Harriette Geisinger, of New Philadelphia, Ohio.

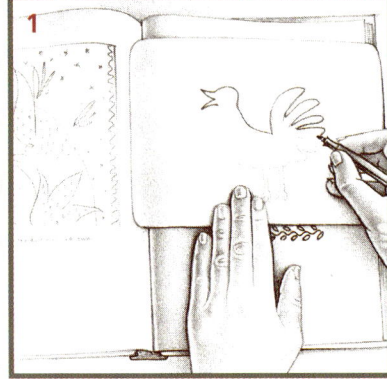
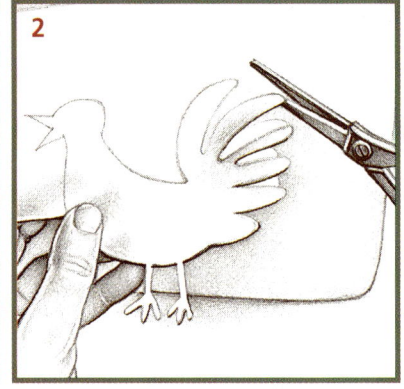
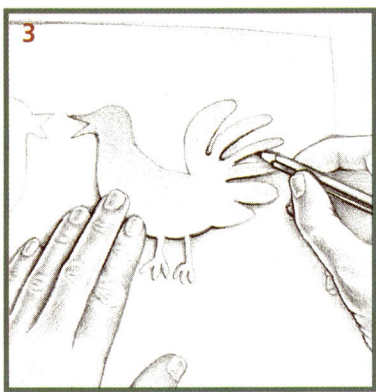

1. Lay the liner over the design and trace the outline with a permanent pen.

2. Cut on the marked outline with scissors.

3. To use the template, trace around the edge. Unlike cardboard templates, this edge won't wear down with repeated use.

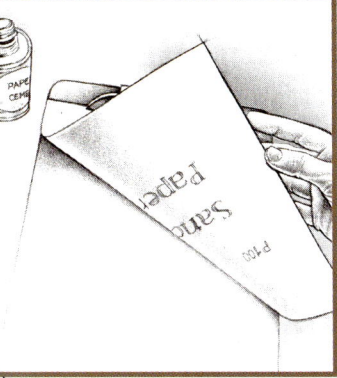 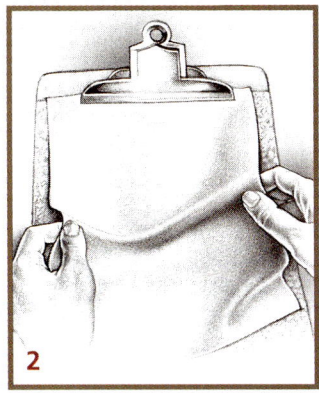  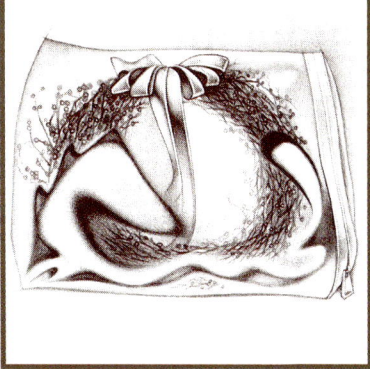

FABRIC CLIPBOARD
To transfer small designs to slippery fabrics, Ione M. Rodnick, of Crescent City, California, devised a special clipboard.

1. **Using rubber cement, glue fine-grit sandpaper to a legal-size clipboard.**

2. **Clip the fabric to the board and smooth it over the sandpaper.**

3. **Transfer the pattern. The fabric won't shift or slip.**

EASY WREATH STORAGE
Large, plastic blanket bags with zippers are the perfect size and heft for storing wreaths and other bulky decorations out of season. This tip comes from Jessica Flanery, of Burnsville, Minnesota.

  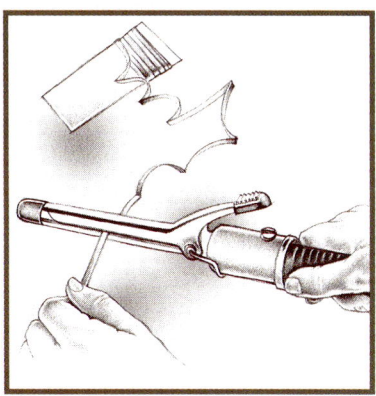

FOAM GLUE SPREADER
Worn-out foam brushes make perfect glue spreaders. Thanks to Victoria George, of Lebanon, Oregon, for this tip.

1. **Pick off and discard all the broken, crumbly foam.**

2. **Use the stick with its remaining foam to transfer and spread glue where you need it. The brush can be rinsed clean with warm water.**

SMOOTH SILK RIBBONS
To press out the kinks, run new silk embroidery ribbon through a curling iron. This method is faster and more convenient than conventional pressing, writes Margery L. Nees, of Marion, Iowa.

 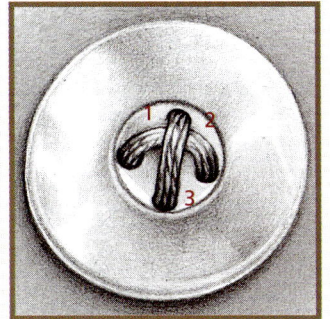  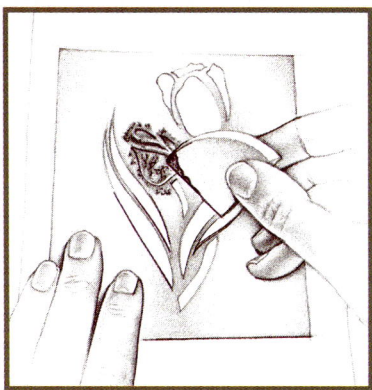

FANCY BUTTON STITCHES
You can perk up ordinary four-hole buttons with some special stitching. Shown above are a box, an arrow, and a French knot tulip. Follow the numbers for the best stitching sequence. Thanks to Twyla Morlan, of Oxford, Iowa, for this tip.

EASY STENCILING
For "pounce" stenciling in small areas, Gail Driscoll, of Worcester, Massachusetts, recommends inexpensive triangular cosmetic sponges. With water-based paints, they can be rinsed and reused.

Quick Home Accents

Pair a paper shade with your favorite lamp base for a fresh lighting effect.

SHADES OF PAPER

Ribbed paper lamp shades, popular in the '50s, are surprisingly modern when combined with bases from other lamps. These lightweight, inexpensive shades are available in a wide variety of shapes and sizes; give off a warm, ambient light; and provide fun, fresh shapes in combination with a variety of table, floor, and pole lamps.

Shown here (left to right) are a pyramidal shade on a deco-inspired ceramic lamp, a free-form cylinder on a steel floor lamp, an urn-shaped shade resting on a wire base, and a flattened globe on a teak base from the early 1960s.

To light each of these shades, we balled up a string of white Christmas lights, then draped the ball of lights on the shade's inner wire frame. Convert the lamp's socket into a plug using a socket adapter. Since these paper shades are not made for use on lamp bases (they're designed to enclose a single hanging bulb), you may need to substitute a different length harp (the pair of metal prongs that supports the shade on the lamp base) for the existing one, or make adjustments to the paper shade's wire frame. (Just make sure the lights do not touch the paper.) The new effect and low cost, however, make it well worth the effort. ◆

COLOR PHOTOGRAPHY:
Carl Tremblay

STYLING:
Ritch Holben

The Perfect Gift

Create a new twist on the traditional shadow box: a glass-backed light box.

KEEPSAKE COLLAGE

Memories make a perfect gift, especially when they're housed in a form that doubles as decorative accent. This glass-backed light box combines several different media for a fun and personalized gift.

To make the light box, we started by removing the back panels from two 8" x 10" picture box frames, or frames with depth to their sides. We used dollhouse hinges to hinge the frames together back-to-back, creating a two-sided glass box frame that stands on its own, and added a miniature latch at the front to hold the box closed.

Next, we had a color Xerox transparency made from a favorite photo (this is easily done at a photocopying center), enlarged it to fit the frame, and mounted it on the glass using double-stick tape. (For variation on this design, make a sepia-toned transparency.) Then we arranged a variety of favorite items inside the frame; some were hung with jeweler's wire, others were hot-glued to the frame's edge, and still others were taped in place. Backlit with a favorite lamp, the translucent image throws a memorable light on our collected items. The box can be displayed open, as shown, or closed and set on a windowsill. ◆

COLOR PHOTOGRAPHY:
Carl Tremblay

DESIGN AND STYLING:
Ritch Holben

GLASSWARE

Fast and Easy Frosted Glassware

Transform ordinary glass into frosted giftware using circles of rubber cement, masking tape stripes, and etching cream.

🌶 BY LILY FRANKLIN

Etching cream can be used to create a matching set of glassware from disparate pieces. Simply repeat the pattern of choice across all the glassware, regardless of its shape or color.

COLOR PHOTOGRAPHY:
Carl Tremblay

COLOR SILHOUETTES:
Daniel van Ackere

ILLUSTRATION
Judy Love

STYLING:
Ritch Holben

I SET OUT TO DECORATE THIS GLASSware with one goal in mind: create a fast and easy way to transform ordinary glasses or bowls into a gift worthy of a wedding or bridal shower. I found the answer in etching cream, which, when used with a mask or stencil, chemically reacts with the glass to leave behind a frosted design.

To keep the design simple but graphically bold, I created polka dots using circles of rubber cement, and stripes using masking tape. The designs can be applied to the exterior of serving pieces such as pitchers, bowls, and platters, or glassware such as tumblers, highball glasses, or stemware.

In order for the designs to look professional, I needed an easy way to create neat and uniform polka dots. My first thought was to use a ready-made mask, such as stick-on dots. The problem, however, is that they only stick well on flat surfaces. A better solution is to create a mask with rubber cement, applied with a blunt-ended and stiff-bristled paint mixing brush. The brush is pushed against the glass while simultaneously rotating it slowly, causing the bristles to fan out, creating a nearly perfect circle of rubber cement. The size of the dots can be controlled by varying the amount of pressure. I used the rubber cement technique to create a design where the polka dots are clear, and the background is frosted. To create the reverse design—frosted circles and clear background—I simply dipped the mixing brush in etching cream.

Polka dots work well on just about any surface, while stripes should be reserved for smooth, less curvaceous shapes. To make the stripes, I used strips of masking tape about one-half inch wide. This may vary, depending on the glass, but as a general rule of thumb, keep the masked and unmasked areas the same width.

The most important factor in choosing glassware is the degree of transparency. Plates and rimmed bowls should be as transparent as possible, as the frosted pattern is applied to the backside of the rim. This prevents moisture and oils in the food from obliterating the decoration. In addition, look for glassware that is sleek and simple in shape, and without surface decoration such as facets or bubbles, which will compete with the frosted design.

Lily Franklin is a designer and writer living in Albuquerque, New Mexico.

INSTRUCTIONS

Note: Before etching colored glassware, practice technique on a disposable glass jar. On tumblers, goblets, and bowls, only frost outer surface; on plates and platters, work on underside. If plate is to be used for decoration only, top of rim may be masked instead for more visible frosting. Note that all masked areas will appear clear on final piece, and all unmasked areas will be frosted.

1. *Mask glassware.* To create masks for stripes and dots, press masking tape or brush rubber cement on clean glassware as described below.

Horizontal stripes: Wrap tape once around rim of tumbler, lining up tape

MATERIALS

- Assorted colored glassware (e.g., tumblers, bowls, and plates)
- Armour Etch cream

You'll also need:
rubber cement; ½"-wide masking tape; ½"-diameter paint mixing brush; 1"-wide soft-bristled brush; newspaper; sink; rubber gloves; goggles; scissors; small wood blocks; ruler; permanent marker; dishwashing liquid; and disposable glass jar.

Making Horizontal Stripes

A. Wrap masking tape around the rim of the glassware.

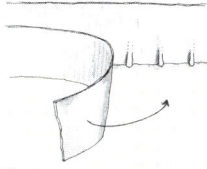

B. Stretch out the top edge of the tape to hug any tapered glassware.

C. If the bottom edge still crinkles, create a new tape edge with a second piece of tape.

D. Repeat the process to create additional horizontal stripes.

Creating Vertical Stripes

E. Align the end of the tape with the bowl's rim, then press the tape in place.

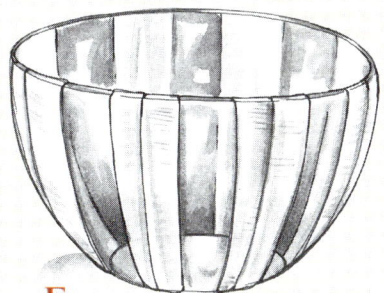

F. For wider stripes, double up the tape.

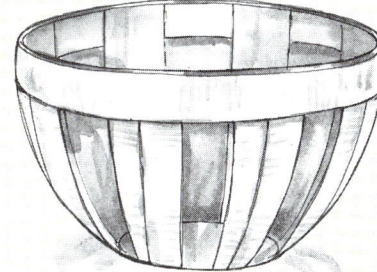

G. Wrap tape around the glassware's rim to protect it from the etching cream.

Making Polka Dots

H. Dip a brush in rubber cement, and twirl it on the glass surface.

I. Place additional rubber cement dots randomly.

edge with rim of glass (*see* illustration A, above). If tumbler is tapered, stretch top edge of tape slightly (like crepe paper) to discourage creases along bottom edge (illustration B). Once tape is positioned, press firmly in place and smooth both edges with fingernail until well-adhered. If bottom edge is flawed by creases or gaps, create new lower edge by overlapping second band of tape by at least 1/8" (illustration C). Repeat process to create striped pattern, allowing about one inch of space in between strips, until you reach base (illustration D).

Vertical stripes: Using permanent marker, mark inside rim of glassware into fourths or other even increments. Align cut end of tape with rim on outside of bowl, even with mark, then press tape down side (illustration E). Repeat process at each mark. For broader stripes, lay down overlapping tapes in same way (illustration F). Note that space between tapes will decrease from top to bottom, depending on degree of bowl taper. Once all vertical stripes are in place, run piece of tape around rim, lining up edges, to protect it from etching cream (illustration G).

Clear dots: Dip mixing brush into rubber cement. Hold brush handle perpendicular to glass surface, touch bristles down on glass until they fan out slightly, then rotate handle, twirling bristles in circle (illustration H). Use more pressure to create larger dots, less pressure for smaller dots. Do not apply rubber cement too thickly, as it can run. Position dots randomly, spacing them 2 to 3 dot widths apart (illustration I).

Frosted dots: Frosted dots are made like clear dots, except the brush is dipped in etching cream instead of rubber cement. (*See* step 2, below.)

2. *Etch glassware with cream.* Follow etching cream safety precautions. Work in well-ventilated area, and wear long sleeves, gloves, and goggles. Set one piece of glassware on several layers of newsprint on counter next to sink; prop plates on small wood blocks for easy lifting. Using 1" brush and working quickly, apply layer of etching cream about 1/8" thick to unmasked portions of glassware. For even etching, complete entire application as quickly as possible, so all cream can work for approximately same length of time. Let cream set 2 to 3 minutes, or time length determined by test run. When time is elapsed, move glassware to sink and immediately rinse off cream under stream of warm water, taking care not to splash. Remove all traces of cream. Peel off tape and/or rubber cement masks, wash piece in soapy water, and let dry. Repeat to etch remaining glassware. ◆

These plates use a clear polka dot design. To create the reverse effect—frosted polka dots—use circles of etching cream instead of rubber cement.

LOW-SEW

Velvet Peaches

These lifelike peaches resemble the real thing in shape, color, and texture. The trick: stretch cotton velvet.

🍑 BY LILY FRANKLIN

These finished velvet peaches measure about 3" across, giving them more presence in a centerpiece than real peaches.

COLOR PHOTOGRAPHY:
Carl Tremblay

ILLUSTRATION:
Mary Newell DePalma

STYLING:
Ritch Holben

IN DEVELOPING THESE LUSCIOUS-looking velvet peaches, I wanted to create as lifelike a piece of fruit as possible. The key to this process, I discovered, is stretch cotton velvet. The fabric's stretchy backing allows it to give at the seams, which creates a soft, full shape, and the cotton fibers readily hold the dye used to create the realistic coloring. In addition, the velvet's nap resembles peach fuzz.

Each peach is created in four simple steps. First, cut four lozenge-shaped pieces of velvet. Next, machine-stitch the fabric segments together and turn the peach right side out. Third, dye the peach, and fourth, stuff the peach with fiberfill and add a velveteen leaf.

Although cotton stretch velvet is readily available, it may be hard to locate in a light shade, such as white, cream, or butterscotch, that is suitable for dying. If you can't find such fabric, you can substitute stretch velvet made from silk or rayon, or any stretchy cotton fabric, such as velour or brushed cotton. I don't recommend fabrics without stretch, as the seams on the sewn peach will pucker. Avoid stretchy fabrics made with acrylic or man-made fibers other than rayon, since they will not accept the fiber dyes.

I considered dyeing the fabric as one large piece before cutting it into segments and sewing them together, but the seams show a sudden change of color when the peach is assembled this way. A more naturalistic result is achieved if the fabric is dyed after the pieces have been sewn together, but before it has been stuffed. I used Procion fiber-reactive dye, but you can substitute any fabric dye except those designed for vat dyeing, as the dyes must be blended directly on the fabric to create the mottled effect.

Lily Franklin is a designer living in Albuquerque, New Mexico.

INSTRUCTIONS

1. *Cut out peach segments.* Machine-wash velvet and velveteen. Machine-dry on delicate (knit) cycle. Photocopy and cut out patterns for peach segment and leaf. Set leaf pattern aside. Pin peach pattern to stretch velvet, observing grain/nap line, and cut out. Repeat process to cut thirty-two pieces total.

2. *Sew segments together.* Set sewing machine at eight to ten stitches per inch. Pin peach segments, right sides together, in pairs. Using white cotton thread, stitch from A to B as shown in illustration A, next page, pivoting at Y, about 3/16" from edge. Lay two pairs flat. Flip top segment of first pair and bottom segment of second pair to one side (illustration B). Stack

MATERIALS
Yields eight 3½"-diameter peaches

- ½ yard 45"-wide white stretch cotton velvet
- 12" x 12" white cotton velveteen
- White cotton sewing thread
- Green fabric-covered stem wire
- 12 ounces fiberfill
- Procion fiber-reactive dye, 2-ounce container each: Golden Yellow, Deep Yellow, Rust Orange, Marigold, Avocado
- Washable fabric glue
- Peach patterns (see page 44)

You'll also need:
washer and dryer; rubber gloves; particle mask; safety goggles; measuring cup; measuring spoons*; 1-pint jar*; 3-quart bowl; five 4-ounce baby food jars*; 1" soft-bristled brush; newspaper; large plastic sheet; old, clean terry towel; baking soda; paper towels; self-adhesive labels; permanent marking pen; zipper-lock plastic bag(s)*; access to photocopier; sewing machine; iron; scissors; pins; hand-sewing needle; ruler; and 5" doll-making needle.

*Comes into contact with dye; do not reuse with food.

pairs, right sides together, and stitch free edges from B to C (illustration C).

3. *Stitch peach split.* Refold piece with right sides together and raw edges matching. With two AB seams aligned, stitch over previous stitching from B to X (illustration D). Flip stitched sections away from raw edges. To create asymmetrical split, jog raw edges slightly so they don't match, then stitch slightly curved line from X to Y through two layers only (illustration E). Turn peach right side out through top opening. Split will appear along one side and excess fabric will fall to inside of peach (illustration F). Repeat process to sew eight peaches total.

4. *Set up dyeing area.* Line countertop next to sink with newspaper, then spread plastic on top. In bowl, dissolve ½ cup baking soda in 2 quarts warm water. Submerge peaches and velveteen fabric in solution and soak for 5 minutes. Remove peaches and fabric from soda solution, wring until no longer dripping, and set aside on plastic. While peaches and fabric are soaking, prepare dyes. Using permanent marking pen, write five dye names on self-adhesive labels and affix to individual jars. Fill jars with hot tap water. Wearing gloves, particle mask, and goggles, measure and place ¾ teaspoon dye powder in appropriate jar and stir until dissolved. Rinse spoon under running water and dry well with paper towel. Repeat process to mix remaining colors. Set pint jar of clear water in sink for rinsing out brush between colors.

5. *Dye peaches and leaves.* Still wearing gloves and goggles, lay one damp peach on plastic. Using soft brush, dapple Golden Yellow dye onto peach, then squeeze and rumple peach to distribute and soften stains. Rinse brush clean, then work Deep Yellow dye into bare areas. Once an overall blond tone is achieved, apply Marigold dye across one-half to three-quarters of peach to suggest sun ripening on one side. For realistic effect, strive for gradual transition and gradations of color. Intensify middle of blush area with Rust Orange dye, streaking it in with brush and blending edges with fingertips. Repeat to dye remaining peaches. For leaves, dapple Avocado dye onto cotton velveteen, coloring about three-fourths of total area, and work in as for peach background. Fill bare spaces with Rust Orange or Marigold. To set colors, let dyed peaches and velveteen rest 1 hour, then place in plastic bag(s) and seal shut. Remove pieces after 48 hours, rinse in cool water until water runs clear, and lay flat on terry towel to dry overnight.

6. *Make velveteen leaves.* Press avocado-colored velveteen from wrong side. Using leaf pattern, cut eight leaves and eight 2½" x 4" rectangles from velveteen. Protect work surface with plastic. Apply washable fabric glue evenly to wrong side of leaf and set 4" of stem wire along spine (see pattern, page 44). Set velveteen rectangle on top, wrong side down, and press to adhere. Repeat process to glue eight leaves total. Let dry 1 hour or as manufacturer recommends, then trim away excess (illustration G).

7. *Stuff peach and sew closed.* Poke fiberfill through top opening into bottom tip of peach, then fill remainder of cavity until peach is firm and plump. Using hand-sewing needle and 12" length of thread, make tiny running stitches around neck (illustration H). Rethread onto 5" doll-making needle. Insert needle down through neck opening and out at X, drawing neck to inside (illustration I). Rethread onto hand-sewing needle, pull snug, and secure with tiny knot. To end off, reinsert needle into X, draw out at any point, pull thread taut, and snip close to peach surface; loose thread end will disappear into stuffing. Roll peach between your palms to distribute and even out stuffing. Press in on split to indent center seam. Make hairpin bend in leaf stem and insert into opening until it lodges in fiberfill (illustration I); apply a few drops fabric glue at entry point and let dry 24 hours. ◆

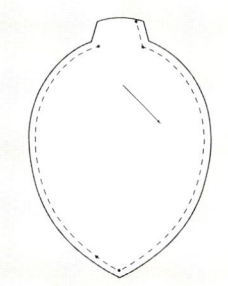

PATTERNS
See page 44 for pattern pieces and enlargement instructions.

Assembling the Peach

A. Sew two peach segments together along one edge, from A to B.

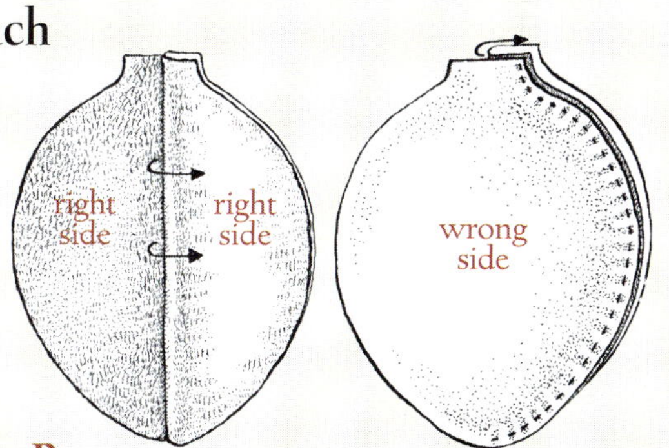

B. Fold back one segment on two pairs.

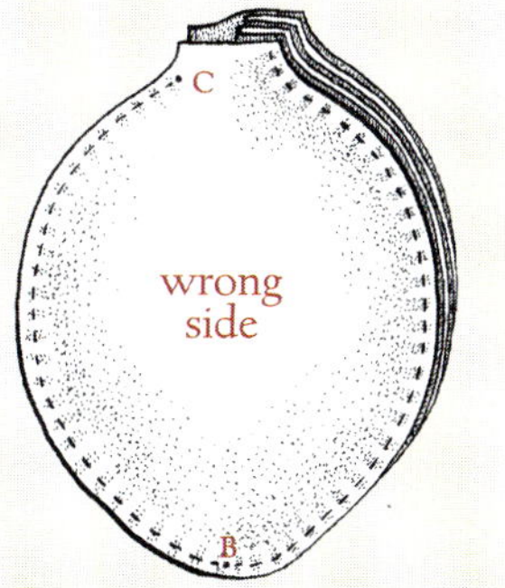

C. Stack the pairs, right sides together, then sew from B to C.

D. Refold the piece, and stitch from B to X.

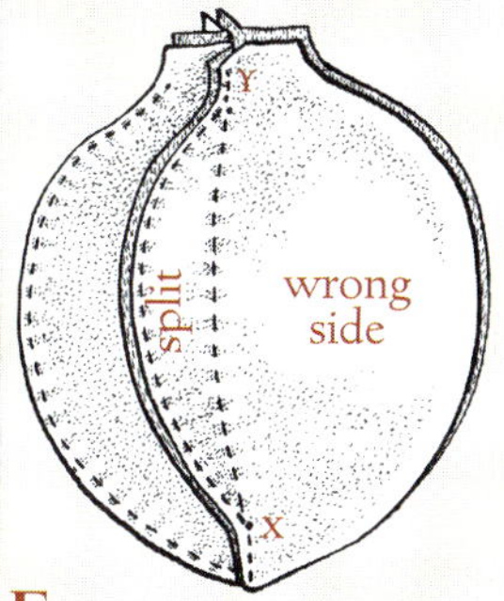

E. Stitch from X to Y to make the two-section split.

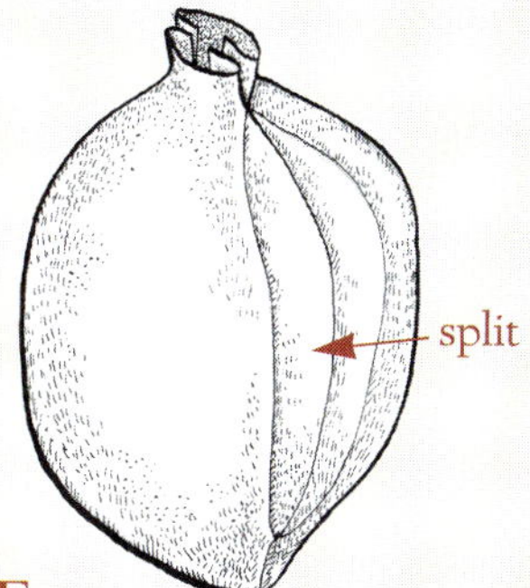

F. Turn the peach right side out. Dye the peach at this stage.

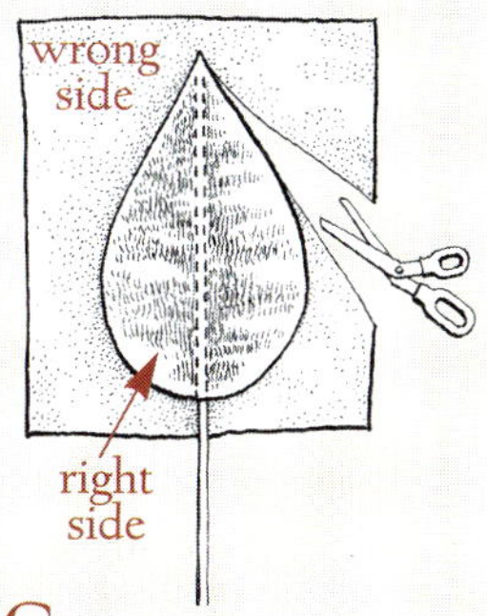

G. Make a two-sided leaf from dyed velveteen.

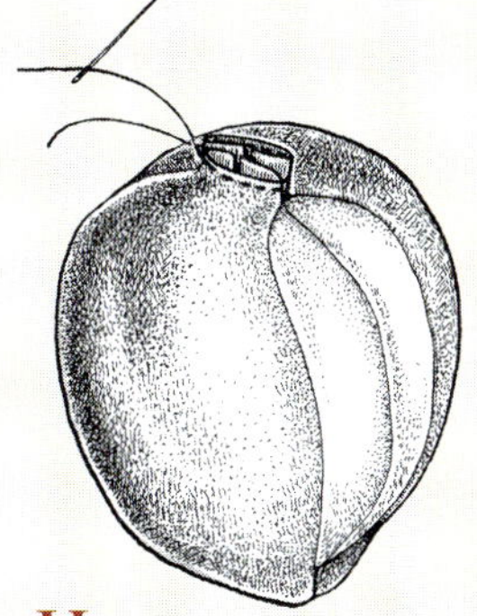

H. Fill the peach cavity with fiberfill, and stitch around the top neck.

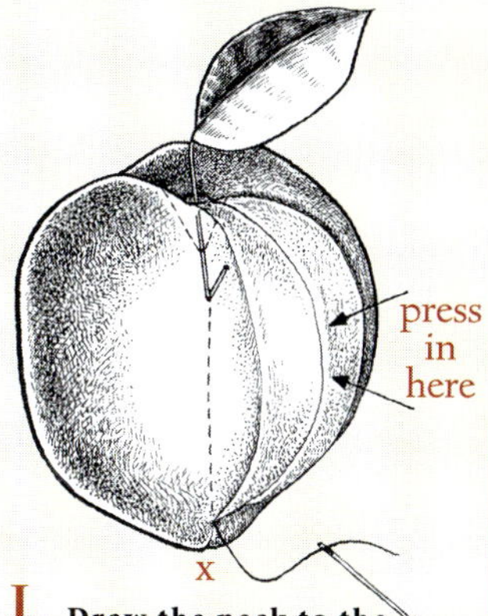

I. Draw the neck to the inside, and insert the leaf.

PAPER CRAFTS

Cut, Fold, and Punch Garden Lanterns

Assemble these festive shades quickly and easily using parchment paper, glue, and specialty hole punchers.

BY ELIZABETH CAMERON

These festive garden lanterns can be assembled from a variety of different papers, including colored or frosted Mylar.

COLOR PHOTOGRAPHY:
Carl Tremblay

ILLUSTRATION:
Michael Gellatly

STYLING:
Ritch Holben

MY GOAL IN CREATING THESE miniature shades was simple: Elevate a common strand of lights to a decorative garden accent. At the same time, because I was not embellishing just one light, the materials had to be inexpensive and the construction technique simple. After much folding and snipping, I settled on a classic open box shade, accented by punched-out stars along the sides.

Although my 7-watt bulbs do not get as hot as the average household lightbulb, it was still important to make sure the sides of the lantern would not touch the bulb. To resolve this issue, I designed the lantern with two flaps at the top that, when glued, hold the paper cube safely centered over the bulb.

Because the box-like lanterns didn't have quite enough pizzazz on their own, I used two specialty hole punchers to punch holes in the paper, which allow tiny slivers of the colored lights to escape. These star-shaped beams of light escape the glowing paper when the lights are lit, and the scattered star shapes make the lanterns more appealing even when unlit.

I tested a variety of papers. At first, I tried a heavy parchment paper for the lanterns. It was translucent enough to allow a mysterious, colored glow, and its weight helped the lantern hold its folded shape. Later, though, nursing blisters after using the hole puncher on this heavy stock, I decided to opt for a lighter-weight paper.

A daytime review of the paper lanterns that had looked so magical the night before revealed that the white glue I had used created lumps and bubbles in the fine paper. Because I intended to leave the strand in place for a month or so, I wanted a neater look when the lights were unlit. So I switched to Yes Stikflat glue for the second strand with excellent results.

Elizabeth Cameron is a freelance writer living in Brighton, Massachusetts.

INSTRUCTIONS

Note: For a long string of lights, make one test lantern following steps 1 through 4 below. Make remaining lanterns assembly line style, completing step 1 for all lanterns, then step 2, etc.

1. *Prefold parchment.* Using X-Acto knife and steel ruler, cut one 6" x 12½" rectangle from parchment for each lightbulb in string. Lay parchment flat with short edges at sides (*see* illustration A, next page). Fold up bottom edge 2½" and crease firmly (illustration B). Open flat, make tick marks 2½" apart on each long edge, then make four creases across parchment to join marks. Fold all creases from same side.

DESIGNER'S TIP

Having a party? It's easy to match the lanterns to your theme. Consider a heavy, brown kraft paper punctuated with leaves for a rustic back porch party, or a heavyweight Japanese unryu paper with snowflake-shaped holes for a winter ski weekend. Parchment paper also comes in a variety of colors, such as soft pink, mint, tan, and baby blue. Lanterns made from any of these colors would work well with white lights.

PAPER CRAFTS

MATERIALS

- Medium-weight parchment paper
- String of 7-watt lights
- Yes Stikflat glue

You'll also need:
star craft punch; star paper punch; self-healing, gridded cutting mat; X-Acto knife; steel ruler; stiff, flat ½" brush; and pencil.

2. *Cut and glue parchment.* Cut the four creases from long crease to nearest edge to make five square flaps (illustration C). Trim end and middle flaps parallel to and ⅞" from long crease (illustration D). Brush glue on one end. Fold parchment, overlapping and gluing ends to make boxy shape (illustration E). Let dry 20 minutes.

3. *Punch stars.* Alternating specialty punchers, punch star-shaped holes at random on four sides of box (illustration F). For some stars, fold box flat and punch through two layers of parchment. To vary star placement, refold box the other way and punch again.

4. *Fit lanterns to bulbs.* Fold in short flaps, and insert bulb between them; if opening is not large enough, trim flaps to correct size (illustration G). Brush glue on one square flap, then overlap flaps and press gently so glue adheres. Hang strand so lanterns suspend down (illustration H). ◆

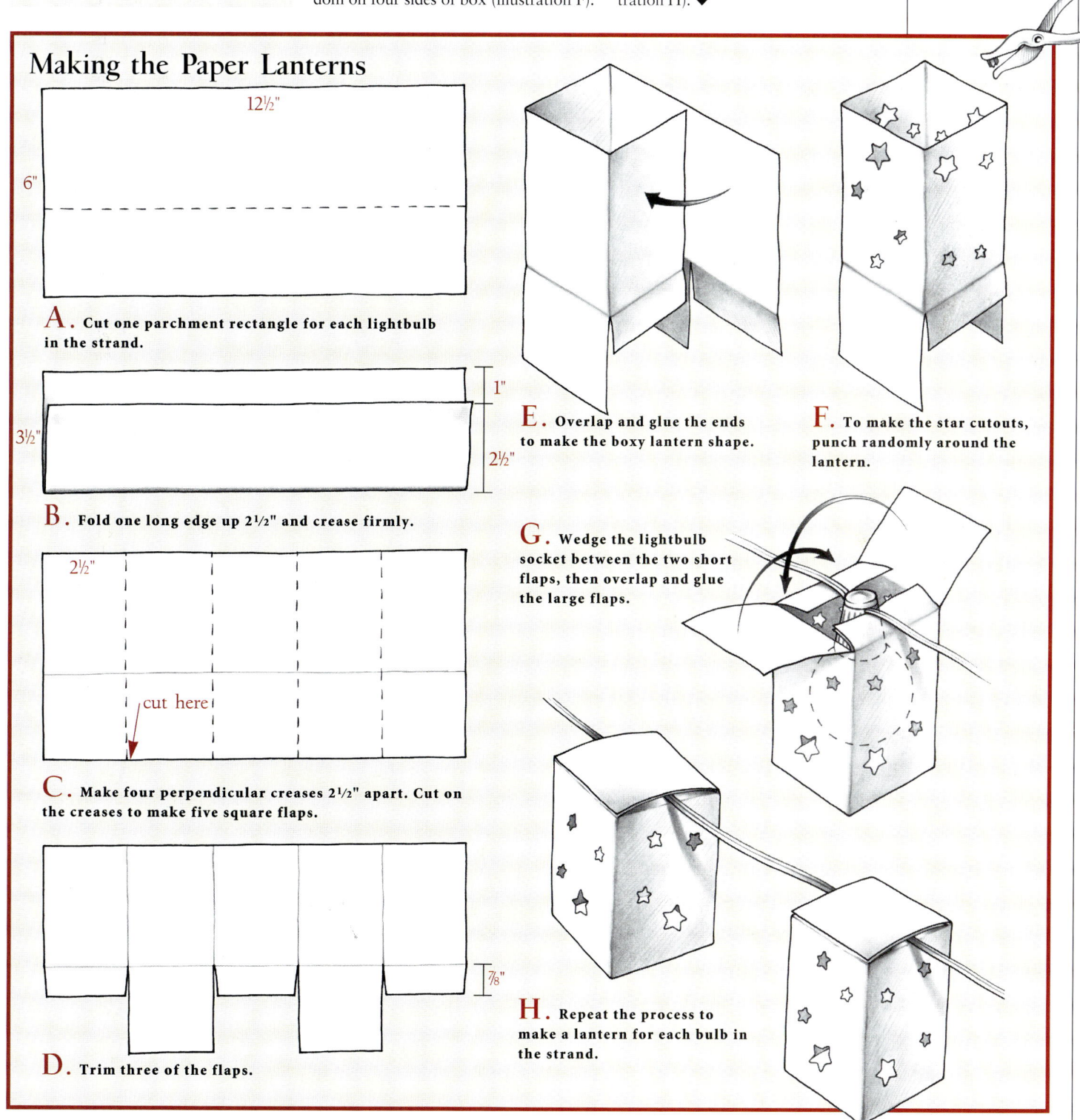

Making the Paper Lanterns

A. Cut one parchment rectangle for each lightbulb in the strand.

B. Fold one long edge up 2½" and crease firmly.

C. Make four perpendicular creases 2½" apart. Cut on the creases to make five square flaps.

D. Trim three of the flaps.

E. Overlap and glue the ends to make the boxy lantern shape.

F. To make the star cutouts, punch randomly around the lantern.

G. Wedge the lightbulb socket between the two short flaps, then overlap and glue the large flaps.

H. Repeat the process to make a lantern for each bulb in the strand.

FAUX FINISHES

1930s Farmhouse Table

Create this vintage patina, reminiscent of an enamel kitchen table, using layers of varnish, paint, and glaze.

BY VI AND STU CUTBILL

The soft, aged finish on this table is created by layering varnish, paint, and glaze. At certain points, the layers are sanded to reveal the underlying color.

MATERIALS
- Wooden table (new or previously finished)
- 1 quart latex primer
- 1 quart ivory matte latex paint (Benjamin Moore #225)
- 1 quart yellow-green matte latex paint (Benjamin Moore #425)
- 1 quart blue-green matte latex paint (Benjamin Moore #431)
- 1 quart latex satin varnish
- ½ cup latex glaze
- ½ cup brown matte latex paint (Benjamin Moore #1057)

You'll also need:
120- and 180-grit sandpaper; drop cloth; lint-free cotton cloths; 1" and 2" natural bristle paintbrushes; paint sticks; 1-pint plastic container; paper towels; spray mister; 2"-wide painter's tape; X-Acto knife; measuring cup; and steel ruler.

DESIGNER'S TIP
When choosing furniture for this finish, keep in mind that it should be fairly straightforward, with minimal turns and shaping in the legs.

COLOR PHOTOGRAPHY:
Carl Tremblay

STYLING:
Ritch Holben

SAY "RUSTIC COUNTRY FINISH," and most people think of chipped and peeling paint. For this table, however, we wanted to create a smoother patina. By using layers of varnish, paint, and glaze, and gently sanding in between, we created the look of a 1930s farmhouse table. The colors we chose are soft and muted, like those found on the appliances and furnishings of that time; the palette includes pea green, bluish green, and ivory.

Vi and Stu Cutbill are one of Canada's leading faux-finishing teams.

INSTRUCTIONS

1. *Sand and prime table.* Protect work area with drop cloth. Remove legs from table. Sand table and legs lightly with 120-grit sandpaper, following wood grain. Remove dust with lightly misted paper towel. Brush on primer, then let dry 1 hour, or following manufacturer's recommendations.

2. *Apply "sloppy" varnish coat.* To simulate years of paint buildup, brush varnish onto table in sloppy, uneven coat that is thick in some areas and thin in others. Do not remove rings, sags, or bubbles. Before varnish dries, apply second coat in same "sloppy" fashion over approximately 40 percent of table. Let dry at least 1 hour longer than manufacturer recommends, but preferably overnight.

3. *Paint underlayers.* Brush even coat of ivory paint over entire table. Let dry 1 hour longer than manufacturer recommends. Using 180-grit sandpaper, sand back ivory paint in raised areas to partially expose varnish layer underneath, then remove dust. Using cotton cloth, rub yellow-green paint into wood along grain and let dry 1 to 2 hours. Sand back portions of yellow-green layer to suggest layer of paint that has worn off over time.

4. *Paint ivory border striping.* Press painter's tape around perimeter of tabletop, even with edge, to form large rectangle. To create border stripe, press down additional tape parallel to first tape, allowing ¼" space between them. Using cotton cloth, rub ivory paint in ¼" space between tape strips. Rub ivory paint onto outermost edge of tabletop and one or two turnings on each leg.

5. *Paint green interior.* Using damp, crumpled cotton cloth, randomly dab blue-green paint onto table area bordered by inner tape. To create texture, allow the pattern created by the crumpled cotton cloth to show. Remove tape and let dry 2 hours.

6. *Apply "dirty" aging glaze.* Mix ½ cup glaze and ½ cup brown paint together in pint container. Dip lightly misted cotton cloth into mixture, then rub glaze onto inconspicuous spot on table to test color. Rub glaze lightly onto all surfaces for an overall "dirty" patina. Let dry 2 hours. Sand lightly and unevenly with 180-grit sandpaper, following wood grain, then remove dust as before. Finish with two light, even coats varnish, letting dry 1 hour between coats. Let dry overnight. ◆

PAPER CRAFTS

Antiqued Collage Cards

Tint a watercolor card with coffee, then decoupage a collage of giftwrap and flowers.

BY ELIZABETH CAMERON

THESE ELEGANT COLLAGE CARDS are so easy to make, you may not need to leave the house for supplies. Just assemble blank cards, instant coffee, giftwrap, and a gardening catalog, and you're ready to go.

I started with store-bought watercolor paper cards for the card base, but you can also cut your own cards from paper of a similar weight. To give the cards an antiqued look, I tinted them with a wash of instant coffee. The collage is created by layering on a piece of torn giftwrap, followed by a flower blossom, piece of fruit, or vegetable cut from a gardening catalog.

The elements I selected all impart an antique feel, but the design is eminently adaptable. Select other colors or patterns of giftwrap, and tint the card with a watercolor wash. For the decoupage layers, consider using a page torn from an old book, maps, lace doilies, empty seed packets, or wine labels.

Elizabeth Cameron is a freelance writer living in Brighton, Massachusetts.

INSTRUCTIONS

1. *Tint cards.* Protect work surface with plastic sheet, then lay several sheets of newsprint on top. Using measuring cup, dissolve 1 tablespoon instant coffee in ¼ cup hot water. Lay folded card face up on newsprint. Using large watercolor brush, apply coffee solution along folded edge. Open card, lay it flat, and finish tinting card front, brushing out to edges (*see* illustration A, below). Repeat process to tint all cards. Lay cards flat, then weight with heavy book and let dry overnight.

2. *Prepare paper pieces.* Trace around folded card on right side of giftwrap; mark one rectangle per card. Tear paper within lines to yield irregular piece approximately ¼" to ½" smaller all around than card front (illustration B). From garden catalog, select one 2" to 3" image per card, then cut out image using manicure scissors.

3. *Glue pieces to card.* Lay torn giftwrap face down on newsprint. Apply Mod Podge to back with foam brush, going beyond edges. Center giftwrap, glue side down, on face of card, then rub gently with crumpled paper towel to adhere. Swab any glue that oozes beyond edges. Brush back of flower cutout with Mod Podge and glue on top of giftwrap (illustration C). Repeat process to glue remaining cards, then stack unfolded cards right side up and weight under heavy book for 1 to 2 hours. To seal collage, brush Mod Podge across entire card front; let dry 1 hour. To counteract warping, press very lightly from back with dry iron at lowest setting. ◆

For variation on this design, combine flowers and fruit on one card, or, for another look entirely, substitute canceled postage stamps.

MATERIALS

- Blank watercolor cards with envelopes
- Giftwrap
- Garden catalog
- Mod Podge
- Instant coffee

You'll also need: manicure scissors; large round watercolor brush; 1" foam brush; measuring cup; measuring spoons; plastic sheet; newsprint; paper towels; iron; and heavy book.

COLOR PHOTOGRAPHY:
Carl Tremblay

ILLUSTRATION:
Nenad Jakesevic

A. Antique the card with a tint of coffee.

B. Tear a piece of giftwrap for the collage.

C. Glue the torn paper down, then add a flower.

LOW-SEW

Tufted Napkin Quilt
Stitch up this eye-catching quilt in an afternoon's time using ordinary dinner napkins.

🌶 BY LILY FRANKLIN

The finished twin-size quilt, above, measures approximately 50" by 85". To further coordinate your bedroom furnishings, consider stitching curtains, pillows, or other items from the same napkins.

DESIGNER'S TIP
For a less expensive version of the quilt, use muslin or other plain fabric for the quilt back.

COLOR PHOTOGRAPHY:
Carl Tremblay

ILLUSTRATION:
Mary Newell DePalma

THIS LOVELY PATCHWORK QUILT can be sewn in less than a day's time. The trick: using 21"-square napkins instead of fabric, which saves significant cutting time. The resulting quilt, with its bright and cheery pattern and simple tufting, will brighten any room.

To get started, you'll need to purchase 30 dinner-size napkins. Whatever you choose, the napkins should work together as a family. The napkins in this quilt all share a similar style (casual), the same fabric (100 percent cotton), and coordinating colors. Before sewing the napkins, you'll need to wash, dry, and press them. This will reduce their size to about 17" square.

When selecting batting, be sure to select a product that is suitable for tufting, such as bonded or needle-punched batting. Most battings manufactured today are stabilized in this way, which means the fibers won't shift even though the quilting or tufting stitches are placed far apart—16" to 17" apart in the case of this quilt.

Lily Franklin is a designer living in Albuquerque, New Mexico.

INSTRUCTIONS

1. *Prepare napkins.* To preshrink napkins, machine-wash in cold water, machine-dry, and press well. Using rotary cutter, trim smallest napkin by smallest amount to make a perfect square. Use this napkin as template to trim remaining 29 napkins to match.

2. *Design grid pattern.* On large, flat work surface, lay 15 napkins right side up to form grid measuring 3 napkins across by 5 napkins down. Rearrange napkins as desired, then sketch final design on scrap paper. Stack napkins in three groups by column to preserve order. Repeat process to design grid for quilt back.

3. *Sew five-napkin columns.* Place two napkins from first stack together, right sides facing and edges matching. Pin one edge, then stitch ½" from edge. Repeat to join remaining napkins in stack, making one 5-napkin column (*see* illustration A, next page). Repeat process to sew five additional columns for quilt front and back, referring to sketches as needed to confirm order. Press all seams open.

4. *Sew columns together.* Referring to sketch, place first two columns for quilt front, right sides together. Pin one long edge, then stitch ½" from edge. Repeat to join third column for quilt front (illustration B). Press seams open. Repeat process to join three columns for quilt back.

5. *Assemble quilt.* Stack batting then quilt front face up on flat surface. To pin-baste quilt, insert safety pin through both layers at center of each square (illustration C). To create opening for turning, machine-baste through both layers ½" from one short edge for 20"; basting should be placed roughly in the middle of the top edge. Lay quilt back face down on quilt front, edges matching, and secure with straight pins. Machine-stitch ½"

MATERIALS
- Thirty 20"- to 21"-square napkins
- 72" x 90" (twin-size) batting
- 1 skein embroidery floss
- Sewing thread

You'll also need:
sewing machine; iron; washer and dryer; laundry detergent; rotary cutter; cutting guide; self-healing cutting mat; sewing shears; embroidery needle; straight pins; 15 large safety pins; pencil; and scrap paper.

Making the Quilt

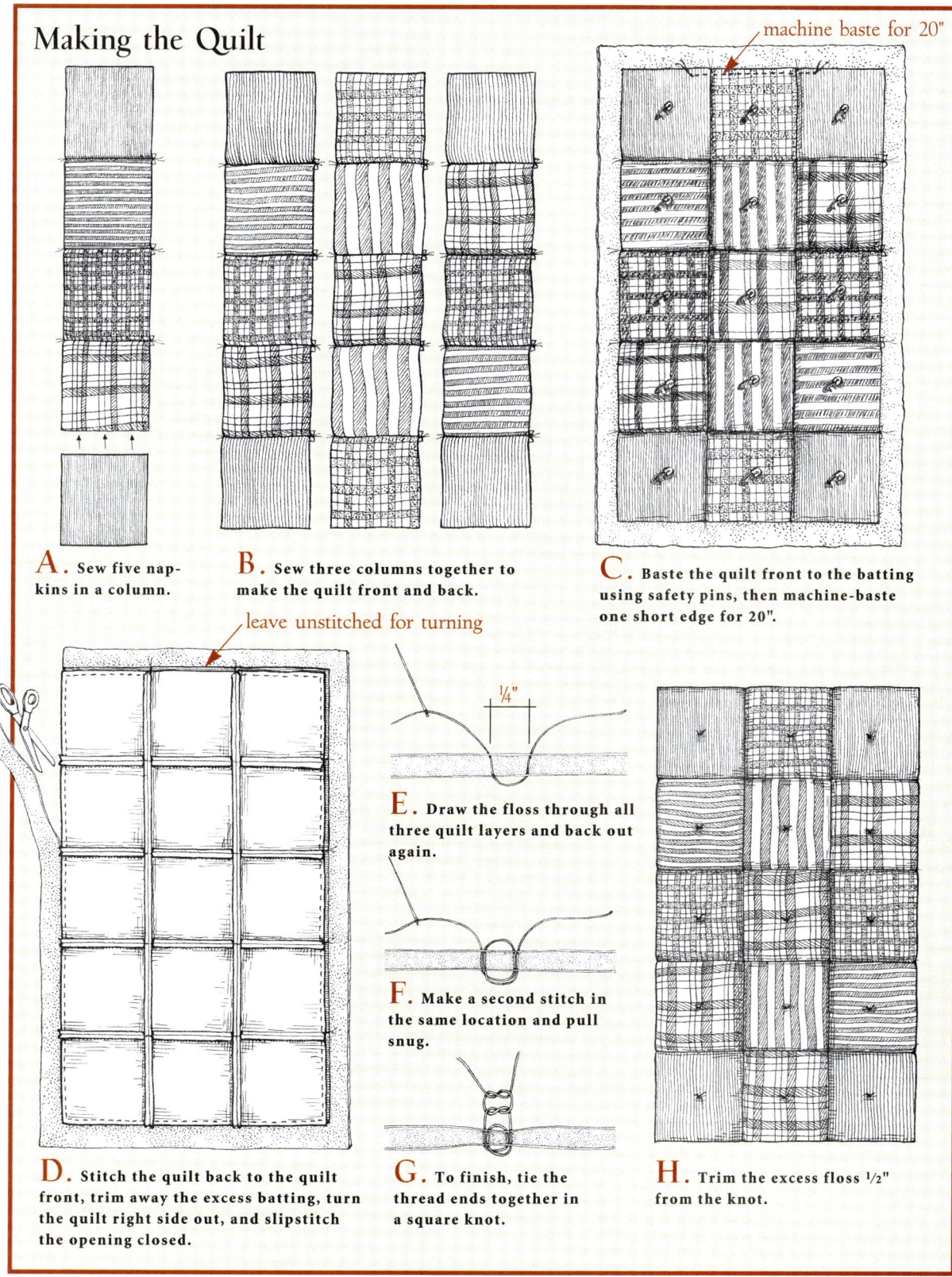

A. Sew five napkins in a column.

B. Sew three columns together to make the quilt front and back.

C. Baste the quilt front to the batting using safety pins, then machine-baste one short edge for 20".

D. Stitch the quilt back to the quilt front, trim away the excess batting, turn the quilt right side out, and slipstitch the opening closed.

E. Draw the floss through all three quilt layers and back out again.

F. Make a second stitch in the same location and pull snug.

G. To finish, tie the thread ends together in a square knot.

H. Trim the excess floss ½" from the knot.

DESIGNER'S TIP

For variation on this design, work up a quilt using just two different napkins, or design each side of the quilt using completely different napkins. To save money, buy odd napkins, closeouts, or one-of-a-kind and discontinued styles.

For a fancier version of this quilt, insert some type of edging between the two sides, such as piping, eyelet, or trim.

from edge all around, but leave machine-basted section open for turning quilt right side out. Trim excess batting as close to stitching as possible (illustration D), then clip corners of quilt and batting diagonally. Turn quilt right side out and slipstitch opening closed along guideline.

6. *Add tufting.* Lay quilt face up. Thread embroidery needle with 36" length of floss. Working one block at a time, remove safety pin, then insert needle down through center of block and draw out ¼" away. Pull through, leaving 3" tail (illustration E). Make second stitch along same path (illustration F), then draw thread snug and cut, leaving 3" end. Repeat to stitch center of remaining blocks. To finish, tie thread ends in square knot (illustration G) and snip excess ½" from knot (illustration H). ◆

HOME FURNISHINGS

Plaid Silk Footstool

Create a small-scale footstool using a square of plywood for the base, foam for loft, and curtain finials for legs.

🌸 BY FRANCOISE HARDY

For variation on this design, substitute a smaller random floral fabric or a damask, then coordinate the paint colors to match.

MATERIALS

- ¾ yard 45"-wide silk fabric
- 1⅜ yard 1"-wide tassel trim
- ¾ yard 45"-wide muslin
- 14" x 14" x 3" medium-density foam
- 22" x 22" polyester batting
- 1¼"-diameter cord-wrapped shank button
- ½" four-hole button
- Four 6"-long wood curtain finials
- 14" x 14" x ¾" piece plywood
- Four ¼" x 3" hanger bolts
- Four ¼" T-nuts
- Dental floss
- 2 ounces Plaid acrylic paint in the following colors:
  Fresh Foliage #954,
  Violet Pansy #440, and
  Crimson #435
- 2 ounces Plaid metallic acrylic paint in the following colors:
  Peridot #671 and
  Rose Shimmer #652
- Tulip Color Point Paintstitching, Pearl White #WH21
- Gold metallic felt-tip pen
- Water-based primer
- Thin cardboard

You'll also need:
½"- and 1"-wide soft-bristled brushes; 1" foam brush; staple gun; hot-glue gun; pliers; hammer; vise; drill with ¼" bit; handsaw; 100- and 120-grit sandpaper; sanding block; pencil; 20"-long ruler; T-square; scissors; 5" doll-making needle; scrap wood blocks; permanent marker; paper towels; masking tape; and serrated kitchen knife.

Other items, if necessary:
four ½"-diameter or smaller furniture glides (for protecting bottom of legs).

COLOR PHOTOGRAPHY:
Carl Tremblay

ILLUSTRATION:
Judy Love

STYLING:
Ritch Holben

Y OU NEED ONLY BASIC WOODworking skills to build this delicate footstool, which has a piece of plywood as its base and curtain finials for legs. If you can handle a handsaw, an electric drill, and a staple gun, you can build this 10"-high stool.

Because the stool has a smaller scale than, say, a sofa ottoman, I was able to take several design shortcuts. For the base, I started with a 14" square of plywood, then trimmed off the corners at a 45-degree angle to yield an octagon. This size piece of wood is easily handled with a handsaw, versus a larger piece of furniture, which might require a table saw.

Since the legs on this diminutive footstool are not going to support the full weight of an adult, they do not need to be as sturdily engineered as those on a larger ottoman, which someone might sit on. I selected a 6" turned maple curtain finial, which, when inverted, makes a beautiful leg. The legs are then attached to the base using hanger bolts and T-nuts, which are easy to work with.

The footstool's small scale also means there is no need for high-density foam. Instead, I used a 14" square block of ordinary foam, about 3" thick; the foam can be trimmed down easily using the stool's base as a template. To soften the edges and to make the final result look a little plumper, I applied a layer of polyester batting, followed by a layer of muslin, over the foam.

Built on a larger scale, the bright, vibrant colors I selected for this footstool would be overwhelming. The small size of this piece, however, means you can use just about any type or color of upholstery fabric. Best bets include bold geometrics in a medium scale, such as a plaid with blocks around 2" to 3". A large, 6" plaid would work better on a couch, while a tiny ½" plaid is better suited to clothing. Stripes can be difficult because they will wrap around the octagon in an odd way. I used a buffalo plaid, which lies in blocks of color and yet wraps around the octagon. (Naturally, if you change the color of the fabric from that shown here, be sure to change the paint colors to match).

The top fabric is applied in the same way as the muslin: pulled taut on one side, then stapled in place. With the top fabric, however, I rolled over the cut edges and used a carded strip for a neat finish. Carded strips can be bought in rolls like tape, or you can make them yourself by cutting pieces of thin cardboard into ½"-wide strips. The strip is inserted in the fold of fabric before stapling in order to keep the edge straight and neat.

Francoise Hardy is a Boston-based writer and designer.

INSTRUCTIONS
Building the Stool Frame
1. *Cut octagonal base.* Lay 14" plywood square flat, smooth side up. Using ruler and pencil, lightly draft two diagonal lines connecting opposite corners. Measure from center intersection 7" along each of four lines and make mark. Using T-square, draft perpendicular line through each mark (*see* illustration A, above). Resulting octagon will measure approximately 5¾" along each edge. Saw off corners on marked lines.

2. *Drill holes for legs and button.* Lay octagon flat, smooth side up. Draft two diagonal lines, perpendicular to each other, to connect opposite corners. At each corner, measure in 1½" and make mark (illustration B). Place scrap wood underneath during drilling to prevent splintering, then use ¼" bit to drill four holes at dots for legs and one hole at center intersection for button. Drill completely through base into scrap wood. Sand surface lightly along woodgrain using 100-grit sandpaper in sanding block. To refine cut edges, run block against them at 45-degree angle.

3. *Test-fit legs.* Position shank of T-nut over each leg hole, then tap in place with hammer until teeth embed and flanges lie flush with wood surface (illustration C). To add hanger bolts to finials, proceed as follows: Secure finial in vise. Using ¼" bit, drill 2" straight into center of leg. Using pliers, screw bolt into opening until just ¾" to 1" of bolt's threaded section remains visible (illustration D). Lay octagon flat, smooth side (stool underside) face up. To test-fit, screw legs into each opening from underside. Legs should lodge perpendicular to base, and stool should not wobble (*see* illustration E, next page).

Painting and Upholstering the Stool
1. *Apply primer.* Start by making painting stand for legs. Using ¼" bit, drill four holes at least 4" apart and ½" deep in scrap wood. Stand legs upside down in holes. Using 1" foam brush and following manufacturer's directions, apply one or two coats primer to stool underside and four legs. Let dry overnight. Sand raised grain with 120-grit sandpaper and remove dust with damp paper towel.

2. *Paint stool underside.* Using 1" soft-bristled brush, apply 3 coats Crimson paint to stool underside, letting dry 20 minutes after each coat. *Note:* Legs will be painted in step 7.

3. *Cut foam, batting, and fabrics.* Lay foam flat, set stool on top, and trace around edges with permanent marker. Using serrated knife, cut foam on marked lines. Screw in legs, stand stool upright, and place foam on top (illustration F). Drape batting over foam. Using scissors, trim batting even with top edge of plywood base and clip out small triangles to reduce bulk at corners (illustration G). To cut muslin, lay it flat, lay batting on top as a template, and cut 2" beyond batting edge all around. To cut silk, lay it flat, determine which part of design will fall at center of stool, and mark with small piece of masking tape. Fold batting into quarters and lay it on silk, placing folded corner at mark and aligning folded edges along lengthwise and crosswise grains of silk fabric. Carefully unfold batting, then cut silk 1" beyond batting edge.

4. *Attach upholstery.* Lay muslin flat, center batting and foam on it, and set stool base painted side up on foam. Unscrew and remove legs. Select muslin edge, cut along straight grain, draw it up onto underside of base, and staple it to center of side edge. Draw opposite edge taut but not tight and staple in same way. Apply several more staples along these two edges until you reach corners. Move two edges to right and repeat process. Staple remaining edges in same way. Screw in legs, turn stool right side up, and trim muslin even with bottom edge of base (illustration H).

5. *Add silk fabric covering.* From thin cardboard, cut eight carding strips each measuring ½" x 5¾". Rest stool on flat surface, padded side up. Lay silk fabric on top face up, with tape marker at center and edges hanging down sides. Fold one straight-grain side edge under, even with lower edge of base. Slip carding strip inside fold to keep it even, then staple silk flat against lower edge, stopping 1" from corners. Repeat to staple opposite edge, pulling silk firm and taut. Move two edges to right and repeat process. Staple remaining edges in same way. To finish corners,

Building the Stool Frame

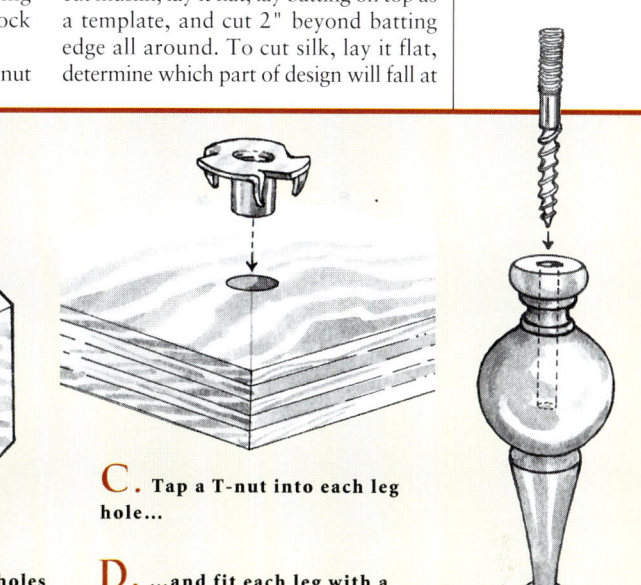

A. Draft an octagon on a square of plywood.

B. Saw off the corners and drill holes for the legs and the center tufting.

C. Tap a T-nut into each leg hole...

D. ...and fit each leg with a hanger bolt.

HOME FURNISHING

Painting the Stool Legs

Top Disk:
Rose Shimmer

Convex collar:
Violet Pansy

Middle ball:
Peridot over Fresh Foliage

Flared cone:
Violet Pansy

Ball foot:
Rose Shimmer

Stripe rings:
Gold marker; dots of fabric paint on widest ring

pull fabric along one edge down and past corner (as if to make a hospital bed corner) and staple down. Tuck excess onto adjacent edge and make fold perpendicular to base. Repeat process at each corner, so folds "pinwheel" around octagon (illustration I). To further anchor fabric, place additional row of staples all around to secure any spots missed on first pass. Tap down protruding staples with hammer.

6. *Add trim.* Thread doll-making needle with 14" length of dental floss. Insert needle through hole in base of stool, up through foam, and draw out at center of silk fabric, removing tape marker as you go. Slip button shank onto floss, reinsert needle back down into cushion at center, and draw it out through hole. Thread floss ends through two holes in ½" button. Tie ends together in single knot, pulling snugly to create tuft on top of stool. Tie floss ends in square knot and snip ends. To conceal staples, hot-glue fringe around edge of base (illustration J).

7. *Paint legs.* Remove legs from stool. Use color silhouette, left, as reference for painting leg. Stand each leg on end so bolt rests on work surface, hold ½" brush against surface being painted, and rotate leg by ball foot. Allow 20 minutes drying time after each coat. Paint middle ball element of each leg with two coats Fresh Foliage, followed by two coats Peridot. Paint flared cone with two coats Violet Pansy. Paint convex collar with three coats Rose Shimmer. Set leg in stand and paint ball foot and top disk with three coats Rose Shimmer. Let dry 1 hour. Brush on acrylic gloss varnish, let dry 15 minutes, brush on second coat, and let dry 1 hour. To stripe rings, nest gold marker tip along crevice and rotate leg. Let dry 30 minutes. Squeeze dots of Pearl White fabric paint directly from applicator onto widest ring, spacing dots ¼" apart. Let dry overnight before screwing legs into stool. If desired, insert glides into bottom of ball feet following manufacturer's instructions. ◆

Upholstering the Stool

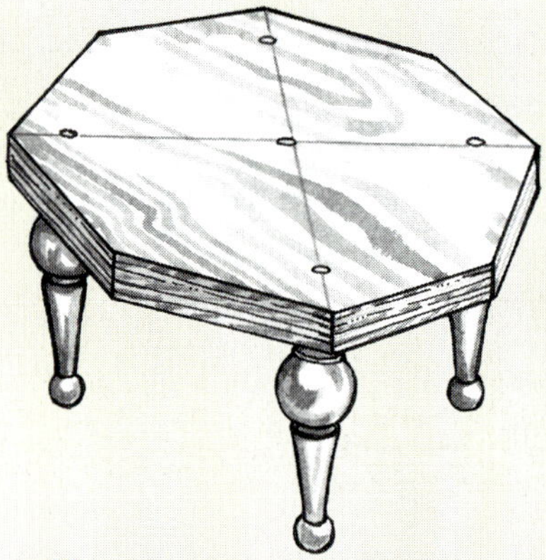

E. Test-fit the legs in the stool base. The stool should not wobble when stood upright.

F. Cut a foam octagon to match the stool base...

G. ...then layer batting over the foam, trim the batting, and clip out the corners.

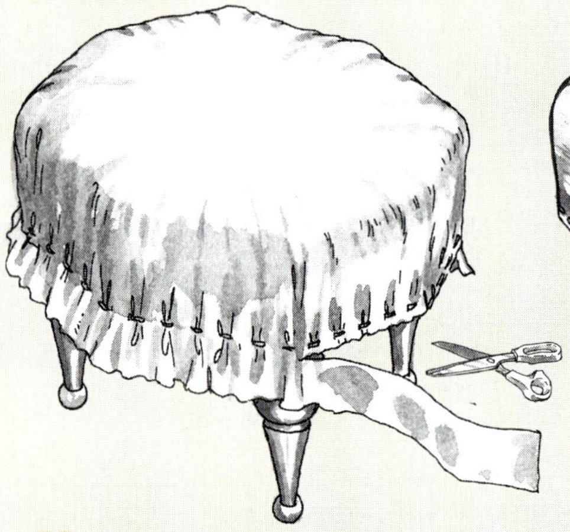

H. Staple muslin over the padding, then trim off the excess.

I. Staple the plaid silk fabric to the stool frame, pleating each corner.

J. Tuft the center of the stool, then glue fringe around the edge.

20   HANDCRAFT ILLUSTRATED • SPRING 1997

Leafy Fern Porch Rug

Decorate any plain fiber rug with a quick reverse-stenciling technique and painter's tape.

BY FRANCOISE HARDY

I LOVE THE NATURAL BEAUTY AND resilience of fiber rugs, but wanted a more colorful version for my three-season porch. To create the leafy fern design shown, I cut leaves and branches from painter's tape, applied them to the rug, and spray-painted the entire rug. The tape pieces are peeled off to reveal the softly patterned design.

For variation on this design, simply cut different shapes from the painter's tape. Use squares, circles and/or triangles to create a more modern design, or cut and apply stripes or zigzags for a children's playroom.

Francoise Hardy is a designer living in Boston, Massachusetts.

INSTRUCTIONS

1. *Prepare work area.* Working in well-ventilated area (or outdoors), spread drop cloth over floor. Unroll rug, and lay flat on drop cloth. If edges remain curled, weight with heavy books overnight.

2. *Cut and apply tape stencils.* Cut 10"- to 14"-long strip of tape from roll. To make stem, cut gentle arc along tape from end to end, then cut parallel arc about ½" away; extreme precision is not necessary (see illustration A, below). From 4"- to 6"-long strip, cut curved spur (illustration B). For leaves, cut lozenge shapes about 3" long and about 1½" to 2" wide (illustration C). Press stems and leaves onto rug surface (illustration D). Cut additional stems and leaves, and press them onto rug, varying their orientation to create free-form design over entire surface except border area. Position small pieces of leaves and ferns to peep in at edges.

3. *Paint rug.* Put on mask and gloves. For optimum coverage, shake teal blue paint can 2 minutes longer than manufacturer recommends. Hold can 8" to 10" from rug surface and spray light, even coat over entire rug. Reshake can every few minutes during spraying. If necessary, immediately spray second coat to even out coverage. Let dry overnight, or as manufacturer recommends.

4. *Mask and paint border.* Mask off center portion of rug using tape and newspaper, leaving natural border free. Spray-paint border using baby blue paint; apply two coats, and let dry as above. Remove tape and air for several days. ◆

Using this one technique, you can decorate a variety of natural fiber or fabric projects, including doormats, floorcloths, or curtains.

Making the Ferns

A. Cut a gently curved stem from the painter's tape...

B. ...then cut a shorter spur stem.

C. Cut a series of 1½" to 2" leaves.

D. Put the pieces together to make a fern.

MATERIALS

- 4' x 6' jute rug
- 12 ounces baby blue Krylon interior/exterior spray paint (for border)
- 12 ounces teal blue Krylon interior/exterior spray paint (for center portion of rug)

You'll also need: 3"-wide painter's masking tape; scissors; newspaper; drop cloth; particle mask; latex gloves; ruler or yardstick; and heavy books.

COLOR PHOTOGRAPHY: **Carl Tremblay**

ILLUSTRATION: **Judy Love**

STYLING: **Ritch Holben**

MIXED MEDIA

Decorative Painted Plates

Forget special glass paints or freehand painting. Decorate these plates using a squeeze bottle and your fingers.

BY LILY FRANKLIN

These 10" plates should not be submerged in water—either through hand washing or in a dishwashing machine. They should only be hung on a wall or used as decorative chargers, or as serving dishes for dry food.

COLOR PHOTOGRAPHY:
Carl Tremblay

ILLUSTRATION:
Judy Love

STYLING:
Ritch Holben

MATERIALS
(for one plate)

- Shell, fruit, or other black and white images
- 10" octagonal smooth clear glass plate
- 9" x 12" piece black felt
- Mod Podge (matte)
- Spray glass frosting (matte)

Paints for Seashell Plate
- 14-milliliter tubes Winsor & Newton gouache in the following colors: Chinese Orange, Flesh Tint, Gold Ochre, and Neutral Gray #4
- 2-ounce FolkArt acrylic paints in the following colors: Bachelor Button Blue, Fresh Foliage, Light Periwinkle, Red Orange, Sunflower, and Warm White
- 2-ounce Accent Crown Jewels acrylic paint, Imperial Antique Gold
- Tulip Colorpoint fabric paint, Ivory Pearl

Paints for Fruit Plate
- 14-milliliter tubes Winsor & Newton gouache in the following colors: Burnt Umber, Gold Ochre, Golden Yellow, Light Purple, Linden Green, Olive Green, and Red Ochre
- 2-ounce FolkArt acrylic paints in the following colors: Aspen Green, Cappuccino, Fresh Foliage, Purple Lilac, Sunflower, and Warm White
- 2-ounce Accent Crown Jewels acrylic paint, Imperial Antique Gold
- Tulip Colorpoint fabric paint, Ivory Pearl

You'll also need:
access to photocopier with enlarger; #4 and #10 round brushes; paint syringes; small sea sponge; watercolor palette; small containers with water; small containers and craft sticks; scissors; steel ruler with cork back; newsprint; graph paper; pencil; sponge; paper towels; and spray glass cleaner.

HAND-PAINTED PLATES SUCH as these might retail for upwards of $100 each. You can make your own at home for a fraction of the cost, however, using decoupage and acrylic craft paint. What's more, there's no freehand painting involved.

To get started, I photocopied a series of shell and fruit images. To simulate the look of old hand-colored lithographs, I tinted the cutouts using a very light wash of gouache, then adhered them to the back of the plates using Mod Podge. To eliminate freehand painting, I used a paint syringe and craft paint directly from a fine-tipped squeeze bottle. To paint the background, I used my fingertip as a spreader, rather than a brush, which will leave marks.

Glass painting is not a new art, and several products exist specifically for this purpose. In the past, for instance, I've used Liquitex Glossies acrylic paint on glass with good success. For this project, though, I needed a wider range of colors. After some experimentation, I discovered that it's possible to use ordinary acrylic craft paints on glass. Proper adhesion is ensured by preparing the glass with a coating of matte frosting spray, which effectively gives the glass some tooth. Most glass paint must be heat-cured, or permanently adhered to the glass, in an oven. This is not necessary with acrylic craft paints, but the painted finish on the plate's back should be sealed with two coats of Mod Podge.

I used a variety of simple techniques to apply the paint. To draw dots and lines, I used extremely fine plastic tips, rather than brushes. The pearlescent paint I selected came packaged in its own squeeze bottle, but any color of paint can easily be transferred to a paint syringe or squeeze bottle. I laid in the gold lines with a brush and a straightedge. This sounds difficult, but it is as easy as running a pencil along a steel ruler. Finally, I applied the solid ground colors using the tip of my finger; a brush, even a soft, flat one, will leave streaks.

Lily Franklin is a designer living in Albuquerque, New Mexico.

INSTRUCTIONS

Note: Do not let paint or Mod Podge harden on tools and brushes. Clean them promptly in warm, soapy water.

Making the Seashell Plate

1. *Cut felt backing.* Turn plate face down and measure across base. Draft square this size on graph paper. Cut out square, position it on plate base, and fold down corners diagonally to match base edges. Use resulting octagon as template to cut matching shape from felt. Set felt backing aside.

2. *Cut out and tint images.* Photocopy one large and eight small shell (or substitute) images, cut out as close to edges as possible, and lay face up on several layers of newsprint. Place small amount each color gouache in watercolor palette and dilute with a few drops of water. (*Note:* When applying color, brush diluted gouache across entire image or, alternately, concentrate color near edges and areas of dense shading; blot up excess wash with paper towel.) On large scallop, using #4 round brush, tint recessed areas between ribs using Neutral Gray #4, then apply Gold Ochre along right half of each recessed area and on rib itself just below growth lines. Tint individual small shells using Neutral Gray #4, Gold Ochre, Chinese Orange, or Flesh Tint; use color to highlight striped patterns. Let dry 30 minutes.

3. *Glue images to plate.* For better paint adhesion, spray back of plate with very light coat glass frosting, following manufacturer's instructions and safety precautions. Let dry 30 minutes. Make sure all images are positioned face up on newsprint. Using #10 round brush, brush thin, even coat of Mod Podge across large image, going beyond edges and onto newsprint. Center image face down on back of plate, immediately check position from right side, and adjust as needed. Rub gently with fingers from back, pressing out all bubbles. Wipe oozing at edges with damp sponge. Once image is smooth, brush thin coat of Mod Podge over back of image, going slightly beyond edge to create seal. Repeat process to glue eight small images around plate rim in turn (see illustration A, below). Let dry to touch, 15 to 30 minutes. Apply two additional thin coats of Mod Podge to all images, letting dry 15 to 30 minutes after each coat.

4. *Paint pearlescent dots.* Clean finger marks from back of plate using paper towel and spray glass cleaner. Set plate face down on newsprint. From this point forward, do not touch plate back with your fingertips; to move plate, rotate newsprint. Working directly from squeeze bottle, apply medium-sized, random dots of Ivory Pearl paint to center octagonal field (illustration B). Use same paint to

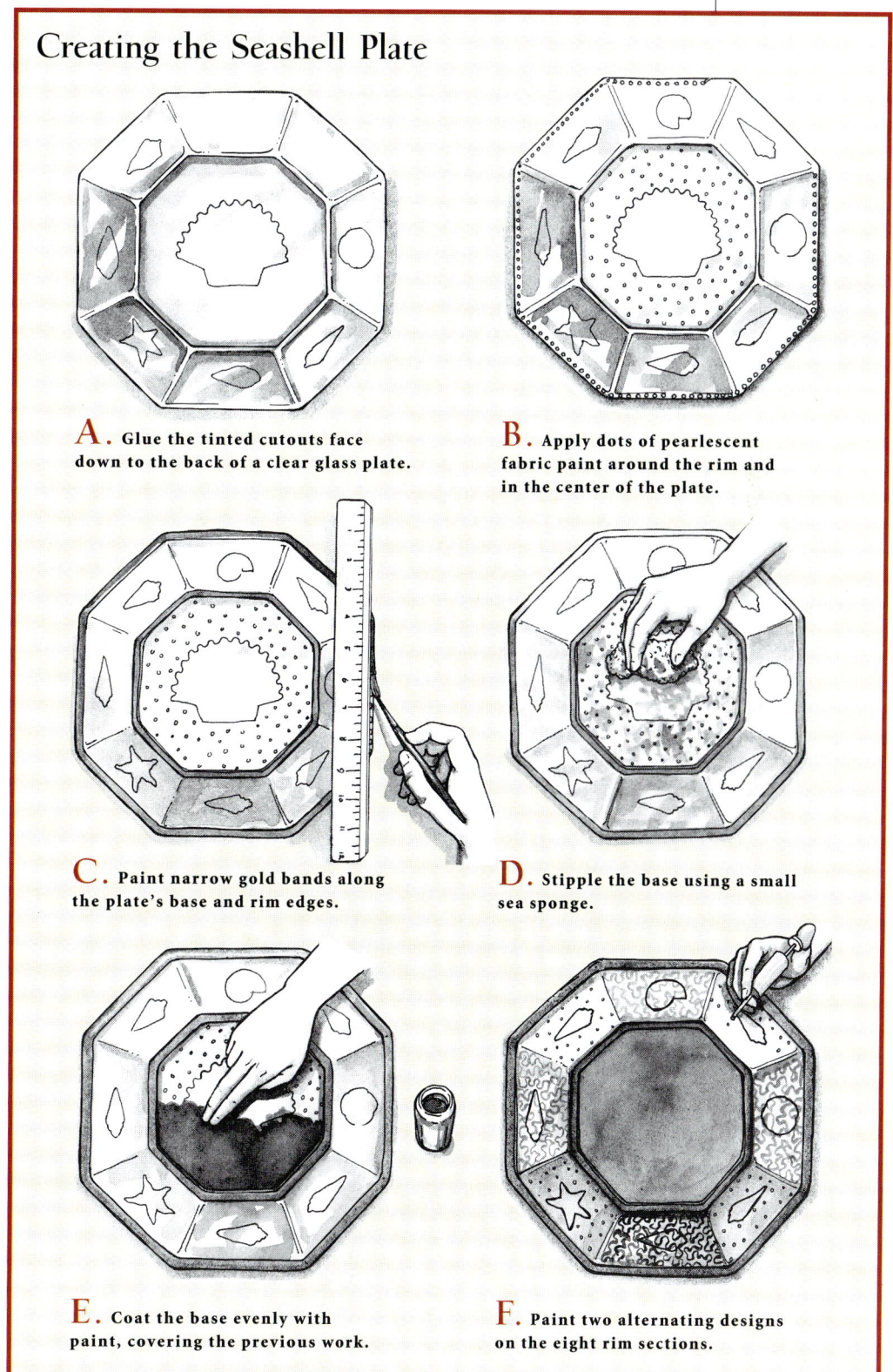

Creating the Seashell Plate

A. Glue the tinted cutouts face down to the back of a clear glass plate.

B. Apply dots of pearlescent fabric paint around the rim and in the center of the plate.

C. Paint narrow gold bands along the plate's base and rim edges.

D. Stipple the base using a small sea sponge.

E. Coat the base evenly with paint, covering the previous work.

F. Paint two alternating designs on the eight rim sections.

MIXED MEDIA

Creating the Fruit Plate

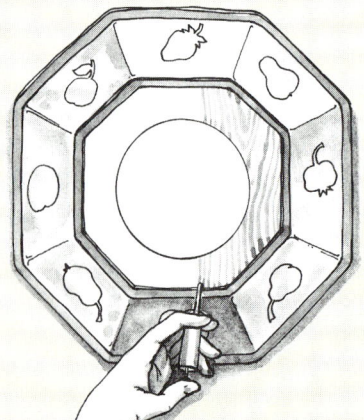

G. To suggest woodgrain, paint wavering vertical lines with a syringe.

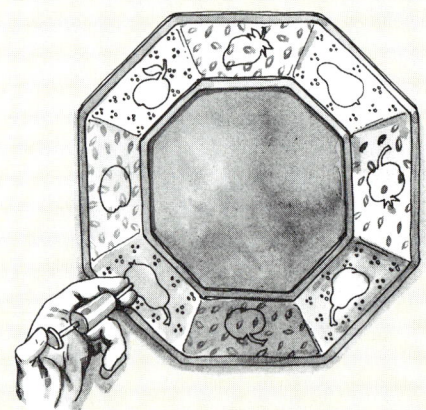

H. Paint green leaf and lilac dot designs alternately around the rim.

Finishing the Plates

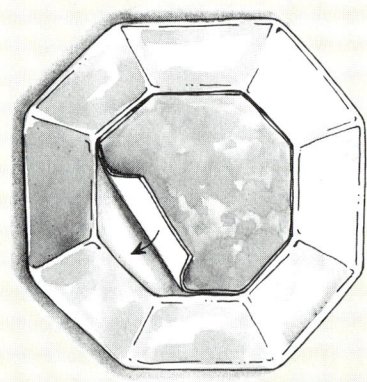

I. Coat the entire plate back, seal it with Mod Podge and add felt backing.

apply small dots of fabric paint ⅜" apart around plate rim. Let dry 24 hours.

5. *Paint gold bands.* Rest steel ruler on base of plate, parallel to and ⅛" from one base edge, then run round #4 brush loaded with Imperial Antique Gold paint along ruler edge. To prevent smearing, paint every other edge; let dry 30 minutes, then repeat process to paint remaining four edges (illustration C). Repeat to paint rim edges. Add second coat of Imperial Antique Gold freehand along all edges and rims. Let dry 30 minutes.

6. *Paint center octagon.* Using damp-dry small sea sponge, stipple Sunflower paint on plate base, stopping at inner gold band (illustration D). Let dry 20 minutes. Then cover entire area with Warm White paint, using fingertip (not brush) to spread thick, even coat (illustration E). Let dry to touch, about 1 hour.

7. *Paint eight rim panels.* Fill one syringe with Fresh Foliage paint. Mix coral paint by combining Red Orange and Warm White in equal amounts, then fill syringe. With green syringe, scribble random, vermiculated pattern across every other rim panel, lightly skimming surface to avoid scrape marks. With coral syringe, fill remaining four panels with random dots (illustration F). Let dry 20 minutes. Coat entire rim with Light Periwinkle, using finger as spreader as in step 6. Let dry 2 hours.

8. *Finish plates.* Using #10 round brush, brush two coats Bachelor Button Blue paint on back of plate, letting dry 30 minutes after each coat. Using #10 round brush, brush two light coats Mod Podge, letting dry 15 to 30 minutes after each coat. Brush one additional coat Mod Podge on base only, position felt backing from step 1 on base, and press gently to adhere (illustration I). Let dry overnight.

Making the Fruit Plate

1. *Cut felt backing.* Same as for Seashell Plate, step 1.

2. *Cut out and tint images.* Photocopy one large and eight small fruit images, cut out as close to edges as possible, and lay face up on several layers of newsprint. Large pear image for center of plate is cut as a medallion. Place small amount of each color gouache in watercolor palette and dilute with a few drops of water. (*Note:* When applying color, brush diluted gouache across entire image or, alternately, concentrate color near edges and areas of dense shading; blot up excess wash with paper towel.) On large pear, using #10 brush, tint fruit Golden Yellow, then darken right edge and stem with Burnt Umber. Using #4 brush, fill turned-back portion of leaves with Linden Green and remainder with Olive Green. Tint berries Gold Ochre, add Golden Yellow or Linden Green highlights, then tint stems Burnt Umber. Tint broadest part of fig Light Purple, crown and stem Linden Green, and twig Burnt Umber. Tint lemon using Golden Yellow and Linden Green, then extend Linden Green into leaf; highlight leaf with Olive Green. Tint one edge of mango using Red Ochre, other edge with Olive Green, and middle with Golden Yellow; tint stem Burnt Umber. Tint plum using Light Purple, then tint stem Olive Green and Burnt Umber. Tint pomegranate using Red Ochre and Gold Ochre and stem Burnt Umber. Tint strawberry Red Ochre and leaf using Olive Green. Let dry 30 minutes.

3. *Glue images to plate.* Same as for Seashell Plate, step 3. Glue large image to center of plate.

4. *Paint pearlescent dots.* Same as for Seashell Plate, step 4. Paint rim only; do not apply dots to center of plate.

5. *Paint gold bands.* Same as for Seashell Plate, step 5.

6. *Paint center octagon.* Brush back of pear medallion with Warm White paint to make medallion opaque. Let dry 20 minutes. Fill syringe with Cappuccino paint. To create woodgrain look, use syringe to apply wavering vertical streaks in area surrounding medallion. Run some streaks back in original direction to suggest knots (illustration G). Use sponge to wipe off any paint that seeps into medallion area. Cover woodgrain area with Sunflower paint, using fingertip (not brush) to spread a thick, even coat. Let dry to touch, about 1 hour.

7. *Paint eight rim panels.* Fill one syringe with Fresh Foliage paint, another with Purple Lilac. With green syringe, draw ⅜"-long lozenge-shaped leaves on every other rim panel. With lilac syringe, fill remaining four panels with clusters of three dots (illustration H). Let dry 20 minutes. Coat entire rim with Aspen Green, using finger as spreader as above. Let dry 2 hours.

8. *Finish plates.* Using #10 brush, brush two coats Aspen Green on back of plate, letting dry 30 minutes after each coat. Continue as for Shell Plate, step 8. ◆

Hand-Painted Parrot Tulips

Transform common silk flowers into a prized variety using watercolor paint.

BY CAROL ENDLER STERBENZ

PARROT TULIPS, EASILY IDENTIFIED by their "flames" of color, make a dramatic flower for display. For a longer-lasting arrangement, I decided to color my own parrot tulips using ordinary silk flowers and watercolor paint.

Tulips, like other silk flowers, typically retail for between $2 and $7 a stem. Although you may be tempted to purchase the least expensive flowers you can find, many of these brands have a plastic or synthetic finish, which will repel the watercolor paint. Instead, look for slightly translucent petals made from 100 percent silk or other fabric without any special coating.

The painting technique used to create the "flames" is simple and forgiving. Apply just enough paint to the bristles to leave a single stroke on the petal. Avoid oversaturating the brush with paint, as this can cause the strokes to bleed. Use the flowers shown, at right, as a reference, or look in your favorite garden and/or bulb catalogs.

INSTRUCTIONS

1. *Set up work area.* Protect work surface with plastic sheet topped with newsprint. Set out brush, squeeze bottle with water, and watercolor palette. Set additional newsprint to one side for scrap.

2. *Load brush with color.* Squeeze small amount of watercolor into palette

THE HISTORY OF PARROT TULIPS

The unique coloration of Parrot tulips actually developed by accident. Some of the first tulip bulbs—single-colored cultivars known as "breeders"—developed a peculiar tendency to break into variegated combinations, where the petals streak, feather, and flame. Once broken, the tulip rarely reverts to its original coloring, and the bulb's offspring retain the new coloration. Today it is known that the broken color was caused by a plant virus, but, at the time, the unexpected breaks further enhanced the flowers' appeal and value. To this day, Parrot tulips are prized for their distinctive coloring.

While we chose to paint red flames on a white tulip, many other varieties of Parrot tulips exist, including those with red flames on yellow tulips.

well. To make paint spreadable, dilute with few drops water. Dip dry brush into paint, then run brush across scrap newsprint to shed excess liquid. When brush runs "dry" (wet but not dripping wet), paint can be applied to tulip petals.

3. *Paint tulip petals.* Bend each petal out and away from stamens. Hold one petal flat against newsprint, outer surface facing up, and bend surrounding petals out of way. Starting at base of petal and moving toward outer edge, run "dry" brush across petal surface. Apply more pressure at beginning of stroke and less pressure at end to create feathering (*see* illustration A). Paint entire petal this way with "dry" brush, reloading brush as established in step 2. Brush additional color onto base as needed to make this area solid (illustration B). Repeat process to paint each petal in turn. Continue until all tulips are painted. ◆

MATERIALS

- 12 white silk ruffle-edged tulips
- 1 tube vermilion watercolor

You'll also need:
#12 round brush; plastic sheet; newsprint; watercolor palette; and water in small squeeze bottle.

COLOR PHOTOGRAPHY:
Carl Tremblay

STYLING:
Ritch Holben

METAL

Chicken Wire Candlecage

Create an onion-dome-like sculpture using ordinary chicken wire, then reinforce the design with armature wire.

BY MICHIO RYAN

This wire candleshade, measuring about 26" high and about 12" wide, makes a dramatic centerpiece. For variation, string colored beads from the honeycombs or surround the base with fresh greens.

DESIGNER'S TIP
To keep down the soot, I recommend using a smokeless, 15" tapered candle with this project.

COLOR PHOTOGRAPHY:
Carl Tremblay

ILLUSTRATION:
Judy Love

STYLING:
Ritch Holben

THIS WIRE CANDLECAGE'S SOPHISticated, curvy shape belies its humble origins: ordinary honeycomb chicken wire. I added several finishing touches using armature wire, but the primary material for this design costs about $4.

Chicken wire, available at hardware stores and home gardening centers, is very easy to work with. It can be cut with ordinary wire cutters, and the wires themselves are thin enough for manipulation by hand. The only drawback I found was a series of rigid support wires that sometimes extend vertically through the wire. If these are present, they can be easily removed early on in the process.

I originally imagined shaping the wire by pressing it over a mold, such as the bottom of a mixing bowl. When I tested this approach, however, the wire crimped up and crumpled, rather than smoothly adapting to the shape of the mold. A much easier way to control the overall shape is to pinch the honeycombs individually between your fingers. When an entire row is pinched so the honeycombs become narrower, that row becomes a smaller circle in circumference, thereby creating a taper in the cylinder. If the next row is pinched more severely, a steeper taper results. Conversely, if the honeycombs are pulled outwards, the design becomes wider. I applied this principle in several different places to give the candlecage its onion-dome-like silhouette.

Once I had created the basic form, I used armature wire to reinforce the base, bind the waist, and add a decorative detail at the top. Armature wire, unlike other kinds of wire, is soft and easy to work with.

INSTRUCTIONS

1. *Prepare chicken wire.* Lay chicken wire flat with cut edges at top and bottom. Using wire cutters, trim straight across bottom edge at base of vertical spirals (*see* illustration A, next page). Count up twenty-eight full honeycomb rows. Count up two more rows, trim base of vertical spirals to yield row of Y-shaped prongs, then trim off left arm of each Y (illustration B). Along entire left edge, grip each vertical spiral with tip of needle-nose pliers and twist two or three times counter to spiral until wires unkink (illustration C). Count thirty-four full honeycombs to right and repeat unkinking along entire right side. If they are present, locate vertical support wires in interior of chicken wire, then remove by snipping out wires as close to spirals as possible. Do not unkink or join will be weakened.

2. *Form cylinder.* Roll chicken wire into cylinder, lining up sides so kinky edges of honeycombs "hook" together. Grip each pair of hooked wires with pliers and twist two or three times to create tight spiral (illustration D). Repeat until edges are fully joined in seamless cylinder about 11" in diameter and about 30" high. Bend straight wire ends at lower edge out and up into small loops (illustration E).

3. *Shape and reinforce base.* Starting at base of cylinder and working one row at a time, use fingertips to pinch individ-

MATERIALS

- 30" x 36"-wide sheet of chicken wire
- 1½"-long metal teardrop bead
- 7' length 11½-gauge (about ⅛"-diameter) armature wire
- 5' length 14-gauge (about 1/16"-diameter) armature wire
- 18-gauge spool wire

You'll also need:
needle-nose pliers; small wire cutters; ruler; and firm 1¼"-diameter cylindrical container (e.g., empty film canister with cap).

ual honeycombs to make them longer and more narrow. Continue reshaping honeycombs in this way for four to five rows up the spiral, gradually compressing and tapering lower end of cylinder until base measures about 6" in diameter (illustration F). To anchor base, bend 19" length of 11½-gauge armature wire into circle so ends butt, rest wire circle on loops around edge of base, and crimp loops around armature wire with pliers. Finally, lace, or whipstitch, base edge with 14-gauge armature wire. For easier handling, use two 18" lengths rather than one long length and run whipping over butted section of armature wire to ensure firm join.

4. *Shape waist.* Pinch in rows 4 and 5 of mesh cylinder further until diameter is reduced to about 1½". Slip empty film case (or substitute) inside pinched section, clasp chicken wire around it, and bind with 28" length of 11½-gauge armature wire (illustration G). Remove film case; mesh will spring out slightly, pressing against wire binding to create waist. Open out mesh above waist to create brandy snifter shape.

5. *Shape topknot.* Cut 5" length of 11½-gauge armature wire. Bend one end into small circle, draw other end through bead, and bend up excess. Cut two 10" lengths of 14-gauge armature wire. Bend each in half and twist around lower bead loop (illustration H). To form collar, compress honeycombs at top edge so mesh tapers toward top, forming onion-shaped dome. To complete sculpture, gather topmost wires, lower bead loop, and loose armature wires into bunch, then bind tightly with 18-gauge wire. Twist 18-gauge wire ends together and clip excess. Conceal this rough binding by wrapping seven or eight turns with 11½-gauge armature wire. Curl ends of four loose armature wires and arrange them equidistantly around bead (illustration I). ◆

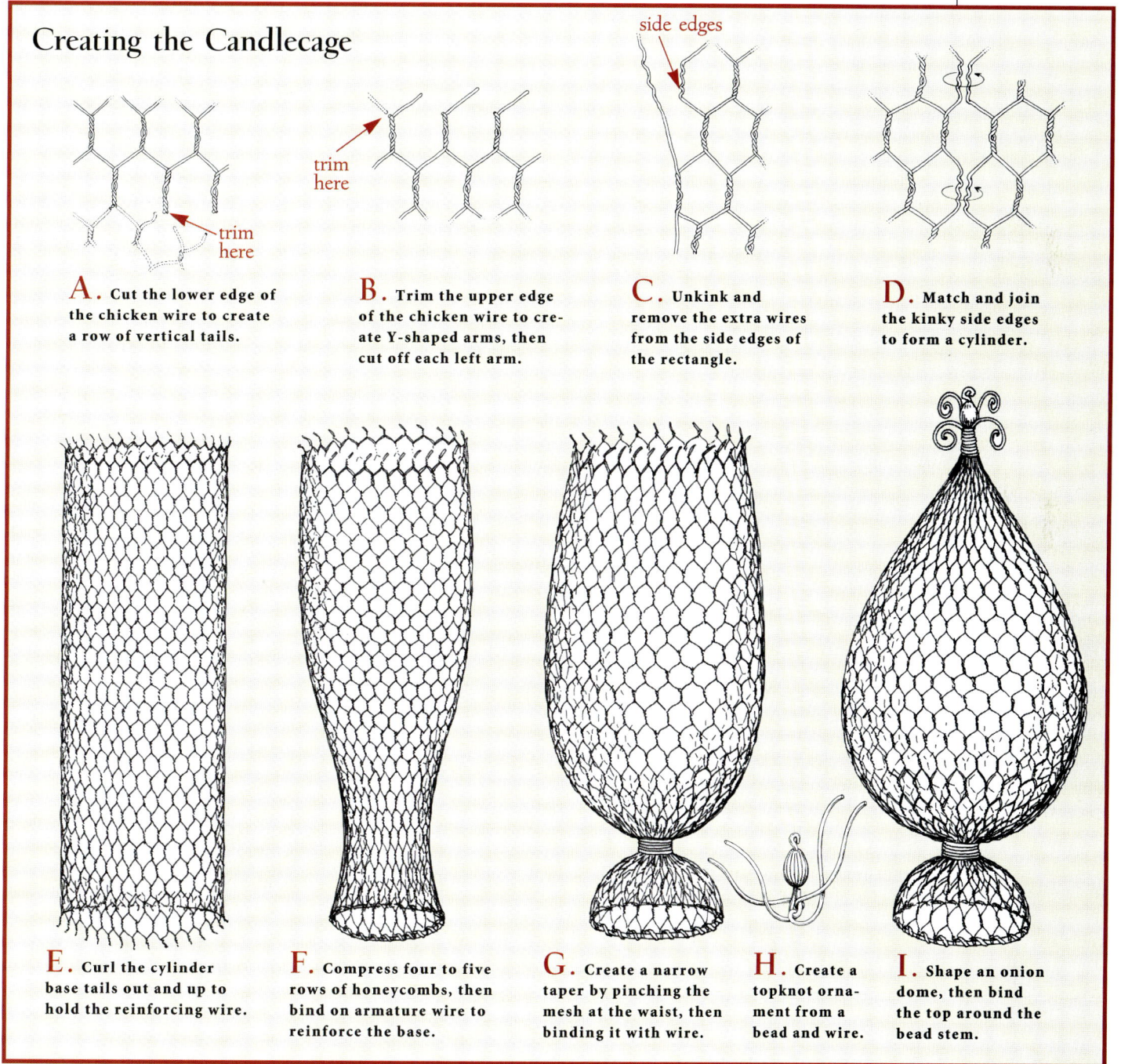

Creating the Candlecage

A. Cut the lower edge of the chicken wire to create a row of vertical tails.

B. Trim the upper edge of the chicken wire to create Y-shaped arms, then cut off each left arm.

C. Unkink and remove the extra wires from the side edges of the rectangle.

D. Match and join the kinky side edges to form a cylinder.

E. Curl the cylinder base tails out and up to hold the reinforcing wire.

F. Compress four to five rows of honeycombs, then bind on armature wire to reinforce the base.

G. Create a narrow taper by pinching the mesh at the waist, then binding it with wire.

H. Create a topknot ornament from a bead and wire.

I. Shape an onion dome, then bind the top around the bead stem.

STENCILING

Vintage Tablecloth

Create your own collectible tablecloth using our fruit and foliage stencils and retro paint recipes.

🍐 BY MICHIO RYAN

The casual, vintage design of this tablecloth works well with the 1930s Farmhouse Table found on page 14 or colorful dinnerware such as Fiestaware.

COLOR PHOTOGRAPHY:
Carl Tremblay

ILLUSTRATION:
Judy Love

SILHOUETTE PHOTOGRAPHY:
Daniel van Ackere

STYLING:
Ritch Holben

MATERIALS

- 1¾ yards 60"-wide white cotton twill fabric
- White sewing thread
- Jacquard Textile Color fabric paint, 4 ounces each: White #123 and Periwinkle #125
- Jacquard Textile Color, 2 ounces each: Yellow Ochre #124, Goldenrod #102, Emerald Green #117, and Ruby Red #107
- Stencil patterns (see page 44)

You'll also need:
two 25" x 36" sheets (or equivalent) .003 Mylar film, frosted on one side; 12" x 12" plate glass; swivel-blade craft knife; X-Acto knife; four 1½" stencil brushes; one ¼" stencil brush; three 4-ounce containers with covers (e.g., baby food jars); old ceramic dinner plate; palette knife with rounded tip; blue, red, yellow, and green colored pencils; mechanical pencil; 5/16"-diameter self-adhesive dots; spray adhesive; quilter's grid ruler; self-healing cutting mat; 1½"-wide masking tape; Scotch Magic tape; plastic dropcloth; plastic wrap; sewing machine; iron; rotary cutter; scissors; dark thread; tape measure; fine-tip permanent marker; washer and dryer; and access to photocopier with enlarger.

THERE'S NO LONGER ANY NEED to scour your local antique store looking for a vintage 1940s tablecloth: Now you can stencil your own using fabric paint mixed to match the colors of that era.

Although four-color stenciling is a multi-step process, over the years I've refined my method for staying organized. I created this tablecloth using three stencil designs: a fruit and foliage border repeat, a pear and peach corner section, and a cherry for the tablecloth's center. I start by making a photocopy of each design, then coloring in the different sections of the design using colored pencils. This helps me understand the color breakout and gives me a color guide to refer back to at all times.

Next, I trace the design onto the cloudy side of Mylar film, making a separate stencil for each color. The border repeat, for instance, requires five stencils, one for each color in the design: periwinkle blue, daffodil yellow, mint green, cherry red, and white. There are several types of film available, but Mylar is the best one for stencils for several reasons: It will not shrink or rip, it is nonpermeable, it yields very crisp edges, and it can be wiped clean with a damp sponge.

I recommend cutting the stencils with a swivel-blade craft knife and a piece of plate glass as a backing. Plate glass is available at glass supply stores; the cost will be nominal for a 12" x 12" piece, and some shops may give it to you for free if it's cut from scrap. Have the glass shop finish the edges so they're not sharp, or cover them with masking tape. Some stencilers tape the Mylar film down and lift and change the blade position as needed to cut the stencil. When cutting sharp curves, I've found that I can cut them more smoothly if I help the blade turn the corner by turning the Mylar rather than trying to twist my hand around the bend.

Stenciling the Tablecloth

While some stenciling projects require very exact registration, the vintage look is more forgiving. The motifs can be placed very approximately; if you look closely at the designs shown at left, you can see that they do not line up exactly. The tablecloth still looks cohesive, however, because the stenciled areas "knit" together visually. In addition, I drew the outside edge of the blue border area as an irregularly curved line. If I had drawn the edges straight, they would have had to be placed in perfect alignment along the edge of the tablecloth. The waviness, on the other hand, disguises even a fairly wide error in placement.

I used Jacquard's Textile Color fabric paint, but mixed the paints to achieve the vintage colors (*see* recipes, page 25). Some stencilers may prefer to hold the stencil in place by hand, but a more foolproof method is to spray the stencil with a very light coating of spray adhesive. This prevents the stencil from creeping, eliminates most bleeding, and gives it traction without affixing it permanently to the fabric.

I applied the paint directly to the cloth using one stencil brush per color. I start by holding the brush straight up and down, then pouncing (dabbing the brush straight down), to deposit a quantity of paint. Then I work the brush in a tight circular motion on the fabric. The circular motion helps to work the paint into the weave of the fabric, preventing the paint from merely sitting on the surface of the fabric, and eliminates bald or thin patches. I hold the brush vertically so the ends of the bristles are all in contact with the fabric's surface, and the action can be rough and fast because the spray adhesive will hold the stencil firmly in place.

tape along seam on both sides to yield large pieces.

3. *Trace blue corner stencil.* Tape corner pattern to smooth work surface. Lay 10" x 10" Mylar piece on top, shiny side down, so minimum 1" margin of Mylar extends beyond design area all around, then tape down. Using permanent marker, trace straight dashed lines and register marks against grid ruler. Trace curved dashed lines freehand, and write "BLUE CORNER" in large block letters along edge of Mylar. Using mechanical pencil, trace outline of blue area only. Untape and remove Mylar (*see* illustration A, above).

4. *Trace red, yellow, and green corner stencils.* To ensure accurate registration in the following steps, stack each new 10" x 10" piece of Mylar on top of the BLUE CORNER, frosted sides up and edges matching, and tape in place. Using permanent marker, trace all dashed lines onto new Mylar.

of a few large shapes, such as pear and lemon, as dashed lines for alignment later. Mark two 4½" x 4½" pieces of film for red and green cherry stencils. On green cherry stencil, use permanent marker to

Cutting the Stencils

A. Mark and cut a stencil for the blue corner.

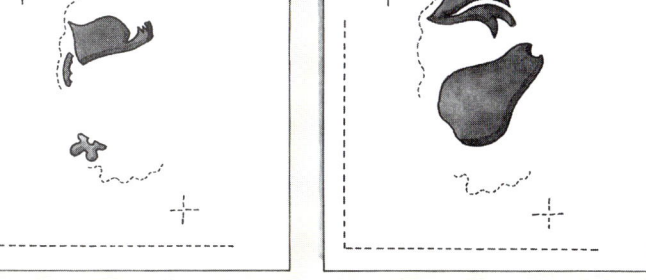

B. Cut separate corner stencils for the red, yellow, and green design areas. Make separate color stencils for the border and cherry designs as well.

INSTRUCTIONS
Making the Stencils

1. *Prepare stencil patterns.* Photocopy and enlarge corner, border repeat, and cherry patterns (*see* page 44). Tape border repeat copies together to yield single pattern measuring 23⅝" long. Using blue, yellow, red, and green colored pencils and following pattern color key, color in each outlined section, including any lightly shaded motifs.

2. *Cut Mylar film.* Using quilter's grid ruler, X-Acto knife, and cutting mat, cut the following pieces from Mylar: four 9"x 25", four 10" x 10", one 7" x 16", and two 4½" x 4½" pieces. If necessary, butt edges of Mylar and apply Scotch Magic

Label films "RED CORNER," "YELLOW CORNER," and "GREEN CORNER." Position RED CORNER film on pattern, align markings, and tape down. Using mechanical pencil, trace outline of all red areas. Repeat process to trace yellow and green designs on their respective films; ignore black areas on leaves (illustration B).

5. *Trace border and cherry stencils.* Label all stencils as you make them. Repeat process outlined in steps 3 and 4 to mark four 9" x 25" pieces of film respectively with blue, red, yellow, and green border designs. To make "white" border stencil, tape 7" x 16" film over border pattern and trace all solid black designs with pencil; then use permanent marker to trace outline

trace cherry outline as dashed line.

6. *Cut eleven stencils.* Lay each film marked side up on plate glass, and cut along pencil lines with swivel-blade knife. For smooth cuts, hold blade steady and rotate film away from you. Cut inside curves and small areas first, then outside curves and large areas. For sharp, crisp corners and angles, cut slightly beyond marked point from both directions. If you make a mistake, repair damaged area on both sides with Scotch Magic tape and recut. Remove and discard all cutout pieces. To confirm that all areas for a color have been cut, lay stencil on top of colored pencil pattern and compare them.

STENCILING

Stenciling the Fabric

DESIGNER'S TIP

For a beginner's version of this project, consider using the cherry stencil alone on a set of napkins. For a more advanced version of this project, use a portion of the border repeat to decorate a set of matching kitchen curtains.

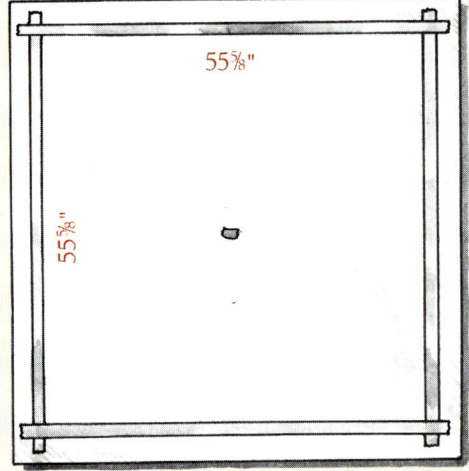

C. Use masking tape to mark the center of the fabric and to define the stenciling area.

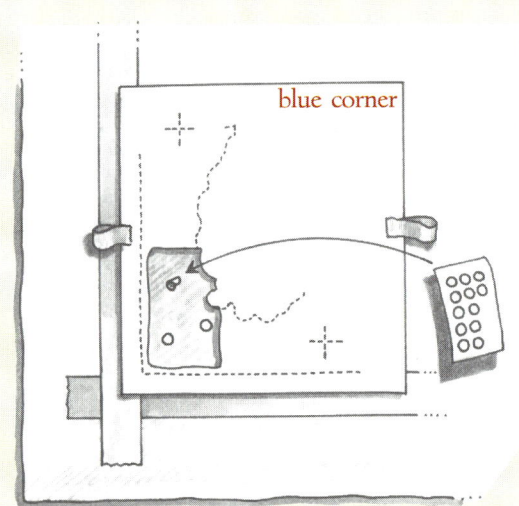

D. Align the corner pattern's dashed lines along the tape edge, then stencil the open areas.

E. Use the border repeat stencil to make a continuous border all around the tablecloth.

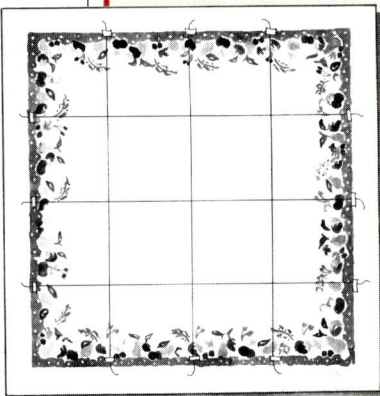

F. To place the cherries, create a grid using the pattern as a reference.

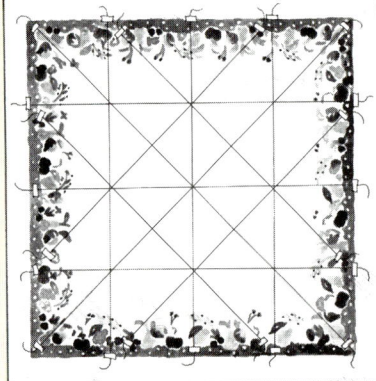

G. Position new threads diagonally, then mark each intersection with a small piece of tape.

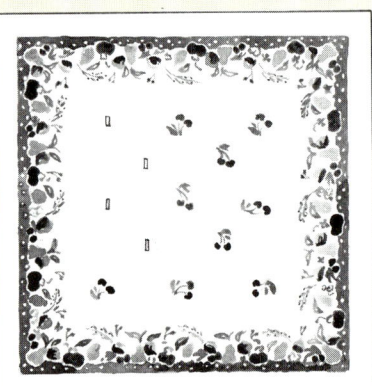

H. Stencil cherries at each marker, turning the stencil at random so each cherry cluster faces a different direction.

Stenciling the Fabric

1. *Mix fabric paint colors.* Custom-mix blue, yellow, and green paint following proportions below. For red stencils, use straight Ruby Red paint. Mix approximately 4 ounces of blue paint and 2 ounces each of green and yellow paints in individual containers. Cap containers to prevent paints from drying out.

Blue: 6 parts Periwinkle, 2 parts White, 1 part Yellow Ochre
Yellow: 4 parts White, 4 parts Yellow Ochre, 1 part Goldenrod
Green: 6 parts White, 2 parts Emerald Green; dull with small amount Ruby Red.

2. *Prepare fabric.* Machine-wash fabric to remove sizing, then machine-dry and press flat. Cut plastic dropcloth to match fabric dimensions. Tape plastic to large, flat work surface. Lay fabric over plastic, pull taut in all directions, and tape down edges. Measure to find center of fabric and mark with small piece of tape. Measure out from center 27 13/16" in each direction and lay down masking tape to create stenciling area 55 5/8" square (illustration C).

3. *Position blue corner stencil on fabric.* To make tab handles, fold and affix tape to opposite edges of blue corner stencil. Apply spray adhesive to wrong (shiny) side of stencil, following manufacturer's directions. Set stencil, adhesive side down, in lower left corner of print area, align dash lines with inside edge of tape, and press to affix. To create decorative white polka dots within blue corner area, press several self-adhesive dots onto fabric within cutout area (illustration D).

4. *Apply paint through stencil.* Transfer small amount blue paint to edge of plate. To load 1½" brush, dip bristles into paint, then swirl bristles on plate in circular motion to shed excess. To stencil fabric, hold brush vertically, pounce bristles inside cutout area of stencil to lay in deposit of paint, then work bristles in tight circular motion, pulling away from cutout edges as much as possible. Continue circular brushwork to distribute paint, work it into fibers, and even out bald or thin spots. When finished, use tabs to peel up stencil in smooth, continuous motion. Wrap brush in plastic wrap to prevent drying. Repeat steps 3 and 4 to stencil remaining three corners.

5. *Stencil blue border repeats.* Position blue border repeat stencil on lower left corner of fabric, aligning dash lines with tape as in step 3; cutout section of stencil will butt blue corner section stenciled in step 4. Apply self-adhesive dots randomly throughout blue area. To keep left corner clear for remaining color stencils, to be added later, locate shaded sections on pattern, then lay masking tape over corresponding cutouts on stencil (illustration E). Apply paint as in step 4. Repeat process to stencil border repeat in three remaining left corners of tablecloth, then remove tape masking cutouts. Repeat process to stencil border repeat in four right corners of tablecloth. Finally, stencil one border repeat to fill opening that remains in middle of each edge. Wash brush and stencils in cool water and lay flat to dry. Let dry 15 minutes. Remove dots with tip of clean palette knife.

6. *Stencil remaining colors.* Using fresh, dry 1½" brush for each color, apply color through remaining stencils in following order: red corner, red border, yellow corner, yellow border, green corner, green border. For each color, mask shaded sections of border repeat stencils (see pattern, page 44) to stencil right corners of tablecloth, then remove masking tape and stencil left corners and middle sections. Let paints dry 15 minutes before proceeding to next color. To add white highlights, lay white stencil on border, aligning dash lines on stenciled fruit. Apply white paint through cutouts with ¼" brush. To highlight fruit in corners, rotate white stencil 45 degrees and repeat. Wash all brushes and stencils. Let tablecloth dry at least 1 hour.

7. *Stencil cherries.* Locate dotted line on colored pencil border pattern. Using marked line on pattern as reference, position dark thread across fabric (from one edge to the other) to cross through corresponding section in stenciled border. Tape down thread ends. Mark each pattern repeat in same way; threads will cross at right angles to form grid (illustration F). Lay new threads diagonally through thread intersections and tape down (illustration G). At each of thirteen intersections, mark position for cherries with new small piece of tape. Remove threads. To stencil, lift tape marker, set red cherry stencil in place, and apply red paint as in step 4. Repeat process to stencil cherries at each marker, turning stencil at random so each cherry cluster faces a different direction (illustration H). Finish by stenciling green cherry leaves.

8. *Heat-set paints and hem edges.* Press fabric from wrong side to heat-set paints. Trim raw edges of fabric evenly using rotary cutter. If selvage is puckered or uneven, trim it off. Narrow-hem all cut edges by machine. ◆

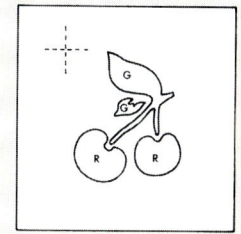

PATTERNS
See page 44 for pattern pieces and enlargement instructions.

COLOR DEVELOPMENT

I. The color sequence shown above captures the general procedure for adding each color to the tablecloth. First, the blue corners and blue border repeats are stenciled, followed by the red corner and border, yellow corner and border, and finally the green corner and border.

DESIGNER'S TIP

Want to stencil a tablecloth larger or smaller than the sample project? By varying the number of border repeats, you can create a square or rectangular border in the size you need.

1 border repeat + 2 corners = 23 5/8"
2 border repeats + 2 corners = 39 5/8"
3 border repeats + 2 corners = 55 5/8"
4 border repeats + 2 corners = 71 5/8"

Arts and Crafts–Style Bandbox

Transform a chipboard craft box into a period piece. Start by giving the lid the look of aged copper, then cover the box with authentic wallpaper.

BY RITCH HOLBEN

Like most Arts and Crafts–style objects, this box is both functional and decorative at the same time.

COLOR PHOTOGRAPHY:
Carl Tremblay

ILLUSTRATION:
Mary Newell DePalma

STYLING:
Ritch Holben

THIS DECORATIVE BANDBOX CAPtures the style of the Arts and Crafts Movement in two ways: The box is covered with an Arts and Crafts–style wallpaper border, and the box's woven top has been treated to simulate the look of aged copper. The resulting piece is true to its nineteenth-century heritage, but will fit in with just about any decorating style.

I started with a chipboard craft box measuring about 5" high and 8" in diameter. To differentiate the lid from the rest of the box, I created the look of aged copper on the woven portion using a patina kit, then painted the rim black. In my search for authentic Arts and Crafts–style wallpaper, I found an outlet for papers from Bradbury & Bradbury Wallpapers, of Benicia, California. This company still hand-prints several original wallpaper designs of William Morris, a leader of the Arts and Crafts Movement. For this box, I chose a frieze section of the Pomegranate series; the border measures 24" wide. (See Sources & Resources, page 48, for information about ordering this and other wallpapers.)

Ritch Holben is a designer and stylist living in Nahant, Massachusetts.

INSTRUCTIONS

1. *Create copper patina.* Follow manufacturer's instructions and safety precautions for Copper Topper and Patina Green. Protect work surface with several layers newsprint. Remove lid from box; set aside box bottom. Wearing latex gloves and goggles and using 1" foam brush, apply two coats Copper Topper to woven section of box lid. Let dry 1 hour after each coat. Apply third coat Copper Topper, let dry until tacky (5 to 10 minutes), then use bristle brush to apply Patina Green over copper surface. Pale green patina will emerge within 10 to 25 minutes. If necessary after that time, apply additional coats Patina Green to intensify verdigris effect. Let dry overnight.

2. *Paint box and lid.* Work on lid first. Using flat or round brush, paint rim that surrounds woven section to match one color in wallpaper background (see illustration A, next page). Paint box bottom, box interior, and lid interior. Let dry 1 hour.

3. *Cut wallpaper border to fit box.* Wrap wallpaper border once around box, overlap 5", and cut with scissors. Fold overlap under until you achieve pleasing

MATERIALS

- 5"-high x 8"-diameter round chipboard box with woven lid
- 7"-wide (or wider) Arts and Crafts–style wallpaper border
- 2 ounces acrylic craft paint (to match one color in wallpaper border)
- Modern Options Copper Topper
- Modern Options Patina Green
- Wallpaper adhesive

You'll also need:
quilter's grid ruler; X-Acto knife; self-healing cutting mat; 1" and 2" foam brushes; ½" disposable bristle brush; ¼" round brush or ½" flat brush; scissors; pencil; paper towels; latex gloves; splash goggles; and newsprint.

pattern transition at seam. Make tick mark on underlap ½" from seam (illustration B). Using grid ruler, X-Acto knife, and self-healing cutting mat, cut strip at fold and at mark. Wrap strip around box, even at bottom edge, and mark strip ⅜" above box rim. Using grid ruler and X-Acto knife, trim strip lengthwise even with this mark (illustration C). Test-fit narrower strip around box lid, even at top edge; trim, if necessary, so strip extends no more than ½" beyond lower rim.

4. *Glue wallpaper strips to box.* Lay strips face down on newsprint. Using 2" foam brush, apply wallpaper adhesive to back of wider strip, brushing out beyond edges for full coverage. Let rest 3 to 5 minutes. Set side of box against middle of strip, matching lower edges (illustration D). Turn box upright. Working from middle out to edges, use paper towel to press strip smooth against box all around; overlap ends to make seam (illustration E). Using scissors, clip into top allowance every ½", then press allowance over onto box rim all around (illustration F). Wipe off any oozing adhesive. Glue narrow strip to lid in same way, pressing allowance onto lower inside rim. Let lid and box dry overnight (illustration G). ◆

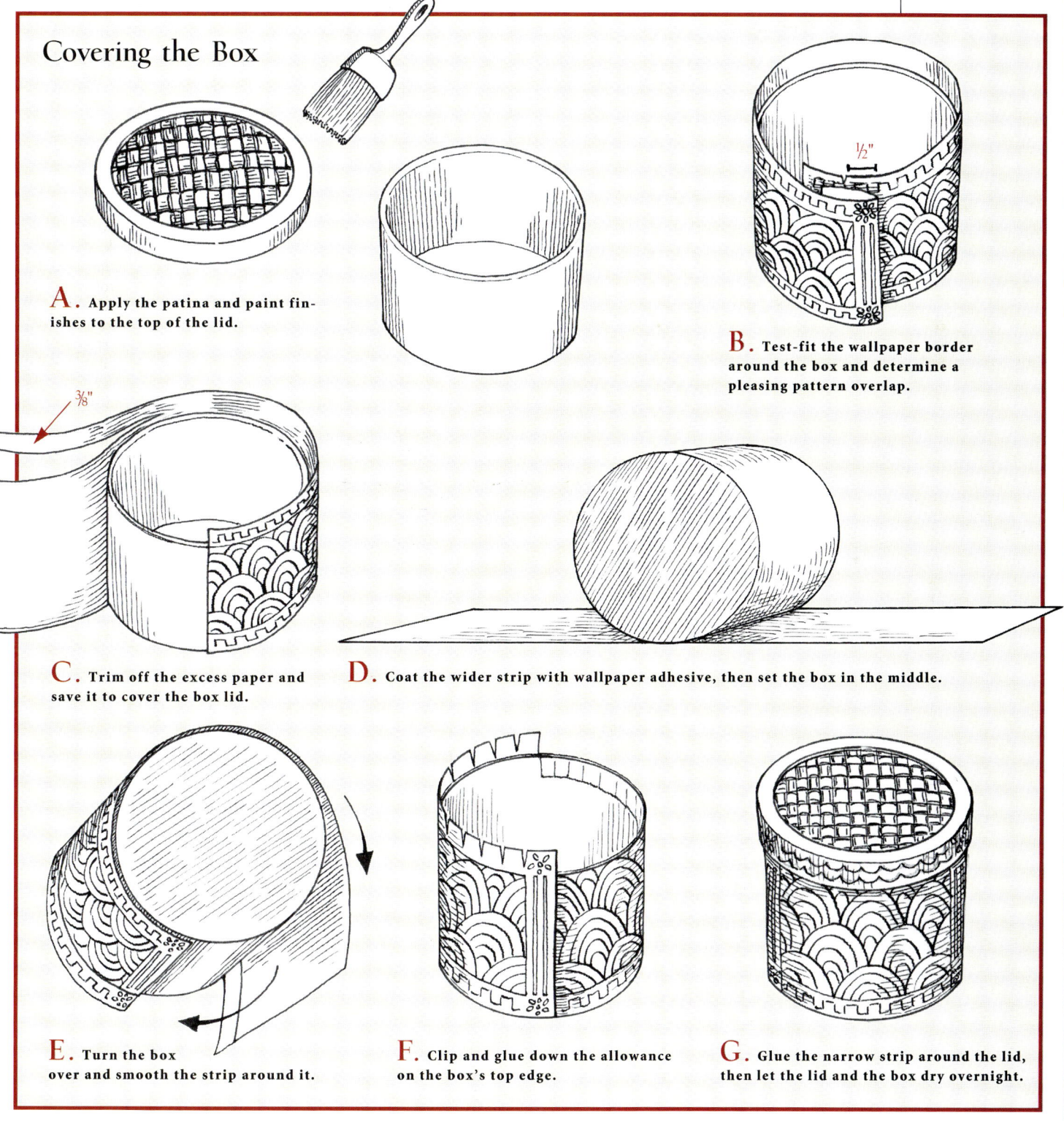

Covering the Box

A. Apply the patina and paint finishes to the top of the lid.

B. Test-fit the wallpaper border around the box and determine a pleasing pattern overlap.

C. Trim off the excess paper and save it to cover the box lid.

D. Coat the wider strip with wallpaper adhesive, then set the box in the middle.

E. Turn the box over and smooth the strip around it.

F. Clip and glue down the allowance on the box's top edge.

G. Glue the narrow strip around the lid, then let the lid and the box dry overnight.

DECORATIVE FOOD

Rose Petal Jelly

Prepare this delicate condiment using roses from your garden.

BY SUSAN LOGOZZO

Rose petal jelly can be made with any variety of deep-colored, fragrant rose, meaning a virtual rainbow of different colored jellies is possible.

COLOR PHOTOGRAPHY:
Carl Tremblay

ILLUSTRATION:
Nenad Jakesevic

STYLING:
Ritch Holben

MATERIALS
Sweet Rose Jelly
(yields 3 cups)

- 4 cups rose petals (see step 1)
- 2½ cups sugar
- 3 tablespoons fresh lemon juice
- 8-ounce package powdered pectin

Even Sweeter Rose Jelly
(yields 4 cups)

- 4 cups rose petals (see step 1)
- 2¾ cups sugar
- ½ cup white grape juice
- 2 tablespoons fresh lemon juice
- 8-ounce package powdered pectin

You'll also need
(for each recipe): 6-ounce jelly jars with mason lids; labels for jars; label marker; 3- to 4-quart nonaluminum saucepan; 8-quart pot; teakettle or small pot; 2-quart bowl with lid; liquid and dry measuring cups; measuring spoons; large stainless steel spoon; soup spoon; tongs; scissors; mesh strainer or colander; ladle; clean dishtowels; and oven mitt or potholder.

EVERYONE LOVES A ROSE; ITS scent and form are unique in the garden. With rose petal jelly, you can transform that same sweet scent into a subtle, delicate flavor.

After comparing more than a dozen techniques, I developed two fast and easy recipes that even beginner jelly makers can handle with ease. The techniques I tested varied quite a bit, considering the main ingredient (rose petals) was always the same. Some recipes called for white grape juice, while others simply used more sugar. Of the two recipes I developed, one includes white grape juice and one does not. The recipe with grape juice is slightly sweeter in a grape jelly kind of way; the alternative recipe uses sugar alone as a sweetening agent.

I tested several recipes that did not call for pectin, which is used to firm up jelly, but the resulting mixtures were more like a syrup. In my tests, liquid and powdered pectin worked equally well, although the powder form (e.g., brand name Sure-Jell) is more readily available in supermarkets.

Note: As with any edible flower, it's important to use organically grown roses, or roses picked from your own garden. Commercially grown roses are usually sprayed with pesticides, which should be avoided at all costs. It's also important to use fragrant roses, and the deeper the color, the better. Good choices for edible roses include the following species: *Rosa rugosa*, *Rosa damascena*, *Rosa* x. 'Alba', and *Rosa eglanteria*. On average, five roses will yield one generous cup of petals. Larger, oversized blooms may yield more, while sweetheart roses will yield less.

Susan Logozzo is a food designer and writer living in Charlestown, Massachusetts.

INSTRUCTIONS
Sweet Rose Jelly

1. *Prepare rose petals.* Pull petals from twenty to twenty-five roses. To prevent bitter taste, snip and discard white base from each petal using scissors (*see* illustration A, next page). Measure 4 cups petals, rinse in mesh strainer or colander under cool running water, then place in 2-quart bowl. Add ½ cup sugar and 2 cups boiling water, stirring gently with stainless steel spoon until sugar is dissolved (illustration B). To develop flavor, cover and let petals stand overnight at room temperature.

2. *Prepare petal syrup.* Pour petal mixture through strainer into 3- to 4-quart nonaluminum saucepan. Press petals firmly with back of stainless steel spoon to extract juice, then discard petals (illustration C).

3. *Sterilize jelly jars.* Place jars and lids in 8-quart pot, add water, and bring to boil. Let boil at least 15 minutes, then turn off heat.

4. *Boil jelly.* Add lemon juice and remaining 2 cups sugar to petal syrup, stirring with soup spoon until sugar is dissolved. Bring mixture to boil over high heat, add powdered pectin, and continue stirring. Bring to full rolling boil that cannot be stirred down, then boil 1 minute. Remove from heat. Skim off foam or skin with stainless steel spoon.

5. *Fill and seal jars.* Use tongs to remove jelly jar and lid from bath. Ladle hot jelly into warm jar, leaving ¼" space at top. Wipe jar rim with clean damp dishtowel, attach lid, and screw on top securely. Repeat to fill remaining jars, setting them on clean dishtowel to cool (illustration D). Label jars and store in cool dry place. Jelly in unsealed container will keep in refrigerator for 2 weeks.

Even Sweeter Rose Jelly

1. Same as Sweet Rose Jelly, step 1, except use ¼ cup sugar and 2½ cups boiling water.

2. Same as Sweet Rose Jelly, step 2.

3. Same as Sweet Rose Jelly, step 3.

4. *Boil jelly.* Add white grape juice, lemon juice, and powdered pectin to syrup, stirring until dissolved. Bring mixture to rolling boil over high heat, and let boil 1 minute. Remove from heat, add remaining 2½ cups sugar all at once, and stir well using stainless steel spoon. Return to heat, bring to full rolling boil that cannot be stirred down, and boil 1 minute. Remove from heat. Skim off foam or skin with stainless steel spoon.

5. Same as Sweet Rose Jelly, step 5. ◆

MAKING THE JELLY

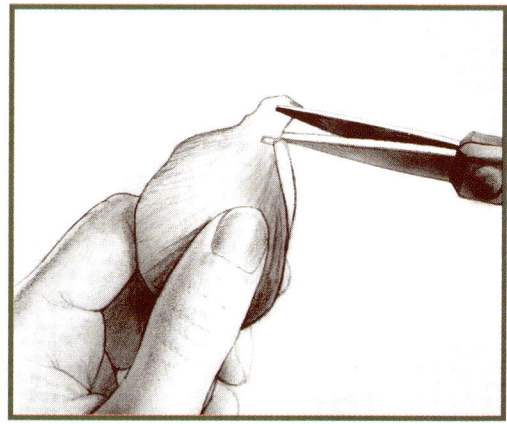

A. Trim off each petal's white base to prevent a bitter taste.

B. Combine the petals, sugar, and boiling water, and let stand overnight.

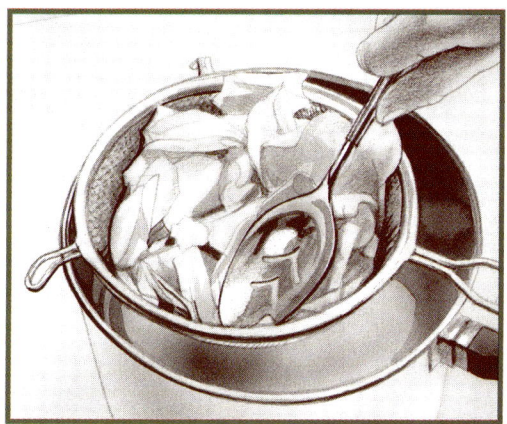

C. Press the petals to extract the juices, add sugar, and boil into jelly.

D. Ladle the jelly into sterilized jars and seal them.

MAKING JELLY WITH OTHER EDIBLE FLOWERS
By Mary Ann Bowers

If you can make jelly using rose petals, can you substitute other edible flowers? The answer, according to many cookbooks, is a resounding yes. In fact, a wide variety of flavors is possible using blossoms from fruit trees, herb blossoms, or edible flowers such as violets.

Petals from fruit tree blossoms, such as apple, lemon, orange, or plum, can all be used to make jelly. Apple blossoms result in a floral and slightly sour-flavored jelly; lemon and orange blossoms offer a citrus flavor. Lemon blossoms can be sweet or bitter, while orange blossoms are often highly perfumed, like orange peel. Plum blossom jelly has a mild flavor, much like flower nectar.

You can also use the blossoms of such herbs and plants as basil, anise hyssop, bergamot, elder, lilac, pineapple sage, and scented geraniums for making jelly. Each of these blossoms is highly flavorful. Basil blossoms are spicy sweet, anise hyssop is licorice-like, and bergamot has an aromatic, tealike flavor. Lilac and pineapple sage blossoms make for fragrant, musky jellies. Elder flowers–which are used to make wine in Scandinavia–are superb for jelly making because of their appetizing scent. I also found several recipes that call for scented geranium blossoms (pelargonium variety) as well as for geranium leaves, which are even more fragrant than the blossoms.

Edible flowers such as violets, pansies, clove carnations, scented white jasmine, primroses, and mimosa are often used to make sweet syrups but can also be used for flavoring jelly. Violets have a sweet taste and, like pansies, are sometimes tangy or spicy as well. For the most part, the taste each blossom imparts will echo the flower's fragrance.

Although marigolds and nasturtiums are popular in decorated salads or other savory dishes, they are not generally recommended for use in making jelly. Instead, they are best chopped and added to cream cheese, omelets, or soufflés.

Mary Ann Bowers is a Boston-based freelance writer and crafter.

MIXED MEDIA

Decorative Sailboat

Create your own nautical accent using a balsa wood hull, dowel masts, muslin sails, and rigging made from string.

BY MICHIO RYAN

This decorative boat measures about 30" long and about 30" high when displayed on its stand. The boat can also be hung on a wall.

COLOR PHOTOGRAPHY:
Carl Tremblay

ILLUSTRATION:
Michael Gellatly

STYLING:
Ritch Holben

MATERIALS

Note: Dimensions are listed in the following order: depth by width by length.

- Five 1/2" x 4" x 24" balsa wood strips
- One 1/2" x 6" x 24" balsa strip
- Three 3/32" x 1/4" x 24" balsa strips
- One 3/16" x 3/8" x 24" balsa strip
- Scraps of 1"-thick balsa wood
- Two 3/8" x 36" dowels
- 1" x 8" x 14" clear pine board
- 2" x 4" aluminum sheet
- 5/8 yard 45"-wide muslin or other unbleached cotton fabric
- Thread to match fabric
- Two pieces 8" x 14" gray felt
- Ball of thin cabled string
- Two 1/4" screw eyes
- 3/4" brads
- 1 1/4" brads
- Drywall screws
- 1 quart white latex enamel
- 2-ounce tube burnt umber acrylic paint
- 2 ounces Plaid FolkArt acrylic craft paint, in the following colors:
  Rusty Nail #914, Harvest Gold #917, and Sterling Blue #441
- Liquitex Acrylic Wood Stain in Cherry
- Durham Hard Rockwater Putty
- Black acrylic craft paint
- Decal-It decal medium
- Spray shellac
- Acrylic sealer
- Wood glue
- Fray preventive

You'll also need:
patterns (*see* page 46); access to photocopier with enlarger; rasp; round file; drill and 3/8" and 1/16" bits; awl; model maker's saw; vise; 36-, 100-, and 150-grit sandpaper; sanding block; utility scissors; manicure scissors; sewing shears or rotary cutter; sewing machine; pins; tapestry needle; quilter's grid ruler; steel ruler; X-Acto knife; finishing nail; Scotch tape; two disposable 1" bristle brushes; #10 round brush; paper towels; carbonless transfer paper; pencil; masking tape; cardboard scraps; rubber bands; hammer; scrap wood block; sponge; magazine; and disposable plastic containers and stirrers.

THIS DECORATIVE SAILBOAT captures the look and feel of an authentic ship model, but without the time, intricate details, and specific skills often necessary with such a project. This sailboat can be assembled for about $25, using a hull made from balsa wood, masts made from dowels, sails sewn from muslin, and string for rigging. Simple finishing details, such as a rudder, gallery, and deck trim, complete the authentic look.

The boat's hull is fashioned from eight layers of balsa wood, cut in progressively smaller shapes. When stacked, the layers form a stepped three-dimensional form, which is then rasped down to create a smooth, finished hull. A rasp, a metal tool, features coarse teeth that shred away the angular edges on the soft balsa wood. Although the rasping portion of this project takes some muscle work, the two sides of the boat do not have to match exactly, making the process more forgiving. I used a coarse rasp for the initial shaping, followed by 36-grit sandpaper to refine the concave areas of the hull. On my finished piece, it took 40 minutes to shape the entire hull and another 5 minutes for final sanding. For best results, hold the hull against the work surface with one hand, leaning into it if necessary using vertical pressure, while rasping with the other hand. For maximum removal, work at roughly a 45-degree angle against the grain.

Although the rasping and sanding can smooth the hull considerably, slight gaps in the joints between the layers of balsa may remain. Tiny gaps are acceptable, and even add to the boat's rustic look, but gaps larger than 1/16" should be filled with putty before sealing and painting.

MIXED MEDIA

Assembling the Boat's Hull

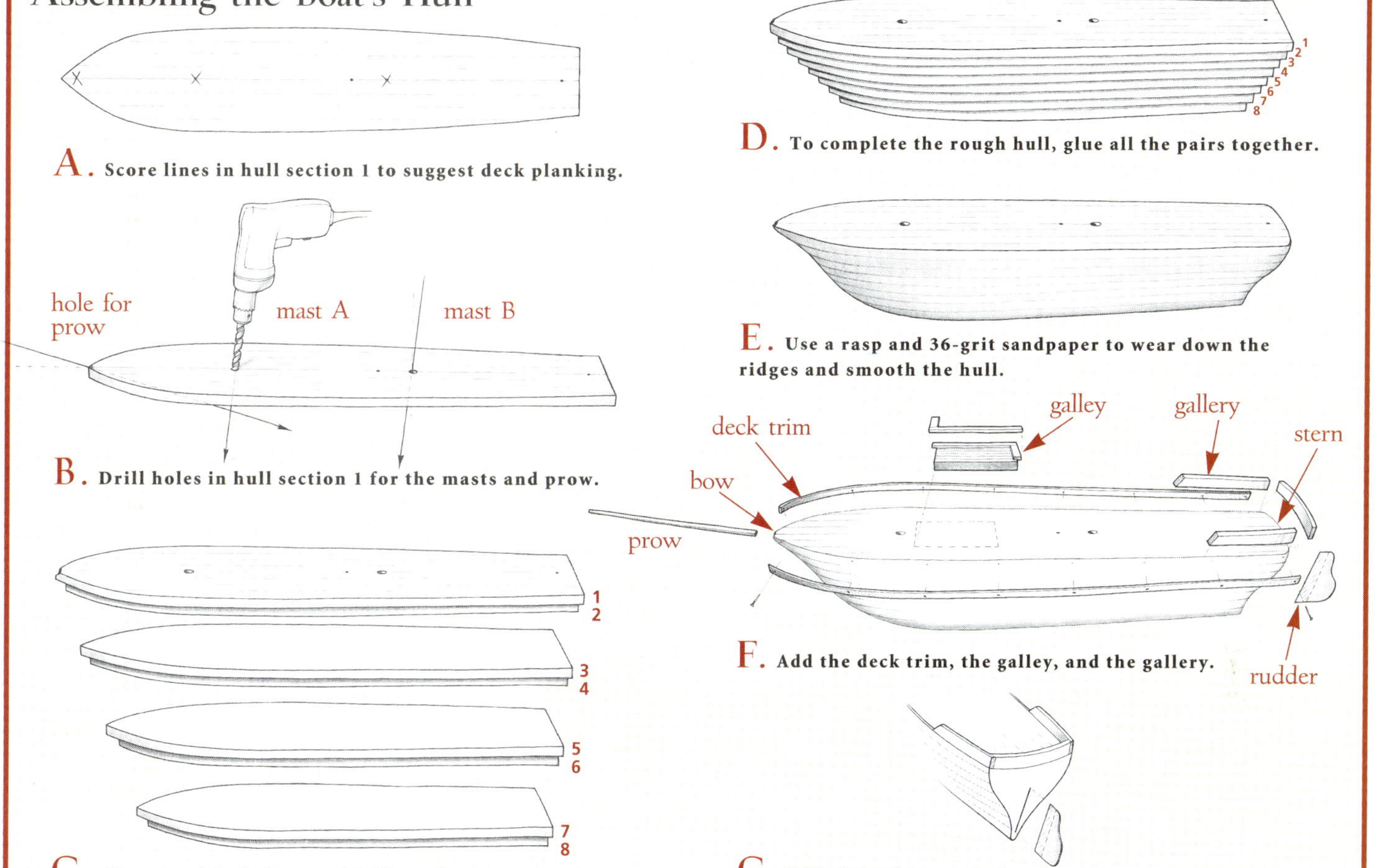

A. Score lines in hull section 1 to suggest deck planking.

B. Drill holes in hull section 1 for the masts and prow.

C. Glue the eight balsa wood hull sections together in pairs.

D. To complete the rough hull, glue all the pairs together.

E. Use a rasp and 36-grit sandpaper to wear down the ridges and smooth the hull.

F. Add the deck trim, the galley, and the gallery.

G. Add the rudder at the boat's stern.

INSTRUCTIONS
Assembling the Boat Hull

1. *Cut balsa pieces.* Photocopy and enlarge hull, galley, rudder, sail, pennant, and bracket patterns (*see* page 46). Tape photocopies together to assemble larger patterns. Set rudder, sail, and pennant patterns aside. Lay hull pattern face up on 4" x 24" balsa strip, slip transfer paper in between, and tape down. Using pencil, lightly trace hull section 1, straight center line (use ruler for guide), "X" markings for masts and prow, and small dots for screw eyes. Repeat process to mark hull sections 2, 3, and 4, each on its own balsa strip. Mark hull sections 7 and 8 and galley on remaining 4"-wide strip. Mark hull sections 5 and 6 on 6"-wide strip. Mark four brackets on 1"-thick balsa wood scrap. Using model maker's saw, cut out eight hull sections, one galley, and four brackets. Set brackets aside.

2. *Prepare deck and galley.* Lay hull section 1 face up. Using grid ruler and pencil, mark lines ½" apart parallel to straight center line. To simulate deck planks, lay steel ruler along each line, score balsa with X-Acto knife, then run tip of finishing nail along score line to indent wood (*see* illustration A, above). Repeat process to mark and score ⅜"-wide planks on galley. To make mast holes in section 1, set point of ⅜" bit on "X" markings, tilt bit back slightly (5 degrees) toward stern, and drill clear through wood (illustration B). To make prow hole, drill straight down at small dot for ⅛"; anchor bit in this hole, tilt bit toward stern 20 to 25 degrees above deck axis, and drill clear through wood. Use awl to punch pilot hole at each dot for screw eyes.

3. *Glue balsa hull.* Lay eight hull sections flat in size order. Turn section 1 face down and apply wood glue to underside, spreading it with cardboard spatula. Spread glue on top of section 2 in same way, then press glued sections together, referring to pattern for spacing. Repeat process to glue sections 3 and 4, 5 and 6, and 7 and 8 (illustration C). Wipe oozing glue with damp sponge, then tape each pair to work surface to prevent shifting. Let dry 1 hour before removing tape. Next, glue section 2 to section 3 and section 6 to section 7; wipe oozing glue, tape, and let dry as above. To complete assembly, repeat process to glue section 4 to section 5 (illustration D). Let dry overnight.

4. *Shape hull.* Using section 1 holes as a guide, drill down about 1½" into sections 2 and 3 to deepen holes for masts and prow. To shape hull, hold hull firmly deck side down on stable work surface, stand alongside it, and run coarse teeth of rasp against woodgrain at 45-degree angle. Strive for long, even strokes rather than small, erratic ones. To ensure symmetrical contours, work evenly all around, rather than completing one area before moving on. As ridges becomes less pronounced, switch to smaller teeth on rasp for slower, more controlled shaping. To develop concave curves below bow and stern, roll 36-grit sandpaper around finger in a tube and rub balsa surface using circular motion. Rub entire surface with 36-grit sandpaper. To wear off scratches, finish with 100-grit sandpaper (illustration E).

5. *Add deck details.* Soak two ¼" x 24" balsa trimming strips under hot running tap water a few minutes until limp. To mold strips in shape of hull, hold each one against side edge of decking, from bow to stern (as shown in illustration F), and secure with tape and rubber bands. Let strips remain in this position 30 minutes, or until dry. To affix strips perma-

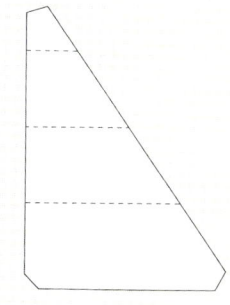

PATTERNS
See page 46 for pattern pieces and enlargement instructions.

MIXED MEDIA

DESIGNER'S TIP

I generated the name decal on this boat using a computer font: 16-point Wide Latin. Then I used Decal-It, a waterborne material, to make the decal. One important note: If you opt for this technique, be sure to photocopy your output to make it waterproof. Ink-jet printer output is not waterproof and will bleed when used with Decal-It.

nently, remove them, apply bead of wood glue to inside edge, and press in place. To further secure trim, tap in ¾" brads every 3" along entire strip.

To make gallery, use X-Acto knife to cut one 2⅝" and two 4½" lengths from ⅜"-wide balsa strip. Trim one end of each longer-length strip at slight angle. Glue shorter strip to deck at stern and two longer strips to deck side edges, so angled ends face bow (illustration F).

Glue galley to deck, plank side up, centering it 1" behind mast hole A. Cut two 2¾" and two 3" strips from ¼" balsa and glue them around galley to form roof (illustration F; see pattern for placement).

6. *Add rudder.* Tape rudder pattern to aluminum, then cut out with utility scissors. File down rough edges with 100-grit sandpaper. To flatten rudder after cutting and sanding, lay on wood block and tap edges with hammer. For better paint adhesion, rough up both sides with 100-grit sandpaper. Lightly draft guideline for rudder straight down middle of stern. Beginning 1" below gallery, slit line with X-Acto knife. Hold rudder perpendicular to stern and press firmly into slit (illustration G).

7. *Assemble masts and prow.* Saw one 36" dowel into 25½" and 10½" lengths. Saw second dowel into 19½", 9", and 7½" lengths. Taper each dowel at one end by laying dowel flat and running sanding block with 100-grit sandpaper along dowel from middle to end, increasing pressure near end. Roll dowel frequently to achieve even taper. Smooth dowels further with 150-grit sandpaper. Label dowels at broad end as follows: Mast A–25½"; Mast B–19½"; Spar B–10½"; Spar A–9"; Prow–7½".

Make small mark on each mast 4" from broad end. Test-fit masts in deck; mark should fall 2½" to 3" above deck level. If necessary, deepen drill holes. Remove masts from deck. Tap each 4" mark gently with hammer to flatten curved surface, secure in vise, then use 1/16" bit to drill clear through mast at mark. Secure spars A and B in vise. Using 1/16" bit, drill ¾" into broad end of each. Run round file across drilled end to create concave impression. To join spars to masts, drive 1¼" brad through hole in mast, lay mast flat so brad points up, and push spar down onto it, lodging brad tip in drilled hole (illustration H). Tap brad down partway with hammer, add dot of glue to exposed portion of brad, then tap down completely. Glue base of prow into hole at bow (illustration F). Set masts aside.

8. *Spackle and seal hull.* To further refine hull, mix water and putty powder together in approximately 1:2 ratio for yogurtlike consistency. Smooth mixture with fingertip over cracks, holes, and dents in hull. Let dry 1 hour, then sand lightly with 100-grit sandpaper. Tape scrap cardboard over prow and rudder to protect them during spraying. Seal hull with three light coats spray shellac following manufacturer's directions; let dry 10 minutes between coats and 30 minutes after final coat. Remove cardboard sleeve from prow and rudder.

Painting the Boat

1. *Make decal.* Compose name by cutting out letters from magazine. Photocopy name. Using decal medium and following manufacturer's instructions, make decal to be added in step 2.

2. *Paint hull and deck.* Using bristle brush, apply white latex enamel to hull, deck, and deck details; do not paint prow or rudder. Let dry 2 hours, then sand lightly with 150-grit sandpaper. Using bristle brush and Rusty Nail paint, paint hull and border around galley roof (use color photo, page 36, for reference). Using Harvest Gold paint and round brush, paint galley roof, deck edging, top and outer edges of gallery, and rudder. Leave deck white. Let paint dry 30 minutes, apply second coat, and let dry 1 hour. Use decal medium to adhere decal to stern, then let dry 1 hour (illustration I).

3. *Antique hull and deck.* Using bristle

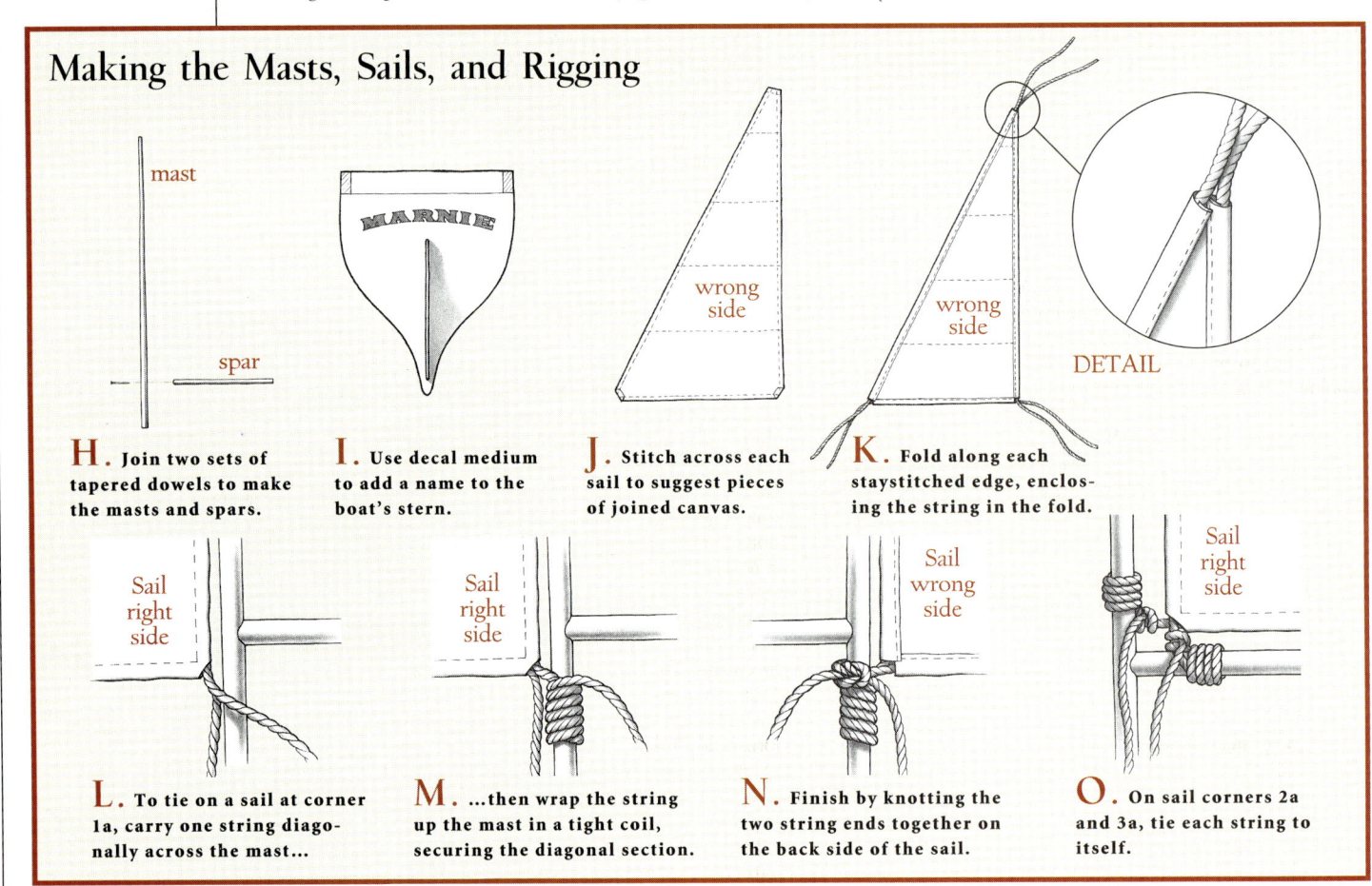

Making the Masts, Sails, and Rigging

H. Join two sets of tapered dowels to make the masts and spars.

I. Use decal medium to add a name to the boat's stern.

J. Stitch across each sail to suggest pieces of joined canvas.

K. Fold along each staystitched edge, enclosing the string in the fold.

L. To tie on a sail at corner 1a, carry one string diagonally across the mast...

M. ...then wrap the string up the mast in a tight coil, securing the diagonal section.

N. Finish by knotting the two string ends together on the back side of the sail.

O. On sail corners 2a and 3a, tie each string to itself.

Final Assembly

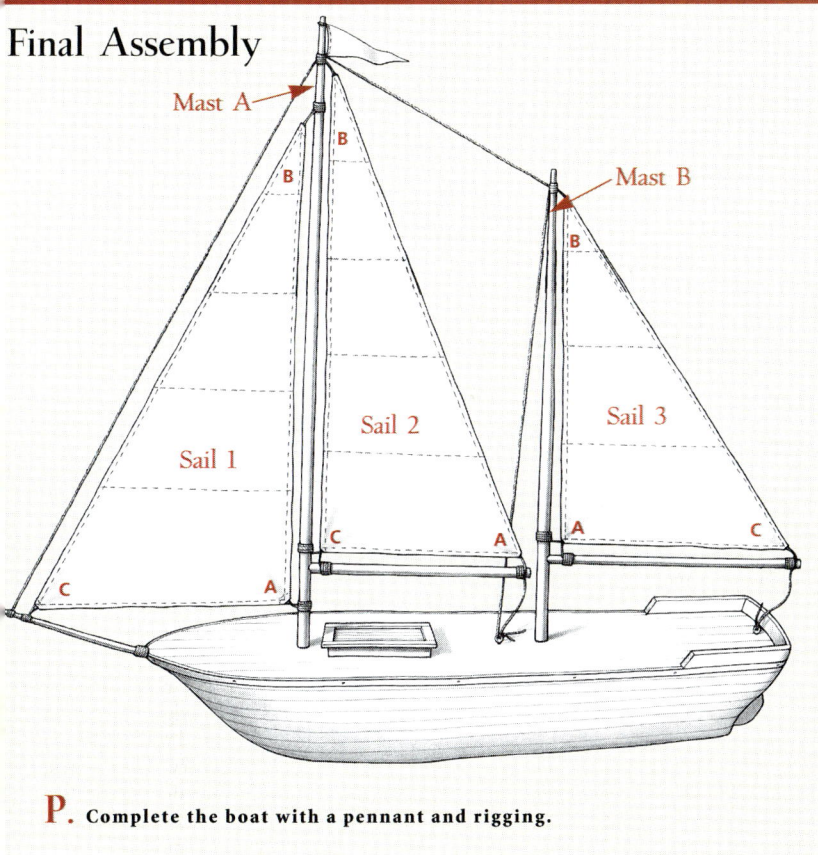

P. Complete the boat with a pennant and rigging.

brush, apply thin coat acrylic sealer over all painted surfaces. In disposable container, combine approximately 1 tablespoon sealer and ¼ teaspoon burnt umber acrylic paint and mix well. Using small piece of crumpled paper towel, rub glaze onto hull in circular motion, as if applying shoe polish. Start at bottom of hull and work up, leaving behind dark pigment in crevices. Let dry 15 minutes, then repeat to antique deck.

4. *Stain prow and masts.* Using crumpled paper towel, apply very light coat wood stain to prow, masts, and spars, rubbing it in as you would shoe polish.

Adding the Sails and Rigging

1. *Cut and sew sails.* Wash and dry muslin, but do not iron. Using patterns prepared earlier and rotary cutter, cut sails 1, 2, and 3 from muslin. To simulate large sails pieced together from canvas sheet, stitch each sail through single layer as indicated on patterns. On each sail, press three short edges ¼" to wrong side, then staystitch ¼" from each long edge (illustration J). For each sail, cut three pieces of string, each one 30" longer than its corresponding sail edge. To make casings for strings, fold edges along staystitching and press toward wrong side. Position string along pressed edge, extending string equally at each end. Fold edge again ¼" toward wrong side, enclose string within fold, and pin. Repeat on remaining two edges, then machine-stitch all around (illustration K).

2. *Cut and sew pennant.* Using round brush and Sterling Blue paint, paint both sides of a 2" x 4" scrap of muslin. Let dry about 30 minutes, or until stiff. Using pattern prepared earlier, cut one pennant from blue fabric. Fold short edge ⅜" to one side as marked on pattern and stitch ¼" from fold. Touch up stitches and cut edges with blue paint.

3. *Join sails to masts.* Lay masts A and B flat with spars at right. Referring to illustration P for position, place sails face up alongside masts. At sail corner 1a, draw vertical string diagonally down across mast A; let second horizontal string dangle free (illustration L). Wrap first string around mast in tight upward spiral, anchoring diagonal section of same string underneath (illustration M). After six to eight wraps, turn assembly over and tie wrapped and free string ends together in tight square knot; do not cut (illustration N). Repeat process to tie corners 1b, 2b, 2c, 3b, and 3c. At corner 2a, wrap vertical string around spar and tie it to itself, then repeat to wrap and tie horizontal string to mast (illustration O). Repeat process to tie corner 3a. Glue masts with sails into appropriate holes and let dry overnight.

4. *Complete rigging.* Twist two small screw eyes into deck at starter holes. Using tapestry needle, poke one loose string from sail corner 2b through pennant casing, wrap string around top of mast, and tie off. To camouflage prow joint at bow, lay 45" length of string along base of prow, leaving 9" tail. Wrap string tightly around prow ¾" above base, then continue wrapping prow in snug downward spiral, securing tail as you go. When wraps reach bow, apply fray preventive along wrapped section, then wrap back over previous wraps to reach starting point. Apply fray preventive once more, wrap back over previous wraps, and tie ends together in tight square knot on prow underside. Tie strings at sail corner 1c to tip of prow, as for sail corner 1a in step 3, above. Finally, tie new 70" length string to tip of prow, run it taut up to mast A and tie just below pennant, run it taut to top of mast B and tie, and run it taut to screw eye in front of mast B and tie. At corner 2c, tie one end to first screw eye. At corner 3c, tie one end to second screw eye. Apply thick dot of fray preventive to all knots, let dry 24 hours, and clip off loose ends (illustration P).

Making the Stand

1. *Attach supports to base.* Lightly draft line down lengthwise center of 8" x 14" clear pine board, then mark perpendicular lines 2" in from each 8" edge (illustration Q). Set brackets on short lines so they touch at center. Rest boat hull on brackets, then adjust bracket positions as needed until deck is level. Trace around each bracket with pencil to mark its position, then remove all pieces. Using 1/16" bit, drill hole through base about ⅜" in from each bracket's outer edge. Drive 2" drywall screw through each hole from bottom of base until tip emerges. Apply glue to bottom of bracket, set in position on base, and drive screw through bracket from underside (illustration Q). Repeat process for remaining brackets. Let dry at least 1 hour, preferably overnight.

2. *Paint base.* Seal brackets and top of base with two coats spray shellac following manufacturer's directions; let dry 10 minutes between coats and 30 minutes after final coat. Using round brush, paint stand with two coats black acrylic craft paint, letting dry 20 to 30 minutes in between coats and 1 hour after final coat. Cut gray felt rectangle ⅛" smaller all around than base, then glue to underside of base. Cut felt scraps to fit on tops of brackets (illustration Q) and glue in place. ◆

Making the Boat Stand

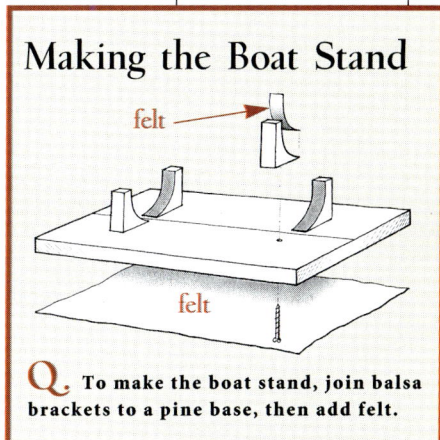

Q. To make the boat stand, join balsa brackets to a pine base, then add felt.

DECOUPAGE

Parisian Fireplace Screen
Cut a silhouette of a floral bouquet from Gatorfoam board, then add your own colorful flowers using decoupage.

BY CAROL ENDLER STERBENZ

The finished fireplace screen measures approximately 23" tall and 23" wide.

COLOR PHOTOGRAPHY:
Carl Tremblay

ILLUSTRATION:
Judy Love

STYLING:
Ritch Holben

MATERIALS

- Floral poster or giftwrap
- 24" x 24" x 3/16" piece Gatorfoam board
- 6½" x 19" x ½" piece Gatorfoam (for stand)
- Black gloss acrylic paint
- Gold metallic acrylic paint
- Mod Podge
- Durham Rock Hard putty
- White tacky glue
- Screen and stand patterns (see page 45)

You'll also need:
X-Acto knife; scissors; manicure scissors; transfer paper; self-healing cutting mat; 2" foam brush; size #10 round brush; 150-grit sandpaper; access to photocopier with enlarger; tape; small disposable container; latex gloves; small stirring stick; old measuring spoons; paper towels; pencil; stapler (or other heavy object); and newsprint.

To decorate the front of the screen we chose a poster of an oil painting from a museum gift shop. You can also use flowers cut from wrapping paper, old greeting cards, or garden catalogs, although the size of the museum poster flowers are more in scale with the fireplace screen. For a finishing touch we added a ladybug, several butterflies, and a snail.

INSTRUCTIONS

1. *Transfer screen and stand patterns.* Photocopy screen and stand patterns (see page 45), enlarging 400 percent, or so short, straight edge of base measures 6½". Tape photocopies together to assemble large patterns. Lay screen pattern face up on 3/16" Gatorfoam board, slip transfer paper in between, and tape down. Trace outline with pencil to transfer design. Position stand pattern on ½" Gatorfoam, aligning long edges, and transfer in same way.

2. *Cut out screen and stand.* Lay Gatorfoam face up on self-healing cutting mat. For easier handling, trim excess Gatorfoam from edge of design with X-Acto knife. To cut out screen, press blade straight down into board along marked lines, and remove cut pieces in sections (*see* illustration A, next page). Repeat to cut out stand.

I'VE RECEIVED SO MANY COMPLIments on the decoupage fireplace screen that I brought home with me from Paris (*see* From the Editor, Winter 1997) that I decided to have one designed in a similar version to give as a gift. This quick and easy project, developed by Elizabeth Cameron, requires only two special materials: a large piece of Gatorfoam board, available in artist supply stores, and a large floral poster.

The original screen was cut from ¼"-thick plywood, but we didn't relish the idea of using the coping saw on such a large piece. Instead, we substituted Gatorfoam board, a material used by architects for building scale models. Unlike other types of foam core, which warp when glue or varnish is applied, Gaterfoam board stands up well to such materials, won't dent, and is easily cut with an X-Acto knife. If you can find black Gaterfoam board, buy it—you'll be able to skip the painting steps.

After cutting the board, we noticed the edges were slightly uneven and very unfinished. To create a smooth, finished surface, we added a coat of Durham Rock Hard putty. Because the screen features tight corners and curves, we found it much easier to apply it using a finger rather than a spackling knife.

3. *Spackle screen and stand.* Mix about 1 tablespoon water and 1 tablespoon dry putty in disposable container. Add more putty until consistency resembles thick pudding. Put on latex gloves. Using fingertip, smooth putty over cut edges of foam on screen and stand; do not apply putty to long gluing edge of stand. Let dry 1 hour, sand spackled areas smooth with 150-grit sandpaper, and wipe off dust.

4. *Paint screen and stand.* Turn screen face down, position stand on it, and trace outline of stand using pattern as reference. Using 2" foam brush, apply 1 coat black gloss paint to screen back, leaving stand area unpainted (illustration B). Let dry 30 minutes. Turn screen face up, and apply two coats black paint to screen front and edges; let dry 30 minutes after each coat. Apply two coats black paint to stand and let dry as above; leave long, straight edge unpainted. Using round brush, paint edges of screen metallic gold (illustration C).

5. *Design bouquet.* Select sixteen to twenty flower and leaf images 2" to 6" across from poster or giftwrap. For easier handling, cut out basic shapes with scissors. Use manicure scissors to cut shapes precisely along printed edges; for easier cutting, hold scissors stationary and move paper. Arrange cutouts collage-style on screen, positioning larger flowers first and inserting leaves between and behind them to create depth in bouquet (illustration D). Continue working until bouquet is full and lush. Remove cutouts one by one from screen; place them face up on newsprint in same relative position, and separate them so they do not overlap.

6. *Glue cutouts to screen.* Using foam brush, apply thin, even coat of Mod Podge to face of each cutout, brushing out beyond edges. Let dry 30 minutes; pieces will curl and then relax. Select last cutout removed from screen in step 5, turn it face down on scrap newsprint, and brush Mod Podge across surface, out beyond edges. Position cutout on screen, glue side down, place folded paper towel on top, and rub gently in circular motion to adhere piece and press out air bubbles. Repeat process, gluing down background cutouts first, then those in foreground, until all cutouts are adhered (illustration E). Let dry 2 hours.

7. *Join stand and seal screen.* Lay screen face down. Apply glue to unpainted stand area on screen and long straight edge of stand. Press stand onto screen, weight with heavy object, and wipe any oozing glue with damp paper towel. Let dry overnight. Stand screen upright (illustration F). Using clean foam brush, apply Mod Podge to all surfaces. Let dry overnight. ◆

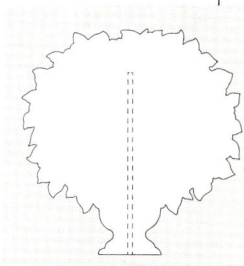

PATTERNS
See page 45 for pattern pieces and enlargement instructions.

Making the Screen

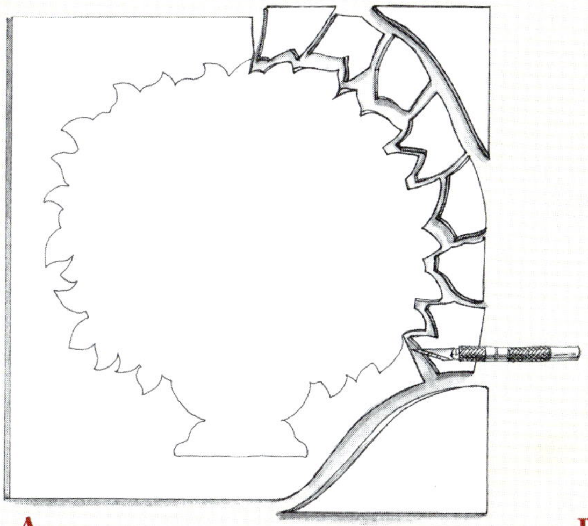

A. Cut the screen silhouette from Gatorfoam board.

B. Paint the screen surfaces black.

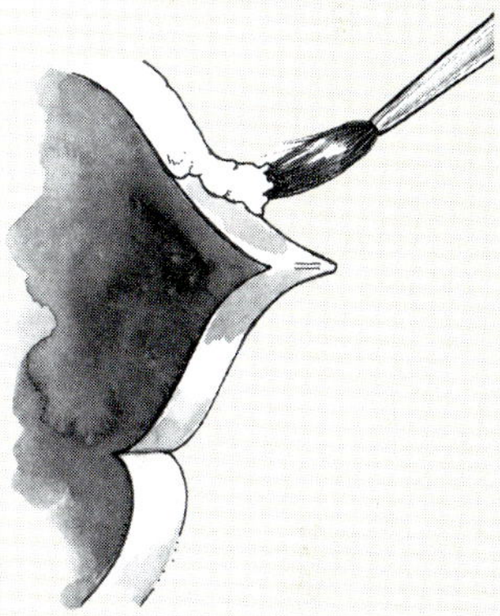

C. Paint the edges metallic gold.

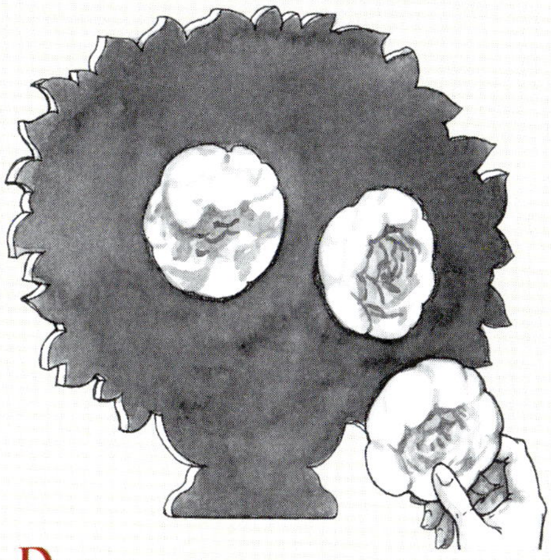

D. Design a bouquet using paper cutouts of flowers and leaves.

E. Glue down the cutouts collage-style.

F. Glue a stand to the back, then finish the screen with Mod Podge.

GARDEN

Broken China Stepping Stones
Construct these weatherproof garden accents using thrift store china, mortar, and tile grout.

🐦 BY ELIZABETH CAMERON

For variation on these stones, substitute a plain plate, and highlight the design with colored tile grout.

COLOR PHOTOGRAPHY:
Carl Tremblay

ILLUSTRATION:
Judy Love

SILHOUETTE PHOTOGRAPHY:
Daniel van Ackere

STYLING:
Ritch Holben

MATERIALS
- Dinner plate with flat, patterned rim (see illustration A, next page, for sample)
- Dessert plate with center motif (see illustration A for sample)
- 11½" x 11½" cement patio square
- 1¾ cups (about 1¼ pounds) dry mortar
- 2 cups (about 1½ pounds) dry exterior grade grout

You'll also need:
trowel (or other flat tool such as squeegee, plastic ruler, or paint stick); grout float (or other smooth, flexible tool such as those listed above); hammer; rubber gloves; particle mask; canvas work gloves; two heavy-duty paper grocery bags; newsprint; old spoons or paint sticks; old measuring cups; old fork; two disposable 1-quart containers; pencil; and sponge.

Other items, if necessary:
soft cloth (for buffing stepping stones).

THESE STEPPING STONES RESEMble intricately inlaid mosaic tile, but without the time and cost associated with such precise work. The stones are easy to make: Buy a variety of inexpensive plates, break them into small pieces, secure the broken pottery to a cement patio square using mortar, and fill in the gaps with exterior grade tile grout.

I started my search for plates in a thrift store and found a treasure house full of low-cost but colorful designs. You can also use china that has been broken or chipped accidentally. To create a more complex design, I used the checked border from a dinner plate and a central fruit motif from a dessert plate on each stepping stone.

Unquestionably, the most difficult part of this project was breaking the first plate. I fought against bringing the hammer down on the plate, which I had safely bundled in a paper bag. Once broken, however, arranging the plate pieces was fun, much like working a puzzle where the pieces don't have to fit exactly. Early on in the design process, I discovered that some parts of the plate are thicker than others, and that the thick and thin parts don't necessarily work well next to each other because they require different amounts of mortar and grout for a smooth overall finish. So I broke off the thinner, usable sections of the plates and discarded the thickest chunks. The slightly curved rim of the plate posed no problem, though, because the small pieces lay virtually flat.

I found cement patio squares at Home Depot for about $1 each. To anchor the broken china to the cement block, I used a thin coat of mortar, then filled in all the spaces in between with exterior-grade tile grout. If you don't already own a trowel and grout float, you can substitute a squeegee, plastic ruler, or paint stick to spread the mortar and apply the grout. I was liberal with the grout, taking care to bury all the sharp edges of the pieces.

Depending on how orderly you choose to be in creating your stepping stone mosaic, the first section of the project (breaking the plates, arranging the pieces, and adhering the broken plate pieces with mortar) will probably take 2 to 3 hours. After the mortar dried overnight, the final grouting process took me less than ½ hour.

Elizabeth Cameron is a freelance writer living in Brighton, Massachusetts.

GARDEN

INSTRUCTIONS

1. *Break plates.* Select dinner and dessert plates (*see* illustration A, below). Fold paper bag flat, with bottom face up. Insert dinner plate into bag face down, so plate back rests against bag bottom. Fold down bag top and anchor it under bottom to make "package" (illustration B). To break plate, put on canvas gloves, set package on cement block, and strike hard several times with hammer (illustration C). Open bag to check progress. Ideal shard size is 1/2" to 2" across. If necessary, refold bag and restrike. To view shards patterned side up, turn bag over, unfold top flap, and tear bag down middle. Repeat process with new bag to break dessert plate.

2. *Design mosaic from shards.* Trace cement block outline on newsprint. Wearing gloves, examine shards and discard any that include protruding rim from plate's underside; if these pieces are large, place them inside new bag and break into smaller pieces. Select pieces from dinner plate border and arrange them around template perimeter, 1/2" in from edge. Reassemble dessert plate motif in center of template. Fill remaining area with broken pieces from either plate. Tighten mosaic, adding extra pieces as needed, until there is approximately 1/8" to 1/4" space between pieces (illustration D).

3. *Cement mosaic pieces to block.* Set cement block on several sheets newsprint. Put on rubber gloves and mask. Pour 1/2 cup cold water in disposable container, add 1 3/4 cups dry mortar (or ratio manufacturer recommends), and mix thoroughly until coarse and thick, like wet sand. Let mortar stand 10 minutes, then dump on center of block. Using trowel or substitute, spread mortar over block surface, making even 1/4"-deep layer. To improve mortar adhesion, use fork to make grooves in surface. Transfer shards, one at a time, from template to block and press gently into mortar to create permanent mosaic (illustration E); strive to make tops of shards even. Let mortar cure 24 hours, or as manufacturer recommends.

4. *Apply grout.* Put on rubber gloves and mask. Pour 1/2 cup cold water in disposable container, add 2 cups dry grout (or ratio manufacturer recommends), and mix thoroughly until coarse and thick, like wet sand. Let grout stand 10 minutes, then dump on center of block. Using float or substitute, smooth grout across block so all crevices are filled (illustration F). Scrape excess grout to edges of block and mold firm, squared-off edge with gloved fingers. Let grout dry 10 minutes, then wipe tops of shards clean with damp sponge. Let grout cure indoors 72 hours, or as manufacturer recommends. If pieces remain hazy, buff with soft, dry cloth. Dispose of excess grout and mortar in mixing containers. ◆

Constructing the Stepping Stones

A. Select a dinner plate (left) with a border design and a dessert plate (right) with a center motif.

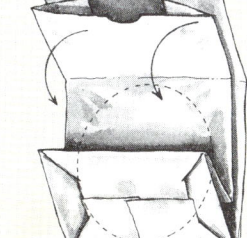 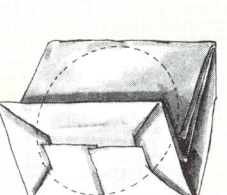

B. Wrap each plate in a brown paper bag.

C. Break the packaged plate with a hammer.

D. Arrange the shards in a mosaic of the original plate patterns.

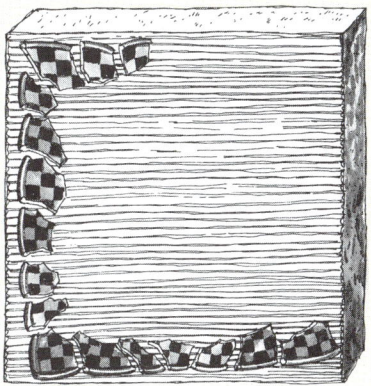

E. Apply mortar to the cement block, then press the shards into it.

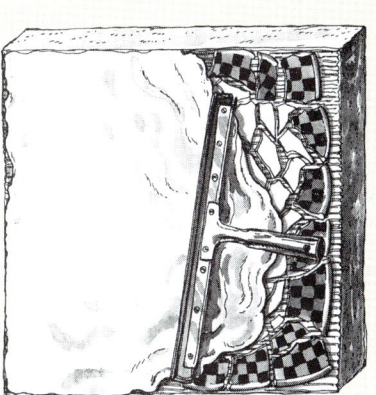

F. After the mortar has cured, apply the grout.

PATTERNS

Spring 1997 Patterns

Velvet Peaches
(*see* article, page 10)

NOTE: PHOTOCOPY ALL PIECES FOR THIS ARTICLE AT 100%

Vintage Tablecloth
(*see* article, page 28)

NOTE: PHOTOCOPY CORNER AND CHERRY PIECES AT 200%.

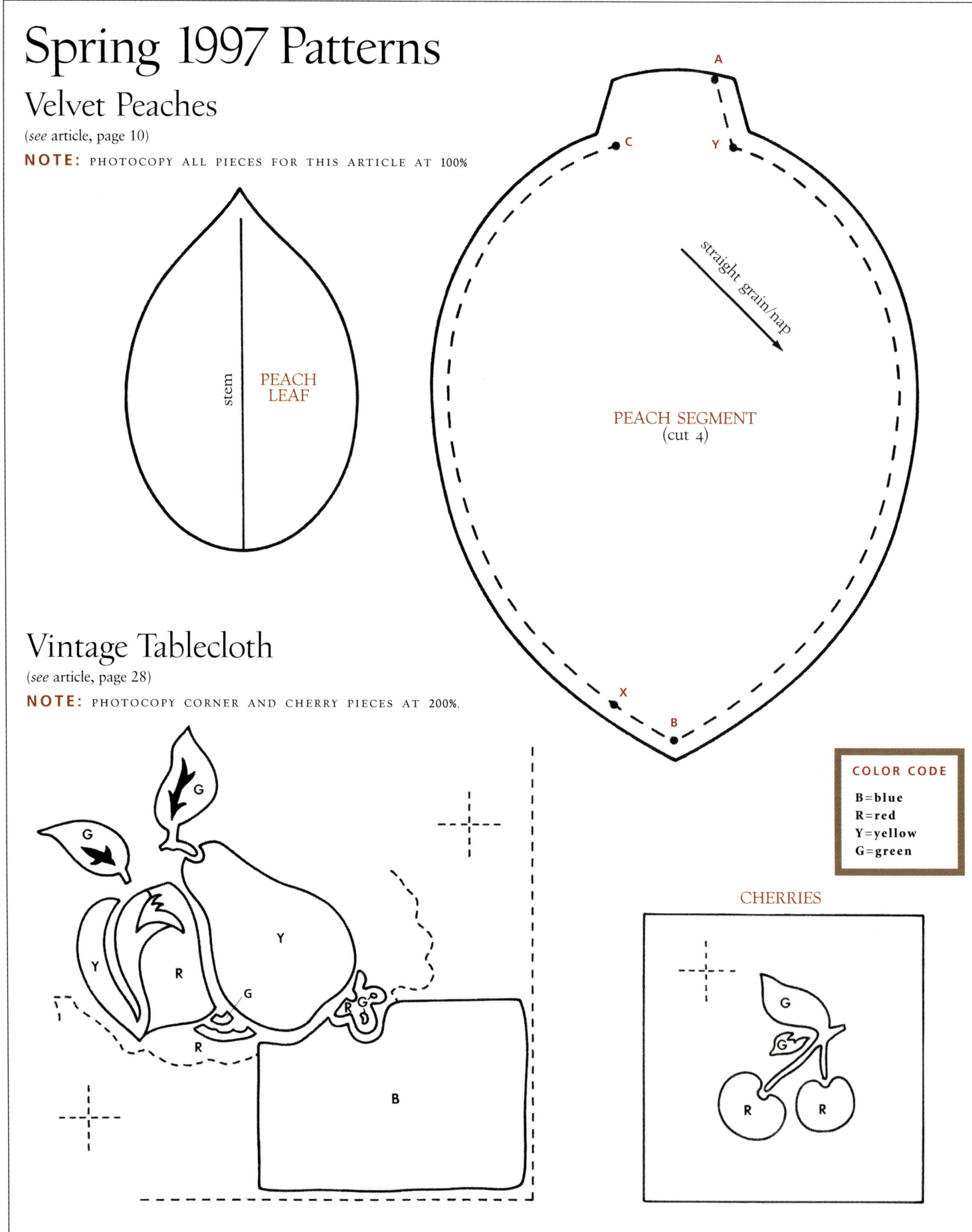

PATTERNS: **Roberta Frauwirth**

PATTERNS

Parisian Fireplace Screen
(*see* article, page 40)

NOTE: PHOTOCOPY ALL PIECES FOR THIS ARTICLE AT 400%.

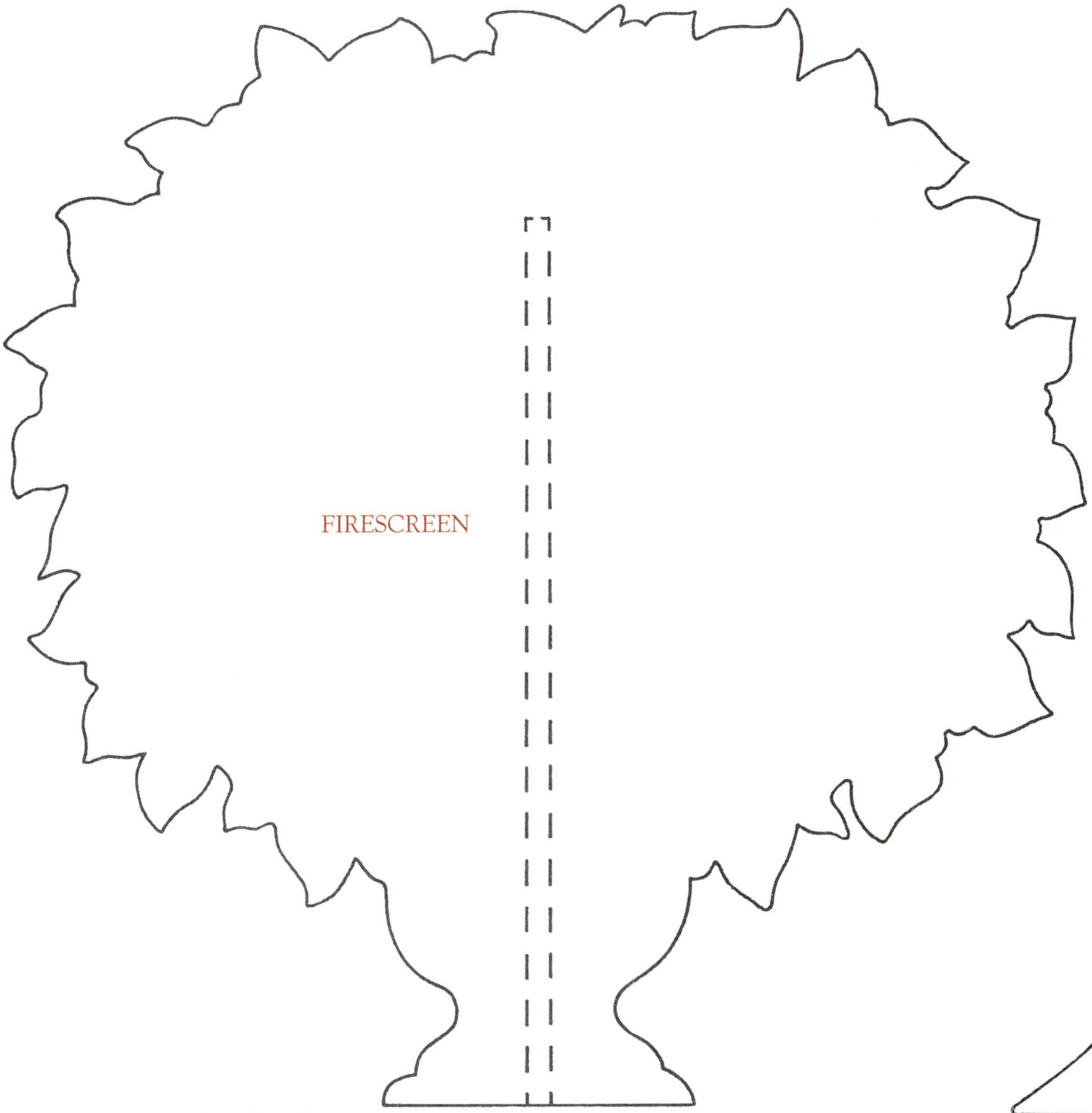

FIRESCREEN

STAND

Vintage Tablecloth
(*see* article, page 28)

NOTE: PHOTOCOPY THIS PIECE AT 400% OR SO OUTER DASHED BORDER MEASURES 23⅝".

COLOR CODE
B=blue
R=red
Y=yellow
G=green

BORDER REPEAT

PATTERNS

Decorative Sailboat
(*see* article, page 36)

NOTE: PHOTOCOPY BRACKET, RUDDER, AND GALLEY AT 100%, PHOTOCOPY HULL AT 400%.

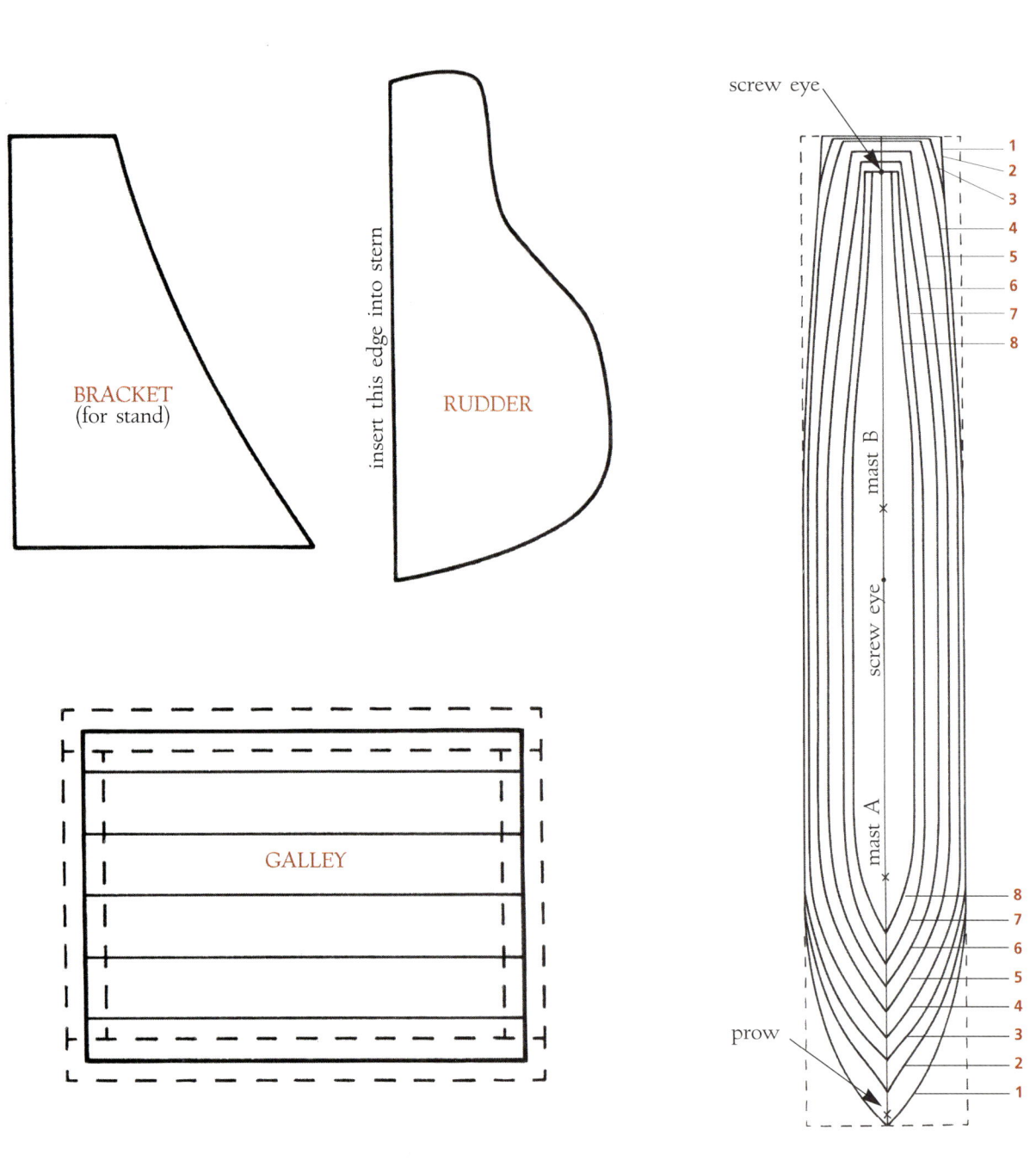

Decorative Sailboat

(see article, page 36)

NOTE: photocopy pennant at 100%, photocopy sails at 200%.

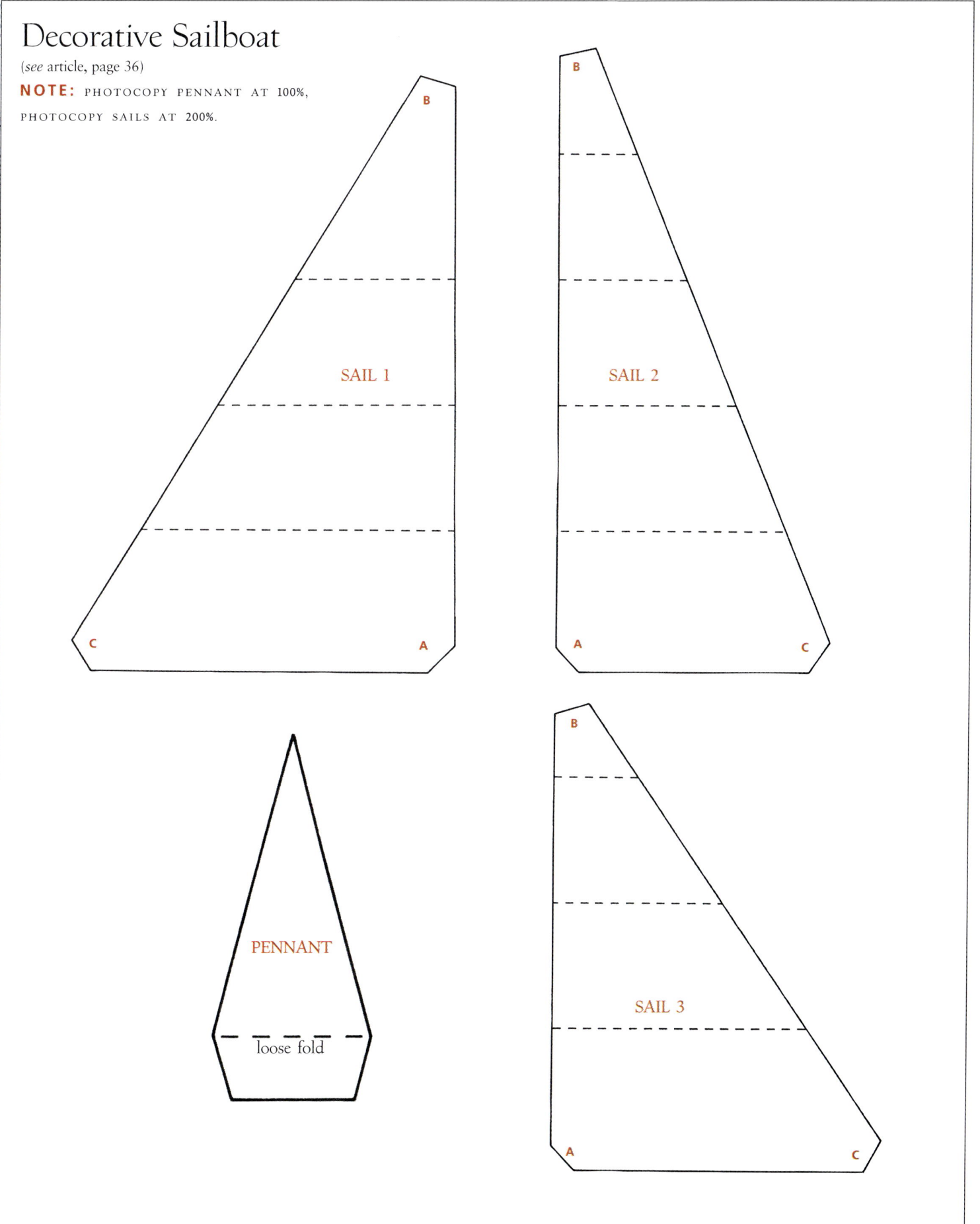

Sources & Resources

The following are specific mail-order sources for particular items, arranged by article.

Most of the materials used in this issue are available at your local craft supply store, florist's, fabric shop, hardware store, or bead and jewelry supply. Generic craft supplies can be ordered from such catalogs as Craft King, Dick Blick Art Materials, Newark Dressmaker Supply, Pearl Paint Company, or Sunshine Discount Crafts. The following are specific sources for harder-to-find items, arranged by article. The suggested retail prices listed here were current at press time. Contact the suppliers directly to confirm prices and availability.

Quick Home Accents, page 6
Japanese lampshades (shade only) from $8 to $24 at the Door Store.

Frosted Glassware, page 8
Glass tumblers in 4½" and 6" sizes ranging from 99¢ to $2 at Lechter's and IKEA.

Velvet Peaches, page 10
Procion fiber-reactive dye from $3.95 for 2 ounces at the Dharma Trading Company. Stretch cotton velvet (custom order) starting at $10.95 per yard from Paterson Silks.

Garden Lanterns, page 12
Medium-weight parchment paper starting at $1.55 per sheet from Kate's Paperie. Strands of 7-watt light bulbs for $15.95 from Just Bulbs. Sixteen ounces of Yes Stikflat glue for $9.25 from New York Central Art Supply. Star craft punch for $3.50 from Dick Blick. Star metal paper punch for $30 from Bookman Enterprise.

Farmhouse Table, page 14
Benjamin Moore matte latex paint starting at $8 per quart from Pearl Paint.

Plaid Silk Footstool, page 18
Interior plywood (14" x 14" piece) for $8 from Metropolitan Lumber & Hardware. Maple wood finials (#22657) for $7.95 each from The Woodworkers' Store. Dressweight muslin for $2 per yard from Paterson Silks. Silk buffalo plaid fabric for $18 per yard at Sunrise Fabrics. Polyester batting for $1.50 per yard from P&S Fabric.

Porch Rug, page 21
Jute rug (#SKU 1061332) for $59 from Pottery Barn.

Decorative Plates, page 22
Winsor & Newton gouache starting at $4.88 for 14-milliliter tube, Accent Crown Jewels acrylics for $1.72 per 2-ounce bottle, Tulip ColorPoint fabric paint for $2.34 per 1.1-ounce bottle, and FolkArt acrylics for $1.24 per 2 ounces all from Pearl Paint.

Candlecage, page 26
Chicken wire for $3.50 per yard from True Value Hardware stores. Armature wire starting at $3.15 for $1/16$" and $4.95 for $1/8$" thicknesses from Pearl Paint. Copper teardrop bead for 75¢ from Canal Surplus.

Vintage Tablecloth, page 28
Mylar film for $2.81 per 24" x 36" sheet and Jacquard Textile Color fabric paint for $2.33 per 2¼"-ounce jar from Pearl Paint. White cotton twill fabric for $13 per yard at Paterson Silks.

Arts and Crafts–Style Bandbox, page 32
Arts and Crafts-style wallpaper borders from $13 per yard from Bradbury & Bradbury Wallpapers. Modern Options Copper Topper at $12.80 per 8 ounces and Patina Green for $8 per 8 ounces from Pearl Paint. Set of three chipboard boxes with plain lids from $7.35 at Sax Arts & Crafts.

Fireplace Screen, page 40
Gatorfoam board sheets from $20.39 at Charrette.

Quick Projects, page 49
Chefmaster Neon Brite liquid paste food coloring for $2.99 per 2-ounce bottle from N.Y. Cake and Baking Distributor. Egg blower device for $6.50 from Surma.

The following companies are mentioned in the listing above. Contact each individually for a price list or catalog.

BOOKMAN ENTERPRISE
P.O. Box 343, La Rue, OH 43332; 614-499-2004

BRADBURY & BRADBURY WALLPAPERS
P.O. Box 155, Benicia, CA 94510; 707-746-1900

CANAL SURPLUS
363 Canal Street, New York, NY 10013; 212-966-3275

CHARRETTE
P.O. Box 4010, Woburn, MA 01888-4010; 800-367-3729

CRAFT KING
P.O. Box 90637, Lakeland, FL 33804; 800-769-9494

DHARMA TRADING COMPANY
P.O. Box 150916, San Rafael, CA 94915; 800-542-5227

DICK BLICK ART MATERIALS
P.O. Box 1267, Galesburg, IL 61402-1267; 800-447-8192

DOOR STORE
940 Massachusetts Avenue, Cambridge, MA 02139; 617-547-8937

IKEA
IKEA Catalog Department, 185 Discovery Street, Colmar, PA 18915; 800-434-4532

JUST BULBS
936 Broadway, New York, NY 10010-6063; 212-228-7820

KATE'S PAPERIE
561 Broadway, New York, NY 10012; 212-941-9816

LECHTER'S
Call 800-60-KITCHEN (800-60-54824) to find the nearest location.

LP THUR
126 West 23rd Street, New York, NY 10011; 212-243-4913

METROPOLITAN LUMBER & HARDWARE
617 11th Avenue, New York, NY 10036; 212-246-9090

N.Y. CAKE & BAKING DISTRIBUTOR
56 West 22nd Street, New York, NY 10010; 212-675-2253

NEW YORK CENTRAL ART SUPPLY
62 Third Avenue, New York, NY 10003; 800-950-6111

NEWARK DRESSMAKER SUPPLY
6473 Ruch Road, P.O. Box 20730, Lehigh Valley, PA 18002-0730; 610-837-7500

P&S FABRIC
355 Broadway, New York, NY 10013; 212-226-1534

PATERSON SILKS
36 East 14th Street, New York, NY 10003; 212-929-7861

PEARL PAINT COMPANY, INC.
308 Canal Street, New York, NY 10013-2572; 800-451-7327 (catalog) or 800-221-6845 x2297 (main store)

POTTERY BARN
P.O. Box 7044, San Francisco, CA 94120-7044; 800-922-5507

SAX ARTS & CRAFTS
P.O. Box 510710, New Berlin, WI 53151-0710; 800-558-6696

SUNRISE FABRICS
264 West 40th Street, New York, NY 10018; 212-768-7438

SUNSHINE DISCOUNT CRAFTS
P.O. Box 301, Largo, FL 34649-0301; 800-729-2878

SURMA
11 East 7th Street, New York, NY 10003; 212-477-0729

TRUE VALUE HARDWARE
Call 800-642-7392 to find the nearest location.

THE WOODWORKERS' STORE
4365 Willow Drive, Medina, MN 55340; 800-279-4441

CORRECTION:
In our Winter 1997 mail-order directory, we listed the Nature's Finest catalog as free. The catalog costs $2.50, although this money is refundable after the first purchase. In addition, Clotilde Inc, a sewing mail-order supplier, has a new address. To order a catalog, write or call the company at B3000, Louisiana, MO 63353-3000; 800-772-2891. ◆

Quick Projects

Create these bold designs with multiple dips or wax-resist techniques.

■ **Hawaiian flowers**
For each flower, create six dots in a circular pattern using wax and a Q-Tip, then connect the dots with wax lines using a thin brush. Dip the egg in blue dye, remove the wax resist, and add pink dye dots with a Q-Tip.

■ **Large polka dots**
Use your fingertip to dab in large rough circles of wax, then dip the egg in green dye. Remove the wax and use a brush to fill in the interiors with pink.

■ **Confetti dots**
Dab in wax dots with a Q-Tip, then dip the egg in pink dye.

■ **Color-blocked plaid**
Dip the egg in yellow dye on its side, then blue on the other side, with no overlaps in between the two colors. Then dip the egg in pink dye at one end; the overlap produces purple and salmon.

■ **Banded with dots**
Create a circle of wax dots around the middle of the egg using a Q-Tip. Then dip the egg in blue dye at one end and pink from the other end. The overlap creates a band of purple.

EGGS FOR THE '90S

Easter eggs. The very thought of them brings back memories of Paas egg-dyeing kits and the smell of vinegar. These eggs are reminiscent of those old-fashioned versions, but we've used bold and simple graphic designs and fresh, bright pastel colors for a more contemporary feeling.

We started with Chefmaster Neon Brite liquid paste food coloring, which offers a more interesting color palette than that found in ordinary egg dyes. The decorations were created using one of two techniques. Some of the eggs were dipped several times in one or more colors, producing either gradations of one color or layerings of multiple colors. For others, we brushed liquid wax (we bought a 2-ounce jar of wax-resist) on the egg and let it dry. The wax creates a barrier between the egg and the dye. After the egg has been dipped in the dye and allowed to dry, the wax is gently rubbed off with a dry paper towel, revealing the pattern.

To get started, empty the eggs of their yolk using an egg blower or hard-boil them and let them cool completely. Specific decorating directions, above, follow the photo clockwise, starting with the blue Hawaiian egg at the top. ◆

COLOR PHOTOGRAPHY:
Carl Tremblay

EGG DESIGN:
Michio Ryan

Vintage Wallpaper Frame

It's no longer necessary to search for an antique frame such as this one; nowadays, you can make your own in a fraction of the time. The distressed effect on this frame is created with two main materials: crackle medium, which makes the frame's painted finish appear worn and chipped, and vintage wallpaper, which gives the piece its dated look.

Start by selecting an acrylic basecoat color and a topcoat color; both should match a color in the wallpaper. Paint the frame with the basecoat color, and let it dry overnight. To create the crackle finish, brush a thin coat of crackle medium onto the face of the frame. Let it stand until the surface turns tacky, then apply the topcoat paint in a spotty manner. The crackling action will begin immediately and intensify over the next 20 to 30 minutes. Let the frame dry for at least 1 hour, then brush on a thin coat of matte acrylic sealer, and let the frame dry overnight.

On a cutting mat, roll out the wallpaper face up. Position the frame on the wallpaper, and lightly trace the frame edges to mark the paper placement later on. Cut the wallpaper approximately 1" beyond the traced frame edges. Turn the cut piece of wallpaper face down. Cover the frame front with a thin layer of wallpaper adhesive. Press the frame in position (face down) onto the back of the wallpaper, adjusting the frame as necessary to match the traced guidelines. Remove any oozing adhesive with a damp paper towel. On a cutting mat, run an X-Acto knife along the inner and outer edges of the frame to trim, and remove any excess paper. Turn the frame face up, and run a wooden roller along the papered surface to press out any air bubbles. Before the wallpaper adhesive dries completely, gently scratch or tear off small sections of wallpaper along the frame's inner and outer edges. Let the frame dry overnight. To simulate wear, sand the torn areas gently with 150-grit sandpaper so they blend into the painted surface, then resand the frame corners and edges.

COLOR PHOTOGRAPHY: **Carl Tremblay** STYLING: **Ritch Holben** FRAME DESIGN: **Pauletta Brooks**

NUMBER SEVENTEEN   FALL 1997

Handcraft
ILUSTRATED

25 FABULOUS USES FOR
Glitter Fruit

PLUS: Fast and Easy Gifts and Ornaments

Jewelry Box Chair
Miniature Upholstered Chair with Hinged Seat Cushion

Foolproof Technique for Glass Mosaic
Create a Keepsake Gift Box Using Glass Gems and Tile Grout

Scottie Dog Cards
Customize Our Silhouette-Style Card to Your Pet

Post-It Books
Suede-Covered Gift Books with Post-It Pads for Pages

The Best Way to Fuse Sheer Fabrics
Attach Chiffon Leaves to a Sheer Window Banner with Paint

Marionette Ornaments
Jointed Sculpey Tree Dolls in 8 Easy Steps

ALSO
Embossed Gift Tags
Miniature Teapot Ornaments
Decorative Wheat Bread
Quick-Sew Linen Chair Slip

NUMBER SEVENTEEN   FALL 1997

Contents

Faux Enamel
Teapots, page 10

Jewelry Box
Chair, page 26

5-Minute Envelope
Liners, page 37

COVER PHOTOGRAPH:
Carl Tremblay
STYLING:
Ritch Holben

These jointed Sculpey dolls make a great gift. See page 18.

FEATURE STORIES

8
FOOLPROOF GLASS MOSAIC
Create a unique box top with glass gems and tile grout, then finish the design with whitewash and brass hardware.

10
FAUX ENAMEL COFFEE- AND TEAPOTS
Create these enamel-like pots using layers of decoupage medium over colorful giftwrap, then complete the effect with spouts and handles made from modeling dough.

13
MINIATURE POST-IT BOOKS
Create a miniature book with four basic materials: a scrap of suede, colored paper, Post-It pads, and contact cement.

14
HARVEST WINDOW BANNER
Create this sheer autumn banner with little to no sewing. The trick: Use fabric paint to fuse the oak leaves in place.

16
DECORATIVE WHEAT BREAD
Use our simple recipe to mix up a loaf of bread, then add a wheat sheaf made from decorating dough.

18
MARIONETTE TREE ORNAMENTS
Assemble these festive jointed dolls using Sculpey thermoset clay, then add facial and costume details using acrylic paint and scraps of fabric.

22
25 USES FOR GLITTER FRUIT
Transform ordinary plastic fruit into a range of home-decorating accents using glue and blended glitter.

24
MAKE YOUR OWN DOG CARDS
Create a set of bold and crisp greeting cards quickly and easily using glossy-coated paper and stationery supplies.

26
JEWELRY BOX CHAIR
Stitch up this unique dresser accent in a weekend using less than a yard of fabric.

29
EMBOSSED GIFT MEDALLIONS
Cut a series of clay tags using a biscuit cutter, then glue on embossed seals.

30
SECRETS OF FROSTING BOTTLES
Transform ordinary glass containers into a set of heirloom perfume bottles using etching cream and decorative cabochons.

32
QUICK FAUX BRONZING
Build a basic frame using pine molding, then create the look of carved antique bronze using an anaglyptic wallpaper border and faux finishing products.

34
PORTABLE DOG BED
This bold and graphic dog bed, sewn from fake dalmation fur, doubles as a carrier for a small dog or puppy.

37
FIVE-MINUTE ENVELOPE LINERS
There's no need for intricate patterns—just trace your envelope for custom-fit liners.

38
DRIED ROSEBUD PINEAPPLE
Build a pineapple-shaped base from florist foam, then cover it with dried rosebuds. A stem made from eucalyptus leaves completes the design.

40
RUBBER-STAMPED LINEN CHAIR SLIP
Create a quick decorating accent using a pair of linen napkins, a rubber stamp, fabric paint, and a rubber stamp ink pad.

IN EVERY ISSUE
NOTES FROM READERS 2
QUICK TIPS 4
QUICK HOME ACCENTS 6
THE PERFECT GIFT 7
PATTERNS 42
SOURCES & RESOURCES 48
QUICK PROJECTS 49
ORGANDY GIFT BAGS BACK COVER

Handcraft ILLUSTRATED

EDITOR
Carol Endler Sterbenz

EXECUTIVE EDITOR
Barbara Bourassa

ART DIRECTOR
Amy Klee

SENIOR EDITOR
Michio Ryan

MANAGING EDITOR
Keith Powers

DIRECTIONS EDITOR
Candie Frankel

COPY EDITOR
Gary Pfitzer

EDITORIAL ASSISTANT
Melissa Nachatelo

PUBLISHER AND FOUNDER
Christopher Kimball

MARKETING DIRECTOR
Adrienne Kimball

CIRCULATION MANAGER
David Mack

FULFILLMENT MANAGER
Larisa Greiner

NEWSSTAND MANAGER
Jonathan Venier

MARKETING ASSISTANT
Connie Forbes

CIRCULATION ASSISTANT
Steven Browall

VICE PRESIDENT PRODUCTION AND TECHNOLOGY
James McCormack

EDITORIAL PRODUCTION MANAGER
Sheila Datz

SYSTEMS ADMINISTRATOR
Paul Mulvaney

PRODUCTION ARTIST
Kevin Moeller

EDITORIAL PRODUCTION ASSISTANT
Robert Parsons

PRODUCTION ASSISTANT
Daniel Frey

CONTROLLER
Lisa A. Carullo

ACCOUNTING ASSISTANT
Mandy Shito

Handcraft Illustrated (ISSN 1072-0529) is published quarterly by Boston Common Press Limited Partners, 17 Station Street, Brookline, MA 02146. Copyright 1997 Boston Common Press Limited Partners. Second-class postage paid at Boston, MA, and additional mailing offices, USPS #011-895. For list rental information, please contact List Services Corporation, 6 Trowbridge Drive, P.O. Box 516, Bethel, CT 06801; (203) 743-2600; Fax (203) 743-0589. Editorial office: 17 Station Street, Brookline, MA 02146; (617) 232-1000, FAX (617) 232-1572, e-mail: hnd-cftill@aol.com. Editorial contributions should be sent or e-mailed to: Editor, Handcraft Illustrated. We cannot assume responsibility for manuscripts submitted to us. Submissions will be returned only if accompanied by a large, self-addressed stamped envelope. Subscription rates: $24.95 for one year; $45 for two years; $65 for three years. (Canada: add $6 per year; all other countries add $12 per year.) Postmaster: Send all new orders, subscription inquiries, and change of address notices to Handcraft Illustrated, P.O. Box 7450, Red Oak, IA 51591-0450. Single copies: $4 in U.S.; $4.95 in Canada and other countries. Back issues available for $5 each. PRINTED IN THE U.S.A.

Rather than put ™ in every occurrence of trademarked names, we state that we are using the names only and in an editorial fashion and to the benefit of the trademark owner, with no intention of infringement of the trademark.

Note to Readers: Every effort has been made to present the information in this publication in a clear, complete, and accurate manner. It is important that all instructions be followed carefully, as failure to do so could result in injury. Boston Common Press Limited Partners, the editors, and the authors disclaim any and all liability resulting therefrom.

From the Editor

A Letter of Thanks to My Children:

It is autumn now and and the lawn in front of my home is almost covered with maple leaves, except for a narrow path that has been cut through the dry layer. I think that some child has cleared the path before me, slipping his little feet under the leaves and kicking them aside as he has walked along. I remember how my children used to do this, and in the briefest of reverie, they are present with me now. It is fitting that I am thinking of them since they have been asking me to tell them what I want for Christmas and I have no answer.

As I walk, I think back to my own childhood and remember asking my mother what she would like for Christmas. "I have everything I need," was her usual reply. I would feel exasperated and disbelieving in light of my long list, numbered and marked with cross-hatched stars indicating the gifts I thought she wanted.

I continue my walk, determined to come up with a reasonable list for my own kids. Yet it is a struggle, for I know that the gifts that have meant the most to me and that I would ask for today, are not even considered "real presents" by my children. I disagree. Genevieve's little house with a roof holding Santa and his sleigh made from business stationery rests on my dresser. She is six and her beautiful face fills the frame of my memory. Then Rodney moves into view. He is holding a sawed-off clothespin, colored with markers to resemble Superman. His four-year-old face is beaming and expectant as he lifts the ornament for me to see. Finally, Gabrielle joins my memory. Her gift card—made of iridescent foil cut into the shape of a snowflake and studded with fake pearls—is signed determinedly in blue pencil—first, middle and last names printed in capitals and surrounded by a big heart. I have saved these gifts, along with other keepsakes, in several journals, one for each child chronicling my pregnancy, their birth, and their childhood.

When I return home from my walk, I begin reading one journal, stopping at the pages that describe Genevieve's first week on this earth. The simple words pull me back in time. I continue to read, stopping to

When my children ask me again what I want for Christmas, I will say, "I have everything I need."

call her on the telephone so that I can read passages to her aloud. We laugh together and I am aware again of our closeness.

I open a second journal and I can hear Rodney's slightly hoarse voice of toddlerhood: "The moon is following us, Mommy. It gonna bite?" We have been riding in our car and he is worried that the moon shining through the window is chasing us home. I finger his little sketch on the page and I smile at the logic of his young mind. Oh, my boy.

A photograph in a third volume moves me back into Gabrielle's life at three year's of age. She has placed a photo in a handmade frame made in nursery school. In it, she is dancing with our poodle, Maxine. Gabrielle has red lipstick on her pouty mouth; Maxine is wearing a plaid dress with her front legs sticking out of the sleeves. I remember that day with the emotional clarity of present time.

The journal goes on for many pages more, when it suddenly ends and I am sad there isn't more to read, to re-experience. But I feel comforted somehow, allowing that the very writing of these simple events indicates that I realized the quicksilver nature of their childhoods and the value I placed on time spent with my children. Reading the details of their lives now serves to sharpen the broad experiences of my life into distinct moments filled with love and belonging. This knowledge is a gift beyond all others, one my children have given to me—that in their very presence, and by its virtue, the gift of fully experiencing my own life has been made possible.

As each autumn approaches I choose to see paths that cut through fallen leaves as proof that children will always be ahead of us, leading the way, and that if we will follow them, we will find once again the important gifts lost in time, gifts that come unwrapped, unbidden, but precious, nonetheless. When my children ask me again what I want for Christmas, I will say, "I have everything I need." It's true. All of life's gifts are already present in the fullness of this moment. Thank you, Genevieve, Rodney and Gabrielle.

With all my love,
Mama

Notes from Readers

Learn to make your own skeleton leaves, select the right type of glitter, or dry flowers in a microwave.

Skeletonize Your Own Leaves

In the Christmas 1996 issue, you displayed a skeleton leaf card. Where can I find the leaf used in this project? If I want to skeletonize the leaf myself, is there a solution that will remove the green part?

ALAN ZIMMERMAN
ROSLYN HEIGHTS, NY

Although we used store-bought skeleton leaves in that project, your question prompted us to find a way to skeletonize leaves, or dissolve the leaf's chlorophyll to reveal its delicate network of veins. After testing a variety of different methods, we recommend the home remedy offered by Beverly Plummer, author of *Earth Presents: How To Make Beautiful Gifts from Nature's Bounty* (Athenium, 1974). After picking fresh leaves, she suggests boiling them in a lye bath. Lye (sodium hydroxide), found in most soap-making supply stores, is an extremely caustic chemical and requires careful use. Make sure to work in a well-ventilated area and wear protective gloves and eyewear at all times.

We tested Plummer's skeletonizing method and found it successful with larger leaves; smaller ones tend to wrap around themselves. Start by pouring 1 quart water into a stainless steel pot, then slowly add 1 tablespoon of lye. (Be sure to use stainless steel; lye reacts with aluminum.) Place the leaves in the mixture and heat over a low setting. When the water and lye begin to boil, continue at a slow boil for 5 to 10 minutes. Watch the leaves carefully to determine when they are ready; they will begin to turn brown and "bleed" into the water. At this point, remove the leaves, rinse in cool water, then lay flat in a metal tray. They will be covered with a black, pulpy material that needs to be scraped away with an old, soft toothbrush. Take care not to rip the leaf's skeleton. After removing the pulpy material, lay the leaf flat, pin its sides down to prevent rolling, and let dry completely.

If you decide to buy skeleton leaves rather than make your own, Black Ink, of Boston, MA, sells a pack of 10 natural papel leaves or 5 fossil leaves for $3.50 per package. To order, write or call the store at 101 Charles Street, Boston, MA 02114; 617-723-3883.

Locating Glass Ball Ornaments Year-Round

Glass ball ornaments are always available right before Christmas, but I want to find these items year-round. Is there a source where I can buy them throughout the year, or at least well before December?

VEENA RAGHAVAN
KEW GARDENS, NY

We found a number of mail-order firms that can supply clear glass ball ornaments any time of the year. The National Artcraft Co., a manufacturer and importer in Twinsburg, OH, sells clear, blown glass ornaments in two sizes. A set of four round 3¼" balls retails for $8.25, while a box of six 2⅝" balls sells for $5.95. The ornaments come with gold-colored metal crowns and wire hangers. Contact the company for further information at 7996 Darrow Road, Twinsburg, OH 44087; 800-793-0152.

Eastern Art Glass, a mail-order source in Wyckoff, NJ, also sells a set of six 2⅜" balls for $10.95, or four 3⅛" balls for $12.95. Write or call for a free catalog at P.O. Box 341, Wyckoff, NJ 07481; 800-872-3458.

Since you know you'll be needing glass ornaments throughout the year, another idea is to buy bulk during post-holiday sales.

Software for Making Greeting Cards

I recently heard of a new software package from a company called DogByte that allows you make your own greeting cards and photo mats. Do you know anything about this package, how it operates, and whether it's worth the investment?

CHRISTOPHER BREESE
SANTA MONICA, CA

We located DogByte's new software package—Frame-It—and took it for a test ride. This is an excellent and virtually foolproof composing tool for craftspeople and amateur artists. Even young children can use the program with a little guidance. The results, however, depend in large part on the computer and printer you are using. Since the program is graphics intensive, the faster the computer's processor and the more memory on the machine, the better.

Frame-It can design picture frames, picture mats, personalized greeting cards, and matching envelopes. It simplifies the layout process by providing preconfigured templates in different styles for each item. These templates can be customized with additional components such as clip art and text. The results are perfect every time because the basic template cannot be altered, prohibiting mistakes in the layout. On the other hand, this also means that you are limited to DogByte's selection of styles and layouts; colors or sizes cannot be changed to accommodate odd-sized photographs or different color schemes. For most of us, however, this is an easy trade-off. The designs are beautiful and well composed, and they vary widely in style and theme, from cuddly and cute ("Animalia," frolicking puppies) to elaborate and gorgeous ("Florentine," richly colored arabesque scrolls).

The software's images are precise and well-defined, so the quality of the final output depends on the printer. A color laser printer will produce the best results. Not having such an option, we considered taking a disk to a copy center such as Kinko's for output. The program, however, only works when the software is loaded on the machine connected to the printer, so this wasn't possible. On a brighter note, however, the starter kit comes with samples of interesting papers, envelopes, and ribbons, so you can create unusual and fun greeting cards right away.

A Windows 3.1 or 95 version of the software retails for $49.99. The software is available at computer retailers such as COMP USA and Computer City as well as craft chains such as Michael's. For more information, contact the company at 800-936-4298.

Locating Clear Dinnerware

I love the look of decoupaged glassware. I am looking for a source of plain glass plates and platters, something like the Octime line by Arcoroc. My sources in this area have been depleted. Can you help?

CHRIS BLAIR
GERMANTOWN, TN

Like the glass plates used in "Decorative Painted Plates" (Spring 1997), octagon-shaped glass plates make wonderful frames for designs. We looked into retail locations that sell the Octime line by Arcoroc, well-known for its octagon shape. We found Durand Glass International of Millville, NJ, which produces but does not sell this line of glassware. The company does provide a detailed, national listing of retail stores that carry this product including Lechters, Michael's, and Walmart. To find the store nearest you, write or call Durand International, Wade Boulevard, Millville, NJ 08332; 609-825-5620.

Selecting a Styrofoam Cutter

I need to cut shapes, such as stars and moons, out of styrofoam. I've heard about styrofoam cutters and would like to try one. Can you direct me to a source?

DOROTHY NELSEN
GARFIELD, AR

Cutting styrofoam can be extremely messy and uneven if done with an electric knife or regular utensil. Unlike an electric knife, a styrofoam cutter melts into the styrofoam to form clean edges and smooth lines. (This will save you the time and hassle of picking up the small bits of styrofoam that flake off.)

Nasco Arts & Crafts carries the Wonder Cutter, a cordless, battery-operated hobby tool for $8.90, or a 13" high styrofoam cutter for $70.25. The company claims the Wonder Cutter can cut any shape within seconds using a small, heated wire. The styrofoam cutter sits on a cutting platform with a blade and is designed for larger pieces. For more information or to order a catalog, call or write Nasco, 901 Janesville Avenue, P.O. Box 901, Fort Atkinson, WI 53538-0901; 800-558-9595.

Sizing up Glitter Grades
I'm working on a glitter project and the glitter I'm using seems very rough. What are the differences between the various types of glitter sold in craft stores?
ANN DWYER
MISSOURI CITY, KS

Choosing the right glitter for your project often depends on your taste in color, sheen, and size. Although many glitters look similar when viewed in a container, there are very real differences in the size and shape of the individual particles.

In general, there are three categories (by size) of glitter: large, regular or fine, and, most recently, microfine. Microfine glitter is half the size of fine glitter, and is less reflective, meaning it shows more of the color of the glitter and the object it covers. According to Jones Tones, Inc., a producer of glitter in Pueblo, CO, use microfine glitter for a more sophisticated finish, since the extremely fine particles cover the surface more evenly and completely than larger grades.

Regular and large glitter particles reflect light with more intensity per particle, giving the project a reflective, slightly more choppy surface. Regular glitter, the most common type found in stores, can be used to cover any project. Large glitter is more confetti-like in appearance; the particles can be hexagon, star, oval, or square in shape.

As for your glitter appearing rough, it may be a metallic glitter. Glitter made from metal gives a bright sheen to projects, but that may not be your goal. If so, switch to glitter made from mylar polyester (plastic). Whatever type you use, be sure to read the label closely and follow the manufacturer's instructions.

Make Your Own Antique Fabric
I recently stained napkins with tea, and I love them. Now, I want to try giving an antique look to my tablecloth. What do you suggest?
JEN WRIGHT
BOSTON, MA

We suggest a method used by costume designers to create authentic-looking materials for theatrical productions. All you need to antique your own natural-fiber fabric (vs. polyester fabrics, which don't dye well) is fabric dye, according to Virginia Aldous, an assistant costume designer for the Huntington Theater Company in Boston, Massachusetts. Commercial dyes sold in grocery stores, such as Rit or Tintex, will work well.

The dye color that you choose to buy depends on the color of the article you want to antique and how strong an effect you want. For instance, if the tablecloth is white, pick a tan or cream dye, suggests Aldous. If the cloth is a dark color, then dye with its complimentary color (the opposite color on the color wheel). For a bright red fabric, for example, she would use a light green dye.

To make the dye bath, prepare a half-and-half solution of dye and water in a large container. Set the tablecloth aside. Start by testing scraps of the material to determine the length of time and number of dips to get the vintage effect you want. Remember, the longer the fabric stays in the dye, the darker it will become. When you achieve what you want, wash the fabric in cold water until the water runs clear, then heat-set the color in your dryer on a high/hot setting.

Like all natural fabrics, the tablecloth will shrink, so be sure to begin with a larger piece than needed. Also, wash the tablecloth before you dye it in order to remove any finish on the fabric.

Pressing Flowers in a Microwave
I'm looking for a fast and easy way to press flowers. Can you help?
DEBORAH RANGLEY
BURLINGTON, VT

We recently tested a new product on the market called Microfleur, which is designed to dry flowers in just seconds using a special press and a microwave.

We tested the product with a carnation, a mum, and a daisy. Each flower was placed in the "pack," a press-like device containing two plates and two heavy felt pads. Following the manufacturer recommendations, we microwaved the flowers for 20 seconds in a 900W microwave on a normal setting. The flowers were not completely dry after 20 seconds, so we put them in for another 15 seconds at the same setting. Each flower came out of the pack dry. The mum and the carnation stayed vibrant and fresh-looking but the white daisy, although still bright white, appeared brown along one edge from overheating.

The process is fast and easy, but you have to be careful with exposure time. Like any technique that deals with delicate materials, timing, practice, and patience are important.

Microfleur is available through mail-order. The press comes in two sizes, a 5" square for $21.95, or a 9" square for $35.95 (shipping and handling charges range from $3 to $5). For more information, write or call Microfleur, 1281 Kimmerling Road #5-265, Gardnerville, NV 89410; 888-883-5387.

Finding the Pop for Christmas Crackers
My friends and I have searched high and low for Christmas cracker "snaps," the things used to make the pop noise. Do you know of any company that sells them in the United States?
CATHERINE CAMPAIGNE
BERKELEY, CA

Christmas crackers are a wonderful way to add to the holiday festivities. Crackers are made of crepe paper, cardboard, tape, decorative ribbon, and a snapping device. They are usually filled with candy, gifts, or written riddles that "pop" out when the cracker is opened with a quick pull. All of the materials are easily found, except for the snap that makes the surprise bang. We checked with a large number of retailers and manufacturers, but couldn't find a source in the United States that sells cracker snaps in bulk. We also contacted Hawkins by Post, in Norfolk, England, a country known for this long-time holiday tradition. Due to exporting laws, however, the company is not allowed to transfer these "explosive" cracker snaps to the United States.

To solve this dilemma locally, check local gimmick or joke stores for old string joke poppers—anything that makes a snap sound when the cracker opens. Party supply stores also sell Christmas cracker kits, which combine all the necessary materials, including snaps, into one package.

Artificial Outdoor Topiaries
I would like to make a large, outdoor topiary that will withstand weather. Would an artificial material work well, or do I have to use live boxwood or other evergreen?
BEVERLY C. THORINGTON
DANVILLE, IA

An outdoor topiary needs to be strong, sturdy, and durable for all weather conditions. Even though it stands outside, your construction options aren't limited. Florists and gardeners say either real or artificial materials are compatible with the outdoors. In our experience, however, we prefer using live boxwood or evergreen to artificial alternatives. Although it requires more attention, a live topiary has a natural durability in changing weather. Winter is the main concern, when a topiary should be either kept indoors or protected with plastic.

Maintaining a live topiary with pruning, watering, and fertilizing takes time. But maintenance is relatively easy with boxwood and evergreen. For information on how to maintain and construct a live topiary, check out *Quick and Easy Topiary and Green Sculpture* (Storey Communications, Inc., 1996), by Jenny Hendy. The book details the many styles of pruning and using chicken wire to mold shapes. ◆

ATTENTION READERS

Need advice on a craft or home decorating project?

Drop us a line, and we'll find the answer. Although we can't respond to every letter we receive, we will try to publish those letters with the widest appeal. Please include your name, address, and a daytime telephone number with your question. Write to:

Notes from Readers
Handcraft Illustrated
17 Station Street
Brookline, MA 02146

Quick Tips

PUMPKIN CANDLE
For less scorching, cut a Halloween pumpkin at the bottom instead of the top and set it over the candle. The candle sits low in the cavity, making the top inside of the pumpkin less likely to burn. Thanks to Susan Donohue, of Plattsburgh, New York, for this suggestion.

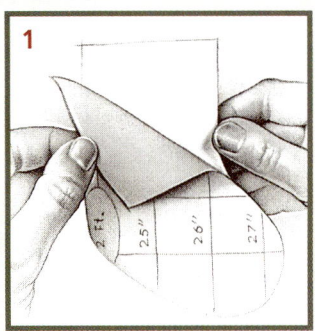 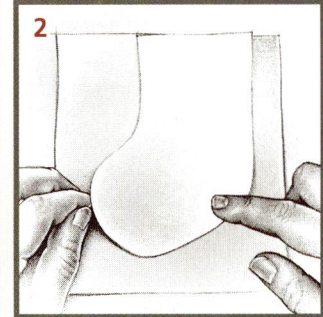
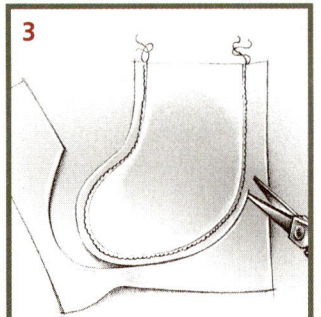 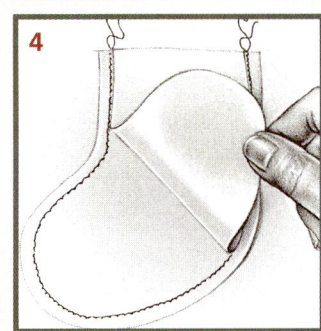

SEWING MULTIPLES
Robin Jaslow, of Westfield, New Jersey, shares her method for sewing multiples from the same pattern.

1. Make the basic pattern from contact paper. Peel off the backing...

2. ...and press the pattern on a double layer of fabric.

3. Machine-stitch along the pattern outline, then trim off the excess.

4. Peel off the pattern to reuse it.

ATTENTION READERS

Calling All Crafters
We're always in need of unique quick tips. Do you have a craft, sewing, or decorating technique that saves time or money? Send it our way! We'll give you a one-year complimentary subscription for each Quick Tip that we publish. Send your tip to:

Quick Tips
Handcraft Illustrated
17 Station Street
Brookline, MA 02146

Please include your name, address, and daytime phone number with all correspondence.

ILLUSTRATION:
Harry Davis

 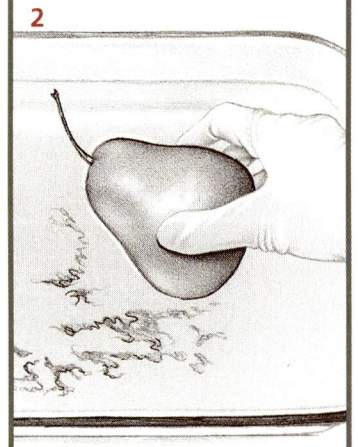 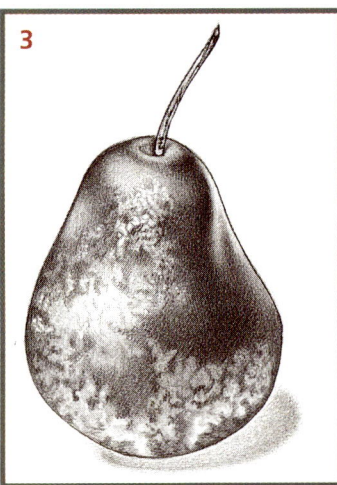

QUICK GOLD LEAFING
Jeanne Graham, of Baltimore, Maryland, shares this quick method of "gold leaf" antiquing.

1. Spray a small amount of metallic gold paint into a pan of water.

2. Dab the item to be gilded onto the water surface. The paint that adheres will form a speckled or webbed pattern.

3. Let the section dry, then repeat as necessary to coat the entire piece.

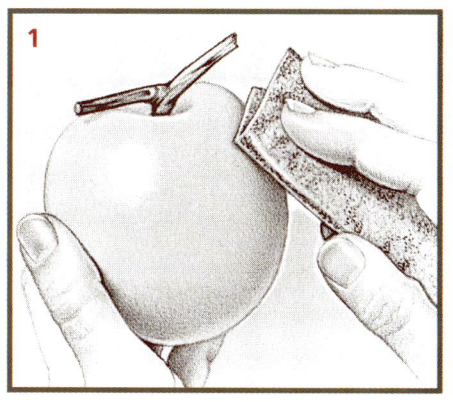 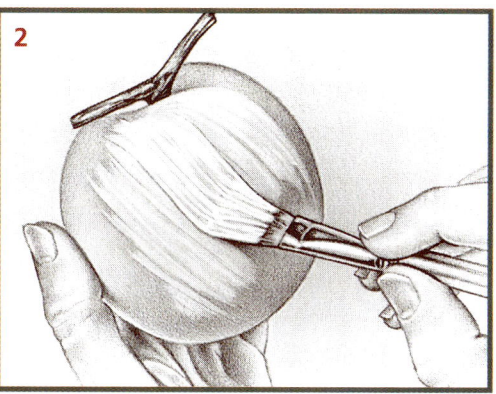

PAINTING ON PLASTIC
Acrylic craft paints don't always stick to plastic surfaces. Angeline Dziwirski, of Eastpointe, Michigan, tells how to improve the bond. Before you paint, follow the sequence below or try either method alone.

1. **Sand the plastic with medium-grit sandpaper to roughen up the surface and give it some tooth.**

2. **Seal the plastic by brushing on a light coat of white craft glue.**

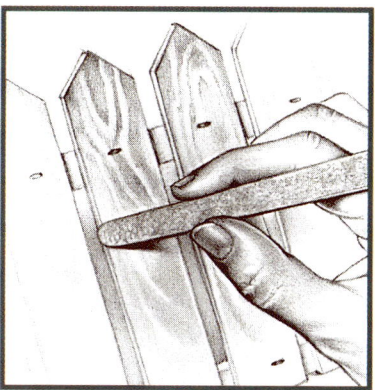

SANDING TIGHT SPOTS
Use an emery board to sand awkward nooks and crannies, writes Barbara Niese, of Marion, Ohio.

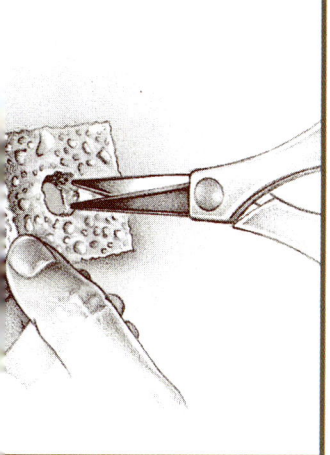 

PREVENTING SPILLS
Use a sponge base to prevent small bottles or vials from spilling, writes Lynn Siedelmann, of Aurora, Colorado.

1. **Cut an opening in a piece of sponge.**

2. **Fit the vial in the opening. The sponge will hold the vial upright even if accidently tipped.**

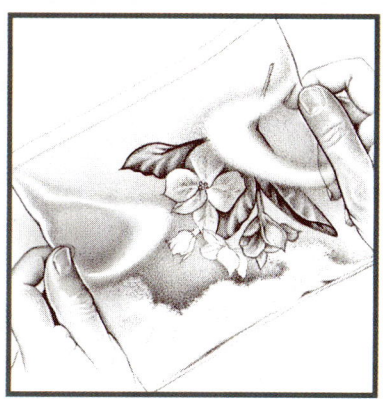

CLEANING SILK FLOWERS
Looking for a quick and easy way to clean the dust off your silk flowers? Simply place them in a plastic zipper-lock bag, add some salt, and shake gently, writes Rachel Pillar, of Saint John, U.S. Virgin Islands.

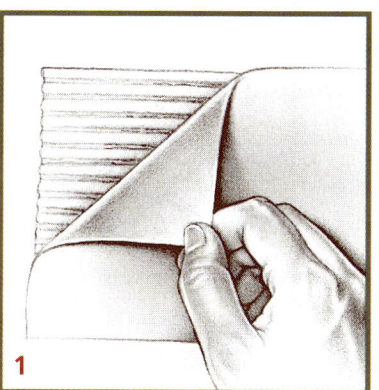 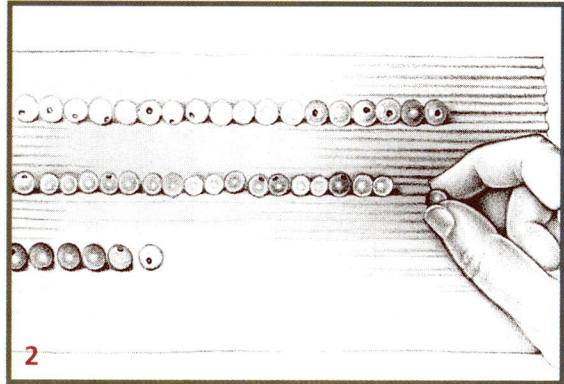

FAILPROOF BEAD STRINGING
Use this tip to keep beads lined up in their proper stringing order. Thanks to Kim Goldsberry, of Cleveland Heights, Ohio, for this suggestion.

1. **Peel off the outer layer from a piece of corrugated cardboard.**

2. **Line up the beads in the grooves.**

SCENTED HANDMADE PAPER
You can add subtle fragrance to your handmade papers by sprinkling strong-scented herbal tea (such as Celestial Seasonings) into the slurry. This tip comes from Pamela Swan, of Roseau, Minnesota.

Quick Home Accents

Create a modern decorating idea with an old material: Transform pressed tin into collars for pillar or votive candles.

TIN CANDLE COLLARS

COLOR PHOTOGRAPHY: **Carl Tremblay**

DESIGN AND STYLING: **Ritch Holben**

These pierced tin candle collar are made from pressed wall and ceiling tiles, designs primarily Victorian in style. The collar can be used at the base of a pillar candle, or surrounding a votive candle. Tin is inexpensive, malleable, and forgiving. It can be used as is or patinated to resemble aged copper, bronze, or rusted iron.

To make the collar, purchase a 4-foot section of pressed tin cornice with an embossed design; such tin is available at builder's supply stores or architectural restoration outlets. Wear heavy gloves when cutting or working with tin, as the edges can be very sharp until finished. To determine the necessary length of metal sheet for the collar (you select the width when you purchase the tin), select a pillar candle, measure its circumference, and add 1". Cut the tin with tin snips. To punch the holes, place the sheet on a piece of scrap board for support, then use a large nail and a hammer to follow the pressed design. To finish the edges, move to the edge of a work table and hammer a ½" lip on each short side of the sheet over onto itself. Using a sturdy can as a base, shape the collar with a rubber hammer. Interlock the bent edges, then gently tap the seams tight to hold the edges together. ◆

The Perfect Gift

Assemble a custom greetings box using a variety of stationery store supplies.

THE WRITE GIFT

To encourage your friends or family to stay in touch, consider a gift with payback: the "Time Flies… Winter Greetings Box."

We started with a cigar box, available in a wide variety of shapes and sizes for as little as 50¢ at local tobacco shops.

To cover the cigar manufacturer's logo and decorate the box's cover, we created a multimedia collage. Our collection, revolving around the "time flies" theme, includes a poem, handwritten on paper with a deckled edge; blue sky and clouds cut from a magazine advertisement; snowflakes rubber-stamped using copper ink; and old clockwork hot-glued over a self-adhesive clock face.

Inside the box, we assembled all the materials necessary for the recipient to create his or her own personalized greeting cards—from stationery and a quill pen to a custom-made rubber stamp with the family name and year on it.

Make the contents as elaborate as you like; we added blank cards and envelopes, postage stamps, rubber-stamping pads, additional rubber stamps, sealing wax, and an initial seal. Or, personalize the contents to the talents and interests of the recipient. ◆

COLOR PHOTOGRAPHY:
Carl Tremblay

DESIGN AND STYLING:
Ritch Holben

FALL 1997 • HANDCRAFT ILLUSTRATED   7

BOXES

Foolproof Glass Mosaic

Create a unique pavé box with glass gems and tile grout, then finish the design with whitewash and brass hardware.

🌶 BY ELIZABETH CAMERON

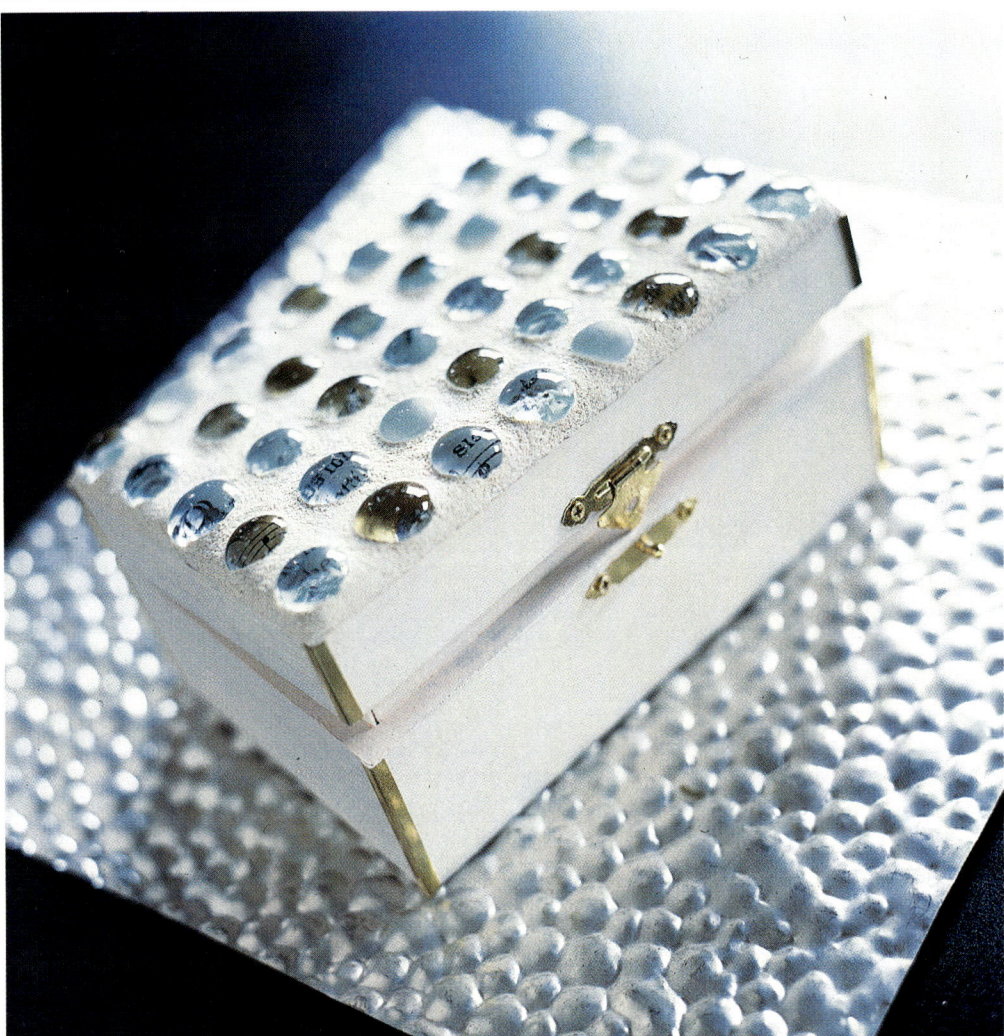

You can personalize your pavé gift box by magnifying invitations, ticket stubs, letters, maps, or other printed memorabilia. If the paper is too thick to glue in place, peel off the extra plies or make photocopies.

COLOR PHOTOGRAPHY:
Carl Tremblay

ILLUSTRATION:
Michael Gellatly

STYLING:
Ritch Holben

MATERIALS

- Wooden box with hinged lid, approximately 4" x 6" x 3" high
- 50 clear (and/or lightly tinted) glass flat marble "gems"
- Printed matter (books, sheet music, etc.)
- Two 10" x 1/8" brass right-angle strips
- Miniature brass catch
- White exterior sanded grout (at least 1 cup)
- 2 ounces white acrylic craft paint
- 2 ounces metallic gold acrylic craft paint
- Instant coffee
- Armour Etch etching cream
- Decoupage medium
- Matte acrylic sealer
- Aleene's Thick Designer Tacky glue

You'll also need:

1/4" disposable brush; 1/2" soft, flat brush; 1" foam brush; latex gloves; watercolor palette; disposable pint container; small paint stick; measuring cup; mug; teaspoon; 150-grit sandpaper; hacksaw; metal file; scissors; fine-tip permanent marker; pencil; newspaper; newsprint; scrap cardboard; paper towels; soft, dry cloth; and hammer or screwdriver

Other items, if necessary:
access to photocopier (for copying printed matter).

THIS PAVÉ GIFT BOX MIXES SEVERAL media—a plain wooden box, paper cutouts, glass gems, brass trim, paint, and tile grout—for a strikingly beautiful effect.

The construction technique is simple and straightforward. Start by cutting out paper squares containing words or phrases, graphical symbols or musical notes, then glue them onto the bottom of transparent glass gems. Next, glue those papered gems, as well as frosted and painted ones, to the top of a wooden box. Third, create a smooth surface on the box top by grouting the spaces in between the gems. Last, whitewash the box, add a brass catch, and attach brass trim at the corners.

When shopping for materials, keep these points in mind. Choose a wooden box in which the lower box is no more than 1/2" deeper than the lid. This is important because the gems and grout add significant weight to the box lid, and a box with a fairly deep lid will not tip backward when opened. When selecting glass gems, choose those that are clear or lightly tinted. This is because light will pass through the gems from only one direction on the finished box (the bottom of each gem will be covered with paper, and the sides blocked by grout), causing dark-colored gems (i.e., green or blue) to remain dark on the box top. Lastly, for the grout, choose an exterior sanded tile grout in order to enhance the earthy feel of the box.

Elizabeth Cameron is a freelance writer living in Brighton, Massachusetts.

INSTRUCTIONS

1. *Count and sort gems.* Arrange gems on box lid in grid formation, 1/8" to 1/4" apart, to determine count needed to fill surface (*see* illustration A, next page). Remove gems from lid and set aside; add two or three additional gems for design flexibility.

2. *Frost and paint gems.* Set five or six gems from step 1 on scrap cardboard. Following manufacturer's instructions and wearing gloves, use 1/4" brush to spread etching cream across top surface of gems. Let set 10 minutes, then rinse gems under running water to reveal frosted surface. Repeat process to frost reverse side. Discard cardboard and brush; remove gloves. Select three or four gems from step 1. Using ½" soft flat brush, paint flat underside using gold paint; color will be visible when gem is viewed from above. Set frosted and painted gems aside.

3. *Select and prepare images.* Place clear gem from step 1 on printed page. Slowly move gem over surface to magnify different images, select certain words, etc. Pencil squares around interesting images, then cut out square with scissors (illustration B). Cut one image per clear gem. Place approximately one-half of images face up on several layers of newspaper. Dissolve 1 teaspoon instant coffee in mug of hot tap water. To create antique appearance, use foam brush to apply coffee wash over images. Let dry 30 minutes.

4. *Glue images to gems.* Lay images face up on newsprint. Using foam brush, apply thin coat decoupage medium across face of one image. Press one clear gem flat side down on image (illustration C), turn gem over, and press paper from flat side to adhere and remove all air bubbles. Repeat process for all images and gems. Wash brush. Let gems dry at least 1 hour. Using scissors, trim off excess paper even with each gem edge (illustration D).

5. *Glue gems to box.* Set box on work surface with hinges at back. Arrange frosted, gold, and clear gems on box lid in grid formation as in step 1. Rearrange stones as needed so all words and letters face you and similar stones are not adjacent to one another. (You will have a few stones left over.) Once design is set, lift one gem, apply decoupage medium to underside, and press gem back into position until adhered. Repeat process to glue down all gems into position (illustration E). Let dry overnight.

6. *Apply grout between gems.* Put on gloves and set box on several layers of newspaper. In disposable container, use paint stick to stir 1 cup dry grout into ⅛ cup water, or follow manufacturer's proportions and instructions. Let grout set up to 5 minutes or until stiff, firm, and gritty. Spread grout over gem-covered lid using gloved finger. Poke grout down between gems, first tracing all long rows, then all short rows. Remove excess grout; keep working areas between gems until grout surface is smooth and round gem tops are visible. At lid edges, mold grout flush to surface. Let dry 30 minutes. To remove grout film, polish tops of gems with soft, dry cloth. Let dry overnight, then polish gem tops again.

7. *Whitewash box.* Sand sides and bottom of box lightly with woodgrain to remove stray grout, then remove dust with damp paper towel. To make whitewash, dilute 1 teaspoon white paint with water until milky. Using foam brush, apply wash to outside of box, let dry 20 minutes, then open box and apply wash to inside. Prop box open and let dry 1 hour. Using foam brush, apply sealer to all painted surfaces.

8. *Attach brass fixings.* Fit brass right-angle strip onto one box corner, lower edges even. Using marker, make tick marks on brass strip at box/lid crack and lid top. Saw brass strip at marks. Repeat process to mark and cut eight brass pieces total. File sawed ends to remove burrs. Using glue, affix each brass strip to appropriate box corner; remove oozing glue with damp paper towel. Attach catch over box/lid crack using hardware (nails or screws) provided by manufacturer (illustration F). ◆

HISTORICAL TIDBIT

The name of this box originates with the french verb paver (to pave). Pavé is used to identify a surface that has been paved.

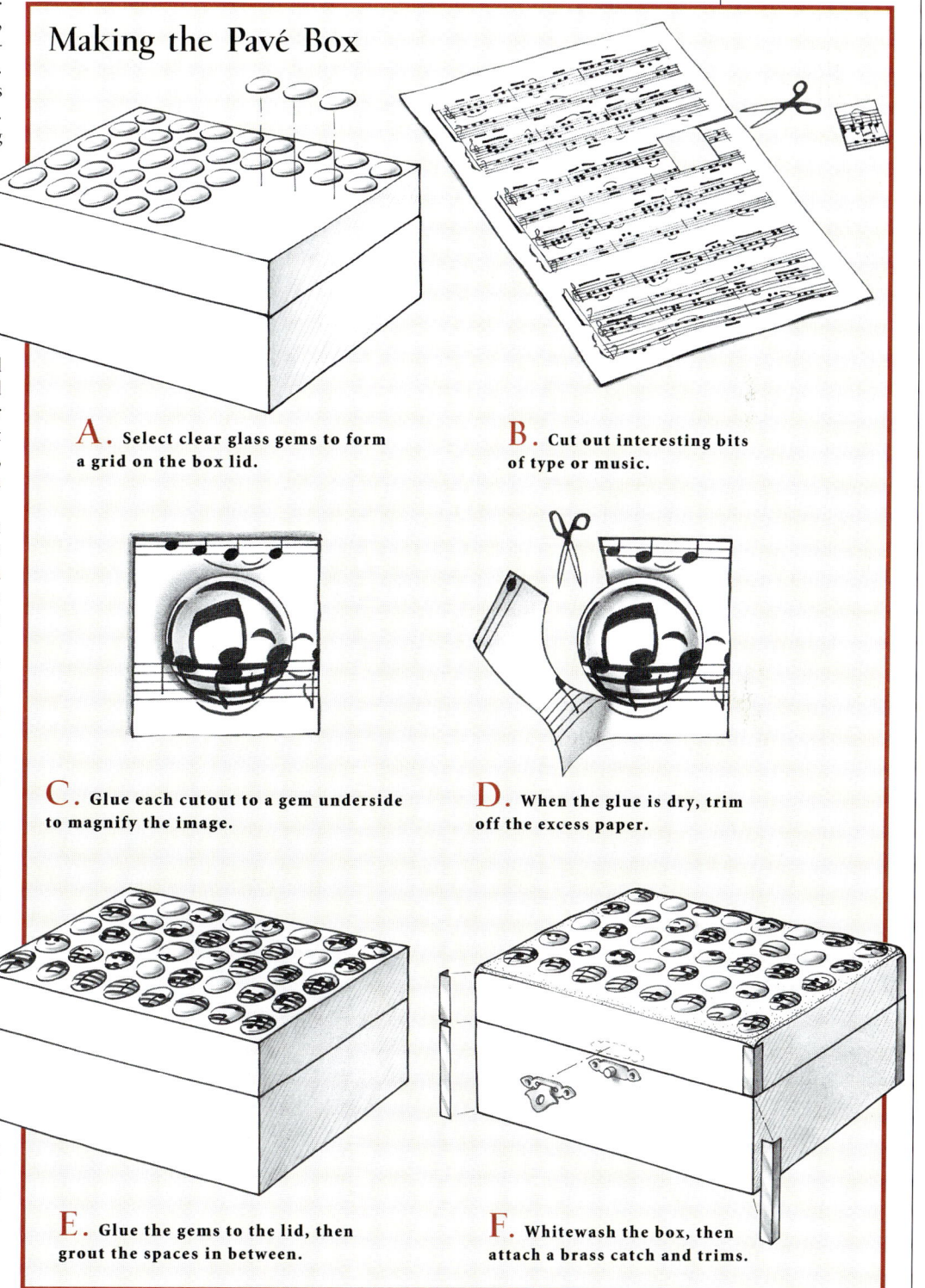

Making the Pavé Box

A. Select clear glass gems to form a grid on the box lid.

B. Cut out interesting bits of type or music.

C. Glue each cutout to a gem underside to magnify the image.

D. When the glue is dry, trim off the excess paper.

E. Glue the gems to the lid, then grout the spaces in between.

F. Whitewash the box, then attach a brass catch and trims.

MIXED MEDIA

Faux Enamel Coffee- and Teapots
Create these miniatures using decoupage medium and giftwrap.

BY MICHIO RYAN

For variation on these designs, mix and match the elements. Use the coffeepot lid on a teapot, for instance, or use the teapot's spout on the coffeepot.

COLOR PHOTOGRAPHY:
Carl Tremblay

ILLUSTRATION:
Michael Gellatly

SILHOUETTE PHOTOGRAPHY:
Daniel van Ackere

STYLING:
Ritch Holben

MATERIALS
Yields 2 teapots and 1 coffeepot

- Giftwrap
- 4 ounces Crayola Model Magic lightweight modeling dough
- 11" x 11" piece 1-ply chipboard (e.g., empty cereal or cracker boxes)
- 5" x 7" piece 2-ply chipboard
- Four 1/8" brass screw eyes*
- Two 6mm jump rings*
- 2 ounces DecoArt Dazzling Metallics Glorious Gold acrylic paint
- Plaid Royal Coat Decoupage Finish
- Aleene's Thick Designer Tacky glue
- Nylon thread

*For Swing-Handle Teapot

You'll also need:
teapot and coffeepot patterns (*see* page 42); X-Acto knife; steel ruler; self-healing cutting mat; scissors; manicure scissors; 2 tweezers; 100-grit sandpaper; 1/2"-wide soft flat brush; small round brush; needle; transfer paper; newsprint; masking tape; pencil; dinner plate; paper towels; and access to photocopier with enlarger.

Other items, if necessary:
file (for smoothing contact point on dough pieces).

SIMPLY PUT, REAL ENAMELED coffee or teapots cannot be made at home. You can create a very convincing miniature facsimile, however, with four basic craft materials: chipboard, giftwrap, decoupage medium, and modeling dough.

I started by making a three-dimensional chipboard pot using a flat pattern. To create the look of enamel, I covered the pot with giftwrap, followed by several layers of semiglossy decoupage medium. To complete the illusion, I made spouts, handles, lids, and feet from modeling dough, then painted them gold.

Chipboard makes the ideal substrate material for these pots because it is easy to cut and is quickly glued into a three-dimensional form with a smooth and bondable surface for decoupage. The resulting pot is also hollow, which makes for a lightweight ornament.

I attached the giftwrap to the chipboard teapot using decoupage medium. I tested several different brands of medium for this project, including Mod Podge and Accent's Clear Glaze, but in the end decided on Plaid's Royal Coat Decoupage Finish. This decoupage medium levels reasonably well and dries to a semigloss sheen.

To make the lids, spouts, handles, and feet, I used Crayola Model Magic lightweight modeling dough. This dough's whipped texture translates into very lightweight modeled parts. If the spout and/or handles were modeled from a heavier clay, such as Sculpey or Fimo, they would make the teapots top-heavy. In addition, the Model Magic dough remains water-soluble even when dry, meaning you can easily touch up dents, wrinkles, or fingerprints using a moist finger.

INSTRUCTIONS
Making the Side-Handle Teapot
1. *Cut chipboard and paper.* Photocopy teapot body and side strip patterns (*see* page 42). Lay side strip pattern on 1-ply chipboard perpendicular to chipboard grain, slip transfer paper underneath, and tape down. Trace outline using pencil and ruler. Remove pattern and transfer paper. Transfer two body outlines to 2-ply chipboard in same way. Cut out all three pieces with scissors. Using pattern as reference, score dashed line on side strip using X-Acto knife, cutting mat, and ruler. Remove several laminated layers, leaving behind thin paper tab for gluing, on "wrong" (non-smooth) side of chip-

board. For each chipboard piece, cut corresponding piece from giftwrap approximately ¼" larger all around. Set giftwrap cutouts aside.

2. *Assemble chipboard teapot.* To render chipboard side strip more flexible, hold it flat against counter or tabletop, perpendicular to edge and smooth side up. Slowly pull free end down and off edge, curling strip as you go. Lay strip concave side up. Run bead of glue on each long edge and on tab. Set a teapot body on middle of each edge, then roll strip up around bodies from both sides, following contours (*see* illustration A, below). Overlap and glue down paper tab at top. For temporary hold as glue dries, apply bits of masking tape where needed. Let dry at least 1 hour, then remove tape.

3. *Sand and seal teapot.* Using manicure scissors, trim off any strip edges that jut beyond teapot sides. Sand joints smooth. To seal pot against warping, smooth very thin coat decoupage medium over entire surface with fingertip. Set teapot on washable surface and let dry 1 hour. If necessary, resand and reseal.

4. *Model handle, spout, lid, and feet.* Knead approximately ½ ounce dough until warm, soft, and pliable. To shape pieces, work on dinner plate or similar smooth, hard surface. For side handle, roll ¾" ball into 4" sausage, taper one end, and bend into a "C." Wind tapered end into tight curlicue (illustration B). For spout, shape ¾" ball into 2½"-long cone, bend cone into gently undulating "S," and snip off tip with scissors (illustration C). For lid, roll one ¾" ball and two ⅜" balls. Compress ¾" ball and one ⅜" ball into rounded disks and stack them. Shape remaining ball into teardrop and set on top (illustration D). For feet, roll four pea-sized balls. Referring to illustration F, press all pieces onto teapot. To eliminate cracks or nicks in dough pieces, rub wet finger over surface until smooth. Let pieces dry in position on teapot for several hours or until dough forms slightly stiff shell. Remove pieces from teapot and set aside. Let all pieces dry 24 hours.

5. *Glue giftwrap to chipboard teapot.* Lay giftwrap cutouts from step 1 face up on newsprint. Using flat brush, apply very thin coat of decoupage medium to each one, brushing out beyond edges. Let dry 30 minutes. Turn cutouts face down. Brush medium on each teapot body cutout and corresponding surfaces of chipboard. Press cutouts against chipboard and rub gently to remove air bubbles; let dry 30 minutes. Trim cutout edges even with chipboard all around (illustration E). Repeat process to apply giftwrap side strip to chipboard teapot; overlap strip ends at bottom of teapot.

6. *Join and paint dough pieces.* Glue dry dough handle, spout, lid, and feet made in step 4 to teapot (illustration F). If pieces do not fit teapot snugly, sand or file contact point as needed. If lid pieces have separated, glue them together. Let glue dry 30 minutes. Using flat brush, apply thick layer of decoupage medium to dough pieces; let dry 30 minutes. Brush on second layer; let dry 1 hour. Using small brush and gold paint, paint all dough pieces. Let dry 20 minutes. Apply second coat if needed.

7. *Attach hanging cord.* Thread needle with 8" length of nylon thread. Draw needle and thread through lid and tie thread ends together.

Making the Swing-Handle Teapot

1. *Cut chipboard and paper.* Same as Side-Handle Teapot, step 1.

2. *Assemble chipboard teapot.* Same as Side-Handle Teapot, step 2.

3. *Sand and seal teapot.* Same as Side-Handle Teapot, step 3.

4. *Model handle, spout, lid, and feet.* Same as Side-Handle Teapot, step 4, except model top-mounted swing handle instead of side handle: Roll ¾" ball into 3" sausage, taper both ends until sausage is 5" long, and bend into an upside-down "U." Wind each tapered end into tight curlicue (illustration G). Hold handle over teapot and refine arc to fit.

5. *Glue giftwrap to chipboard teapot.*

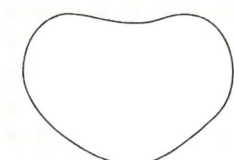

PATTERNS

See page 42 for pattern pieces and enlargement instructions.

DESIGNER'S TIP

If you make these teapots for use as Christmas ornaments, consider adding some extra sparkle to your giftwrap. You can easily add small dots or stars, for instance, using gold paint and a very fine brush.

Assembling the Side-Handle Teapot

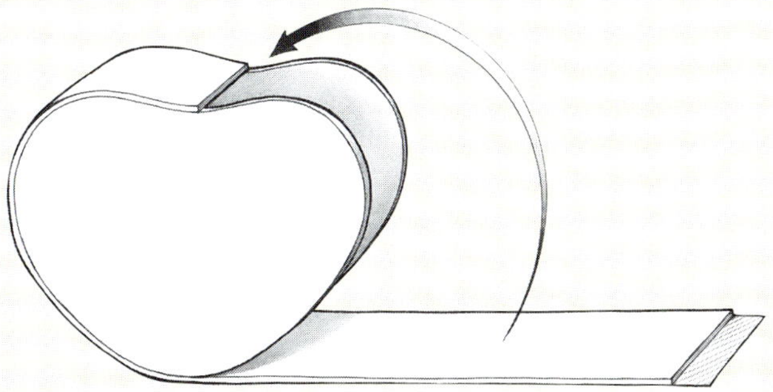

A. Glue the chipboard pieces together.

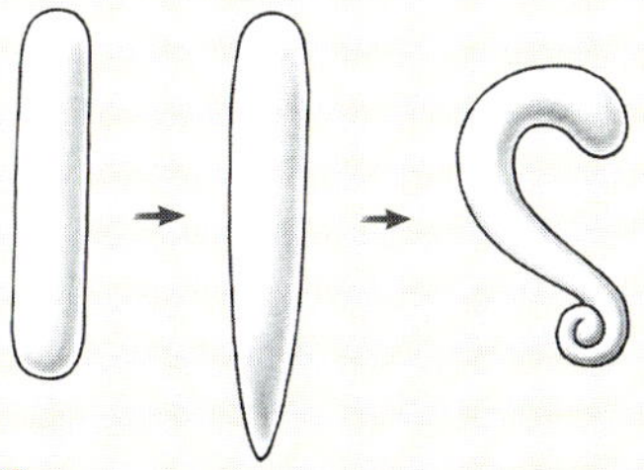

B. From modeling dough, make a side handle,...

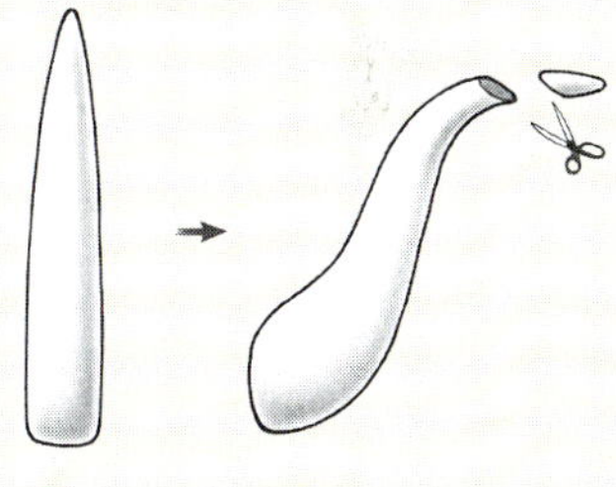

C. a spout,...

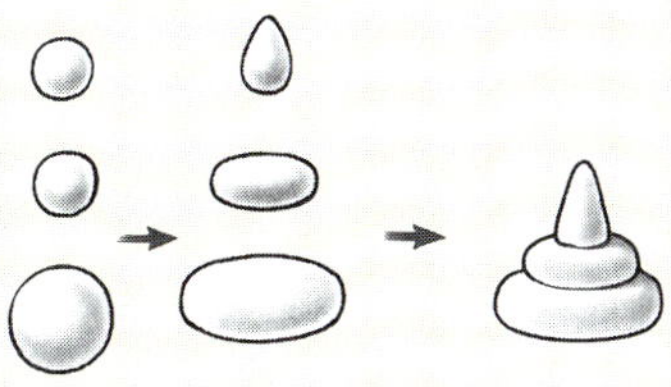

D. and a teapot lid.

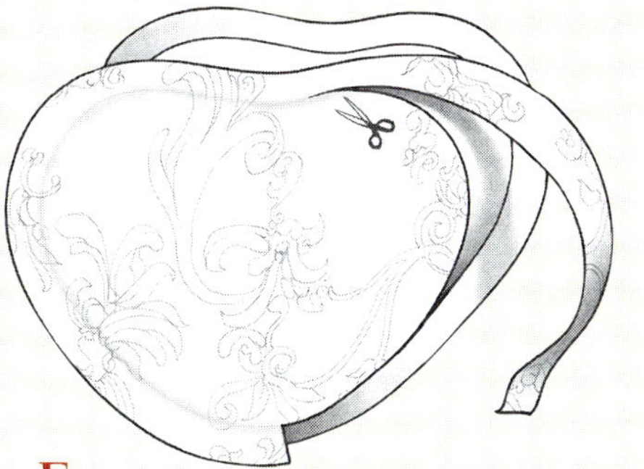

E. Glue giftwrap to the chipboard base and trim the edges.

F. Glue the modeled dough pieces to the teapot.

MIXED MEDIA

Making the Swing-Handle Teapot

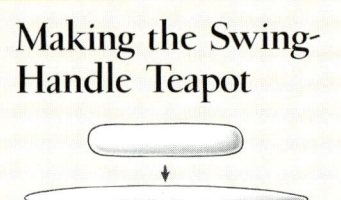

G. Model a swing handle instead of a side handle.

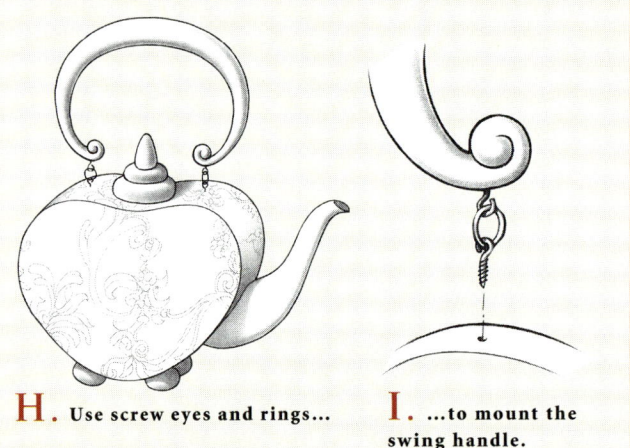

H. Use screw eyes and rings...

I. ...to mount the swing handle.

Same as Side-Handle Teapot, step 5.

6. *Join and gild spout, lid, and feet.* Same as Side-Handle Teapot, step 6. For swing handle instructions, proceed to step 7.

7. *Paint and join swing handle.* Using illlustration H as reference, pierce hole at each end of swing handle with needle. Hold handle in position above pot and pierce two corresponding holes in pot. Squeeze dot of glue over each hole, then push screw eye through glue into hole. Wipe off excess glue with damp paper towel. Seal swing handle with two coats decoupage medium and paint gold as in "Making the Side-Handle Teapot," step 6. To attach handle, join screw eyes with jump rings, using two pairs of tweezers to open and close rings (illustrations H and I). Tie 8" length of nylon thread to swing handle for hanging cord.

Making the Coffeepot

1. *Cut chipboard and paper.* Photocopy coffeepot pattern (*see* page 42). Lay pattern on 1-ply chipboard so arrow runs along chipboard grain. Slip transfer paper underneath and tape down. Trace straight solid and dashed lines with ruler and pencil. Trace curving lines freehand. Remove pattern and transfer paper. Using X-Acto knife, mat, and steel ruler, score dash lines. Cut out with scissors on solid lines. Using one "arm" of chipboard as template, cut four corresponding pieces from giftwrap each approximately ¼" larger all around than arm. Cut one 1⅜" square from giftwrap. Set giftwrap cutouts aside.

2. *Assemble chipboard coffeepot.* To render chipboard arms more flexible, hold each one flat against counter or tabletop, perpendicular to edge and smooth side up. Slowly pull free end down and off edge, curling arm as you go. When all four arms are curled, turn template over and repeat process from other side. To shape coffeepot, bend chipboard on score lines, fold arms up, and manipulate so curved edges meet (illustration J). Run a bead of high-tack glue on each edge; hold middle section with tape, if necessary, until glue dries (illustration K). Let dry at least 1 hour, then remove tape.

3. *Sand and seal coffeepot.* Same as Side-Handle Teapot, step 3.

4. *Model handle, spout, lid, and feet.* Knead approximately ½ ounce dough until warm, soft, and pliable. To shape pieces, work on dinner plate or similar smooth, hard surface. For handle and spout, use illustrations B and C, page 11, for reference, but keep pieces elongated to fit on coffeepot. For handle, roll ¾" ball into a 4" sausage, taper one end, and bend into a "C." Wind tapered end into tight curlicue. For spout, shape ⅞" ball into 4" sausage, bend sausage into gently undulating "S," and snip off tip with scissors. Referring to illustration N, press handle and spout onto opposite seams of coffeepot, touching down on outward curves. For lid, shape ¾" ball into 2½" cone. Taper pointed end and wind into tight curlicue. Press cone onto top of coffeepot to seal opening. Roll four pea-sized balls and press onto lid at each seam (illustration L). To eliminate cracks or nicks in dough pieces, rub wet finger over surface until smooth. Let pieces dry in position on coffeepot for several hours or until dough forms slightly stiff shell. Remove pieces from coffeepot and set aside. Let all pieces dry 24 hours.

5. *Glue giftwrap to coffeepot.* Lay giftwrap cutouts from step 1 face up on newsprint. Using flat brush, apply very thin coat of decoupage medium to each one, brushing out beyond edges. Let dry 30 minutes. Turn cutouts face down. Brush thin coat of medium on one coffeepot "arm" cutout and corresponding surface of chipboard coffeepot. Press cutout against chipboard and rub gently. Repeat process to glue arm cutout to opposite side of coffeepot; let dry 30 minutes. Trim cutout edges even with chipboard curved and top edges; fold lower edge onto pot bottom (illustration M). Repeat process to paper two remaining coffeepot sides. Using straight scissors, trim square piece slightly smaller than coffeepot bottom, then glue in place.

6. *Join and gild dough pieces.* Same as Side-Handle Teapot, step 6; refer to illustration N for position.

7. *Attach hanging cord.* Same as Side-Handle Teapot, step 7. ◆

Assembling the Coffeepot

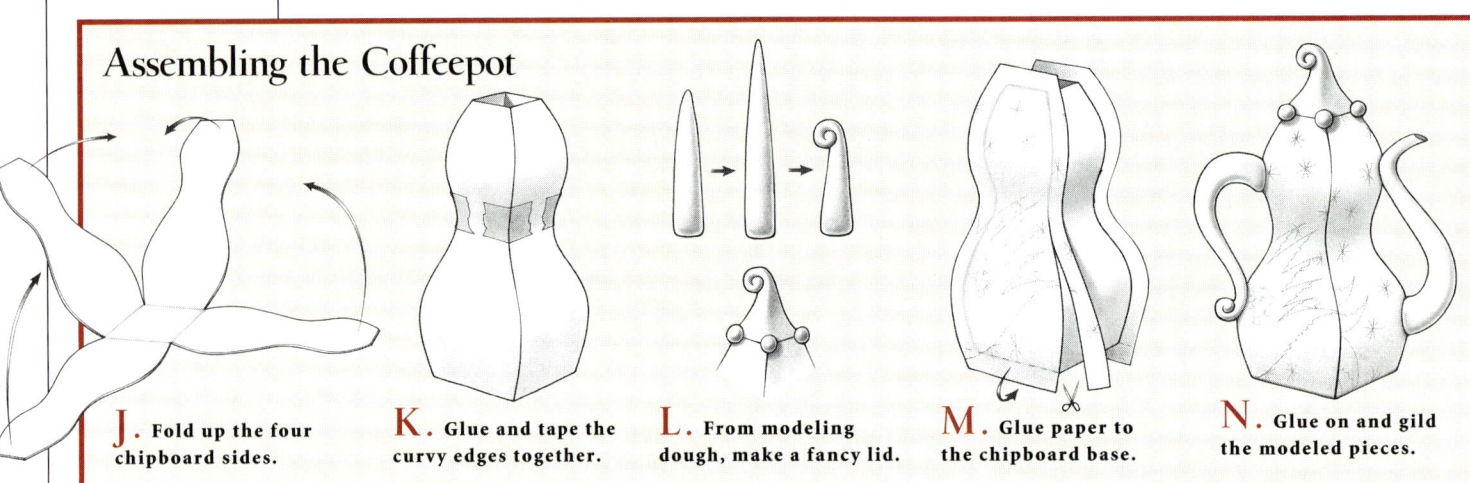

J. Fold up the four chipboard sides.

K. Glue and tape the curvy edges together.

L. From modeling dough, make a fancy lid.

M. Glue paper to the chipboard base.

N. Glue on and gild the modeled pieces.

PAPER CRAFTS

Miniature Post-It Books

Create a collection of tiny books using suede scraps and Post-It pads.

BY LILY FRANKLIN

MATERIALS
- Post-It notepads
- Scraps of colored suede or Ultrasuede
- Medium-weight colored paper
- Contact cement

You'll also need: liner patterns (*see* page 46); X-Acto knife; steel ruler; rotary cutter; self-healing cutting mat; quilter's acrylic grid ruler; disposable bristle brush; pencil; and newsprint.

The designs shown here create energy by using contrasting colors of suede, paper, and Post-It pads. For a coordinated design, match all three materials.

If you're looking for a great little stocking stuffer, this may be it. Each of these miniature books has a scrap of suede for a reusable cover and a Post-It pad for pages. When the pages run out, simply insert another pad.

Post-Its are available in a wide range of colors and sizes. I found pads in bright neon colors at an office-supply store; traditional yellow, blue, and pink pads are easily found in drugstores. Suede can be purchased in small quantities at craft stores such as Michael's; a 3" x 5" piece sells for about $3.

Lily Franklin is a designer and writer living in Albuquerque, New Mexico.

INSTRUCTIONS

1. *Organize materials.* For each book, select suede scrap for cover, colored paper for liner, and pad for pages.

2. *Cut liner.* Referring to diagrams (*see* page 46) for dimensions, lightly draft liner on colored paper. Lay colored paper on mat. Using steel ruler and X-Acto knife, cut out along solid lines and score lightly on dashed lines. Crease score lines. Repeat process to cut one liner per pad.

3. *Glue liner to suede.* Lay suede right side down on newsprint. Lay corresponding liner on newsprint with scored side facing up. Brush contact cement onto each piece; brush cement beyond liner edges. Let cement dry 3 to 5 minutes or until tacky. Set liner on suede and press gently to adhere. Wrap glued pieces around Post-It pad, liner on inside, and crease score lines to hug spine. Remove pad, lay cover on mat with liner facing up, and rub with palm of hand to create firm bond. Use rotary cutter and grid ruler to trim suede even with liner edge all around (*see* illustration A, left). Repeat process for each pad.

4. *Attach suede thong.* Mark two short lines on front cover (*see* diagrams for position). Slit lines by drawing X-Acto knife against steel ruler. Using rotary cutter and grid ruler, cut 3/16"-wide thong from suede for each book; cut 11" thongs for small books and 14" thongs for medium and large books. Draw thong through slit, and knot end (illustration B).

5. *Glue pad to cover.* Brush contact cement on inside spine of cover and spine of pad. Let dry until tacky (3 to 5 minutes) then press edges together (illustration C). Wind thong around book and tuck in end. Repeat process for each pad. ◆

Making the Book

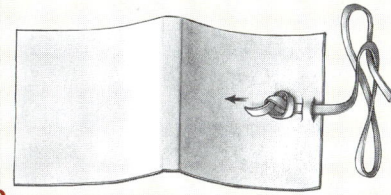

A. Glue a colored paper liner to the suede cover, then trim off the edges.

B. Slit the cover and attach a thong.

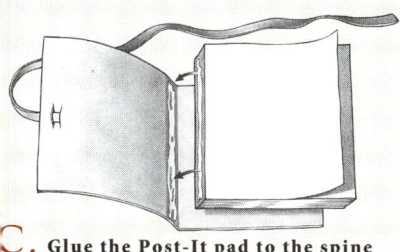

C. Glue the Post-It pad to the spine of the inside cover.

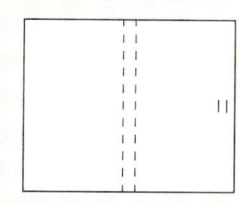

DIAGRAMS
See page 46.

COLOR PHOTOGRAPHY:
Carl Tremblay

ILLUSTRATION:
Michael Gellatly

STYLING:
Ritch Holben

LOW-SEW

Harvest Window Banner

Create a custom-fit autumn banner with minimal sewing. The trick: Use fabric paint to fuse the oak leaves in place.

🍂 BY MICHIO RYAN

MATERIALS

- 1 to 3 yards 45"-wide metallic gold sheer nylon fabric (see step 1)
- ⅜ yard 45"-wide sheer bronze lining fabric
- Sheer nylon remnants in any three fall colors (e.g., persimmon, plum, yellow-ochre, mustard, citron, rose madder, olive, or aubergine)
- Tulip Colorpoint fabric paints to match remnant colors
- Thread to match banner fabrics
- Spring tension rod to fit window opening
- 3- to 4-foot-long ⅜" dowel (see step 5)

You'll also need:
leaf patterns (*see* page 46); sewing machine; iron; rotary cutter; self-healing cutting mat; steel measuring tape; small handsaw; light table (or use window during daylight hours); tweezers; freezer paper; newspaper; masking tape; sharp scissors; permanent marker; pencil and paper; and access to photocopier with enlarger.

This window banner can be made to cover an entire window opening, or used to cover the lower half of a window with blinds in place.

COLOR PHOTOGRAPHY:
Carl Tremblay

ILLUSTRATION:
Mary Newell DePalma

STYLING:
Ritch Holben

THIS SEASONAL WINDOW BANNER, which features colorful autumn leaves scattered across a sheer, gold panel, requires minimal sewing. Although the leaves look as though they've been appliquéd in place, I actually used fabric paint to fuse them onto the background fabric.

The banner is designed to hang from an inexpensive tension rod much like a café curtain, except the banner is stretched taut to fill most of the window opening. I started by purchasing just over 2 yards of sheer gold nylon fabric for the background, then cut a series of contrasting leaves from different colors of the same fabric. I had originally intended to zigzag the leaves in place using clear monofilament thread, or to glue the leaves to the background using a lightweight spray adhesive. The first idea involved too much sewing, however, and the second idea would not survive laundering.

In designing the banner, however, I stumbled on my solution for attaching the leaves. I had planned on outlining the leaves using fabric paint in order to seal the fabric's raw edges and give the leaves a clear outline. Most fabric paints must be heat-cured in order to render them both permanent and washable. Even after they have dried to the touch, they are still heat-sensitive; if you press them with an iron, for instance, they will melt, then restiffen when cool. After some testing, I discovered that if I used an iron that was cool enough not to melt the sheer fabric but hot enough to melt the fabric paint, I could use the iron to fuse the leaf in place. The melted paint oozes through the mesh of the background piece, and when it cools it binds the two layers of fabric precisely at the edges of the cut leaf.

When purchasing fabric paint, look for pearlescent paint that matches the color of the leaf fabric as closely as possible. I recommend Tulip Colorpoint Bead Paint; the line offers a wide range of colors, a relatively stiff paint consistency, and fine tips on the dispenser. I tested ordinary craft paint extruded from a fine-tipped tube, but the paint was too watery and bled through the sheer fabric.

When tracing over the leaf designs with the fabric paint, move fairly quickly to ensure a fluid, even line. If you go too slowly, your hand may shake, causing the line to waver. The paint will come out in a thin stream, but the pressing process will flatten the lines, making the finished leaf outlines thicker.

INSTRUCTIONS

1. *Cut panel to size.* Measure window opening width and height (e.g., 42" x

68"). Purchase sheer fabric yardage 8" longer than window height (e.g., 68" plus 8" equals 76", or about 2⅛ yards). Subtract ½" from original window width and 1" from window height to determine finished panel size (e.g., 41½" x 67"). Add 2" to finished panel width and 6" to finished panel length to determine cut panel size (e.g., 43½" x 73"). Jot down all dimensions. Using cutter and self-healing cutting mat, cut panel from sheer yardage to match cut panel size (e.g., 43½" x 73"). Cut two strips from lining fabric that measure the finished panel width by 6" long (e.g., 41½" x 6").

2. *Sew sheer panel with channels.* Press one long edge of each lining strip ½" to wrong side. Lay panel wrong side up. Center lining strips along top and bottom edges, so panel extends 1" at each side. Machine-stitch lining ½" from raw edges of sheer panel (*see illustration A, below*). Fold and press each side edge of panel ½" to wrong side. Fold and press again, then topstitch to secure (illustration B). Fold top and bottom edges along stitching line, and press toward wrong side (illustration C). Fold top edge of panel to meet bottom edge of lining, then topstitch edge through all layers to secure (illustration D). Repeat on bottom of panel.

3. *Prepare leaf appliqués.* Make 12 photocopies of leaf appliqué pattern (*see page 46*). Make four copies at 100% (about 5½" long), four at 145% (about 8" long), and four at 180% (about 10" long). To vary final design, turn several copies face down against window (to see reverse image), and trace from wrong side with marker to make mirror image design. Tape patterns to flat work surface. Rough-cut a piece of sheer remnant for each leaf pattern, varying colors and sizes. Lay remnant over pattern, and tape down securely along edges; leaf will be visible through sheer overlay. Trace each leaf outline and spine with matching paint (illustration E). Let paint dry overnight or at least 12 hours. Remove tape. Using scissors, cut out each leaf along paint outline (illustration F). Peel off paper pattern, using tweezers to pick off any paper that remains stuck.

4. *Fuse appliqués to panel.* Lay panel right side up on large work surface. Arrange leaves on lower half of panel, painted surface facing down; vary color placement and direction to create windblown look. Lay freezer paper (shiny side up) on top of newspaper, then slip freezer paper/newspaper padding underneath panel behind any leaf. Lay second sheet of freezer paper shiny side down on top of leaf. Set iron at lowest dry setting, then press gently to soften paint and fuse leaf to panel. Check progress after 1 minute; if fusing has not occurred, increase temperature one setting and try again. Repeat process to fuse all leaves to panel (illustration G). Let paint cool slightly before removing freezer paper.

5. *Hang panel.* Following manufacturer's directions, insert tension rod in top channel and mount in window opening. Saw dowel to measure panel width minus ½". Insert dowel in bottom channel to hold panel steady. ◆

PATTERNS

See page 46 for pattern pieces and enlargement instructions.

Sew the Banner's Channels

BANNER OVERVIEW

Illustration A shows circled portion above

A. Sew a lining strip to each end of the panel.

B. Hem each long side edge.

C. Fold and press the top edge.

D. Fold again and topstitch to form the channel.

Appliquéing the Leaves

E. Trace each leaf outline on sheer nylon with fabric paint.

F. When the paint is dry, cut out each leaf.

G. Use an iron to fuse the leaves to the sheer panel.

DESIGNER'S TIP

Prices for sheer fabrics range from $3 to $30 a yard, depending largely on the fiber content. The metallic fabric I purchased for $2.99 a yard is made from nylon, while pricier versions use silk. For this project, I found the nylon-based fabric easier to work with.

DECORATIVE FOOD

Decorative Wheat Bread

Use our simple recipe to mix up a loaf of bread, then add a wheat sheaf made from decorating dough.

BY SUSAN LOGOZZO

The decorating dough used to form the wheat sheaf shown here includes all-purpose and whole wheat flour, salt, and water. For a darker dough, add a small amount of sifted cocoa powder with the flour.

COLOR PHOTOGRAPHY:
Carl Tremblay

ILLUSTRATIONS A-C:
Michelle Amatrula

ILLUSTRATIONS D-F:
Michael Gellatly

STYLING:
Ritch Holben

MATERIALS

Bread Dough
- 2/3 cup warm water (110 degrees maximum)
- 1 package active dry yeast
- 1 cup warm buttermilk
- 3 tablespoons vegetable oil, plus extra for bowl
- 2 1/2 teaspoons salt
- 1 tablespoon sugar
- 2/3 cup whole wheat flour
- 3 to 3 1/2 cups all-purpose flour, plus extra for surfaces
- 1 egg white (to brush on loaf)
- Small amount cornmeal

Decorating Dough
- 3/4 cup whole wheat flour
- 3/4 cup all-purpose flour
- 1/2 teaspoon salt
- 1/2 cup plus 1 tablespoon warm water

You'll also need:
mixing bowl; small- and medium-sized bowls; wet and dry measuring cups; measuring spoons; baking sheet; large wooden spoon; fork; pastry brush; instant-read thermometer; plastic wrap; ruler; electric mixer; and sharp scissors.

Other items, if necessary:
dough hook for electric mixer (for kneading bread).

IF YOU CAN WORK WITH CLAY, THEN you can make this loaf of decorative wheat bread. The process is simple, even for beginning bakers: Prepare the loaf of bread, then shape a wheat sheaf from decorating dough. Before baking the bread, arrange the wheat sheaf on top. The finished loaf is both beautiful and tasteful.

My bread recipe includes buttermilk, which enhances the taste and the texture of the bread. I added whole wheat flour for taste and color, although the dough can be made entirely with all-purpose or bread flour. The bread bakes at 400 degrees so the crust will set up quickly.

The decorating dough, made with two types of flour, salt, and water, is very easy to work with. You can roll it out like clay and cut it freeform or with cookie cutters; any variety of shapes, including flowers, geometrics, leaves, or simple decorative designs, is possible. You can also roll out the dough and cut it into thin strips, which you can then braid or mold into other shapes, such as animals or fish.

To attach the wheat sheaf to the loaf, I used egg whites, but water will also work. You can also apply the wheat sheaf or other decorations to any unbaked loaf of bread as long as the loaf is sturdy enough to bear the weight of the decorations.

Susan Logozzo, a food consultant, lives in Charlestown, Massachusetts.

INSTRUCTIONS

1. *Mix dough.* Pour warm water into small bowl, sprinkle in yeast, and stir with fork. In mixing bowl, add buttermilk, oil, salt, and sugar. Using electric mixer, mix in whole wheat flour and yeast mixture until smooth. Mix in 2 cups all-purpose flour until well blended.

2. *Knead dough.* If using mixer with dough hook, mix in 1 cup all-purpose flour and knead for 5 minutes; add more flour if needed until dough pulls away from sides of bowl. Then transfer dough

MAKING THE BREAD

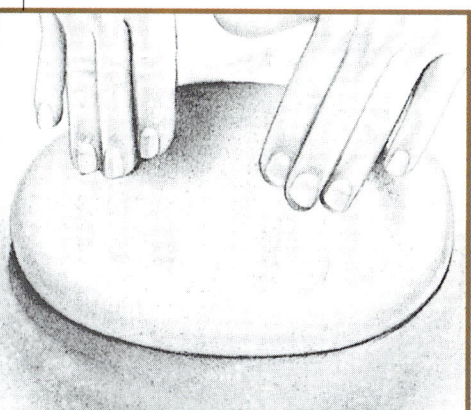

A. Shape the loaf into an oblong rectangle, about 1" thick.

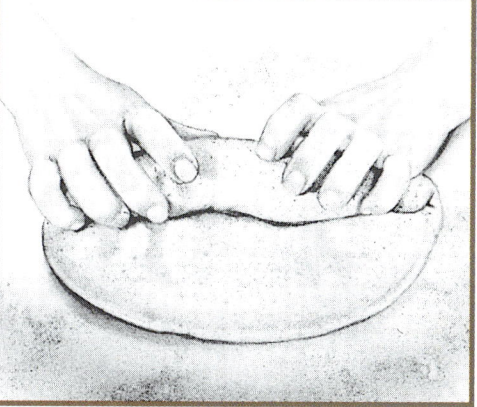

B. Roll the dough into a cylinder, pressing down so the dough sticks to itself.

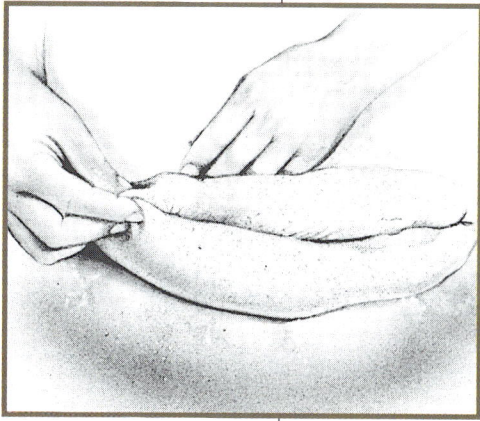

C. Turn the dough seam side up and pinch it closed.

to lightly floured countertop and knead by hand 2 to 3 minutes until dough is soft, smooth, and elastic. To knead dough without dough hook, use wooden spoon to mix in flour until dough pulls away from sides of bowl. Transfer dough to lightly floured countertop and knead by hand 10 minutes.

3. *Let dough rise.* Set dough in lightly oiled medium-sized bowl, cover with plastic wrap, and let rest in warm (75 degrees), draft-free area 1½ to 2 hours or until dough doubles in size. Punch down dough, re-cover with plastic, and refrigerate overnight.

4. *Shape loaf.* Ease chilled dough from bowl onto lightly floured countertop and let rest 15 minutes. Shape dough into oval (see illustration A, above), then roll long side of dough into cylinder (illustration B) and pinch closed (illustration C). Rub baking sheet lightly with oil and sprinkle with cornmeal. Turn loaf seam side down and set loaf on baking sheet. Cover with plastic wrap, and let rest in warm, draft-free area for 1½ hours or until puffy. While loaf is rising, mix decorating dough.

5. *Mix decorating dough.* In mixing bowl, use fork to combine whole wheat flour, all-purpose flour, and salt. Using electric mixer, gradually blend in warm water to form smooth, firm dough. Shape dough into smooth disk, wrap in plastic, and refrigerate ½ hour. (Excess dough may be refrigerated for up to 2 weeks.)

6. *Make wheat sheaf.* Pinch off and roll small amount chilled dough into 1½"-diameter ball. Roll ball into 4"-long sausage, then roll half of sausage into narrow stem about 4" long; shape broad end so tip is somewhat pointed. To make individual grains, angle small, sharp scissors toward stem; make cut #1 in base of broad section. Move scissors to right and left to make cuts #2 and #3 (illustration D). Continue cutting broad section, progressing toward tip, to suggest stem of ripened wheat (illustration E). Snip off excess at tip. Cover stem with plastic wrap to prevent drying. Repeat to make five stems total.

7. *Bake bread.* Preheat oven to 400 degrees. Brush loaf with egg white. Gently lift individual wheat stems and arrange on top of loaf as shown in color photograph. From excess decorating dough, shape ¼" x 4" thin sausage, then tie loosely around stems at middle (illustration F). Twist the dough to finish. Brush stems with egg white. Bake bread 35 to 40 minutes or until deep golden brown. To determine whether bread is done, tap bread for hollow sound and/or insert thermometer into side of bread (thermometer should register 200 degrees). ◆

Shaping the Wheat Sheaf

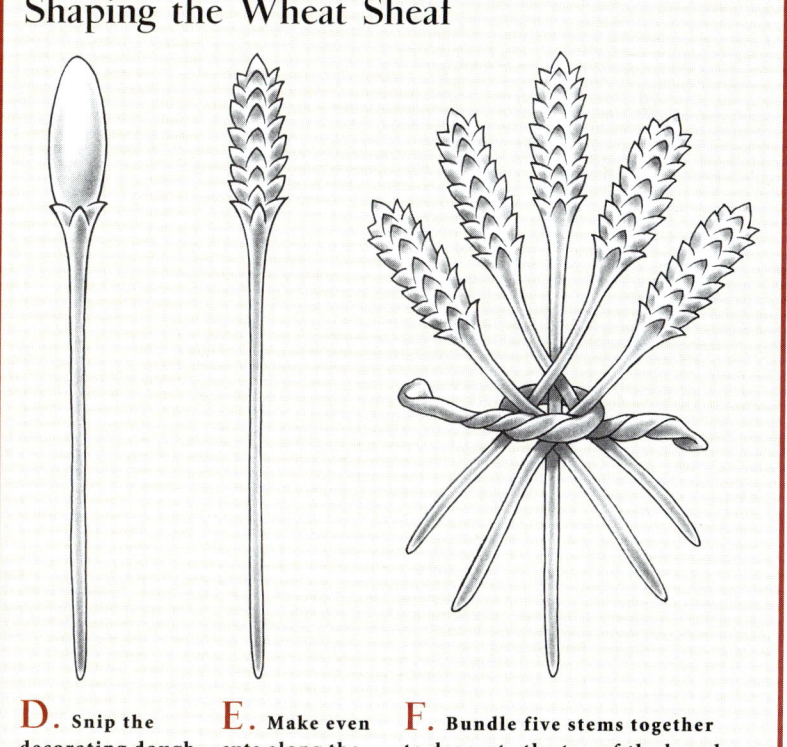

D. Snip the decorating dough with sharp scissors to make each angled cut.

E. Make even cuts along the entire stem to suggest ripened wheat grains.

F. Bundle five stems together to decorate the top of the bread.

DESIGNER'S TIPS

■ For variation on this design, consider glazing the bread loaf, which you can do before or after baking. For a prebaking glaze, brush egg yolk, egg white, or a mixture of both over the loaf; add coffee for a darker finish. For a glaze solution after baking, bring 1 cup water plus 2 tablespoons cornstarch to a boil, brush the glaze over the decorations, and let it dry.

■ The decorating dough in this article can also be used to make decorations, ornaments, candlesticks, and so forth. Place the items on a baking sheet and bake them at 350 degrees for 15 to 20 minutes or until they are hard and dry. After a few days the items will harden to a ceramic-like consistency. If desired, varnish the pieces with a wash of egg white before or after baking. The items, which should not be eaten, will last up to 3 years.

ORNAMENTS

Marionette Tree Ornaments

Assemble these festive jointed dolls using Sculpey clay, then add facial and costume details using acrylic paint and scraps of fabric.

🐚 BY MICHIO RYAN

The finished dolls measure about 6" high. For variation on their costumes, substitute different colors of Sculpey III clay and fabric.

MATERIALS

Male Doll
- 2 ounces Sculpey III thermoset clay in each of following colors: White #001*, Flesh #092*, Tan #301*, Gray #342, Translucent #510*, and Bronze #1085
- Two 4mm wiggle eyes
- Five 5mm black pompoms
- One ¼" brown pompom
- Eight ¾" coil pins
- 16" strong, thin cord
- 2 ounces black gloss acrylic paint*
- 2 ounces rose acrylic paint*
- Aleene's Thick Designer Tacky glue

Female Doll
- 2 ounces Sculpey III thermoset clay in each of following colors: White #001*, Flesh #092*, Tan #301*, Translucent #510*, and Purple #1003
- 5" x 19" piece striped silk charmeuse
- Scrap of coordinating chiffon
- ½"-wide x 3½"-long pink ribbon
- ¼"-wide x 1"-long white lace insertion
- 2½"-wide x 3"-long sheer gold metallic ribbon
- 1 skein pale yellow pearl cotton
- Yellow sewing thread
- Two 4mm wiggle eyes
- Eight ¾" coil pins
- 20" strong, thin cord
- 2 ounces pale green acrylic paint
- 2 ounces black gloss acrylic paint*
- 2 ounces rose acrylic paint*
- 1¼ ounces Tulip Pearl fabric paint, Snow White
- Aleene's Thick Designer Tacky glue

*One package/container will make both dolls

You'll also need: small detail brush; small round paintbrush; X-Acto knife; needle-nose pliers; two small wood blocks; two dinner plates; demitasse spoon; butter knife; baking sheet; aluminum foil; toothpicks; 5"-long doll-making needle; hand-sewing needle; ruler; pencil; scrap of cardboard; tracing paper; and scissors.

COLOR PHOTOGRAPHY:
Carl Tremblay

ILLUSTRATIONS:
Michael Gellatly

SILHOUETTE PHOTOGRAPHY:
Daniel van Ackere

STYLING:
Ritch Holben

My GOAL IN DESIGNING THESE jointed male and female figurines was simple: create a tree ornament that resembles a miniature marionette doll, in the style of a traditional European puppet theater. The material that makes these dolls an at-home craft project, versus one for the experienced ceramist, is Sculpey III thermoset clay.

This project can be divided into two general stages: making the separate parts for each doll (i.e., head, torso, legs, and arms), and the assembly process, in which the parts are strung or jointed together. The individual parts are very easy to shape, as each starts from a simple geometric form such as a sphere or a cylinder. The head is a ball, for example, without the need for a neck; the hanging string joins the head and torso. Although the individual parts do not need precise finishing, it is important that you shape them in proportion to each other. I've included general guidelines for sizing the parts in order to create a well-proportioned ornament.

In researching the materials needed to make the doll, I kept several considerations in mind. The ideal clay had to be lightweight so the ornament was not too heavy; it also had to be easy to form, good at holding impressed details, and strong enough so that the wired joints would not crack or rip.

Any brand of thermoset clay such as

Sculpey, Cernit, or Fimo would have worked for this project, but my personal preference turned out to be Sculpey III because it proved the easiest to knead into a usable consistency. *Note:* Some of the parts require surface decoration, such as the male doll's jacket opening, which you cut with an X-Acto knife. I found that it is nearly impossible to incise sharp lines into clay that is soft and warm from repeated handling. To firm up the surface, I refrigerated the dough for 30 minutes.

Once you have created all the individual pieces, you can bake them en masse. Sculpey III hardens when baked in a home oven at 275 degrees for 10 to 20 minutes. The parts should be left to cool, after which you can add the details. These include some painted highlights, a piece of fabric wrapped around the female doll's waist to form a skirt, hair assembled from embroidery thread, and so forth.

Assembling the Ornaments

I used two different kinds of joints for the marionette dolls. The first type, made from coil pins, connects the limbs to each other or to the trunk. Unlike most ceramic clay, which is fired at such a high temperature that any embedded joint would disintegrate, Sculpey does not have this limitation. This means the tiny wire joints can be embedded into the unbaked clay, the parts baked, and the doll assembled by looping the wires together, with no drilling necessary.

String is used for the second type of joint. To attach the doll's head to the torso, and to provide the ornament with a hanging device, I ran a string through the head and collar and out through the bottom of the doll's torso, where I knotted it. To create the holes in the head and torso, I used a long doll-making needle.

INSTRUCTIONS

Note: Each 2-ounce package of Sculpey III is scored in four bars. Use the butter knife to slice off individual bars or fractions of bars as needed. To keep the dough clean, knead and roll it on a dinner plate using clean hands.

Making the Male Doll

1. *Model head.* To make flesh tone dough, knead together ½ bar Translucent, ¼ bar Flesh, and ¼ bar Tan Sculpey until completely blended. For head, roll two-thirds flesh tone mix into ⅞"-diameter ball. To make nose, pinch off small amount from reserve, knead until very warm and soft, and shape into ½"-long cone. Press cone onto center of head and smooth for seamless join (see illustration A, below). To mark eyes, use pencil point to make two impressions ½" apart and slightly above nose. For each ear, roll ¼"-diameter ball from reserve, flatten into disk, then press onto side of head at nose level (illustration B). For mouth, slice arc into face with X-Acto knife, about ¼" below nose. Press bowl of spoon on lower edge of incision to create open smile (illustration C). Set remaining flesh tone mix aside.

2. *Model hat.* Knead ¾ bar Bronze Sculpey until soft, roll into ball, and flatten into 2½"-diameter pancake. Using X-Acto knife, slice and remove a three-eighths pie-shaped segment. Roll remaining five-eighths piece of clay into cone, overlapping cut edges at base. Smooth overlap at top to define tip of hat; pinch and flare rim, rippling it to make floppy brim (illustration D). Press hat onto head with split brim slightly off-center and cocked back to reveal eyes. Set head aside.

3. *Model torso.* Knead 2 bars Gray Sculpey until soft, roll into ball, then roll into 1"-diameter x 1¼"-long cylinder; tap ends on plate to flatten (illustration E). Lay cylinder on side, set index finger ⅜" from one end, and roll cylinder back and forth under finger to form off-center hourglass 1¾" long (illustration F). Tap both ends again to flatten. Compress cylinder slightly to make round ends more oval-shaped.

4. *Model collar.* Mix 1 bar Translucent and ⅙ bar White Sculpey until soft. Break off slightly less than half and roll into ¾"-diameter ball. Flatten ball into 1⅝"-diameter by 3/16"-thick pancake. Using X-Acto knife, make ⅜"-deep cuts ¼" apart around edge. Use thumb to dimple center (illustration G). Pinch edge, gently splaying collar petals. Stand torso upright and press collar on top, like mushroom cap (illustration H). Place head and torso on plate and refrigerate 30 minutes. Once torso is cold and firm, use X-Acto knife to incise single line down center front for jacket opening and three flared lines on torso back to suggest pleats. Return torso to refrigerator. Set remaining white mix aside.

5. *Model arms.* For each hand, roll ½"-diameter ball from reserved flesh tone mix, then flatten into ½" x ¾" oval-shaped disk. Using X-Acto knife, slit narrow end to section off thumb, then model thumb and mitt (illustration I, next page). For each arm, knead ½ bar Gray Sculpey until soft and roll into 1½"-long sausage. Taper one end, and join to wrist end of hand; length from shoulder to fingertip should measure about 2". For each cuff, knead ⅛ bar Bronze Sculpey until soft, roll into 2"-long snake, then press flat to make strip 2½" long by ½" wide. Wrap

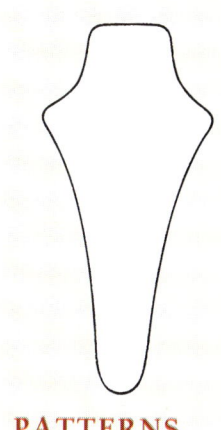

PATTERNS
See page 46 for pattern pieces and enlargement instructions.

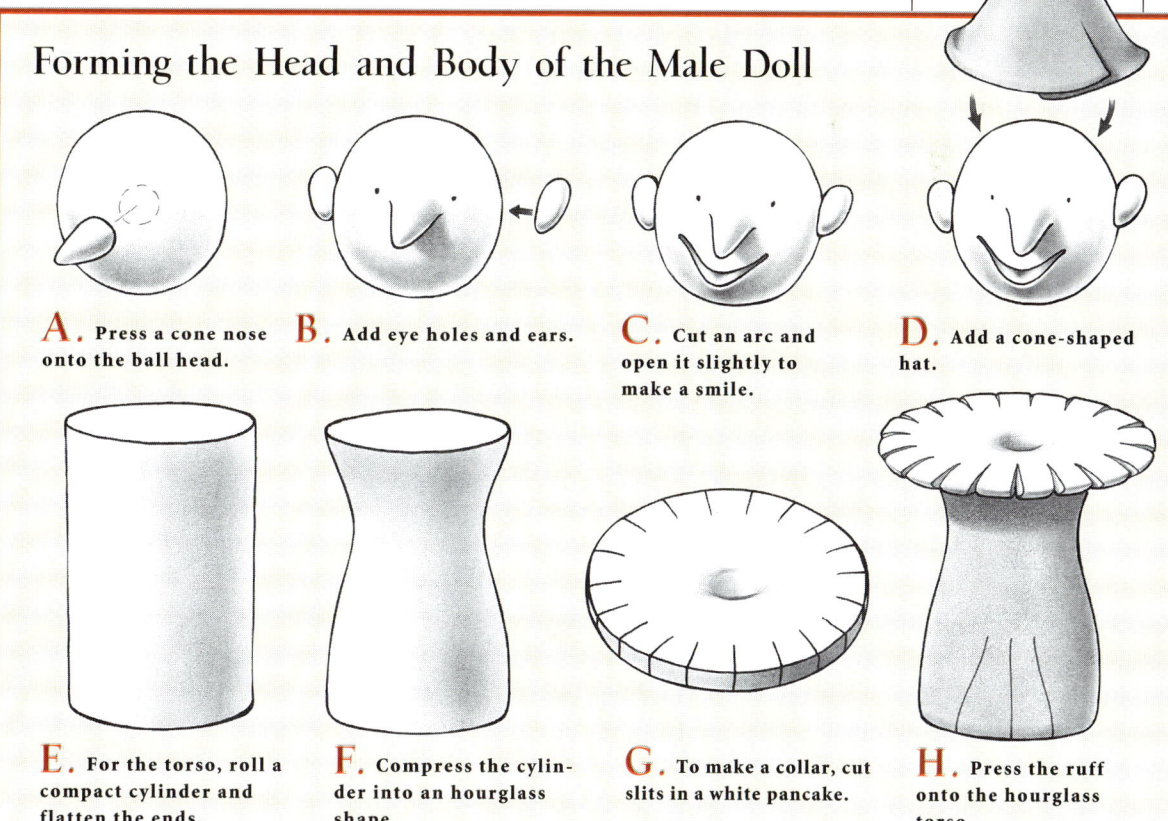

Forming the Head and Body of the Male Doll

A. Press a cone nose onto the ball head.

B. Add eye holes and ears.

C. Cut an arc and open it slightly to make a smile.

D. Add a cone-shaped hat.

E. For the torso, roll a compact cylinder and flatten the ends.

F. Compress the cylinder into an hourglass shape.

G. To make a collar, cut slits in a white pancake.

H. Press the ruff onto the hourglass torso.

ORNAMENTS

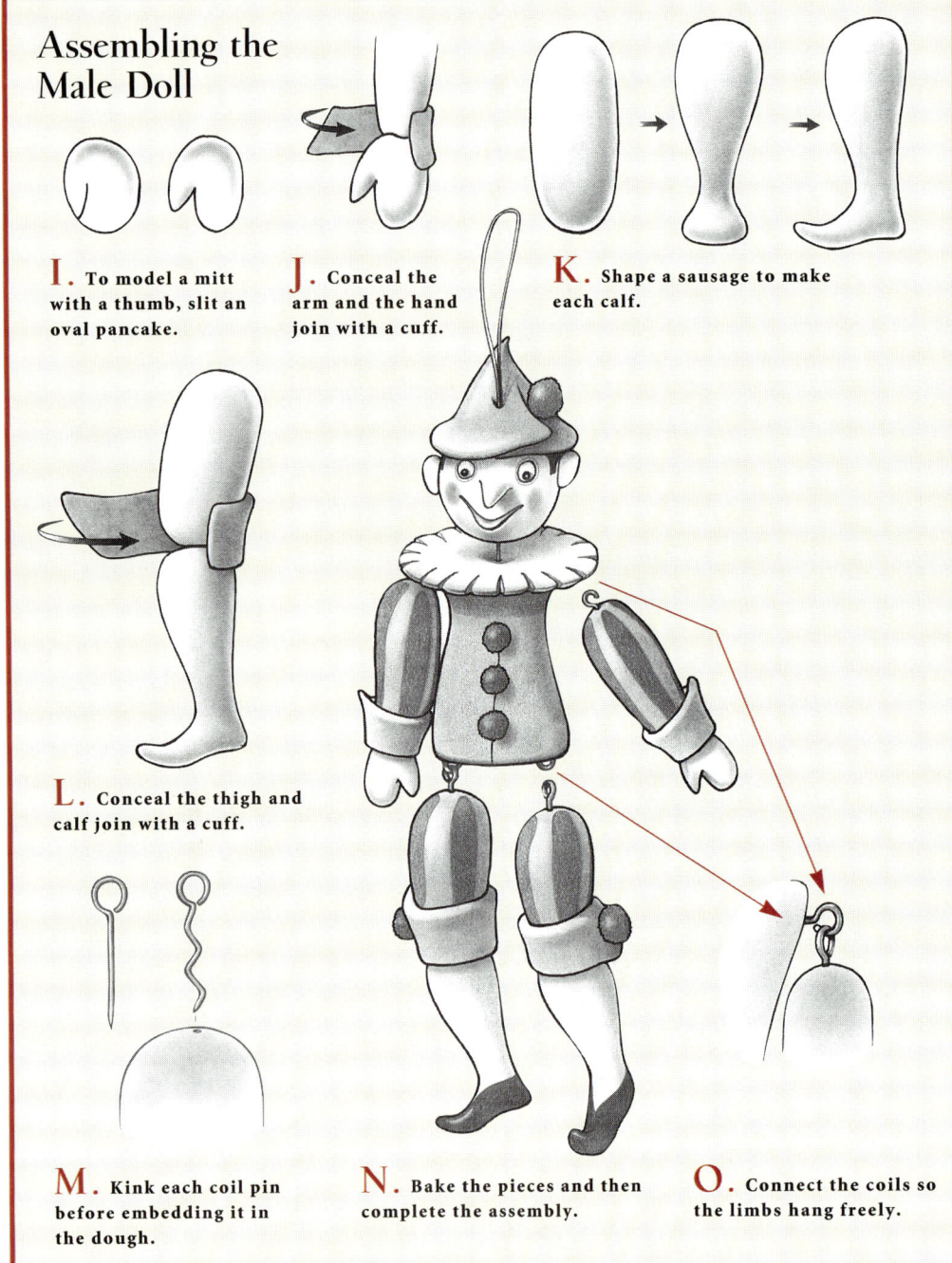

Assembling the Male Doll

I. To model a mitt with a thumb, slit an oval pancake.

J. Conceal the arm and the hand join with a cuff.

K. Shape a sausage to make each calf.

L. Conceal the thigh and calf join with a cuff.

M. Kink each coil pin before embedding it in the dough.

N. Bake the pieces and then complete the assembly.

O. Connect the coils so the limbs hang freely.

sponding pins in ends of arms and legs; double-check position of pins against torso to make sure they will connect.

Note: To bake both dolls together, complete Female Doll steps 1 through 8, then proceed to step 9.

9. *Bake modeled pieces.* Preheat oven to 275 degrees. Place all modeled pieces on foil-lined baking sheet (torso upright on wood block). Bake 10 to 20 minutes; begin checking progress after 10 minutes to avoid scorching. Let cool on baking sheet 30 minutes or until pieces are hard and cool to touch.

10. *Add face and clothing details.* Using detail brush, apply rose paint to cheeks and inside of mouth. Brush black paint onto head for sideburns and hair and onto feet for slip-on style shoes. Using round brush, paint four evenly spaced rose stripes on each gray sleeve and pants leg. Let paint dry 30 minutes. Glue wiggle eyes to face. Glue three black pompoms down torso center front and one to each pants cuff. Glue brown pompom to hat (illustration N). Let dry 1 hour.

11. *Join pieces together.* Cut 16" length of cord. Hold ends together, insert ends down through hat and out through torso. Tie ends in knot. Pull loop above head to lodge knot inside torso. Push head flush to collar and tie overhand knot as close to hat as possible. To join arms and legs, open coil on arm or leg with pliers, slip it around corresponding coil on torso, and press closed (illustrations N and O).

Making the Female Doll

1. *Model head.* To make flesh tone color, knead together 1¼ bars Translucent, 1¼ bars White, ¼ bar Flesh, and ¼ bar Tan Sculpey until completely blended. For head, break off about one-fifth of flesh tone mix and roll into ⅞"-diameter ball. Proceed as for Male Doll, step 1; make nose slightly smaller and upturned and omit ears (illustration P, next page). Set remaining flesh tone mix aside.

2. *Model hat.* Knead ½ bar Purple Sculpey until soft, then divide in half. Roll one piece into ⅝"-diameter ball, then flatten into ¾"-diameter by ¼"-thick pancake. Roll remaining Sculpey into 3½"-long snake, press flat, and wrap strip around pancake to make pillbox-style hat (illustration Q).

3. *Model torso.* Trace torso pattern (*see page 46*) and cut out with scissors. Roll small amount flesh tone mix into 1¾"-diameter ball, then roll ball into 3"-long cylinder and flatten to about ⅝" thick. Lay torso tracing on top, run butter knife along template outline, and remove excess dough (illustration R). Model torso with fingers, rounding off and smoothing edges and tapering lower stem.

4. *Model sleeves.* Mix 1 bar Translucent and ⅙ bar White Sculpey until soft. For

cuff around wrist, ending at outside edge; trim excess at angle with scissors, allowing cuff to flare out slightly (illustration J).

6. *Model legs.* Divide remaining white mix from step 4 in half. For each calf, roll one 1¼"-long sausage. Lay sausage on side, set index finger at one end, and roll gently to form drumstick with knobbed handle. Pull one side of knob into sharp point for toe; knee-to-heel length should measure about 1⅜" (illustration K). For each thigh, knead ½ bar Gray Sculpey until soft, roll into 1¼"-long sausage, and flatten slightly. Press calves onto thighs at slight angle. Make knee cuffs as for wrist cuffs in step 5 (illustration L).

7. *Make string holes.* Remove head and torso from refrigerator. To make hole for central string, insert doll-making needle into center front of hat, push down through center of head, and draw out at neck. Repeat process to make hole through collar/torso. Reinsert needle into hole at bottom of torso for ½" and wiggle it around to widen hole slightly.

8. *Add coil pins.* Using pliers, kink shafts of eight coil pins (illustration M). Insert two pins into torso at shoulders for arms and two in flat torso bottom for legs; to prevent distortion to collar, set torso upright on block of wood narrow enough to fit between pins at base. Insert corre-

sleeves, break off slightly less than half of mixed Sculpey, divide this dough in half, and roll into two ¾"-diameter balls. Push toothpick through upper torso, and trim ends to extend ½" at each side. Push white ball onto each end, lodging balls against shoulders (illustration S). Place torso on wood block (to avoid crushing balls) and refrigerate 30 minutes. Remove from refrigerator. Using X-Acto knife, make five vertical slits on each sleeve. Gently press each ball between fingers to pucker slits open (illustration T). For each cuff, knead ⅛ bar Purple dough until soft, roll into 3"-long snake, and press flat. Wrap cuff around base of sleeve, ending at outside edge; trim excess at slight angle with scissors. From mixed white reserve, pinch off and roll two ⅛"-diameter balls; press one ball onto each cuff for button. Place head, cap, and torso on plate (elevate torso on wood block), and refrigerate 30 minutes.

5. *Model arms.* For each arm, roll small amount flesh tone mix into ½"-diameter ball, then roll into 1¼"-long sausage. Lay sausage on side, set index finger at one end, and roll gently to form drumstick with knobbed handle (illustration U). Flatten each knob slightly to make hand, then slit edge with X-Acto knife to define thumb; make hands in mirror image. Taper arm toward wrist, then curve upper arm slightly about ¼" from end to suggest elbow.

6. *Model legs.* Divide remaining white mix from step 4 in half. For each calf, roll 1¼"-long sausage. Lay sausage on side, set index finger at one end, and roll gently to form drumstick with knobbed handle (illustration V). Pull one side of knob into sharp point for toe; thigh-to-heel length should measure about 2". Model each leg to suggest calf, knee, and thigh.

7. *Make string holes.* Remove head, hat, and torso from refrigerator. Place hat temporarily on head. To make hole for central string, insert doll-making needle into hat crown, push down through center of head, and draw out at neck. Repeat process to pierce through center of torso, maneuvering needle past toothpick; draw out about 1" at bottom but do not remove needle.

8. *Add coil pins.* Using pliers, kink shafts of eight coil pins as with male doll (illustration M). Using illustration W for pin position, insert two pins into lower sleeves and two pins into lower torso at each side. Insert corresponding pins in ends of arms and legs; double-check position of pins against those on torso to make sure they will connect.

9. *Bake modeled pieces.* Same as Male Doll, step 9; rest torso on wood block to avoid flattening sleeves. Remove doll-making needle when torso is completely cool.

10. *Add bodice, shoes, and facial features.* Load small round brush with pale green paint. Working freehand, paint scoop-necked bodice on torso; apply two coats for even coverage. Using detail brush, apply rose paint to feet to suggest slip-on shoes, then paint two crescents on upper and lower part of mouth for lips. Dilute paint with water to blush cheeks. For lashes, use detail brush and black paint to make single strokes up and away from eye indents. Glue wiggle eyes to face. Glue white lace insertion down center front of bodice. Using applicator nozzle, apply beads of white fabric paint directly to neck edge of front bodice. Let dry 24 hours.

11. *Add hair and veil.* Cut a 1¾"-wide strip of cardboard. Wind pearl cotton around strip about twenty times; then trim off excess. Using hand-sewing needle and yellow thread, "sew" wrapped strands together. Slide locks off cardboard; do not cut loops. Glue sewn end of locks to top of head, being careful not to hide stringing hole. For veil, glue 3" square of gold ribbon to head.

12. *Join pieces together.* Same as Male Doll, step 11, except start with 20" cord; refer to illustrations O and W.

13. *Make skirt.* Finger-press short ends of charmeuse ½" to wrong side. Fold piece in half lengthwise, right side out, and press. Hand-baste through both layers ⅜" from raw edges, draw up basting thread, and gather until edge measures about 3". Restitch to secure gathers. Glue skirt around waist section of torso, overlapping ends at back (illustration W). Glue pink ribbon around waist, concealing stitches, and hand-tack at back. To pouf out skirt and add body, glue chiffon scrap to lower torso. ◆

Making the Female Doll

P. Model the female doll's head similar to the male's head.

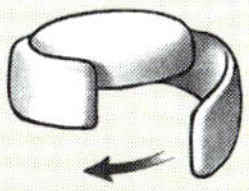

Q. To make a pillbox-style hat, wrap a strip around a pancake.

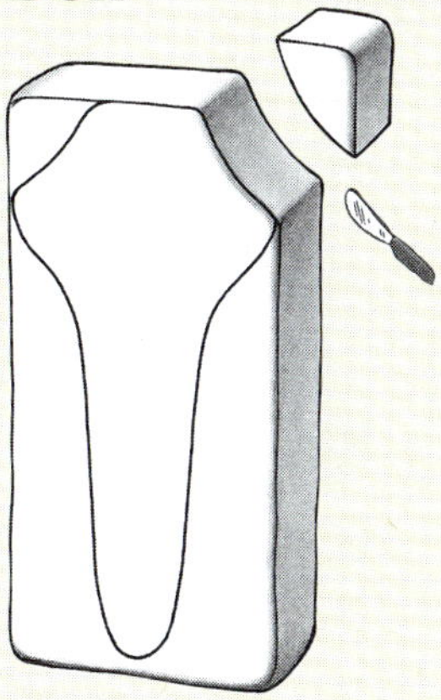

R. Use a template to cut the doll's torso.

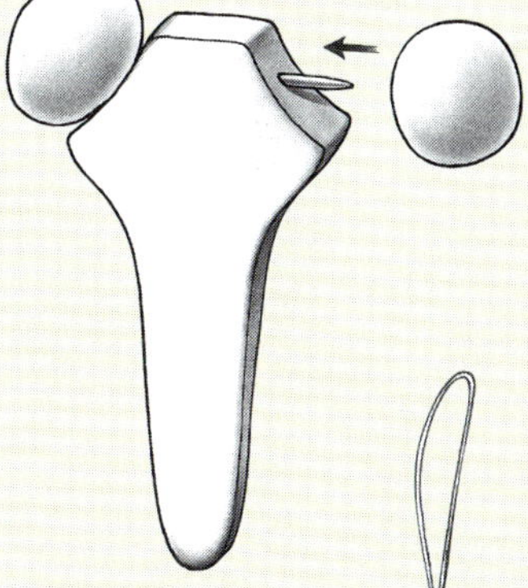

S. For the sleeves, join balls to the torso at each shoulder.

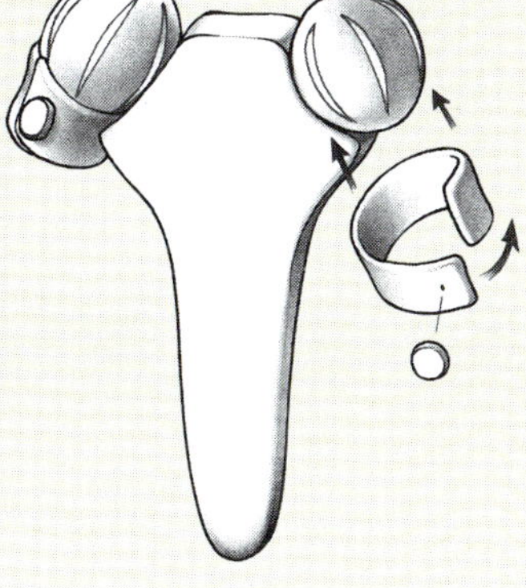

T. To style the sleeves, slit each ball and add a cuff.

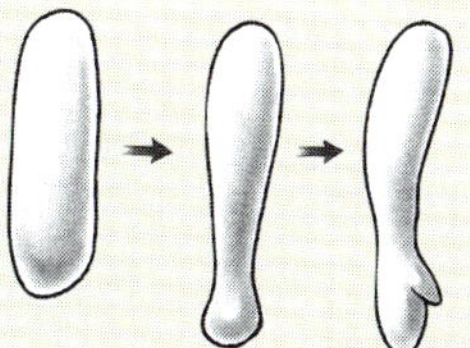

U. Shape a sausage to make each arm.

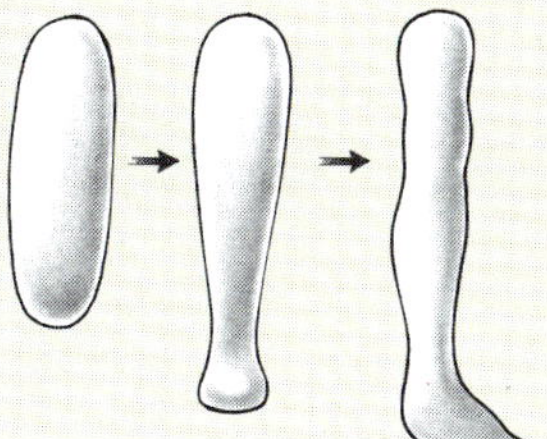

V. Shape a sausage to make each leg.

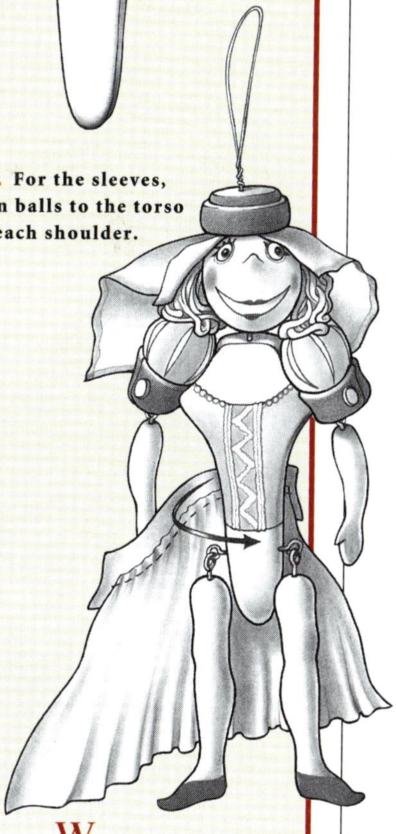

W. Bake the pieces and complete the assembly.

COVER STORY

25 Uses for Glitter Fruit

Transform ordinary plastic fruit into a range of home-decorating accents using glue and micro glitter.

🍂 BY GENEVIEVE A. STERBENZ

MATERIALS

- Artificial pears, grapes, and apricots with leaves
- Jones Tones polyester glitter in following colors: Micro Silver PY02, Micro Gold PY04, Violet PY08, Bronze PY10, Willow Green PY25, Moss Green PY26, Lilac PY27, and Wedgewood PY31
- Jones Tones metallic glitter, Yellow Green MT15
- White all-purpose craft glue (such as Sobo)

You'll also need:
1" foam brush; plastic palette; waxed paper; clean scrap paper (1 sheet per glitter color); and clothesline with clothespins or florist foam bricks.

These glitter grapes look fairly realistic. For variation on this design, consider making fantasy fruit, or fruit with colors not found in nature.

COLOR PHOTOGRAPHY:
Carl Tremblay

ILLUSTRATION:
Harry Davis

COLOR PHOTOGRAPHY, PAGE 23:
Daniel van Ackere

STYLING:
Ritch Holben

GLITTER, ONCE FOUND ONLY IN classrooms, has come of age. Like acrylic paint, today's glitter is available in a myriad of beautiful colors. Furthermore, the tiny particles found in microfine glitter can be blended, much like paint, to create realistic shading.

To get started, you'll need an assortment of plastic fruit, all-purpose craft glue, and several colors in different shades of microfine glitter. The key to creating beautiful fruit is to blend different colors of glitter. Contrasting or complementary colors can be used on the fruit itself (to create highlights or sun-ripened spots) or on the leaves.

I discovered three basic techniques to create realistic shading effects. First, for small highlights, apply glue directly from the nozzle in a squiggly band or dot, smooth out the glue with a foam brush, and sprinkle on the glitter. (I used this technique on the small pears and the grapes, above.) For larger patches of color (e.g., the ripe area on a piece of fruit), brush glue onto the fruit and sprinkle with glitter. Then brush the remaining area with glue and sprinkle that with a different color of glitter. Lastly, for patches with more blended coloration, apply glue as in step 2, then sprinkle two different colors of glitter onto the wet glue area. The colors will intermingle in an overlap area, much like the speckling on a real piece of fruit. (I used this technique on the apricots, next page.)

When shopping for plastic fruit, you may come across clusters of fruit as well as individual pieces. Either type is suitable for this project. If you choose clusters, simply hold the additional pieces and leaves out of the way and apply the glue and glitter to one fruit at a time. You should also allow about one hour's drying time before proceeding within a cluster so that fruits with wet glue and glitter don't rub against one another. Individual fruits are somewhat easier to handle. They can be coated with glitter first, allowed to dry, and then twined or wired together to complete a cluster.

Genevieve A. Sterbenz lives in New York, New York.

INSTRUCTIONS

Note: Follow the instructions below to decorate the fruits shown on these two pages. The instructions can be easily adapted for similar fruits. As you finish applying each glitter color, use scrap paper to funnel excess glitter back into its container for reuse.

Small Pears

1. *Apply glue to pear.* Squeeze glue into palette. If pear is part of cluster, hold leaves and other fruit aside. Using foam brush, apply glue to surface, rotating pear for full coverage (*see illustration A, next page*).

2. *Apply glitter to pear.* Hold pear over sheet of clean scrap paper. Sprinkle Micro Gold glitter onto wet glue, rotating pear for full coverage (illustration B). Shake or tap gently to shed excess glitter onto

COVER STORY

paper; do not touch glittered surface. Clip pear stem to clothesline so glitter does not touch other fruit or leaves in cluster; let dry 1 hour undisturbed. Repeat steps 1 and 2 to glitter remaining small pears.

3. *Add highlights.* Squeeze glue directly from nozzle onto pear in a squiggly band, a dot, or other irregular pattern (illustration C). Smooth and blot bead of glue with foam brush. Hold pear over clean scrap paper, sprinkle Violet glitter onto wet glue, and tap off excess. Repeat to add Bronze glitter highlights. Repeat process to highlight remaining pears. Let dry 1 hour as above.

4. *Add glitter to leaves.* Lay leaf face up and flat on waxed paper. If leaf is part of cluster, hold other leaves and fruit aside. Apply glue to leaf surface using foam brush. Hold leaf over scrap paper, sprinkle Moss Green glitter over wet glue area, and tap off excess. Apply glitter to front of as many leaves as possible while keeping them separate, then let dry 1 hour, as in step 2. Repeat process as needed to cover all leaf fronts. When dry, coat leaf undersides with Willow Green glitter. On some leaf undersides, create two-tone effect: Brush glue on interior area of leaf only and coat with Moss Green or Bronze glitter. Next, brush glue on remaining outer border and coat with Willow Green glitter (illustration D).

5. *Add glitter to stems and navels.* Apply glue directly from nozzle to stems and navels; smooth and distribute with foam brush. Sprinkle wet glue areas with Bronze glitter, then tap off excess. Set fruit on its side on waxed paper to dry, avoiding contact with freshly glued areas.

Grapes

1. *Apply glue to grapes.* Same as Small Pears, step 1. Coat about half of grapes in cluster; do not let grapes touch each other.

2. *Apply glitter to grapes.* Same as Small Pears, step 2, but use Violet glitter. Repeat steps 1 and 2 to apply Lilac glitter to remaining grapes in cluster.

3. *Add highlights.* Same as Small Pears, step 3, but use Wedgewood glitter to highlight some of the grapes.

4. *Add glitter to leaves.* Same as Small Pears, step 4. Coat leaf fronts with Moss Green or Willow Green; coat undersides with Willow Green or Micro Silver.

5. *Add glitter to stems and tendrils.* Same as Small Pears, step 5.

Large Pear

1. *Create glitter shading.* Squeeze glue into palette. Identify shaded, or well-ripened, areas on plastic pear, then use foam brush to apply glue to these areas only. Hold pear over sheet of scrap paper. Sprinkle Yellow Green glitter onto wet glue, rotating pear as needed. Shake or tap gently to shed excess glitter, but do not touch glittered surface.

2. *Apply glitter to remainder of pear.* Hold pear by stem. Using foam brush, apply glue to remainder of pear surface, working around glitter already in place. Hold pear over new sheet of scrap paper, sprinkle Micro Gold glitter onto wet glue, and tap off excess. Clip pear by stem to clothesline or stand upright in florist foam brick; let dry 1 hour.

3. *Add glitter to leaves.* Same as Small Pears, step 4, but coat leaf fronts and undersides with Moss Green.

4. *Add glitter to stem and navel.* Same as Small Pears, step 5.

Apricots

1. *Create highlights.* Squeeze glue into palette. Identify unripe (white, yellow, or green) areas on surface, then use brush to apply glue to these areas. If fruit doesn't have natural markings, brush glue around base and/or stem. Hold apricot over sheet of scrap paper. Sprinkle Micro Gold glitter onto some areas of wet glue, then shake off excess. Move to clean sheet of scrap paper and sprinkle Willow Green glitter over remaining wet areas, causing gold and green glitters to blend. Shake or tap gently to shed excess glitter, but do not touch glittered surface.

2. *Apply glitter to remainder of apricot.* Same as Large Pear, step 2, but use Bronze glitter. Repeat process on remaining apricots.

3. *Add glitter to leaves.* Same as Small Pears, step 4. Coat front and underside of larger leaves with Moss Green glitter; coat smaller leaves with Willow Green glitter.

4. *Add glitter to stems and navels.* Same as Small Pears, step 5. ◆

The pears (left) and apricots (right) illustrate two different techniques for applying glitter.

USING YOUR GLITTER FRUIT

DECORATE:
- garlands
- wreaths
- candlesticks
- place settings
- mirrors
- sconces
- banisters
- doorknobs
- chair backs
- curtain finials
- gift baskets

USE AS:
- package decorations
- hostess gifts
- napkin rings
- mistletoe

- guest room accents
- Christmas tree ornaments
- party favors

ARRANGE:
- within a centerpiece
- scattered across a sideboard
- along a mantel
- hanging from a chandelier
- clustered in a large glass bowl
- on the corner of a picture frame or mirror
- hanging from a door knocker

MAKING THE GLITTER FRUIT

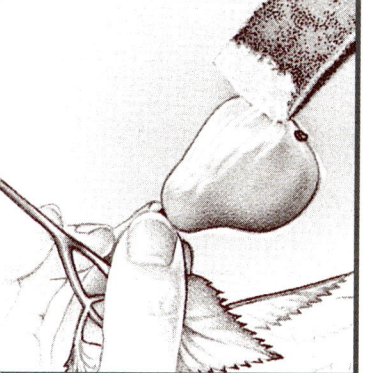

A. Spread glue over the entire piece of fruit.

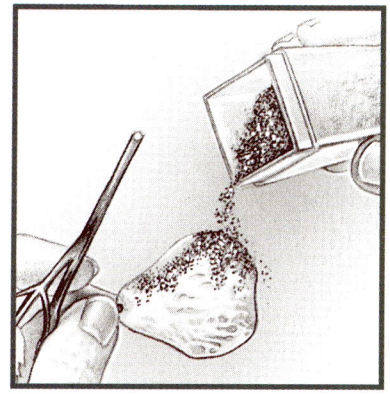

B. Sprinkle on glitter, rotating the fruit for complete coverage.

C. To add highlights, apply glue directly from the nozzle.

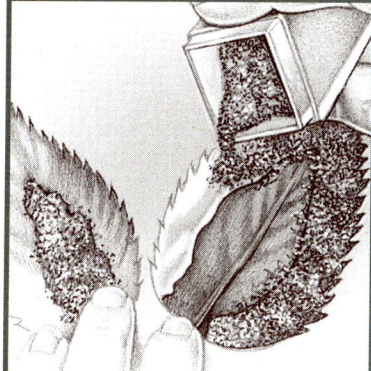

D. For distinct contrasts, apply the glue and glitter separately.

PAPER CRAFTS

Make Your Own Dog Holiday Cards

Create a set of bold and crisp cards quickly and easily using our Scottie dog pattern, glossy-coated paper, and stationery supplies.

BY LILY FRANKLIN

For the card shown above, we used standard A10 envelopes. To make a set of party invitations, reduce the cards to fit an A6 envelope (commonly used for thank-you notes).

MATERIALS
Yields five 5¼" x 7¼" cards

- 20" x 27" Chromalux black glossy 65-pound (heavyweight) paper (reverses to matte white)
- 8" x 10" 65-pound cream paper
- Red and green plaid giftwrap
- 5 size A10 envelopes
- 1⅔ yard ¾"-wide red plaid ribbon
- Five 4mm wiggle eyes
- Fifteen ⁵⁄₁₆"-diameter white self-adhesive dots
- 5¾" x 12" green self-adhesive liner pad

You'll also need:
Scottie and miniature envelope patterns (*see* page 42); X-Acto knife; steel ruler; self-healing cutting mat; scissors; manicure scissors; hole punch; bone folder or wooden dowel; pencil; 1-ply chipboard; 2 to 3 sheets white copier paper; newsprint; black fine-tip permanent marker; metallic gold felt-tip permanent marker; red felt-tip permanent marker; glue stick and access to photocopier with enlarger.

DESIGNER'S TIP
There are two ways to personalize this card. Write a greeting on the inside of the card in the customary manner and/or write a note inside the miniature envelope in the dog's mouth.

COLOR PHOTOGRAPHY:
Carl Tremblay

ILLUSTRATION:
Michael Gellatly

STYLING:
Ritch Holben

LOOKING FOR A MAKE-AT-HOME holiday card with a fresh and contemporary feel? Consider this black Scottie dog card, which only requires paper, ribbon, and a few stationery supplies.

The success of this project, in large part, depends on the paper you select. The paper stock must be stiff enough to stand up when made into a card; at the same time, it should be thin enough so that both layers can be cut at the same time without shifting. Keeping these qualities in mind, I selected 65-pound (heavyweight) Chromalux glossy-coated paper. The glossy coating adds a slick touch to the finished project, and because the paper is only color-coated on one side, the white back of the paper makes a good "inside" for the card. One note of caution: This paper is easy to scratch and readily shows finger marks. To prevent this, use a piece of white scrap paper to protect the surface while cutting.

The Chromalux paper is also reasonably inexpensive. A single 20" x 27" sheet, priced at $3.15, will yield five strips measuring just about 5½" high. Translated into a cost per card, that's about 60¢. Glossy paper of this type is frequently used for mounted presentations and graphics purposes and can be found in graphic design, drafting, and art supply stores.

I also searched for a quick way to add the dog's facial details. I found my answer in a stationery supply store. The green holly foliage on the card is made from green self-stick felt lining that is used to prevent lamps, boxes, and so forth from scratching tabletops. To create the serrated edge, I used an ordinary hole punch, then peeled the backing off and stuck the leaves on the dog. The berries are made from dot stickers. I colored them with a red felt-tip permanent marker, then stuck them on the card.

For the dog's eyes, I used wiggle eyes, such as those found on dolls. These 4mm eyes are thin enough to go through the post office without trouble. They are actually too small if used by themselves, so I used a white dot sticker to give the eye more surface area.

Lily Franklin is a designer living in Albuquerque, New Mexico.

PAPER CRAFTS

Making the Scottie Dog Card

A. Lay a cardboard template on folded paper to cut each Scottie card.

B. Glue a plaid ribbon with a mock bow around the Scottie's neck.

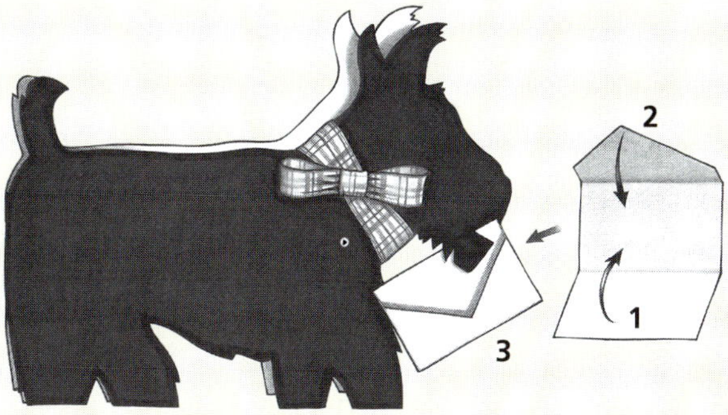

C. Glue a miniature envelope to the Scottie's jaw and foreleg.

D. Finish with a wiggle eye and self-adhesive holly leaves and berries.

DESIGNER'S TIP

This card design can be altered for other dog breeds. Start by locating a silhouette of your dog's breed for making a pattern. Consider tracing copyright-free designs, stickers, stencils, images in dog magazines, embroidery or applique patterns, photographs, or the like.

Note: for this card design to work, the card's fold should appear at the dog's backside. For breeds other than the Scotty, which don't have a straight silhouette along the back legs, this may require some modification. Once you've created your pattern, purchase paper that matches your dog's coat color, or layer paper to create multicolor designs.

INSTRUCTIONS

Note: Glossy paper scratches and picks up fingerprints easily. To prevent blemishes, keep the work surface free of dust or grit and avoid touching the glossy surface unnecessarily. To handle the paper, use white paper as a buffer.

1. *Make Scottie and envelope templates.* Photocopy and enlarge Scottie and miniature envelope patterns (*see* page 43). Rub glue stick across back of patterns, press onto chipboard, and rub to adhere. Lay chipboard on mat. Using X-Acto knife, cut on marked outlines; run blade against ruler to cut straight edges.

2. *Cut card silhouettes.* Lay black paper face down on newsprint. On white side, draft five 5⅜" x 15" rectangles. Cut out rectangles using scissors. Fold each rectangle in half crosswise, white side facing in, and crease using bone folder. Place one rectangle on mat. Set Scottie template on top, aligning dashed line (at dog's backside) with folded edge (*see* illustration A, above). To cut out card, run X-Acto knife blade along edge of template, pressing firmly to cut through both layers. Cut from two directions to make sharp points and notches. Smooth curled edges with bone folder, using separate sheet of white paper as buffer. Repeat process to cut five cards total.

3. *Add ribbon collar.* For each card, cut one 4½" and one 7" length of ribbon. Wrap 4½" ribbon around dog's neck (card front only), pleat ends at front, and glue to secure. Fold one end of 7" ribbon into 2" loop, glue securely, then wrap remainder around middle and glue (illustration B). Glue mock bow to collar. Repeat process for each card.

4. *Cut and add miniature envelope.* Lay heavyweight cream paper on mat, lay miniature envelope template on paper, and trace around edges with pencil. Cut out using knife and ruler. Run gold metallic marker along steel ruler and diagonal edges to highlight envelope flap. Fold envelope on dashed lines (illustration C) so gold-edged flap falls outside. Using manicure scissors, cut jaw slit (see Scottie pattern) on card front. Slip envelope in behind lower jaw, then glue to jaw and foreleg. Repeat process for each card.

5. *Add wiggle eye.* Press hole punch through 5/16" white self-adhesive dot to cut slightly smaller dot. Remove backing and press smaller dot onto card front at eye position (*see* Scottie pattern). Glue 4mm wiggle eye to lower area of white dot. Repeat process for each card.

6. *Add holly and berries.* For holly, cut two 1¼" x ¾" ovals from green self-adhesive liner. To make prickly holly leaves, cut edge of oval all around with hole punch. For berries, use red marker to color two white self-adhesive dots. Peel backing from holly leaves and berries and press onto card below bow (illustration D). Touch black permanent pen to each berry near edge to mark stem depression. Repeat process for each card.

7. *Line envelope.* Open envelope, lay flat on giftwrap, and trace around edge with pencil. Cut out liner with scissors, trim side edges slightly, and slip into envelope (*see* "Five-Minute Envelope Liners," page 37, for further reference.) Fold down envelope flap, creasing liner as you go. Trim flap edges of liner to fall about ½" inside envelope flap, clearing gummed section. Secure liner to envelope flap and interior using glue stick. Make one lined envelope per card. ◆

PATTERNS

See page 43 for pattern pieces and enlargement instructions.

LOW-SEW

Jewelry Box Chair

This miniature upholstered chair features a hidden jewelry compartment. You can sew it using less than a yard of fabric.

BY MICHIO RYAN

MATERIALS

- ½ yard 45"-wide bark cloth fabric
- ¼ yard 45"-wide moiré fabric
- 1 yard ¾"-wide crimped moss fringe
- 4"-diameter crocheted doily
- ½" covered button
- ⅜" two-hole button
- Ribbon to match bark cloth
- Thread to match bark cloth
- Fiberfill
- 4" x 5" batting
- Four 1¼"-diameter wooden ball knobs
- 2-ply chipboard, at least 11" x 13"
- 1-ply chipboard, at least 3" x 4"
- High-tack white glue
- Masking tape

You'll also need:
jewelry box chair patterns and chipboard diagrams (*see* pages 44 and 45); sewing machine; sewing shears; hand-sewing needle; pins; X-Acto knife; steel ruler; self-healing cutting mat; pencil; grid ruler; hot-glue gun; awl; stiff brush; and access to photocopier with enlarger.

This miniature chair measures about 9" high at the back and about 9½" wide from arm to arm. The jewelry box is located under the seat cushion.

COLOR PHOTOGRAPHY:
Carl Tremblay

ILLUSTRATION:
Mary Newell DePalma

STYLING:
Ritch Holben

THIS MINIATURE CHAIR, WHILE charming on its own, has a secret: a tiny 3" x 4" jewelry box hidden under the hinged seat cushion. Although the piece resembles a real piece of furniture, there is no carpentry or upholstering involved. Instead, the chair is sewn like a soft sculpture; the interior structural strength comes from several small pieces of chipboard.

The sewing portion of this project is minimal and forgiving. With the exception of the seat cushion, there are very few square-cornered seams on the chair, so the sewing does not need to be geometrically accurate for the overall design to hold its shape.

I used a rectangle of double-ply chipboard, inserted at the bottom of the chair, to provide the necessary structure. The chipboard keeps the sewn and stuffed portions of the chair from going out of shape and serves as the base to which the jewelry box is mounted.

The seat cushion forms the lid of the jewelry box, so it must open to give clear access to the contents. If it were hinged to open upward and backward like a conventional jewelry box, it would not open very wide because both the cushion and the chair back are upholstered. The lid could also be entirely removable, but this makes its closure less secure. Instead, I made the cushion open forward, in the way a sleeper sofa opens. This places the sewn hinge at the front of the seat cushion, which presents a neat, straight finish when the lid is closed.

INSTRUCTIONS
Cutting the Pieces

Note: The patterns for cutting the fabric pieces, found on pages 44 and 45, must be photocopied and enlarged. The diagrams on page 45, a reference for drafting the remainder of the chair pieces on chipboard, do not require photocopying.

1. *Cut fabric pieces.* Photocopy and enlarge eleven patterns. Use patterns to cut the following pieces from bark cloth: two backrests (one with extra allowance), two front rolled arms (reverse one), two back rolled arms (reverse one), two side arms (reverse one), one apron, one base, one hinge, and one seat cushion. From moiré, cut one box strip, one box floor, and one lid/hinge lining.

2. *Cut chipboard pieces.* Referring to five chipboard diagrams, draft following pieces on 2-ply chipboard: one base, one box, one box floor, and one box lid. Draft one box lid underside on 1-ply chipboard. Cut out all pieces using X-Acto knife, steel ruler, and mat. Score box dashed lines. Use awl to punch four holes in base and one hole in box lid as indicated on diagrams.

Sewing the Chair

Note: Use the patterns as reference for stitching particulars.

1. *Sew backrest and apron.* Pin two backrests right sides together. Machine-stitch curved edge, beginning at straight edge and pivoting at dots. Clip into seam allowance at dots and notch curved seam allowance (*see* illustration A, below). Remove pins and turn backrest right side out. Machine-baste side edges from A to B (illustration B). Fold apron right side out, as indicated on pattern, with D dots aligned. Machine-baste side edges from C to D (illustration C). Set backrest and apron aside.

2. *Sew arms.* Pin back rolled arm and side arm right sides together, matching dots A and E. Machine-stitch from A to E, easing to fit, then notch curved seam allowance (illustration D). Pin front rolled arm to opposite end, right sides together, matching dots C and F. Stitch from C to F, then notch seam allowance (illustration E). Repeat process to make second arm in mirror image. Remove pins and turn both arms right side out (illustration F).

3. *Join arms and backrest.* Lay backrest flat, longer side face down. Slip one backrest "tab" into AB opening at back arm; if side arm does not butt backrest, use mirror image arm instead. Turn piece wrong side out and sew arm from A to B, catching tab in seam. Repeat process to join other arm to opposite side (illustration G).

4. *Join arms and apron.* Turn piece right side out. Holding apron so longer side is at back, slip tab into CD opening at front arm. Turn piece wrong side out and sew arm from C to D, catching tab in seam. Repeat process to join apron to opposite arm (illustration H). Note that all four

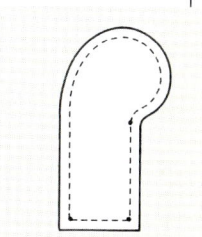

PATTERNS
See pages 44 and 45 for pattern pieces and enlargement instructions.

Sewing the Chair

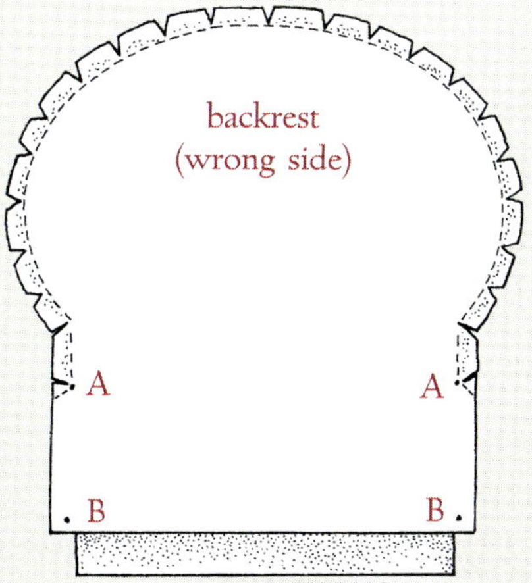

A. Sew the two backrests together.

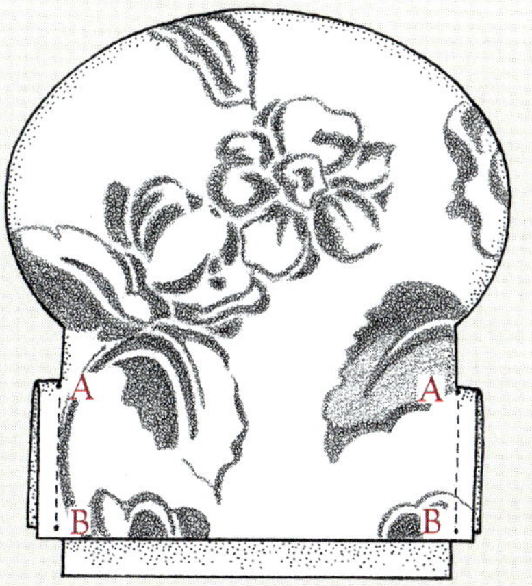

B. Turn the backrest right side out and machine-baste the side edges.

C. Fold the apron and machine-baste the side edges.

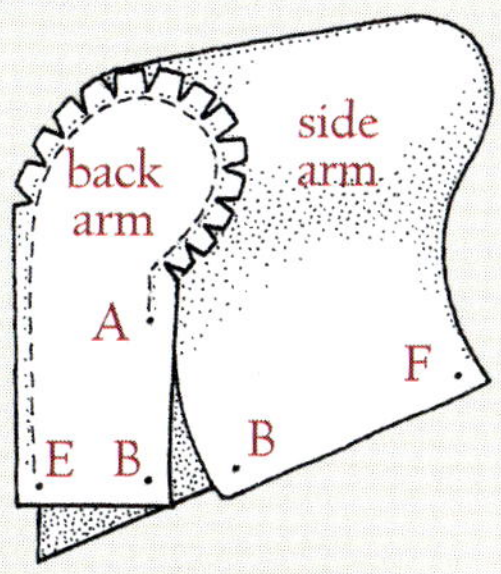

D. Sew one back rolled arm to a side arm.

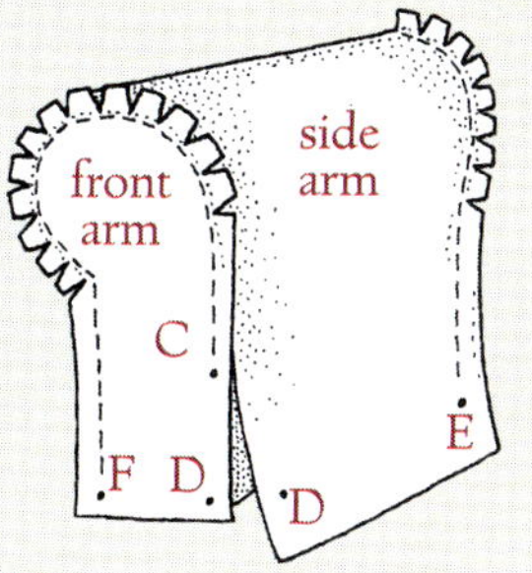

E. Sew a front rolled arm to the other end.

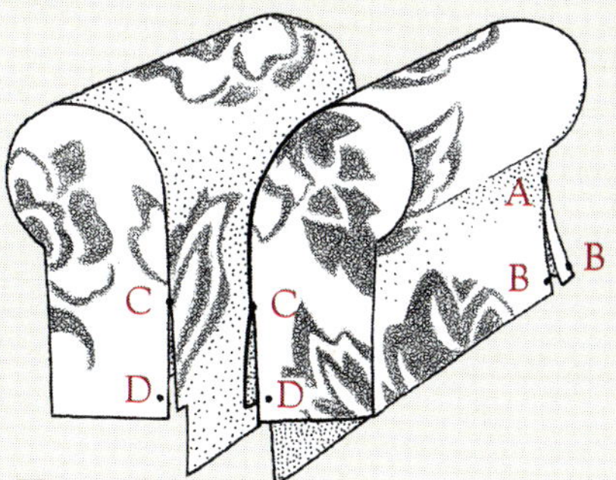

F. Sew a second arm in mirror image, then turn both arms right side out.

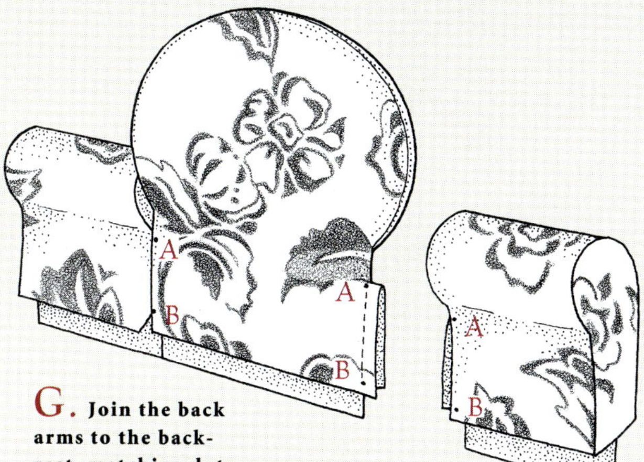

G. Join the back arms to the backrest, matching dots A and B.

H. Join the front arms to the apron, matching dots C and D.

LOW-SEW

DESIGNER'S TIP

When selecting fabric for this project, look for a large-scale pattern, but not one so large that it overwhelms the chair. Many rose heads on floral upholstery prints, for example, will be almost as large as the entire chair. Instead, look for a floral print with bouquets and smaller roses.

If possible, select a loosely woven upholstery fabric such as a bark cloth or a cotton blend. These fabrics have enough weight to resemble upholstery while still being flexible enough at the seams to prevent puckering. Avoid chintzes, backed fabrics, and dress fabrics.

extensions drop down into middle of chair.

5. *Join base.* With chair still wrong side out and extensions flipped out of the way, pin base to lower edge of chair sides and front, right sides together. Machine-stitch these three edges, pivoting at corners and backtracking at beginning and end; leave back seam open. Remove pins.

Assembling the Chair

1. *Add base and ball feet.* Screw ball feet into four holes in chipboard base to test fit, then remove. Stuff fiberfill into arms and backrest until chair is firm and plump but not stiff. Insert chipboard base into opening at chair back and position on fabric base. Slip-stitch opening closed. Using awl, pierce holes in base fabric to correspond to holes in chipboard. Squeeze small amount of glue into each hole, then screw in ball feet (illustration I).

2. *Line jewelry box with moiré.* Fold chipboard box on score lines and tape corners to make shallow box. Using stiff brush, apply glue to four outside walls. Position moiré box strip right side facing outwards at one corner, extending ½" beyond corner and box bottom, and press to adhere. Glue strip around box, overlapping ends at starting point (illustration J). Fold and glue lower allowance onto outside bottom of box. Glue top allowance to inside walls, tucking neatly at inside corners and letting excess fall onto inside bottom.

3. *Add jewelry box floor.* Lay moiré box floor wrong side up. Brush glue onto chipboard box floor, center it glue side down on moiré box floor, and press to adhere. Fold and glue moiré allowance onto chipboard, corners first, then edges. Brush glue evenly across this surface. Press piece, glue side down, into box (illustration K).

4. *Make padded chair seat.* Use chipboard box lid as template to cut same-size piece from batting. Lay bark cloth seat cushion wrong side up, then center batting and box lid on top. Fold and glue bark cloth allowance onto chipboard, corners first, then edges, same as jewelry box floor. Let dry 20 minutes. To tuft seat, thread needle with 7" length of button thread. Draw needle from underside up through center hole, through covered button shank, and back down through hole. Slip needle from thread. Run each thread tail through separate hole in two-hole button, pull snug, and tie off.

5. *Assemble jewelry box.* Lay moiré lid/hinge lining wrong side up. Glue chipboard box lid underside to lining (*see* pattern for position); fold and glue allowance onto chipboard on three sides only. To make ribbon tab, fold 2½" strip of ribbon in half and glue to lid underside. Fold and glue short edges of bark cloth hinge (*see* pattern). Glue bark cloth hinge to hinge section of lining, wrong sides together. Glue lid cushion to lid section of lining, sandwiching hinge in between (illustration L). Fit lid on box, then glue hinge to side and underside of box (illustration M).

6. *Complete chair.* Smooth backrest, side arm, and apron extensions onto floor of chair and glue down. Brush glue onto bottom of box and press onto chair floor, with hinge against apron. Glue hinge to apron. Using hot-glue gun, affix doily to backrest. Glue fringe to lower edge of chair all around (illustration N). ◆

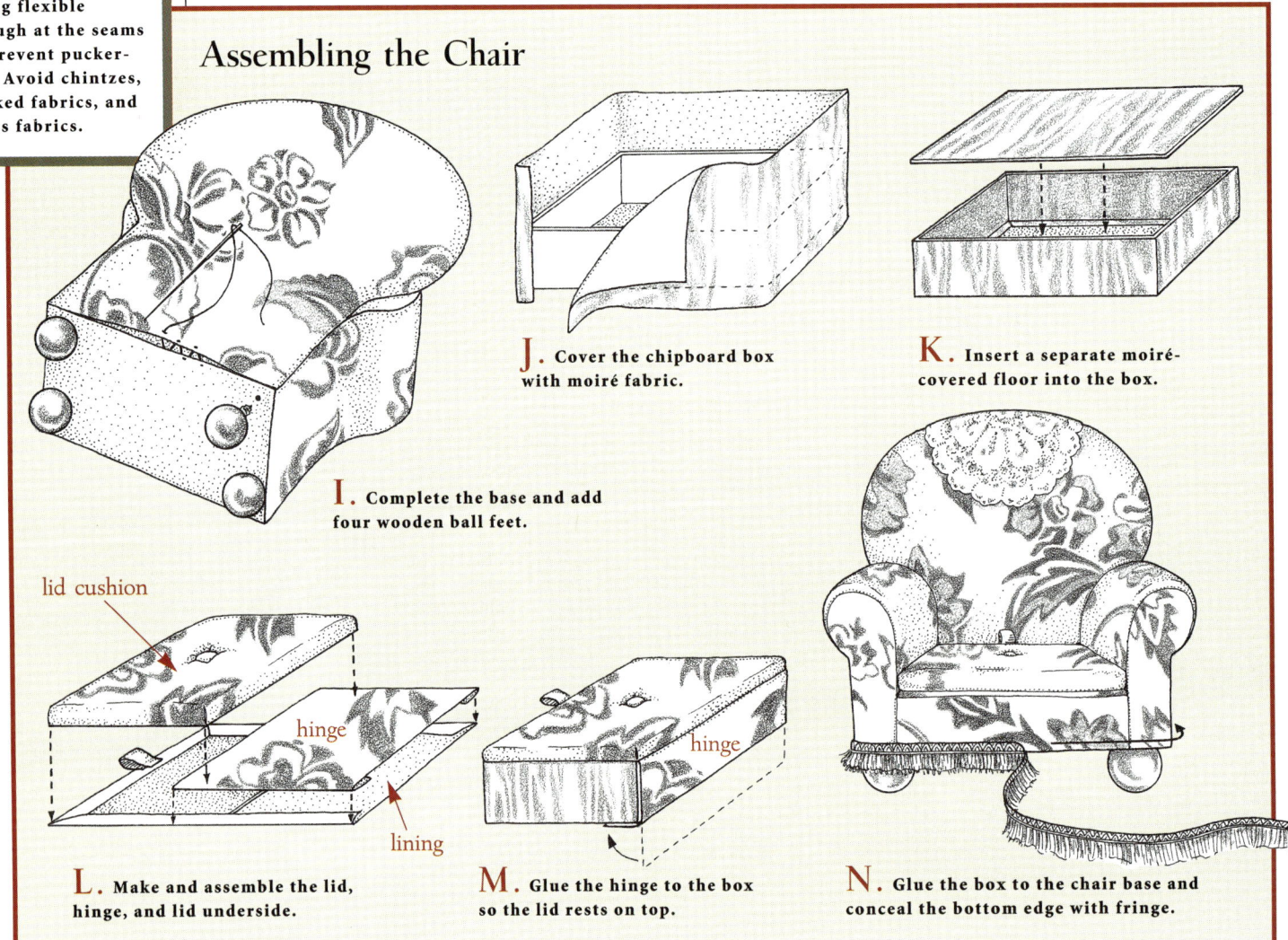

Assembling the Chair

I. Complete the base and add four wooden ball feet.

J. Cover the chipboard box with moiré fabric.

K. Insert a separate moiré-covered floor into the box.

L. Make and assemble the lid, hinge, and lid underside.

M. Glue the hinge to the box so the lid rests on top.

N. Glue the box to the chair base and conceal the bottom edge with fringe.

MIXED MEDIA

Embossed Gift Medallions
Cut a series of clay tags using a biscuit cutter, then glue on embossed seals.

COLOR PHOTOGRAPHY:
Carl Tremblay

ILLUSTRATION:
Harry Davis

STYLING:
Ritch Holben

BY LILY FRANKLIN

THESE SMALL DECORATED DISKS, made with thermoset clay, make an elegant but simple gift tag. After the gift has been opened, the tags can be removed from the package and hung on a Christmas tree or holiday wreath.

Making the tags is very quick and easy. I started by cutting small disks from modeling clay using a 1¾" biscuit cutter (you'll need about 1 ounce of clay per disk). For best results, roll out the dough on freezer paper. After the disks have baked, sand them smooth using an emery board, then glue on an embossed paper seal.

Lily Franklin is a designer and writer living in Albuquerque, New Mexico.

INSTRUCTIONS

1. *Roll out dough.* Knead clay, roll into ball, and flatten into pancake. Lay sheet of freezer paper flat, shiny side up. Hold down paper at each side with lattice strip and lay clay pancake in middle. Rest ends of rolling pin on lattice strips and roll out pancake to even ¼" thickness (*see illustration A, below*).

2. *Cut medallions.* Press biscuit cutter into rolled dough to cut as many medallions as possible (illustration B); lift off scrap dough and set aside. Line baking sheet with aluminum foil. Lift freezer paper from work surface, peel back paper until medallion underside rests on hand, then transfer disk to baking sheet. Reroll leftover dough and cut new medallions.

3. *Add wire hanging loops.* Cut 2" length of wire. Bend wire around pencil, grip ends with pliers, and twist together into tight spiral. Slip loop off pencil and clip stray ends close to spiral. Press spiraled stem into medallion edge until only loop remains visible. Repeat for remaining medallions.

4. *Bake and decorate medallions.* Preheat oven to 275 degrees. Bake medallions 10 to 20 minutes, checking progress regularly toward end to prevent scorching. Let cool several hours or overnight. Using emery board, smooth rims and sand imperfections. To finish, brush high-tack glue on back of cutouts and affix to face of each medallion using tweezers (illustration C). Add "To/From" text on back of tag using gold marker. To add gold stretchy cord, fold cord in half and tie cut ends together. Insert folded end of cord through wire loop, open loop about 1" to 2", insert tied ends through loop and pull tight. ◆

This round medallion measures about 1¾" across. For variation on this design, use a miniature holiday-shaped cookie cutter.

MATERIALS
Yields twelve medallions

- 12 ounces white Sculpey III modeling clay
- 26-gauge brass wire
- 12 embossed gold metallic paper cutouts, up to 1½" high
- High-tack glue
- Gold stretchy cord

You'll also need:
1¾" round biscuit cutter (or substitute); two ¼" x 1" x 14" lattice strips; rolling pin; baking sheet; aluminum foil; freezer paper; needle-nose pliers; wire cutters; emery board; tweezers; small round brush; round-barreled pencil; ruler; and fine-tipped gold marker.

MAKING THE GIFT TAGS

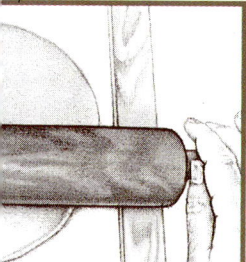

A. Roll out the clay.

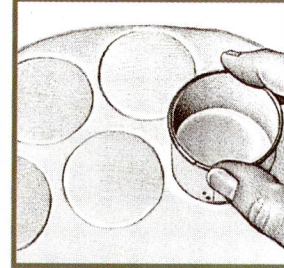

B. Cut the medallions using a biscuit cutter.

C. Finish the tag with an embossed paper seal.

GLASS

Secrets of Frosting Perfume Bottles

Transform ordinary glass containers into a set of heirloom perfume bottles using etching cream and decorative cabochon beads.

BY LILY FRANKLIN

The cylinder (left) and ovoid (right) bottles shown above measure about 5 inches and 3 inches high, respectively.

MATERIALS

Cylinder Bottle
- Small apothecary bottle with glass stopper
- 1 sheet aluminum leaf
- Plaid Liquid Leading glass paint, Gold #15151
- 2 ounces Armour Etch cream
- 2 ounces Wunda (or japan) size
- 4 ounces Accent Waterbase Crystal Clear Glaze

Ovoid Bottle
- Ovoid perfume bottle with glass stopper
- 7 to 10 opaline 5mm round cabochons
- 1 sheet composition gold leaf
- Plaid Liquid Leading glass paint, Gold #15151
- 2 ounces Armour Etch cream
- 2 ounces Wunda (or japan) size
- 4 ounces Accent Waterbase Crystal Clear Glaze
- Beacon FabriTac glue

You'll also need:
1/4"-, 1/2"-, and 1"-wide masking tape; 5/16"-diameter self-stick circles; #4 round sabeline brush; 3/4" foam brush; butter knife; cotton swab; rubber gloves; safety goggles; scissors; and white paper.

DESIGNER'S TIP

For more information on etching glass, see "Fast and Easy Frosted Glassware," page 8, Spring 1997.

COLOR PHOTOGRAPHY:
Carl Tremblay

ILLUSTRATION:
Michael Gellatly

STYLING:
Ritch Holben

THIS PROJECT USES WHAT I CALL the Cinderella principle: start with an ordinary glass flask, then use everyday craft materials to turn it into a beautiful, decorative perfume bottle. To achieve this transformation, I used etching cream for frosted effects, aluminum leafing for a rich, metallic finish, and glass cabochons for several drops of jewellike color.

The success of this project depends in large part on finding the right containers. The ideal bottles should be made of clear glass and have little to no surface decoration. (For mail-order options, see Sources and Resources, page 48.) If you can't find a bottle that matches the flea market finds I selected, follow the instructions for the bottle type that most closely resembles yours. One other important note: If your bottle has heavy casting seams (usually visible at the sides), it should not be leafed, as the metallic foil will only emphasize those areas. Such seams become virtually invisible under frosting, however.

The two bottles shown above illustrate basic rules of thumb regarding how to match a pattern to your bottle's shape. You can decorate a cylinder-shaped bottle with a wrap-around pattern such as a plaid; the absence of corners makes this a relatively quick and easy pattern to create. For a rounded shape with compound curves, an all-over pattern will be easiest, since such a shape will be hard to lay out with a rigid pattern.

If you plan to leaf your bottles, be sure to use size (the glue used to adhere the metallic leaf) that forms an invisible adhesive coating. Ordinary leaf size has a strong orange-brown tint, which will show up on clear glass. I recommend Wunda size, which is milky white when wet but dries clear.

Lily Franklin is a writer and designer living in Albuquerque, New Mexico.

INSTRUCTIONS

Note: Before you begin, wash bottle and stopper in warm, soapy water to remove residues. Air-dry, preferably overnight.

Making the Cylinder Bottle

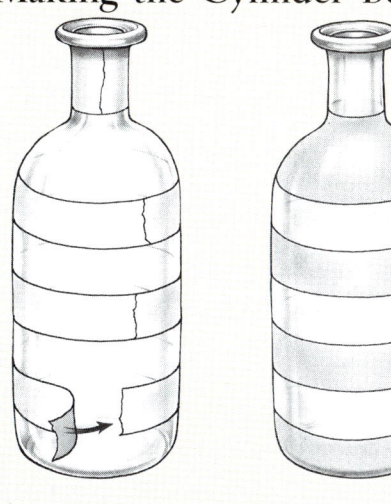 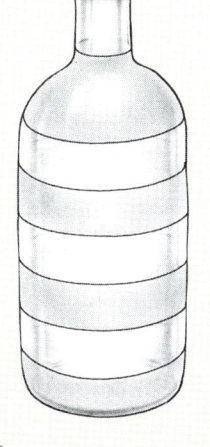 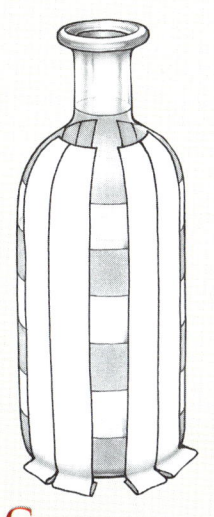 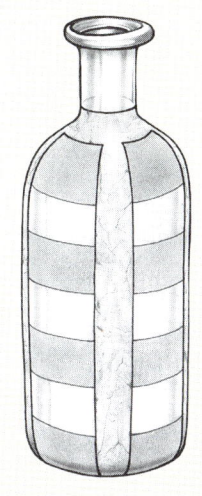 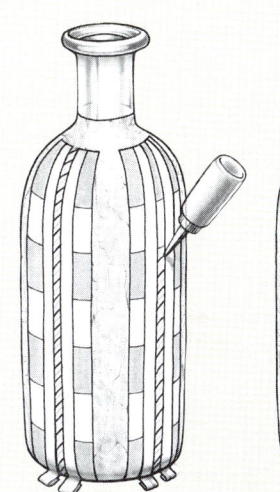 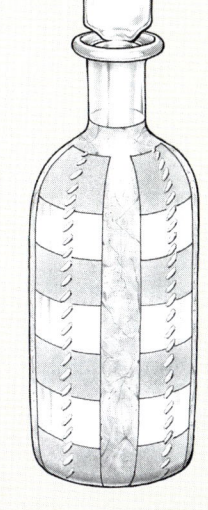

A. Use tape to mask off horizontal bands.

B. Frost the unmasked areas using etching cream.

C. Adhere the tape vertically to make four wide bars.

D. Apply aluminum leaf to the narrow unmasked areas.

E. Add glass paint between two bands of narrow tape.

F. Peel off the tape promptly after painting.

Decorating the Ovoid Bottle

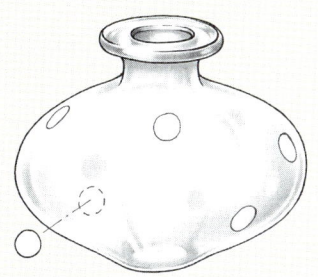 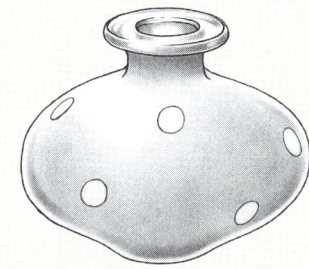 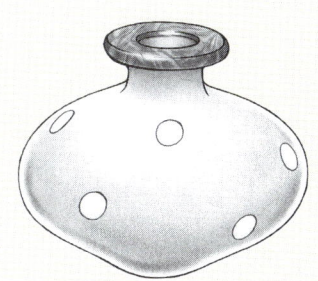 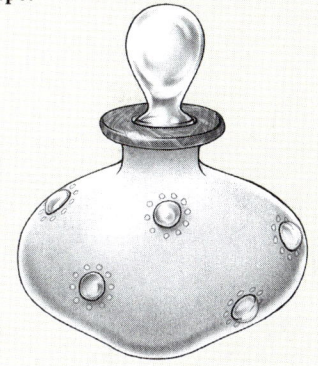

G. Apply self-stick circles to the bottle at random.

H. Frost the bottle with etching cream to create clear circles.

I. Decorate the flange with composition gold leaf.

J. Glue a cabochon to each clear circle, then add small dots of paint.

Decorating the Cylinder Bottle

1. *Mask horizontal bands.* Wrap ½"-wide masking tape around topmost portion of bottle, overlapping tape at starting point; stretch edge of tape if necessary to hug curved glass. Repeat process to apply parallel bands of tape around bottle one tape width apart. Repeat to tape bottle neck (*see illustration A, above*).

2. *Frost horizontal bands.* Following manufacturer's instructions and wearing gloves and goggles, apply Armour Etch cream to unmasked areas with foam brush. Let cream set 3 to 5 minutes. Wash off cream and remove tape to reveal etched bands (illustration B). Wash glass in soapy water and dry thoroughly.

3. *Mask vertical bars.* Starting just below neck, affix length of masking tape down side of cylinder. For clean line at top, cut tape with scissors; for easy removal, fold excess tape at bottom back on itself to make tab. Repeat to affix three additional tape lengths, for four bars that divide bottle vertically into quadrants. Increase width of these bars by adding new tape; overlap long edges until space between bars is reduced to about ½" (illustration C). (If bottle circumference is small, you may not need additional tape).

4. *Leaf vertical bars.* Using #4 brush, apply thin coat of size to unmasked areas. For clean line, run brush alongside tape edge; try not to brush over it. Apply size to collar and lower portion of bottle neck. Remove tape. Using butter knife, transfer sheet of aluminum leaf to white paper. Tear leaf into postage-stamp size pieces. When size reaches proper tack (10 to 15 minutes), transfer pieces of leaf to sized areas using fingertip, then tamp down with brush (illustration D). Let dry 1 hour, then buff gently with cotton ball. To seal and protect leafed sections, brush on thin coat of Accent waterbase glaze; do not seal frosted or clear areas. Let dry at least 1 hour.

5. *Paint gold accents.* Affix two lengths ¼" masking tape ⅛" apart down center of each open vertical section. Make a series of thin, angled lines by applying plaid glass paint directly from dispenser to unmasked area (illustration E). Remove tape immediately after painting to reveal final plaid design (illustration F).

Decorating the Ovoid Bottle

1. *Mask circles.* Press 5/16" self-adhesive paper dots on bottle surface, randomly spaced about 1" apart (illustration G).

2. *Frost bottle.* Refer to Cylinder Bottle, step 2. Frost entire bottle up to neck flange. Remove dots during washing (illustration H).

3. *Leaf bottle flange.* Refer to Cylinder Bottle, step 4. Brush size onto entire flange. Substitute gold composition leaf for aluminum leaf (illustration I).

4. *Add cabochons and gold accents.* Squeeze small dot of glue onto one clear circle. Pick up opaline cabochon with tweezers, set into glue and press down gently with cotton swab. Repeat process for remaining circles. Apply Plaid glass paint directly from dispenser to make circle of small dots around each bead (illustration J), then let dry 15 minutes. ◆

> **DESIGNER'S TIP**
>
> I don't recommend applying glue to surfaces that have been frosted with etching cream. To keep some areas clear, I adhered small 5/16" stationary label dots to the ovoid bottle before applying the etching cream. This creates a small circle of clear glass where the cabochons can be glued in place.

FRAMES

Quick Faux Bronzing with Wallpaper

Build a basic frame using pine molding, then create the look of repoussé bronze using an anaglyptic wallpaper border and a faux finish.

BY RITCH HOLBEN

If you don't have access to a power miter saw, or you want to save time and effort, consider having a frame shop build the basic frame for you. The cost is about $5 per corner.

COLOR PHOTOGRAPHY:
Carl Tremblay

ILLUSTRATION:
Judy Love

STYLING:
Ritch Holben

IF YOU'RE LOOKING FOR AN INEXpensive way to create the look of antique bronze, this project is for you. This faux metal frame requires just three primary materials: wood molding for the frame itself, paintable anaglyptic wallpaper border for an embossed relief effect, and three faux finishing products to create the antique patina.

The frame's construction can be broken into three rough stages. The first stage, the most time-consuming portion of the project, centers around building the frame from molding. First, measure the artwork to be framed, or select a standard size for the frame. Then use these measurements to determine how much molding you'll need to purchase. I selected 4"-wide extension jamb molding, a common pine window jamb molding found at lumber yards. This type of molding is pre-routed along one edge, which makes a perfect rabbet for the frame's glass, artwork, mat, or mirror.

Once you've purchased the molding, it must be miter-cut (cut on a 45-degree angle) using a power miter saw. If you don't own this type of saw, you can have a frame shop cut (and join) the corners for you. I joined the corners of my frame using flat angle brackets and finishing nails.

Once the basic frame is assembled, you can move to the second and third portions of the project: covering the frame with cut pieces of anaglyptic wallpaper border, and faux finishing the paper surface.

Ritch Holben, a craft designer, woodcrafter, and photo stylist, lives in Nahant, Massachusetts.

INSTRUCTIONS

Note: If you don't have access to a power miter saw, have a frame shop build the frame for you (steps 1, 2, and 4).

1. *Determine frame size.* Jot down figures as you do this step. First, measure artwork, including any mat or border (e.g., 13½" x 13½"). Subtract ½" from each measurement to account for rabbet overlap (e.g., 13" x 13"). Add two jamb molding widths, or 8", to determine finished frame dimensions (e.g., 21" x 21"). To determine length of jamb molding required, add the two dimensions, multiply by 2, and add 4" (e.g., 88"). Round up to nearest foot (e.g., 8 feet).

2. *Miter-cut frame pieces.* Put on safety goggles. Using power miter saw, crosscut molding in half. Reset saw for 45-degree right miter-cut (cut will slant from lower left to upper right). Stack pieces evenly, place in saw bed with rabbet edges toward you, and miter-cut right end. Measure and mark top edge to match one frame dimension from step 1. Reset saw for 45-degree left miter-cut, lay piece in saw bed with blade on mark, and make miter-cut for left end. Repeat process to saw two sides to match other frame dimension (*see* illustration A, next page).

3. *Mark wallpaper border pieces.* Use frame pieces as templates to mark wallpaper border pieces. Lay border face up on flat surface. Stand one frame piece on edge of border, perpendicular to work surface, and adjust to center design (illustration B). Lay frame piece face down so border extends evenly beyond each long edge. Using pencil, lightly trace diagonal edge of miter-cut at each end (illustration C). Repeat to mark a second, identical section on border. Mark two identical border sections for remaining two frame pieces in same way, for four lengths total.

MATERIALS

- 5-yard package Graham & Brown Super Fresco leaf prepasted wallpaper border, #92779
- Modern Options Blonde Bronze
- Modern Options Flemish Gray
- Modern Options Copper Topper
- Modern Options Primo Primer
- 4"-wide extension jamb molding (see step 1 to determine length)
- Eight flat angle brackets
- 32 wood screws (to fit brackets)
- Eight ¾"-long finishing nails
- Glazier's points
- Sawtooth picture hanger
- Latex primer
- Wood glue

You'll also need:
power miter saw; hammer; screwdriver; awl; X-Acto knife; steel ruler; self-healing cutting mat; hard rubber brayer; paint stirrer; masking tape; rubber gloves; safety goggles; large shallow disposable pan; three 1" foam brushes; sponge; pail of clean water; and paper and pencil.

4. *Miter-cut wallpaper border pieces.* Lay border marked side up on self-healing cutting mat. Select fullest or most interesting motif along one diagonal mark. Using X-Acto knife, cut around motif. Next, using steel ruler, cut along diagonal line as marked, but do not cut through motif. As you approach longer (outer) edge, cut diagonally clear to edge; on shorter (inside) edge, cut perpendicular to edge as shown in illustration D. Repeat to cut remaining border pieces.

5. *Assemble frame.* Lay four wood pieces face down on flat surface. At each corner, butt pieces and hold snug; if possible, have partner help. Position flat angle brackets across seam at inside and outside corners. Using bracket as template, punch holes in molding with awl. Remove brackets, apply wood glue to each miter-cut edge, bring edges together, and screw brackets in place (illustration E). On outside edge, tap two finishing nails into each corner. Blot oozing glue with damp sponge. Let dry at least 1 hour, but preferably overnight.

6. *Glue border to frame.* Using foam brush, cover frame front and inside and outside edges with latex primer. Let primer dry 1 hour. Following manufacturer's instructions, soak each border piece in bucket of water for 30 seconds. To prepare border, remove from water, fold adhesive sides crosswise onto each other without creasing, and let rest 5 minutes. Unfold border, position flat on right side of frame, and smooth down with damp sponge. Repeat process all around, overlapping motif at each corner and butting diagonal edges (illustration F). Tape down inner and outer edges, if necessary, and let dry overnight. Remove tape. If edges pop up, secure with wood glue (illustration G).

7. *Create antique finish.* Following manufacturer's instructions, and wearing rubber gloves and safety goggles, apply one coat Primo Primer to frame front and inside and outside edges; let dry 1 hour. Apply three coats Blonde Bronze followed by three to four coats Flemish Gray; let dry at least 1 hour after each coat. To color raised portion of design, pour small amount Copper Topper in shallow, disposable pan, roll brayer through solution, then roll onto frame. To tone down highlights, brush on one coat Flemish Grey. Let dry overnight. Following manufacturer's instructions, mount artwork in frame using a glazier's points, then add hanger to back of frame. ◆

DESIGNER'S TIP

Using a prepasted wallpaper border eliminates the messy step of applying adhesive by hand. To activate the paste, I used a process called booking. Start by soaking the border in water, then folding it so the prepasted areas touch one another. The paste should reach maximum stickiness in about 5 minutes.

Making the Frame

A. Miter-cut four frame pieces from jamb molding.

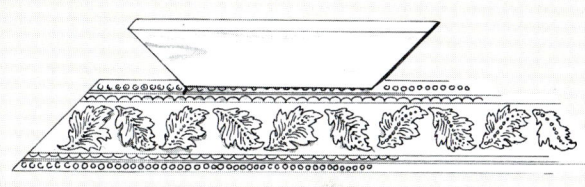

B. Use a cut piece of molding to determine how the wallpaper border pattern will fall on the finished frame...

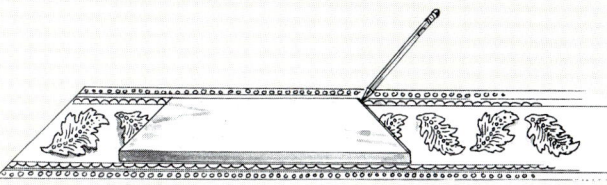

C. ...then use the piece of molding as a template for marking the border.

← Cut perpendicular to edge here

D. Miter-cut the border, but let the motif extend at one end.

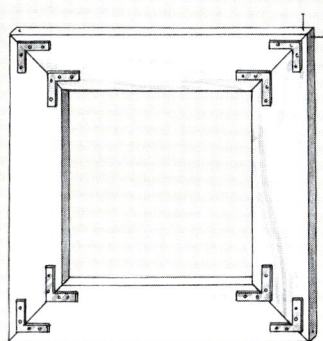

E. Join the frame pieces together on the back side.

F. Paste the border strips to the front of the frame.

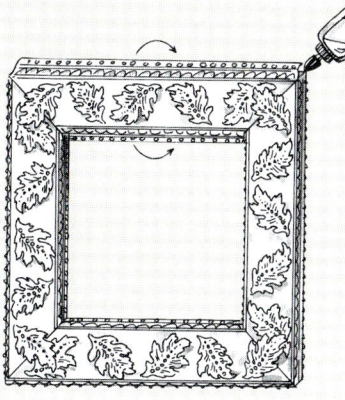

G. Glue down any loose inner and outer edges with wood glue.

H. Antique the frame with a decorative faux bronze finish.

PET ACCESSORIES

Portable Dog Bed

This bold and graphic dog bed, sewn from fake dalmation fur, can also be used as a carrier for a small dog or puppy.

🐾 BY MICHIO RYAN

This soft and cozy dog bed measures about 9 inches high by 15 inches wide by 18 inches long. The bed can be sewn with or without straps.

MATERIALS

- 1 1/8 yards 60"-wide fake dalmation fur
- 1 1/2 yards 45"-wide Thermolam Plus interlining
- 1/2 yard 45"-wide red polyester fleece
- 14" x 20" piece 2-ply chipboard
- White, red, and black sewing thread
- 5/8 yard black oval corded elastic
- Four black 7/8" four-hole coat buttons
- 42" bootlace
- Dog bed patterns (see page 47)

Portable version only:
- Two 3 1/2" x 5 1/2" pieces black crocodile-patterned vinyl
- 3 1/2" x 5 1/2" piece medium-gauge acetate
- 11' x 1"-wide red polypropylene webbed strap
- Four 1" black plastic single bar slides
- 1" chrome D-ring
- Small chrome leash clip
- Bone-shaped nameplate pattern (see page 47)
- Index card

You'll also need:
access to photocopier with enlarger; grip bodkin; straight pins; sewing machine; sewing shears; seam ripper; X-Acto knife; hand-sewing needle; steel ruler; self-healing cutting mat; and pencil.

Portable version:
T-pins; rubber bands; tape; matches; hole punch; tweezers; and tracing paper.

COLOR PHOTOGRAPHY:
Carl Tremblay

ILLUSTRATION:
Mary Newell DePalma

STYLING:
Ritch Holben

THIS DOG BED, DESIGNED FOR A small dog or puppy, can be made two different ways. For a bed that doubles as a carrier, attach the red webbing straps to the bed's side. Or leave off the straps for a functional and fashionable dog bed. In either design, the top edge of the bed is rolled down and secured with four buttons. On the portable version, the rolled-over edge conceals the carrying straps.

The construction process for this lightweight bed is actually quite simple. For the walls of the bed, I cut two similar pieces of fake dalmation fur. The exterior wall and the bottom of the bed are lined with Thermolam Plus interlining, then all three pieces are sewn together to create the basic bed. To create a soft but firm floor for the bed, I inserted a circle of chipboard into a removeable red fleece cover. This floor piece can be taken out of the bed, and both the bed and the red fleece floor cover can then be washed. For the finishing touches I added red straps, black buttons, and a black vinyl bone-shaped nameplate.

Sewn in a different fur (e.g., tiger or leopard) this bed could be adapted for a cat. Whatever fabric you select, make sure it—as well as the inset materials you select—is washable.

INSTRUCTIONS

Note: Follow all steps below to make portable dog bed. To make bed only, without carrying handles and name tag, omit steps 2, 8, and 9.

1. *Cut out fabric and chipboard pieces.* Photocopy and enlarge dog bed wall and floor patterns (*see page 47*). Observing cutting line, fold line variations and fur nap arrows, use patterns to cut the following pieces: From fur, cut one outside wall,

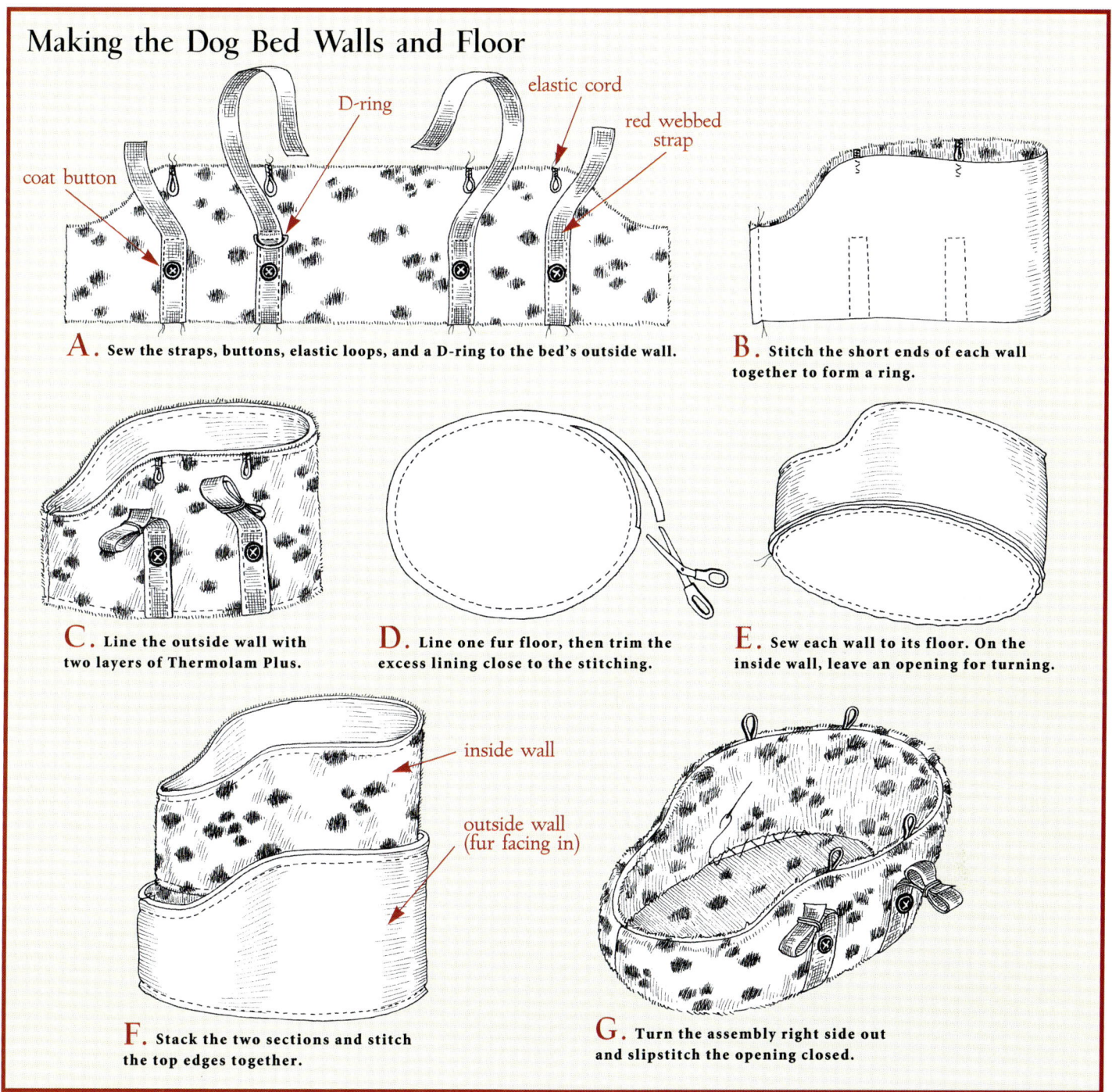

Making the Dog Bed Walls and Floor

A. Sew the straps, buttons, elastic loops, and a D-ring to the bed's outside wall.

B. Stitch the short ends of each wall together to form a ring.

C. Line the outside wall with two layers of Thermolam Plus.

D. Line one fur floor, then trim the excess lining close to the stitching.

E. Sew each wall to its floor. On the inside wall, leave an opening for turning.

F. Stack the two sections and stitch the top edges together.

G. Turn the assembly right side out and slipstitch the opening closed.

one inside wall, and two floors. From Thermolam Plus, cut two walls and two floors. From polyester fleece, cut one floor. Trace floor on chipboard, rest chipboard on cutting mat, and score and cut on marked line with X-Acto knife.

2. *Sew straps to outside wall.* Cut webbed strap into two 14" and two 52" straps. To prevent raveling, hold lit match near each cut end to sear and melt fibers. Lay fur outside wall face up on flat surface. Referring to pattern, pin straps to fur using T-pins. Starting at bottom edge of fur, topstitch one strap edge for 7", pivot and stitch across strap, pivot again and topstitch down opposite strap edge (*see* illustration A, above). Repeat for each strap. Join leash clip to D-ring, slide D-ring down one long strap to stitching, and stitch across strap to lock it in place.

3. *Sew buttons and elastic to outside wall.* Referring to pattern, sew button to outside wall at each X (if bed has straps, stitch directly through strap webbing). Cut four 4½" lengths of elastic cord. Hold ends of each length together, and zigzag to top edge of fur as marked (illustration A). If bed has straps, fold each strap into small bundle and secure with rubber band to keep straps out of the way during sewing process. Plastic slides will be added in step 6.

4. *Sew Thermolam interlining to fur.* Fold each fur wall in half, right sides facing, and machine-stitch short edges together to form a ring (illustration B). Set fur inside wall ring aside. Turn outside wall so fur faces out. Pin both Thermolam walls, for double thickness, to wrong side, matching edges all around; overlap Thermolam edges at seam to ease fit. Machine-baste ⅜" from top and bottom edges through all thicknesses (illustration C). Lay one fur floor face down, lay two

PET ACCESSORIES

Assembling the Dog Bed

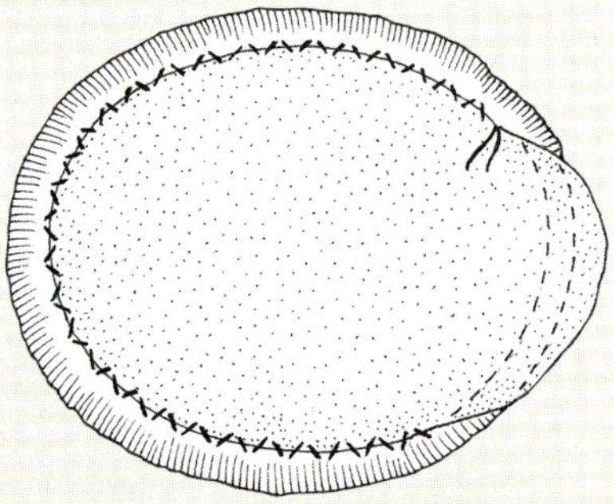

H. Zigzag the raw edge of the fleece to make a channel.

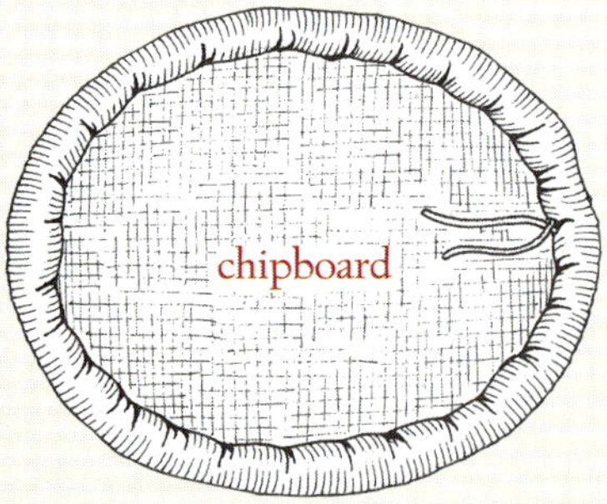

I. Thread a bootlace through the channel, then tie the fleece snugly around the chipboard floor.

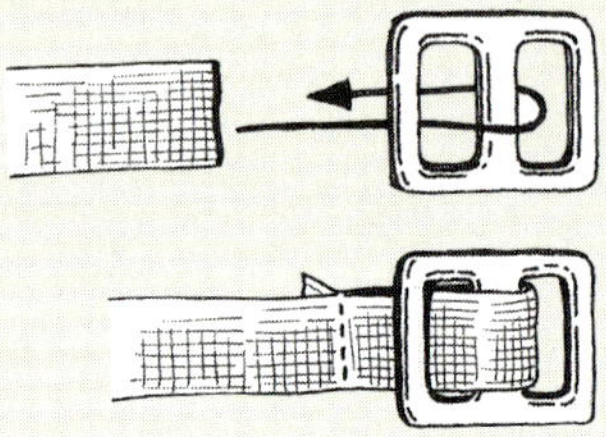

J. Join each short strap to a slide.

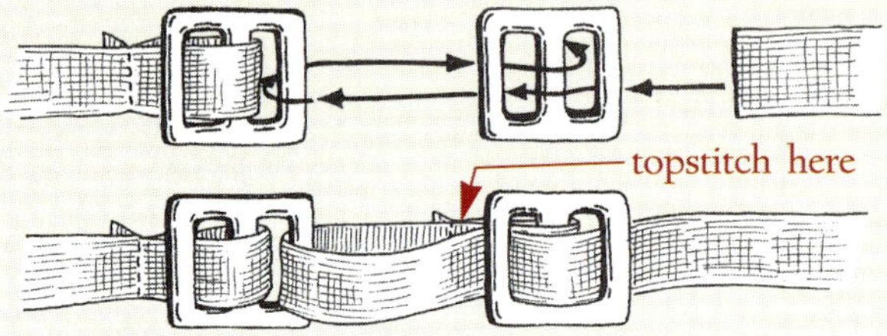

K. Thread each long strap through both slides. *topstitch here*

L. Stitch the bone outline, then trim off the excess.

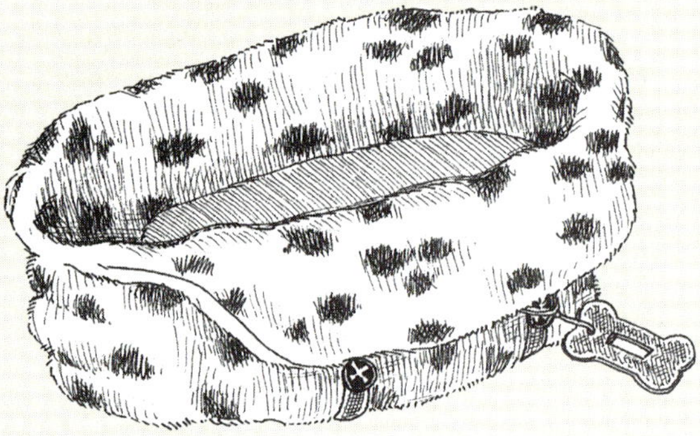

M. Button down the top edge to use the carrier as a bed.

DESIGNER'S TIP
To save time but keep the dog bed personalized, purchase a luggage tag instead of making the patent leather bone tag, and loop it onto one of the straps.

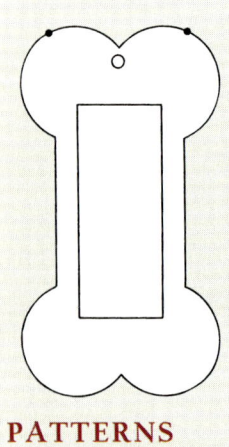

PATTERNS
See page 47 for pattern pieces and enlargement instructions.

Thermolam floors on top, and machine-baste ⅜" from edge all around. Using scissors, trim Thermolam only close to stitching (illustration D).

5. *Join walls and floors.* Stand outside wall upright, fur side in. Pin Thermolam-lined floor to lower edge, matching dots as indicated on pattern. Machine-stitch all around, easing to fit (illustration E). Repeat to join unlined (inside) wall and floor, but leave 10" opening in seam for turning right side out.

6. *Join outside and inside walls.* Stand outside wall/floor upright, fur side in. Lower inside wall/floor into it, fur side out (illustration F). Pin top edges together, matching dots and seams. Machine-stitch all around, easing to fit. Turn right side out through 10" opening. Stand bed upright, adjust and align fur, then slip-stitch opening closed (illustration G).

7. *Make floor insert.* Set machine for long, wide zigzag stitch. Fold edge of fleece floor 1" to wrong side and zigzag raw edge all around to make channel (illustration H, above). To open channel for bootlace drawstring, pick out a few stitches with seam ripper. Using grip bodkin, thread bootlace through channel. Lace fleece wrong side up, center chipboard floor on top, and draw bootlace ends together, cinching fleece around chipboard (illustration I). When fit is snug, tie off lace ends. Set floor insert aside.

8. *Attach slides.* Make sure straps don't twist as you add slides. Wrap end of each short strap once around slide center bar, then topstitch to secure (illustration J). Insert long strap through second slide, loop it around end bar of first slide, then loop it around center bar of second slide. Topstitch to secure (illustration K).

9. *Make tag.* Trace tag pattern (see page 47). Use ruler to draft rectangular window opening. Tape tracing to right side of one 3½" x 5½" piece of crocodile vinyl. Using X-Acto knife and steel ruler, cut out window opening. Stack vinyl pieces wrong sides together, slip acetate in between, and tape together. Using matching thread, machine-stitch bone outline between dots. Punch hole at open end one layer at a time. Cut away excess ⅛" beyond stitching (illustration L). Tear off tracing paper, using tweezers to remove small bits. Trim index card to fit tag, write pet's name on it, and insert in tag. Attach tag to snap clip.

10. *Finish bed.* Set floor insert into carrier. To use carrier as bed, fold down top edge to form collar and slip elastic loops around buttons. Tuck straps up under collar (illustration M). ◆

PAPER CRAFTS

Five-Minute Envelope Liners

There's no need for intricate patterns—just trace your envelope for custom-fit liners.

❧ BY ELIZABETH CAMERON

I LOVE THE LUXURY OF LINED envelopes, but am rarely willing to pay much for such elegance. So I set out to handcraft an envelope liner that was both inexpensive and fast enough to to make in quantity. I discovered that the envelope itself makes a natural pattern for the liner, making the process simple no matter what type of envelope you use.

My first attempts to glue the liner into the envelope were failures—I couldn't get the piece of decorative paper to slide into the envelope after it had been coated with glue. But then I realized that gluing the flap portion of the liner to the corresponding portion of the envelope was adequate. I also used a glue that dries clear, doesn't soak the paper, and dries flat (e.g., Elmer's School Glue).

For variation on these designs, think creatively. Try a page from an Asian or Russian newspaper, pages from an outdated atlas, handmade paper, and old map, or a decorative shopping bag.

Elizabeth Cameron is a freelance writer living in Brighton, Massachusetts.

INSTRUCTIONS

1. *Cut basic liner.* Open envelope, lay flat on decorative paper, and trace with pencil (*see* illustration A, below). Cut out with scissors.

2. *Custom-fit liner to envelope.* Using scissors, trim a scant 1/16" from each side edge of liner. Slide liner down into envelope until bottom edge touches envelope's bottom inner fold. If necessary, retrim sides to ease fit. Hold envelope and liner flaps together and carefully fold down to crease liner along envelope's flap. Unfold envelope and liner and lay flat. Fold down edges of liner to expose gummed section of envelope flap; number and orientation of creases will depend on shape of flap. Remove liner from envelope and cut along creases, rounding points and corners as desired (illustration B).

3. *Glue liner to envelope.* Reinsert liner in envelope. Fold down liner flap, then slip scrap paper underneath to protect envelope back. Brush glue across back of liner flap, press flap back into position against envelope flap, and smooth with fingers (illustration C). Weight under heavy book 1 hour. ◆

If you're planning to line a large quantity of envelopes, use the directions to make a basic pattern from which to trace and cut the remaining liners.

MATERIALS

- Envelopes
- Decorative paper
- Clear glue

You'll also need: pencil; scissors; stiff, flat 1/2" brush; scrap paper; and heavy book.

COLOR PHOTOGRAPHY:
Carl Tremblay

ILLUSTRATION:
Michael Gellatly

STYLING:
Ritch Holben

Making the Envelope Liners

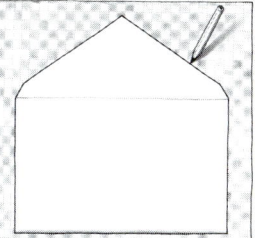

A. Trace and cut out an envelope liner from decorative paper.

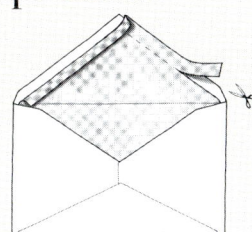

B. Crease and trim the liner flap to expose the envelope's gummed edges.

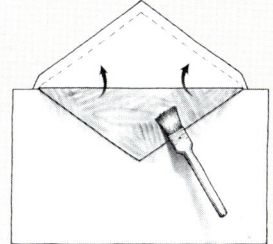

C. Glue the liner flap to the envelope flap.

DRIED FLOWERS

Dried Rosebud Pineapple

Build a pineapple-shaped base from florist foam, then cover it with dried rosebuds. Add a stem made from eucalyptus leaves.

🌶 BY CAROL ENDLER STERBENZ

This rosebud pineapple centerpiece works well for any season. For a different look entirely, cover the pineapple-shaped base with moss, miniature pinecones, or holiday foliage.

MATERIALS

- 250 to 275 dried rosebuds with stems
- 80 to 100 seed eucalyptus leaves, 2" to 3" long, on branch
- 2 florist foam bricks (about 2¾" x 4" x 8")
- Old pencil, about 4" long
- Aleene's Thick Designer Tacky glue

You'll also need: long-bladed knife; paring knife; lightweight pruning shears; steel ruler; permanent marker; stiff brush; and heavy book.

INSTRUCTIONS

1. *Build pineapple base.* To make straight cuts in florist foam, lay ruler on foam surface and run long-bladed knife perpendicular to ruler edge. Use illustration A, next page, as reference for cutting foam block into three pieces. First, trim both bricks to measure 7" long; set one aside (#1). Slice the other in half lengthwise to yield two 1⅜" x 4" x 7" pieces; set one aside (#2). From scrap, cut 1" x 1" x 4" block (#3). Using brush, apply glue to one 4" x 7" surface of block #1 and factory-cut 4" x 7" side of block #2. Press glued surfaces together (illustration B), weight with book, and let dry 1 hour.

2. *Carve pineapple form.* Stand glued foam block upright. Using marker, draw 1¼"-diameter circle on center of top end and 3¼"-diameter circle on opposite end. Using paring knife, shave off corners and straight edges (illustration C). Next, taper cylinder at top and bottom to meet circles; make form squat and full at bottom and narrower at top (illustration D).

3. *Add foam stem.* Dip eraser end of old pencil into glue, then insert pencil into block #3 until just 2" is showing (illustration E). Shave off edges of block #3 to make tapered stem with rounded top about 3" long (illustration F). Dip pointed end of pencil into glue and press it down into pineapple form (illustration G).

4. *Attach dried rosebuds to form.* Using shears, snip each rose stem 1" below calyx. Press stem into pineapple form at base. Add second rosebud in same way, butting first rosebud. Repeat process, adding rosebuds one by one (illustration H). Work up from base to cover entire pineapple form.

5. *Attach leaves to stem.* Using shears, snip individual eucalyptus leaves from branch, leaving ½" stems. Insert one leaf stem into foam stem at base. Add second stem in same way, adjacent to but staggered from first stem, so leaves can flare out. Repeat process, adding stems one by one and proceeding up until entire stem is covered (illustration I). ◆

DESIGNER'S TIP

To save money while shopping for materials, consider recycling several old dried flower arrangements for this project.

COLOR PHOTOGRAPHY:
Carl Tremblay

ILLUSTRATION:
Mary Newell DePalma

STYLING:
Ritch Holben

THIS PINEAPPLE-SHAPED DRIED flower design is not only quick and easy to assemble but also offers a fresh and different way to use dried or silk flowers.

The construction technique is very straightforward. I started by building a pineapple-shaped base using blocks of florist foam. Next, I covered the pineapple body with dried rosebuds. Last, I created a pineapple-like stem using dried seed eucalyptus leaves.

For variation on this design, you could cover the body with other types of dried or silk flowers. For a small-scale design such as this one (the finished pineapple measures about 9" high), look for flower heads that are small and compact, such as strawflower, cockscomb, small-petal hydrangea, and so forth. For the pineapple stem, consider substituting dried grasses or fern fronds. You can also cut off the stem from a live pineapple, let it dry 5-6 days, and use it as a stem for this centerpiece. When working with alternative materials, use a real pineapple as a reference to ensure that your piece has the correct proportions.

DRIED FLOWERS

Making the Pineapple Centerpiece

A. Cut three blocks to size from florist foam.

B. Glue blocks #1 and #2 together.

C. Shave off the corners and edges with a paring knife.

D. Continue shaving and shaping to make a squat pineapple form.

E. Glue a 4" pencil into the end of block #3.

F. Shave the edges of block #3 to make a rounded stem.

G. Attach the foam stem to the body of the pineapple.

H. Insert the rose stems into the foam pineapple.

I. Create a pineapple stem by inserting eucalyptus.

HISTORICAL TIDBIT

The pineapple is perhaps the most enduring symbol of hospitality. In the 15th century, exploring Spaniards knew they were welcome in a Caribbean village if a pineapple was placed at its entrance.

Colonial women arranged vast amounts of foods in tiers and on pedestals, then crowned the table with the distinctively shaped pineapple. The exotic fruit had such a reputation for rarity and expense that colonial confectioners sometimes rented pineapples to hostesses before selling them to other households for consumption. Because it was so sought after, guests at a feast where pineapple presided felt especially honored, and the pineapple came to represent welcome, good cheer, warmth, and family affection.

The pineapple was also used outside the home by returning sea captains, who speared a pineapple on the main gate posts of their homes to signal their return and as an open invitation to visitors. In the same vein, plantation owners carved pineapples into the wooden gate posts at the plantation entrance and wove them into table linens.

Rubber Stamping on Linen

Create a quick decorating accent using a pair of linen napkins and a rubber stamp.

☙ BY FRANCOISE HARDY

When selecting your rubber stamp, look for one with bold, graphic shapes, such as the 3" x 4½" leaf stamp we used. An image featuring delicate lines will lose clarity when viewed from a distance.

COLOR PHOTOGRAPHY:
Carl Tremblay

ILLUSTRATION:
Judy Love

STYLING:
Ritch Holben

MATERIALS
Yields 1 chair slip

- 2 natural-colored linen hem-stitched dinner napkins
- Four ¼" round glass beads
- Two 6mm oval glass beads
- Thread to match napkins
- Cream heat-set (washable) fabric paint (e.g., Jacquard)

You'll also need:
leaf rubber stamp; chocolate brown rubber stamp ink pad; brayer; flat pan; white paper; size 10 round watercolor brush; pencil and paper; masking tape; sewing machine; iron; press cloth; rotary cutter; acrylic grid ruler; self-healing cutting mat; tape measure; hand-sewing needle; fabric-marking pencil; pins; and scissors.

INSTRUCTIONS
Printing the Leaf Border

1. *Determine dimensions for fit.* Use illustration A, next page, as reference while measuring chair. Measure around chair back at widest part (e.g., 36") using tape measure; if back is curved, hold tape flat against curved area while measuring. Divide by 2 to determine width of chair slip (e.g., 18"). Measure from top of chair to lower edge of chair back, then add 1" to 3" for desired chair slip drop (e.g., 12"). Jot down measurements.

2. *Test-stamp border design.* On white paper, draft horizontal line equal to chair slip width. Load rubber stamp with ink, align it on baseline at left, and press down to stamp image. Trace stamp block outline with pencil, then lift up stamp (illustration B). Rotate stamp 180 degrees, realign it one space to right, and stamp again (illustration C). Repeat process to stamp four-leaf border (illustration D). If spacing between leaves pleases you, proceed to step 3. To tighten spacing, measure gap between leaves (illustration D) and make new test border as follows: Stamp first leaf and trace outline as before. For second leaf, align stamp edge to left of penciled edge by a length that equals or is smaller than the gap measurement; stamp remaining leaves at same spacing (illustration E). Cut out test border with scissors.

3. *Stamp cream leaf border.* Tape linen napkin right side up to flat work surface. Center stamped test border on one hem edge and tape down. Turn flat pan face down. Place small amount fabric paint on pan bottom and roll brayer through paint until fully loaded. Shed excess paint by rolling on clean area of pan, then roll brayer across rubber stamp to coat all raised areas. To print border, position stamp so lower edge butts top of hem-

LOOKING FOR A FAST AND EASY way to dress up an everyday dining room chair? You can make this tasteful chair slip in a few hours using two linen napkins and a rubber stamp.

To create a slightly three-dimensional effect, I stamped the leaves on the napkin using a two-part process. I started by stamping the leaves using cream-colored washable fabric paint. Then I stamped a second image, slightly offset, using chocolate brown rubber stamp ink. I stamped four images on the front of the chair slip (the side facing the table) and a single image on the chair's backside, but you can vary this design as desired.

I chose linen napkins because I was drawn to their edging detail as well as to the look and feel of the fabric. In addition, linen has a fine, flat weave that works well with rubber stamping. In addition, make sure the width of the napkin is greater than the width and thickness of the chair back.

Francoise Hardy is a Boston-based artisan and crafts person.

stitching and side edges line up with test border pencil lines. Gently press down stamp, then lift up. Reload stamp and repeat to print remaining images, rotating stamp 180 degrees after each print (illustration F). Tape second napkin to work surface, then mark center of one edge with pin. Load rubber stamp with paint as before, then stamp single image along center of edge. Wash stamp promptly with soap and warm water and dry thoroughly. Use brush and cream paint to touch up weak or broken areas within stamped images on both napkins. Let napkins dry in taped-down position for at least 1 hour or overnight.

4. *Stamp chocolate brown leaves.* To offset print and create shadow effect, remove tape from test border, slide test border ¼" to ⅜" to right, and retape. Load stamp with brown ink from pad. Align lower edge of stamp with lower edge of hemstitching; align side edges with test border pencil lines. Press down to stamp image. Reload stamp and repeat, rotating stamp 180 degrees after each print (illustration G). Print single shadow overlay on second napkin as before. Let dry overnight. To set color, press both napkins with hot dry iron and press cloth.

Sewing the Chair Slip

1. *Cut chair slip pieces.* Refer to chair slip measurements from "Printing the Leaf Border," step 1. Using ruler and fabric marking pencil, draft three sides of rectangle on each napkin so that rectangle is 1" wider than chair slip width (e.g., 19"), and ½" longer than chair slip drop (e.g., 12½"). Note that printed edge will form lower edge of chair slip; be sure leaf design is centered on this edge. Using rotary cutter, ruler, and cutting mat, cut out both pieces on three sides (illustration H).

2. *Sew seams.* Pin pieces together, right sides facing and edges matching. Machine-stitch raw edges on three sides; leave hemstitched edge open. To box corners, open each corner, fold corner so seams align, then stitch diagonally across corner 1" from point (illustration I and detail). Turn chair slip right side out. Finger-press creases to define boxy shape.

3. *Add beads.* Cut 6" length of thread. Knot one end, then draw thread into oval bead, lodging knot inside hole. Thread on two round beads, then tack bead strand to lower edge of chair slip at side seam. Repeat at opposite edge (illustration J). Place chair slip over back of chair. ◆

> **DESIGNER'S TIP**
>
> For a holiday variation on this design, subsitute cream-colored liner napkins, silver fabric paint, and gold stamping ink.

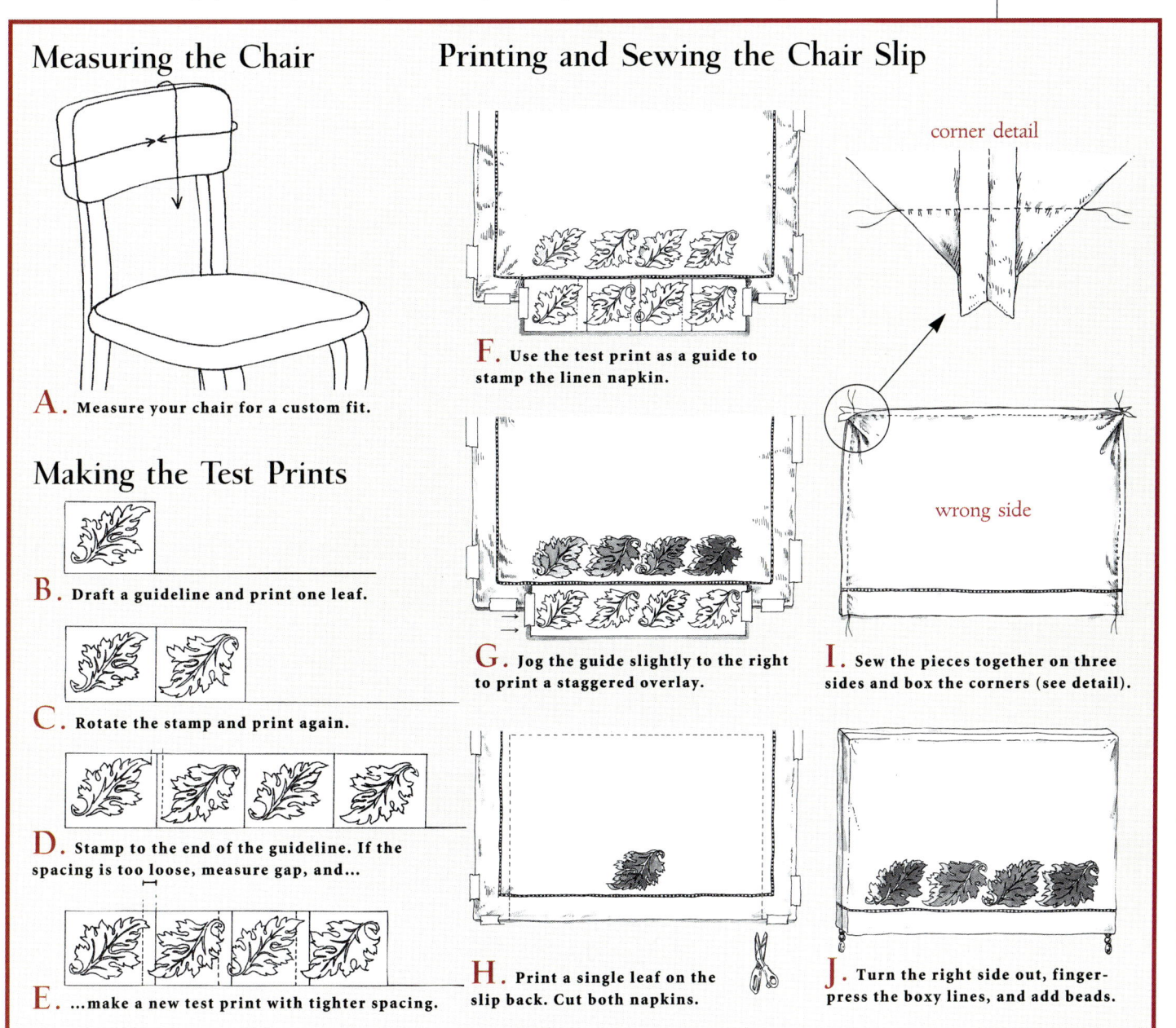

Fall 1997 Patterns

Faux Enamel Coffeepot and Teapots

(*see* article, page 10)

NOTE: PHOTOCOPY ALL PIECES AT 100%

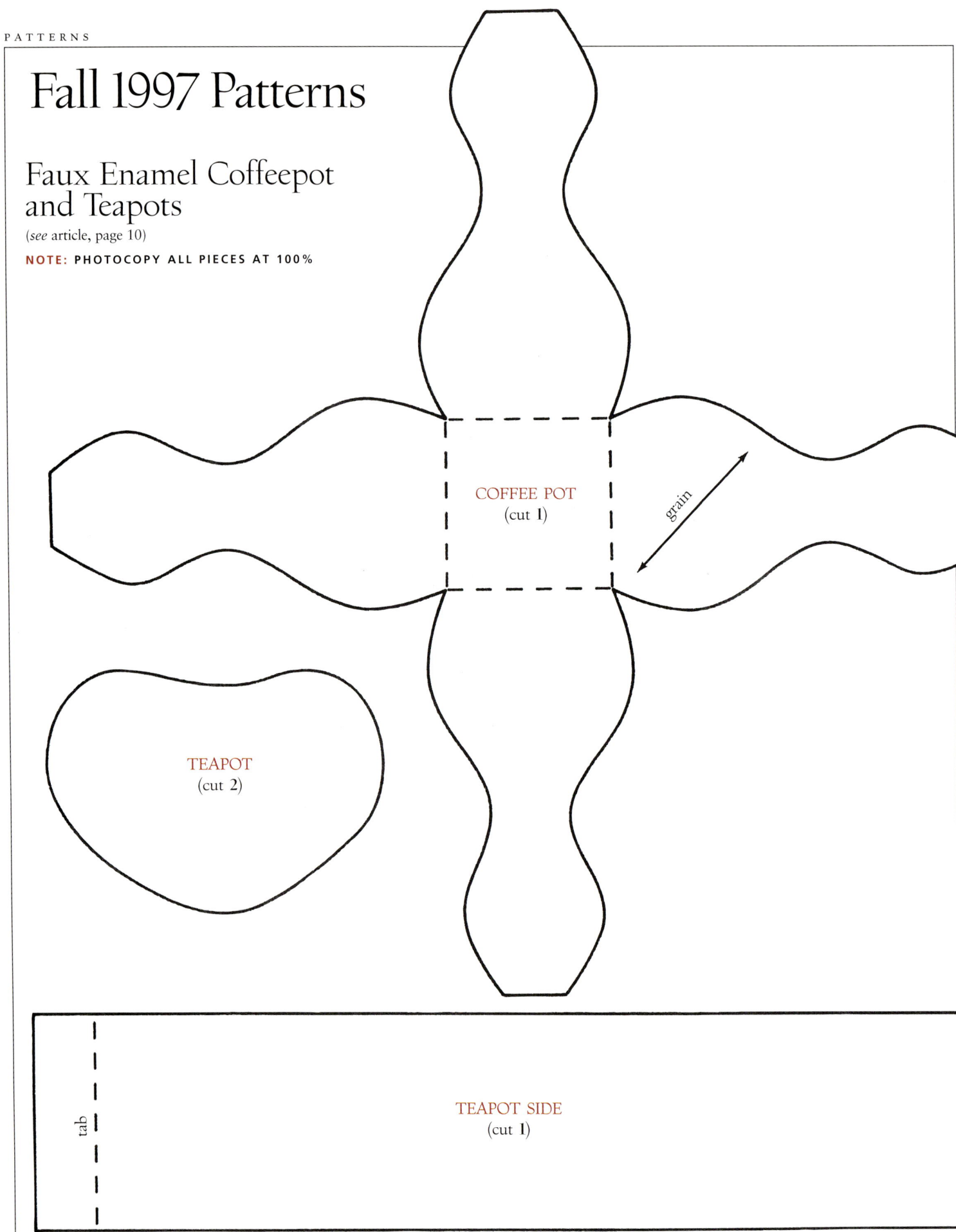

Scottie Dog Holiday Cards

(*see* article, page 24)

NOTE: PHOTOCOPY ALL PIECES AT 100%

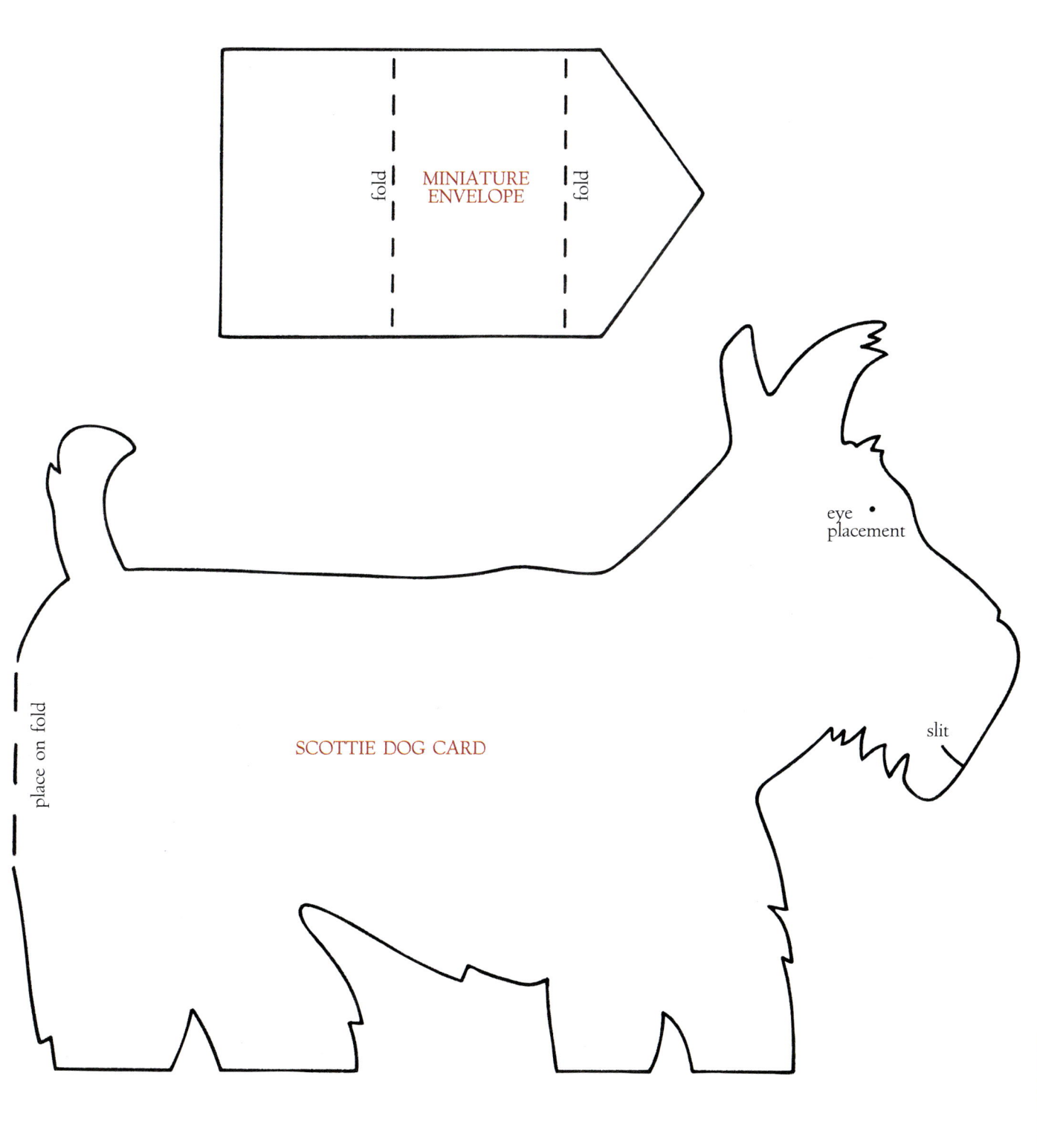

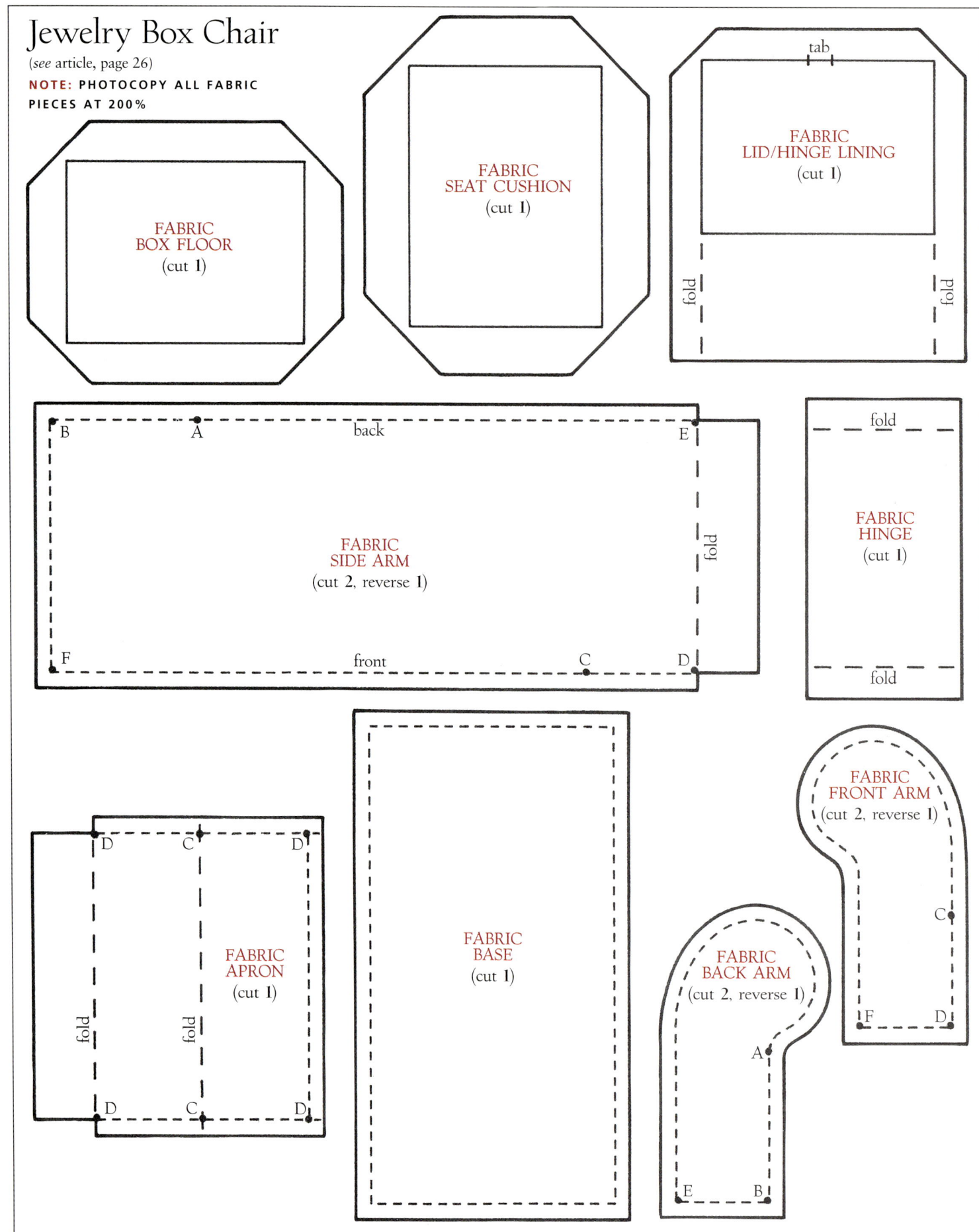

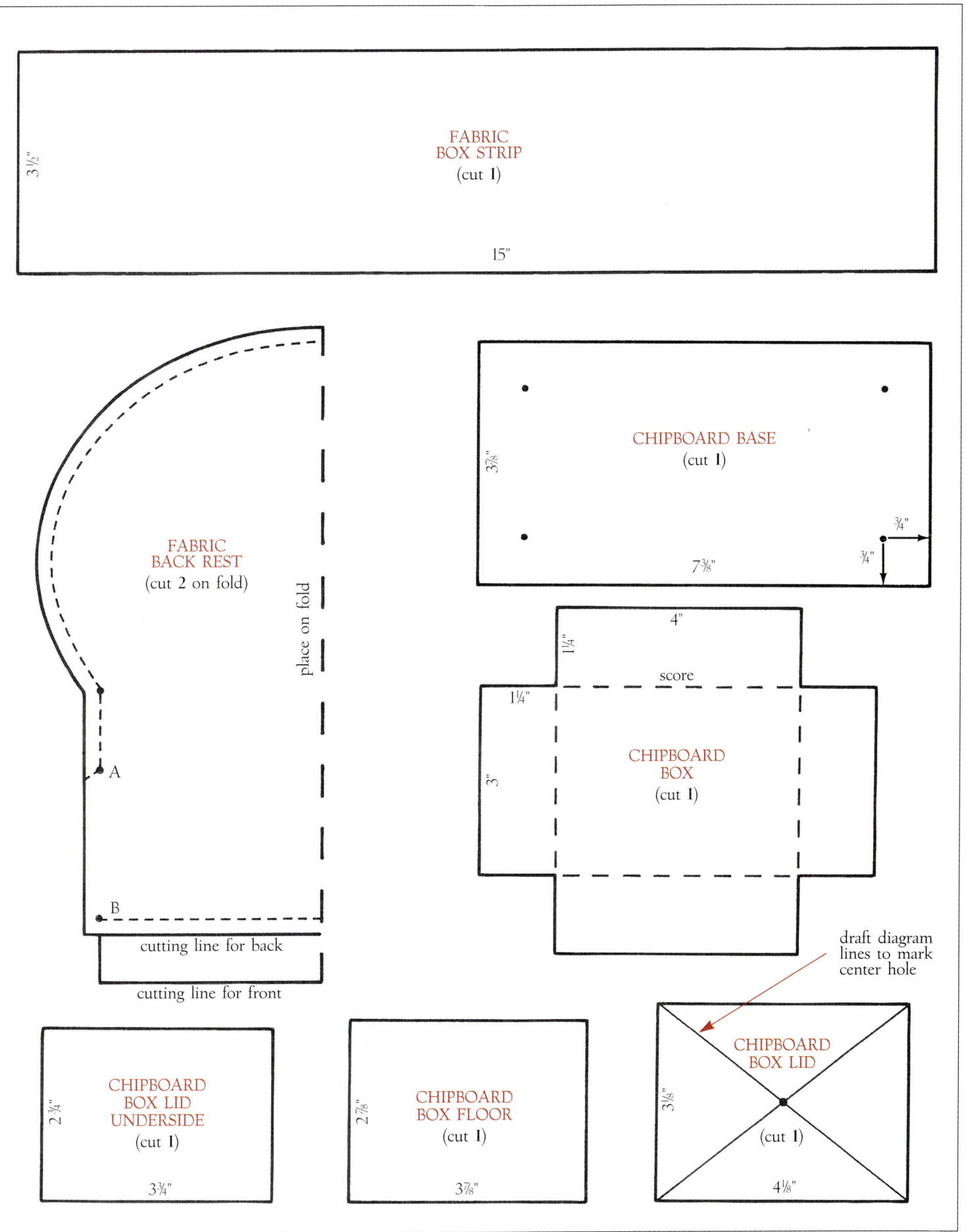

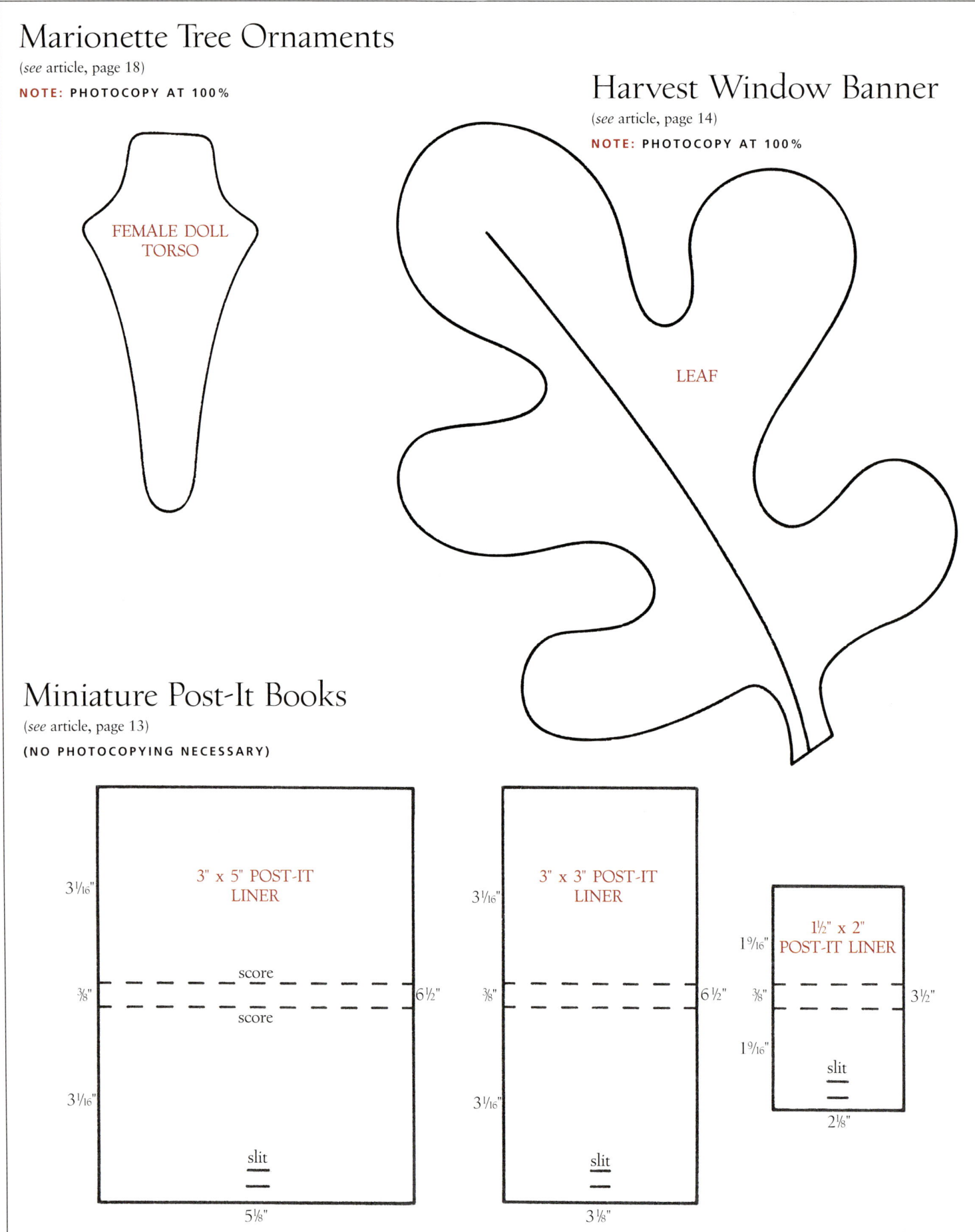

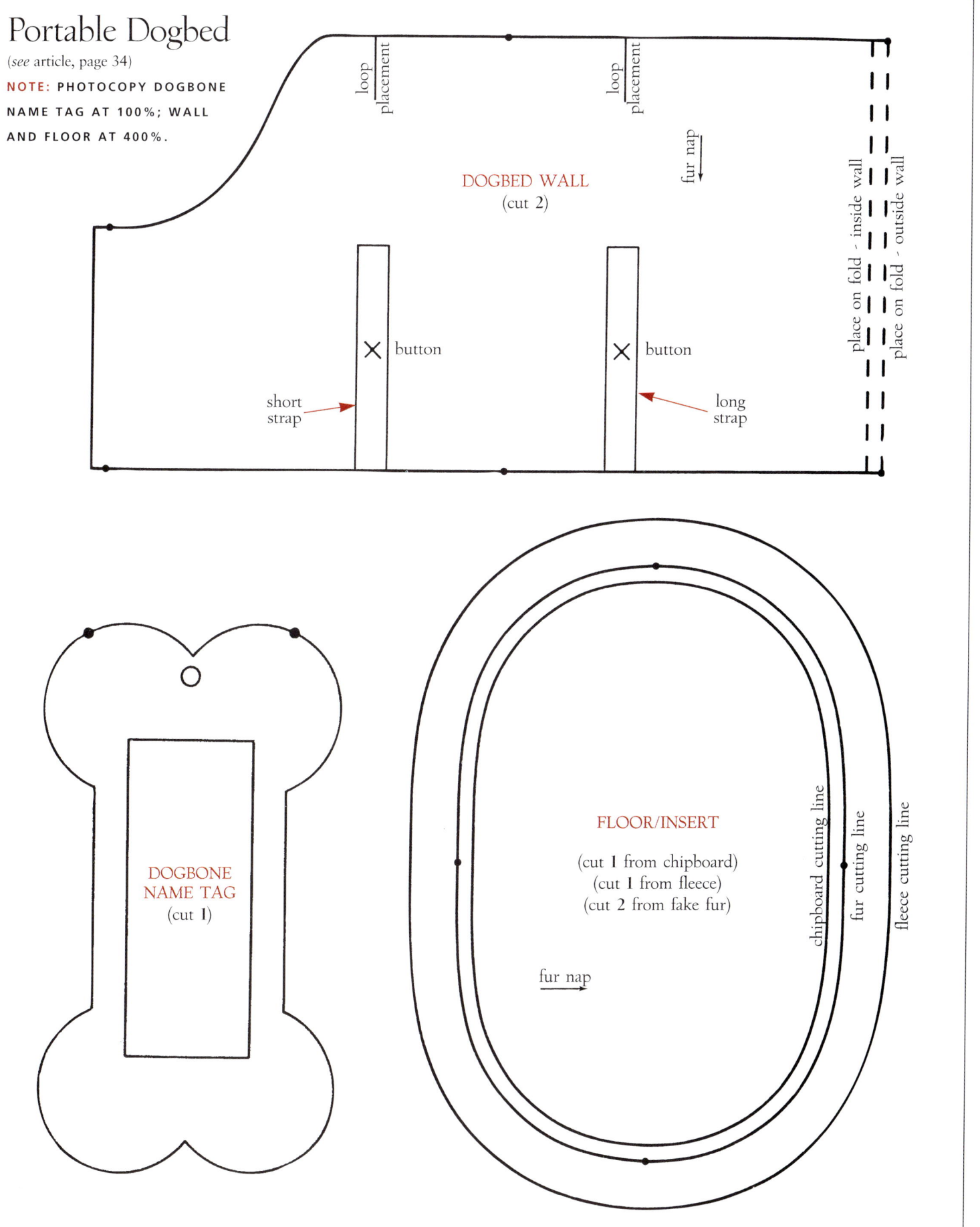

Sources & Resources

The following are specific mail-order sources for particular items, arranged by article.

Most of the materials used in this issue are available at your local craft supply store, florist, fabric shop, hardware store, or bead and jewelry supply. Generic craft supplies can be ordered from such catalogs as Craft King, Dick Blick Art Materials, Newark Dressmaker Supply, Pearl Paint Company, or Sunshine Discount Crafts. The following are specific sources for harder-to-find items, arranged by article. The suggested retail prices listed here were current at press time. Contact the suppliers directly to confirm prices and availability.

Quick Home Accents, page 6
Pressed tin cornice from $5.50 to $19 per 4-foot section at Lynn Lumber.

Pavé Gift Box, page 8
Classic wooden box for $9.62 from Pearl Paint. Aleene's Thick Designer Tacky glue for $2.15 per 4-ounce jar from Craft King. Assortment of colored glass marbles starting at $6.40 from Nasco Arts & Crafts.

Faux Enamel Coffeepot and Teapots, page 10
Crayola Model Magic lightweight modeling dough for $3.80 per 4-ounce-tube from Pearl Paint. Giftwrap sheets (stock varies) starting at $2 from Kate's Paperie. Plaid Royal Coat Decoupage Finish for $3.99 per 8-ounce jar from Sunshine Discount Crafts.

Post-It Books, page 13
Ultrasuede 6" x 9" scraps for $10.25 per 5-piece collection of colors, or individual 9" x 12" scraps for $4.25 from Nancy's Notions Ltd.

Harvest Banner, page 14
Metallic sheer nylon fabric from $2.99 per yard and opaque lining fabric for $2.99 per yard from P&S Fabric.

Marionette Tree Ornaments, page 18
Sculpey III modeling clay for $1.43 per 2-ounce bar from Pearl Paint. Silk charmeuse fabric starting at $18.95 per yard from Paterson Silks.

Glittery Fruit, page 22
Microfine glitters starting at $3.49 per one ounce container from Jones Tones.

Dog Cards, page 24
Black, heavyweight glossy paper (#10-4320) for $1.79 per 20" x 26" sheet from Charrette. Plaid giftwrap (seasonal item) for $2.50 per sheet from Kate's Paperie. Wiggle eyes (4mm) for 47 cents per 32-piece set from Nasco Arts & Crafts.

Jewelry Box Chair, page 26
Bark cloth for $10 per yard from Shor International, Inc.

Embossed Gift Tags, page 29
Sculpey III modeling clay for $1.35 per 2-ounce bar and Plaid Royal Coat Decoupage Finish for $3.79 per 8-ounce jar from Sunshine Discount Crafts.

Frosted Bottles, page 30
Clear glass apothecary bottles (varying sizes and prices) from Scientific Specialties Service, Inc. Armour Etch cream for $5.50 per 3-ounce bottle from Eastern Art Glass. Round cabochon paste stones for 15 cents each at Metalliferous. Wunda Size synthetic size for $6 per 2-ounce jar, Accent's Waterbase Crystal Clear Glaze (gloss finish) for $2.99 per 4-ounce jar, and aluminum leaf for $4.20 per 25-sheet booklet, all from Pearl Paint.

Bronze Frame, page 32
Graham & Brown Super Fresco leaf prepasted wallpaper border (#92779) for $5.34 per 15-foot package from Home Depot. Modern Option's Blonde Bronze Base (12-ounce bottle), Flemish Gray (16-ounce bottle), and Copper Topper (8-ounce bottle), all for $12.80 (each) from Pearl Paint.

Portable Dog Bed, page 34
Dalmation faux fur fabric for $20 per yard, red webbed strapping (1-inch-wide) for $2.20 per yard, and Thermolam Plus interlining for $10 per yard, all from Paterson Silks. Chrome D-ring for 70 cents from Canal Surplus. Red polyester fleece for $3.95 per yard from Oppenheim's.

Rosebud Pineapple, page 38
Dried rosebuds for $26 per pound (contains approximately 500 rosebuds) from J&T Imports Dried Flowers. Eucalyptus leaves for $4.63 per 4-ounce bunch from Craft King.

Chair Slip, page 40
Beads starting at 3 cents from Bead-works, Inc. For rubber stamp suppliers, order a copy of Rubberstampmadness for $7.

The following companies are mentioned in the listing above. Contact each individually for a price list or catalog.

BEADWORKS, INC.
149 Water Street, Norwalk, CT 06854; 203-852-9108

CANAL SURPLUS
363 Canal Street, New York, NY 10013; 212-966-3275

CHARRETTE
P.O. Box 4010, Woburn, MA 01888-4010; 800-367-3729

CRAFT KING
P.O. Box 90637, Lakeland, FL 33804; 800-769-9494

DICK BLICK ART MATERIALS
P.O. Box 1267, Galesburg, IL 61402-1267; 800-447-8192

EASTERN ART GLASS
P.O. Box 341, Wyckoff, NJ 07481; 800-872-3458

HOME DEPOT
Call 770-433-8211 for store locations.

J&T IMPORTS DRIED FLOWERS
143 South Cedros, #F, Solana Beach, CA 92075; 619-481-9781

JONES TONES
33865 United Avenue, Pueblo, CO 81001; 800-397-9667

KATE'S PAPERIE
561 Broadway, New York, NY 10012; 212-941-9816 or 800-809-9880

LYNN LUMBER
180 Commercial Street, Lynn, MA 01905; 617-592-0400

METALLIFEROUS
34 West 46th Street, New York, NY 10036; 888-944-0909

NANCY'S NOTIONS LTD.
P.O. Box 683, Beaver Dam, WI 53916-0683; 800-833-0690

NASCO ARTS & CRAFTS
901 Janesville Avenue, P.O. Box 901, Fort Atkinson, WI 53538-0901; 800-558-9595

NEWARK DRESSMAKER SUPPLY
6473 Ruch Road, P.O. Box 20730, Lehigh Valley, PA 18002-0730; 610-837-7500

OPPENHEIM'S
P.O. Box 29, 120 East Main Street, North Manchester, IN 46962-0052; 800-461-6728

P&S FABRIC
355 Broadway, New York, NY 10013; 212-226-1534

PATERSON SILKS
36 East 14th Street, New York, NY 10003; 212-929-7861

PEARL PAINT COMPANY, INC.
308 Canal Street, New York, NY 10003; 800-451-7327 (catalog) or 800-221-6845 x2297 (main store)

RUBBERSTAMPMADNESS
P.O. Box 610, Corvallis, OR 97339-0610; 541-752-0075

SCIENTIFIC SPECIALTIES SERVICES, INC.
P.O. Box 352, Randallstown, MD 21133; 800-648-7800

SHOR INTERNATIONAL, INC.
401 Broadway, New York, NY 10013; 212-274-8910

SUNSHINE DISCOUNT CRAFTS
P.O. Box 301, Largo, FL 3464-0301; 800-729-2878

TOHO SHOJI
990 Sixth Avenue, New York, NY 10018; 212-868-7466

CORRECTIONS:
The wooden trays listed in Notes from Readers (Spring 1997) are no longer offered by S&S. Call the company at 800-243-9232 for information. The Rose Petal Jelly Recipe (Spring 1997) requires a 1.75-oz. package of powdered pectin. ◆

Quick Projects

Decorate your guest towels using cord, silk flower petals, ribbon, or buttons.

Towels shown clockwise from upper left: Silk flower petals on cream-colored linen, ribbon rose and leaf on pink linen, silk cord and beads on moss linen, and running stitch and shirt buttons on soft brown linen.

TOWELS WITH A TWIST

While plain linen guest towels can be quite beautiful on their own, adding an accent such as silk flower petals, ribbon roses, or cord can create a custom look. Follow the directions provided here, or use these ideas as inspiration.

■ **Silk flower petals on cream-colored linen:** Remove the petals from a small silk flower by separating the petals from the stamen. Scatter the petals randomly along one edge of the towel, then pin each petal in place. Hand-tack each petal to the towel, finishing each center with a small seed pearl.

■ **Ribbon rose and leaf on pink linen:** Fold wire-edged ribbon into a rose (see "The Best Way to Make Ribbon Roses," Winter 1996, for specific directions). Tack the rose to the center of the towel, adding green ribbon stems and leaves made from folded ribbon.

■ **Silk cord and beads on moss linen:** Arrange silk cord in loops and curves across the hem of the towel, then secure it with pins. Hand-sew the cord in place, or zigzag on a sewing machine. Use contrasting thread for one look; use monofilament thread for a quieter statement. Hand-sew decorative beads in place.

■ **Running stitch and shirt buttons on soft brown linen:** Use a sewing needle and white embroidery floss to sew a running stitch across the width of the towel's hemline. Arrange two- and three-button groups of small, white men's-shirt buttons along the lower edge, then hand-sew each in place. ◆

COLOR PHOTOGRAPHY:
Carl Tremblay

DESIGN:
Genevieve A. Sterbenz

STYLING:
Ritch Holben

Organdy Gift Bags

Looking for a fresh way to wrap gift sets of household tools, cooking utensils, or bath sundries? Don't hide them in a box—instead, make a delicate organdy gift bag. Later, the bag can be reused to store any number of items, from linens to bath soaps. We filled these bags with a variety of heavy items, but take care not to overload the bag and risk ripping the seams.

    To sew the bag, start by folding one-half yard of 45"-wide organdy in half crosswise, right side out with selvages matching. Machine-stitch the raw edges, then trim the seam allowances 3/8" from the stitching. Turn the bag wrong side out and stitch along the same edges to make 1/2"-wide French seams. Turn the bag right side out. Fold and press the selvage 4" to the inside and topstitch. The finished bag should resemble a small pillowcase. Load the gift items inside, then cinch the top with contrasting wire-edged ribbon.

COLOR PHOTOGRAPHY: **Carl Tremblay**   STYLING: **Ritch Holben**   DESIGN: **Genevieve A. Sterbenz**

NUMBER EIGHTEEN CHRISTMAS 1997

Handcraft
ILLUSTRATED

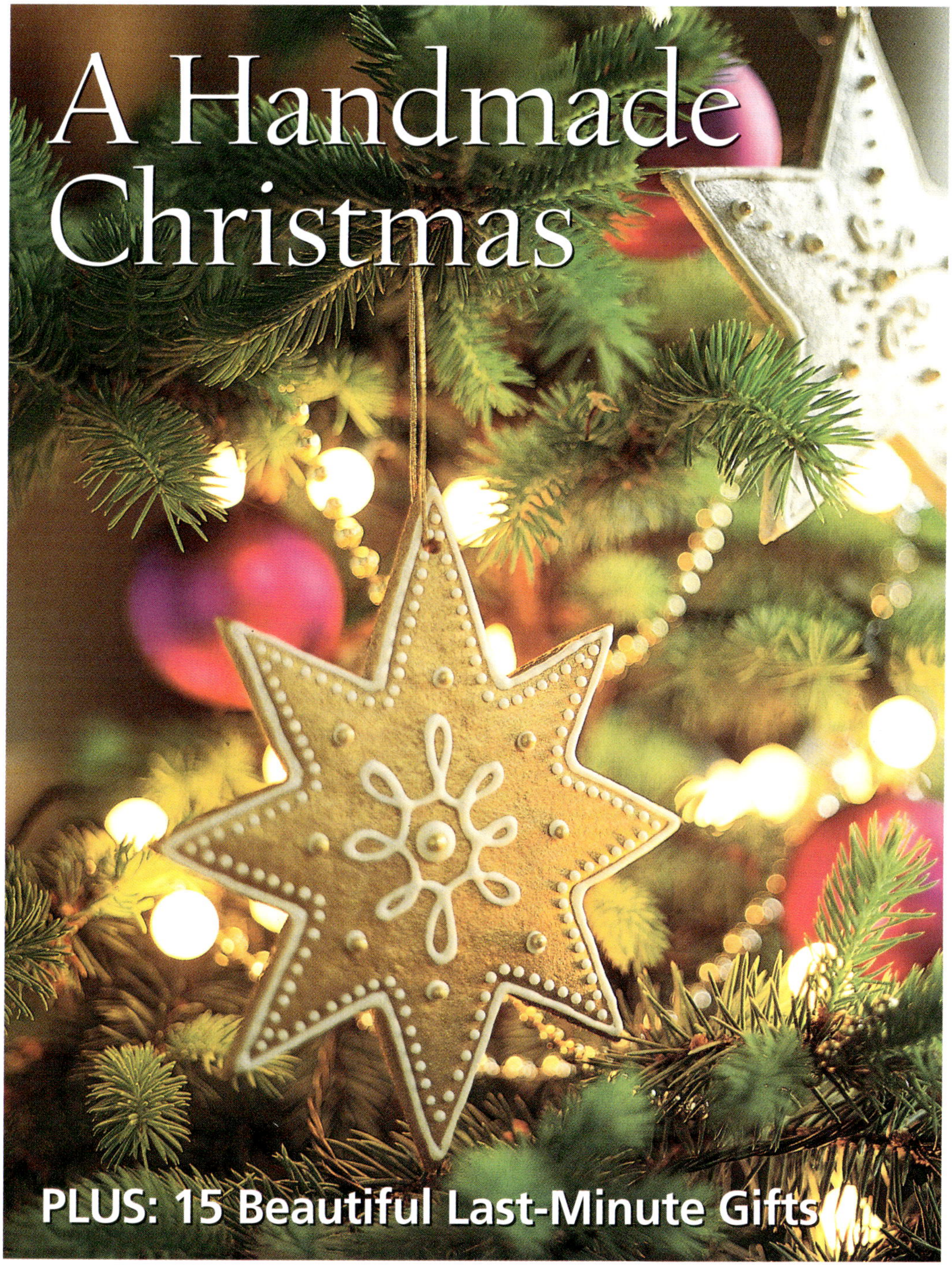

A Handmade Christmas

Gilded Gingerbread Cookies
Transform Ordinary Gingerbread Into Sparkling Ornaments

The Classic White Rose Wreath
The Easiest Wreath Ever

Angel Tree Topper
Crown Your Tree with Our Beautiful Heirloom Decoration

Court Jester Christmas Stocking
Silk Slipper Stands Upright On Its Own

3 Easy Ornaments
Quick Jeweled Cages
Keepsake Silver Bird
Silk Ribbon Tassel

Learn the Secrets of:
Decorating Glassware with Glitter

Gilded Rubberstamp Designs

Transforming Candles with Sheet Wax

PLUS: 15 Beautiful Last-Minute Gifts

Contents

Folded Paper Sleeves, page 10

Classic White Rose Wreath, page 12

10-Minute Christmas Crackers, page 20

COVER PHOTOGRAPH:
Carl Tremblay

STYLING:
Ritch Holben

Create the look of sterling silver with aluminum leaf. See page 13.

FEATURE STORIES

8 ELEGANT SACHETS IN 6 EASY STEPS
Quick-sew these delicate pillows using silk and organza, then fill them with potpourri.

10 FOLDED PAPER SLEEVES
Create these elegant folded "envelopes" using paper and glue.

12 THE CLASSIC WHITE ROSE WREATH
Assemble this holiday wreath by weaving the stems of artificial roses around a wire base.

13 KEEPSAKE SILVER BIRD ORNAMENT
Recreate the look of sterling silver for pennies.

14 THE EASIEST FOUR-PANEL SCREEN YOU'LL EVER MAKE
Use one poster and four wooden plaques for a heavenly hinged mural.

16 HOW TO MAKE LEAFED DESIGNS WITH RUBBER STAMPS
Create beautiful leafed designs on glass.

18 COURT JESTER STOCKING
This Christmas stocking, which stands upright on its own, can be filled to overflowing.

20 10-MINUTE CHRISTMAS CRACKERS
Make these fast and easy classic tabletop decorations with just a few basic materials.

21 JEWELED CAGE ORNAMENTS
Assemble these cagework tree decorations using a simple wrap-and-trap technique.

22 GILDED GINGERBREAD COOKIES
Dress up your holiday gingerbread recipes with a trio of sparkling materials.

24 TERRY CLOTH BABY ANIMALS
Sew your own soft-bodied bunny and piglet.

26 HEIRLOOM ANGEL TREE TOPPER
This elegant tree topper requires ordinary craft materials and practically no sewing.

29 FROSTED GLITTER MARTINI GLASSES
Create a sparkling, heat-fused effect by combining epoxy with microfine glitter.

30 THE LOOK OF BRUSHED STEEL
Scrub aluminum tooling foil with steel wool.

32 DECORATE CANDLES WITH SHEET WAX
Cut your favorite design from a sheet of honeycomb wax, then adhere it to a candle.

34 CANDLE CUP AND RIBBON TASSEL
Make a tassel from candle cups and a wooden ring, then add a ribbon fringe.

35 MERINGUE MUSHROOMS
Pipe these delicate confections from meringue.

36 ZIPPERED SUEDE PURSES
Stitch these bags using a no-pattern technique.

38 BEADED VOTIVE CANDLE HOLDER
Construct this delicate holiday candle holder using brass rods, seed beads, and spool wire.

40 MORAVIAN GLITTER STARS
Holiday accents with chipboard and glitter.

42 MESH NIGHTLIGHT
Transform your nighttime lighting with wire mesh and glass beads.

IN EVERY ISSUE
NOTES FROM READERS 2
QUICK TIPS 4
QUICK HOME ACCENTS 6
THE PERFECT GIFT 7
PATTERNS 43
SOURCES & RESOURCES 48
QUICK PROJECTS 49
PRESSED TIN FRAME BACK COVER

Handcraft Illustrated

EDITOR
Carol Endler Sterbenz

EXECUTIVE EDITOR
Barbara Bourassa

ART DIRECTOR
Amy Klee

SENIOR EDITOR
Michio Ryan

MANAGING EDITOR
Keith Powers

DIRECTIONS EDITOR
Candie Frankel

COPY EDITORS
Amy Finch
Gary Pfitzer

EDITORIAL ASSISTANT
Melissa Nachatelo

EDITORIAL INTERNS
Anne Rein
Jordan Salvatoriello

PUBLISHER AND FOUNDER
Christopher Kimball

MARKETING DIRECTOR
Adrienne Kimball

CIRCULATION MANAGER
David Mack

FULFILLMENT MANAGER
Larisa Greiner

NEWSSTAND MANAGER
Jonathan Venier

MARKETING ASSISTANT
Connie Forbes

CIRCULATION ASSISTANT
Steven Browall

VICE PRESIDENT PRODUCTION AND TECHNOLOGY
James McCormack

EDITORIAL PRODUCTION MANAGER
Sheila Datz

DESKTOP PUBLISHING MANAGER
Kevin Moeller

PRODUCTION ARTIST
Robert Parsons

PRODUCTION ASSISTANT
Daniel Frey

CONTROLLER
Lisa A. Carullo

SENIOR ACCOUNTANT
Mandy Shito

STAFF ACCOUNTANT
William Baggs

Handcraft Illustrated (ISSN 1072-0529) is published quarterly by Boston Common Press Limited Partners, 17 Station Street, Brookline, MA 02146. Copyright 1997 Boston Common Press Limited Partners. Second-class postage paid at Boston, MA, and additional mailing offices, USPS #011-895. For list rental information, please contact List Services Corporation, 6 Trowbridge Drive, P.O. Box 516, Bethel, CT 06801; (203) 743-2600; Fax (203) 743-0589. Editorial office: 17 Station Street, Brookline, MA 02146; (617) 232-1000, FAX (617) 232-1572, e-mail: hndcftill@aol.com. Editorial contributions should be sent or e-mailed to: Editor, *Handcraft Illustrated*. We cannot assume responsibility for manuscripts submitted to us. Submissions will be returned only if accompanied by a large, self-addressed stamped envelope. Subscription rates: $24.95 for one year; $45 for two years; $65 for three years. (Canada: add $6 per year; all other countries add $12 per year.) Postmaster: Send all new orders, subscription inquiries, and change of address notices to *Handcraft Illustrated*, P.O. Box 7450, Red Oak, IA 51591-0450. Single copies: $4 in U.S.; $4.95 in Canada and other countries. Back issues available for $5 each. PRINTED IN THE U.S.A.

Rather than put ™ in every occurrence of trademarked names, we state that we are using the names only and in an editorial fashion and to the benefit of the trademark owner, with no intention of infringement of the trademark.

Note to Readers: Every effort has been made to present the information in this publication in a clear, complete, and accurate manner. It is important that all instructions are followed carefully, as failure to do so could result in injury. Boston Common Press Limited Partners, the editors, and the authors disclaim any and all liability resulting therefrom.

From the Editor

Postscript to "A Letter To My Children":

No doubt, you are used to the ongoing nature of our dialogues, so these extra sentiments will not come as a surprise. But I wanted to be sure to tell you a bit about the traditions that we have shared in our family, and inspire you to continue them, now that you have established nests of your own. I've included a little assignment, hardly the stuff of a Christmas letter, but I thought it worthy of your time. So, let me begin.

When I was a child, my mother taught my sisters and I how to make woven, paper hearts from shiny colored paper. Last Christmas, I was given a slender box, unadorned except for a ribbon and a little card inscribed in my mother's slightly unsteady script, "For Carol." I lifted the lid and in an instant, I was young again, fiddling with paper strips, weaving them into the heart-shaped baskets that now lay flat in the bottom of the box. My mother had collected several of the baskets I had made when I was a child, thinking they would be the perfect gift, now that I had a family of my own. In Scandinavian tradition, the baskets were hung on the tree on Christmas Eve. By morning, they would be filled with candy—sugared fruit slices, dark chocolate rings with sprinkles, and marzipan shaped like little potatoes.

Now, as I held the heart baskets in my hands, the entire scene came back to a time when my sisters and I sat together in our little kitchen, the soft hiss of the radiator forcing heat into the room. Outside, snow fell silently on roofs, and on newly planted evergreens and pudgy hydrants in a just-built post-war neighborhood of the '50s. I used to lie on the floor under the tree and look up through the branches, wishing I could sleep there all night so I could be the first one to taste the sweet confections. But that never happened. I awoke on Christmas morning in my own bed and went downstairs to find the promise those heart baskets kept. My sisters and I would whisper to one another as we filled our mouths and the pockets of our robes, emptying most of the baskets before my parents awoke for breakfast.

As you know it is our custom to exchange one gift that has been handmade, and I decided that this year, the little heart baskets would bear that tradition. As with all traditions, I decided to add something of our lives together, so I am including a handmade woven basket together with some shiny paper in bright colors for you to make a heart basket of your own. If you turn the paper to the dull side, you'll notice little messages, each written with you in mind. I am hoping that woven into your baskets, these words might symbolize the inseparable nature of the philosophy and tradition of our family.

Believe in miracles—they happen every single day in untold numbers.

Here are the messages in their entirety: Fall in love—again and again and again; love helps you grow. And don't forget to turn it in equal measure toward yourself. Do the hard thing—choose the challenging path; it will strengthen you for life's journey ahead. Tell the truth—you won't have to wonder what it is, you'll know it by the peace it brings. Sing—even if you have forgotten the words; hum past the forgotten lyrics or make some up, for a song will heal the heart and make you happy. Believe in miracles—they happen every single day in untold numbers. Some will say "luck," others will say "coincidence," but actually, there is a heavenly conspiracy to bring you all you need; just ask. Give thanks—not because you have more or less than somebody else, but because you are here, and knowing the immensity of this gift, life, will instill in you humility and gratitude, as well as help you spend your time on this sweet planet more wisely. And one more thing. Make something by hand—it will be a dwelling place for your spirit for all time. And as you work, know that you are joining with all before you, and all who will come after you, when all that may be left behind of your walk through life is this testimony, one little paper heart made by your hands. A simple ornament to hang on a tree, yes, but over time, more than that, it will stand as a symbol of tradition, a little place holder in life that embodies all you were and all you were meant to become.

With all my love,
Mama

P.P.S. And to our readers, may you celebrate your holiday traditions surrounded by family, good friends, and the spirit of the season.

Notes from Readers

Learn how to cruise the crafters' Internet, make your craft tool handles easier to hold, protect your Christmas ornaments, or spice up mulled cider.

COMPILED BY MELISSA NACHATELO

Crafts on the Internet
Can you recommend any good web sites for information on crafts? I'm unfamiliar with the Internet and would like to use it for crafting ideas, projects, etc.
JOAN SINGER
TUCSON, AZ

We accessed a number of web sites and found a wide variety of craft and home decorating information. Each web site has something different to offer, but to minimize the time you spend online, we recommend focusing your search on a single subject. Listed below are a few of the web sites we liked best.

www.crafts.com—This site, designed as an all-purpose resource for the general crafter, does its job well. Not only does it offer sound advice, great hints, and a forum for exchanging ideas, it also conveys the friendliness often associated with the craft industry. Post a message on the message board, enter the craft mall, or explore its many links to other sites.

www.michaels.com—Much like its namesake chain of craft stores, this web site offers crafting techniques, ideas, and instructions. You can use the site to locate the closest Michael's location in your area, or find the latest store events and classes on the site's calendar page.

www.decoart.com—Accessing a manufacturer's site like DecoArt's means you're sure to see their products getting promoted. But DecoArt, like many other manufacturers, takes their site a step further by offering ideas about how to use their products. The site also includes seminar schedules, color conversion charts, tips for painting, and detailed project instructions.

www.plaid.com—Like other manufacturers, Plaid's site is filled with production promotions. In addition, the company uses its own products to explain technical terms, and it offers a variety of craft projects and instructions.

www.crafter.com—This site features a comprehensive listing of craft shows and craft malls, organized by city and state, for both professional crafters looking for business opportunities or a craft hobbiest looking for places to shop. Crafter.com can also link you to other related craft sites, chat rooms, and project pages.

Christmas Feather Trees
I recently saw a tree made of feather branches, standing about two feet high. Are you familiar with this kind of tree? I'm interested in finding out more about it.
JUDITH B. EICHORN
BRISTOL, CT

Nicknamed the "Charlie Brown Christmas tree" for its resemblance to the famous Peanuts version, the German feather tree you described is made by wiring goose or turkey feathers to branches. Feather trees originated in late 19th century Germany, where they were used to display the work of German ornament blowers.

Today, feather trees are still being made, and antique versions sell as collectors' items. Dianna Carlson and her husband, Rob, produce trees through their company, the Feather Tree Company. The tree is often considered only a tabletop decoration, says Carlson, but they can reach as high as 8 feet tall. Carlson's $3 catalog features various styles of the tree and a brief description of its history. To order, call or write to the Feather Tree Company, P.O. Box 281, Sun Prairie, WI 53590; 800-831-1999.

Making Easy-Grip Handles
Two years ago, I developed a mild case of arthritis. Since then, it's been difficult to craft using small handles, like brushes and X-Acto knives. Is there a way to make it easier?
ELENA NORWOOD
SEATTLE, WA

When purchasing an X-Acto knife, paint brush, or any other crafting tool, look for those with a wide, non-slippery grasp. Specialty stores and mail-order companies also carry specially-designed X-Acto knives, rotary cutters, and other tools for easier crafting. Try Fiskars' line of Softouch products, designed to reduce fatigue. Vicon Inc., of LaVerne, CA, carries the line's rotary cutter starting at $15.50 for a 45mm blade. Call or write to P.O. Box 7188, LaVerne, CA 91750; 800-938-4266. Nasco Arts and Crafts sells Fiskars' ergonomic scissors starting at $8.95. Write or call, Nasco, 901 Janesville Ave., P.O. Box 901, Ft. Atkinson, WI 53538-0901; 800-558-9595.

If you can't find specialty tools, you can add gripping material to your existing tools. Try coating the handles of your tools with liquid rubber or foam grip for a better hold. Liquid rubber is available in a variety of colors at most hardware stores. Foam grip tubing, used on bicycle handle bars, is available at most bicycle shops.

Finally, here's a quick tip for picking up flat rulers easily: cut a 2" to 3" piece of tape, fold it over about ¾ of the way, sticky sides together, then attach the "tag" to the end of the ruler.

Decorating the Mantel
I want to make a fresh garland for the mantel above my fireplace. I love the look of pine and evergreen but I know these greens will shed their needles. Is there a better choice of fresh greenery that lasts longer?
NICOLE REYNOLDS
PROVIDENCE, RI

Any evergreen that does not have a water supply will eventually dry out and drop its needles. You can mist the foliage with a hand-held mister to prolong its display time, but the water may damage the surface against which the garland is placed. We recommend constructing your garland using lemon or salal branches. These foliage varieties have a rich green color when fresh, and fade to a soft sage green when dry. This way, you can display the garland long after the holidays are over, because it will remain sturdy and attractive when dry. Check with your neighborhood florist for pricing and availability.

Once your garland has dried, you can change the accents to match the season. For the holidays, use clusters of berries as a decoration; later, slip the stems of pink silk roses between the dry branches and add a bow with streamers for a Spring garland. Make sure to keep all decorations away from heat and flame.

Positioning Streamers with Velcro
I have an exterior wreath door decoration with long streamers that get caught in the door as it closes. How can I fix the problem without cutting the streamers short?
DEBRA DERRY
LEXINGTON, MA

Use self-adhesive Velcro to fix the streamers in place. Velcro comes in both dot and strip forms, so you can stabilize ribbon streamers of any width. We purchased a 12" strip of the hook and loop sections for $1.99 in a stationery store, and cut them to fit the ribbon. Velcro dots also work well, coming in a variety of diameters for easy application. Peel the backing off one dot and press it to the door, then align the second fuzzy dot to the back of the streamer. The Velcro can be removed from the ribbon and door surface when the wreath is put away or discarded. If the Velcro leaves adhesive residue on the door, we recommend using an orange oil-based cleaner, available at most hardware stores, to remove the adhesive.

Protecting Ornaments Off-Season
I have kept my ornaments in a hodge podge of different boxes and canisters, and, invariably, a few are broken when I unwrap them each year. Are there boxes designed to protect

ornaments, so that I can store them neatly throughout the year?
MARIA COLLINS
ST. PAUL, MN

We found exactly what you're looking for at Hold Everything, a mail-order company devoted to organized storage. During the fall and through the holidays, the company sells heavy-duty, decorated boxes for storing ornaments, light strands, miscellaneous decorations, and wreaths. The 25" x 13" x 11" ornament box sells for approximately $15. Call or write for a free catalog: Hold Everything, Mail Order Department, P.O. Box 7807, San Francisco, CA 94120-7807; 800-421-2264.

Evergreen Potpourri
As a child, I remember seeing a pillow of pine needles on my aunt's porch couch. I love the smell of fresh pine needles and would love to keep the dry needles from my Christmas tree for use either in potpourri or a sachet. Do I need to treat them in any way?
MELISSA GREEN
FAIRFIELD, CT

The needles of some evergreen varieties will provide a subtle yet pleasant fragrance when dry, but over time the scent will fade. To enhance the smell, add a few drops of essential oil and a fixative to a cup full of needles. A fixative, such as pine cones, will hold the scent for a long period, releasing its aroma sporadically. Then, use our instructions on page 8 to make a sachet, or refer to our recipe, "Christmas Potpourri Demystified" (November/December 1995) to make a potpourri mixture.

Essential oils can be purchased via catalog from A World of Plenty, P.O. Box 1153, Hermantown, MN 55810-9724; 218-729-6761.

Disguising Seams on Ornaments
I'm trying to decoupage Christmas ball ornaments like the ones sold in stores. I can't seem to imitate the shine, and my seams are not well hidden. Do you have any ideas?
ROGER OLIVER
CHERRYVILLE, NC

Before you begin, minimize the chance of unattractive seams by choosing thin paper and small images. Because you're placing a flat image on a rounded surface, larger images tend to crease, and thicker paper sits higher on the ornament's surface.

There are several other tricks for disguising seams. On larger images, make tiny incisions (about ¼"-long) about ⅜" apart along the edges of the image. Then, as you glue the image down, overlap the edges slightly, much like darts in a sewn garment. If you don't want to cut into the image, use manicure scissors to cut around its detailed edge as we did for our decoupage lampshade (see "Rose Decoupage Lampshade," November/December 1993). This will take longer, but the image will curve more easily around the surface. Finally, if trimming and cutting the whole image still leaves unsightly seams, try cutting away a section of the art, then fitting a new image into the cut area like a puzzle piece. This will keep the decoupage on one layer.

Once the pieces are glued down, be sure to seal the piece with a general-purpose decoupage medium such as Mod Podge. This will smooth down any rough-cut edges and fill in any differences in levels. Add several layers to minimize the seams and give the ornament a high-gloss finish.

Washing the Shag Rug
I made the shag rug featured in your Winter 1997 issue (see "Bathroom Shag Rug," page 10) and it looks great, but I'm not sure how to wash it. Can you help?
JUDY BRIGGS
CORVALLIS, OR

To answer your question, we machine-washed the shag rug. The rug, which is made by enclosing strips of jersey-knit fabric into a knitted grid, survived a normal cycle with relatively little fraying or pulls. We did find three strips of the jersey fabric in the dryer's lint trap, however. To minimize this problem, we recommend washing the rug on a gentle cycle and air drying if possible.

Rub-On Transfers
I love the look of rub-on transfers, especially those designed to duplicate the look of hand-painting, like Plaid's Accents on Everything. I can't find them in my local craft store, however. Have you found any mail-order sources for rub-on transfers?
MARY NOEL CAIN
OWENSBORO, KY

Rub-on transfers are available in larger craft catalogs, such as Sunshine Discount Crafts and Craft King. Sunshine Discount Crafts offers a variety of transfers, including more than 30 new designs of Plaid's Accents on Everything. Six-by-seven-inch designs, including hearts, flowers, bears, Santa Claus, etc., are priced at $2.39 each. For a free catalog, write or call Sunshine Discount Crafts at P.O. Box 301, Largo, FL 33779-0301; 800-729-2878. Craft King also offers a wide range of designs, including teapots, bears, cows, pigs, cherubs, flowers, and creative sayings. Prices start at $2.79 each. Write or call the company at P.O. Box 90637, Lakeland, FL 33804; 800-769-9494.

You may also want to experiment with a new product from Loew-Cornell called Tilescapes Rub-On Transfers. This product lets you transfer an image to a bathroom or kitchen tile easily with preset tile dimensions. We tested a rub-on on a 4¼" x 4¼" bath tile and were impressed with the fast and easy results. Tilescapes can be ordered from Alpine Imports; prices range from $4.99 to $19.99. To order, call 800-654-6114 or write Alpine at 7106 North Alpine Road, Rockford, IL 61111.

More on Decorative Bottles
Beautiful, clear glass bottles present wonderful opportunities for decorating. But finding them can be a problem, as Lylian Chen, of Santa Clara, California, noted in our Spring 1997 Notes from Readers. We listed several mail-order sources for decorative bottles, but would like to add a new supplier to that list. The Lavender Lane, in Sacramento, California, carries glass bottles and jars appropriate for a variety of crafts, including painting and etching. The store specializes in hard-to-find herbalware as well as natural essential oils, potpourri, gels, powders, and waxes. We ordered a few of their products and found a good choice of styles and shapes. The selection even includes dainty perfume bottles. To order a $3 catalog, call or write the company at 7337 Roseville Road #1, Sacramento, CA 95842; 888-593-4400.

Spicing Up the Punch
I need an idea for spiced mulled wine. I have this great recipe but it needs a little decoration.
LINDA WAGNER
SACRAMENTO, CA

Spiced mulled wine, with its deep aromatic scent, can be complemented by a number of garnishings, all simple and decorative. You can also spice up the wine itself with cinnamon sticks or tree-shaped apple slices cut from cookie cutters. For fun table decorations, string dried apple slices and dried cranberries around the punch bowl to add holiday cheer. Or, turn the bowl into a centerpiece by laying an evergreen wreath or a festive floral garland around the bowl's base. You can also spice up the wine itself with cinnamon sticks or tree-shaped apple slices cut from cookie cutters.

Locating Glass Prisms
I am interested in purchasing a large quantity of glass prisms, such as the type used on lamp and light fixtures. What do you recommend?
SUE J. ELAM
WELLINGTON, AL

Chandelier crystals can be purchased by mail from Renovator's, a home-decorating supplier, and The National Artcraft Company, a general craft supplier. Renovator's offers scalloped and tapered prisms in a variety of sizes; prices range from $1.50 for a 1½"-long version to $9.95 for a 6" prism. Call or write the company at P.O. Box 2515, Conway, NH 03818-2515; 800-659-2211. National Artcraft also sells a variety of prisms; short crystals with brass hooks start at five for 56 cents. Write or call the company at 7996 Darrow Road, Twinsburg, OH 44087; 216-963-6011. For older, more unique prisms, scour thrift stores, flea markets, and antique shops in your area; be aware, however, that prices can vary depending on the age and condition of the prism. ◆

ATTENTION READERS

Need advice on a craft or home decorating project?
Drop us a line, and we'll find the answer. Although we can't respond to every letter we receive, we will try to publish those letters with the widest appeal. Please include your name, address, and a daytime telephone number with your question. Write to:

Notes from Readers
Handcraft Illustrated
17 Station Street
Brookline, MA 02146

Quick Tips

INSTANT MONEY HOLDER
To prevent checks and gift certificates from spilling out of greeting cards, Harriette Geisinger, of New Philadelphia, Ohio, has devised a ribbon holder.

1. **Tie a ribbon around the front cover and glue down the bow.**

2. **Fold check over ribbon, then glue down the upper and lower edges of the ribbon to hold the check in place.**

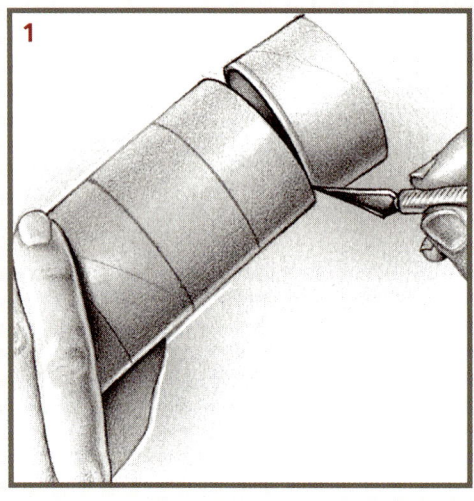

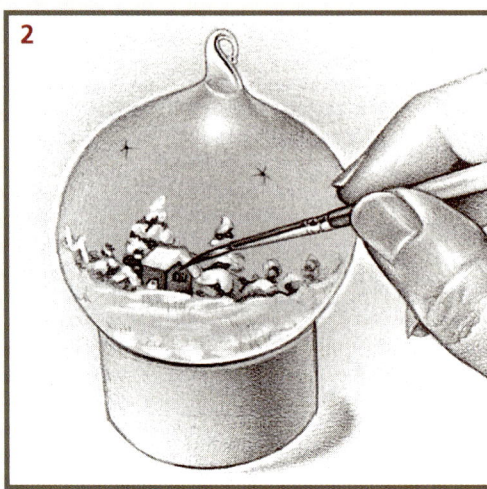

PAINTING STAND
To hold ball ornaments low and steady for painting, Laurey Zoladz, of West Chester, Pennsylvania, uses cardboard tubes.

1. **Mark 1" segments along a cardboard tube, then cut the rings apart.**
2. **Stand each ball in its own ring for easy painting and drying.**

ATTENTION READERS
Calling All Crafters
Do you have a unique craft, sewing, or decorating technique that saves time or money? Send it our way! We'll give you a one-year complimentary subscription for each Quick Tip that we publish. Send your tip to:

Quick Tips
Handcraft Illustrated
17 Station Street
Brookline, MA 02146

Please include your name, address, and daytime phone number with all correspondence.

ILLUSTRATION:
Nenad Jakesevic

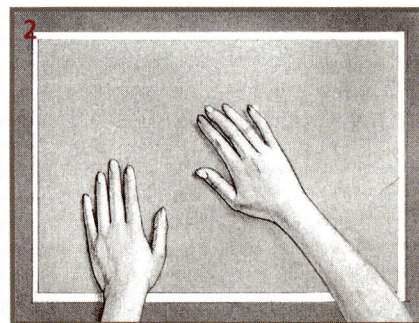

MAKING PLACE MATS
For a set of custom place mats, start with ordinary mat board, writes Connie Calvert, of San Leandro, California.

1. **Brush Yes Stikflat glue onto a 13" x 19" piece of mat board.**

2. **Set the board glue side down on the wrong side of the decorative paper and rub it to adhere.**

3. **Let the board dry for 1 hour, then trim off the excess paper.**

4. **Seal the front, back, and edges with an acrylic matte varnish and let place mat dry according to the manufacturer's instructions.**

4 HANDCRAFT ILLUSTRATED • CHRISTMAS 1997

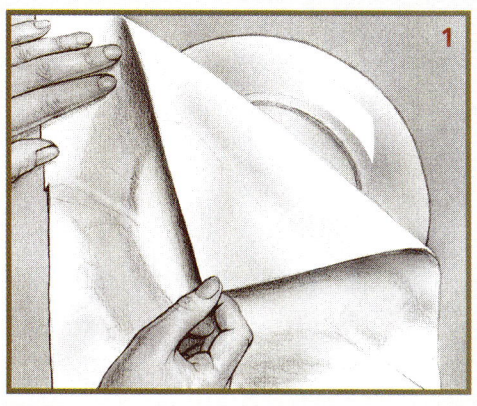 

BREAKING PLATES

Before breaking plates for mosaic projects (such as our Broken China Stepping Stones, Spring 1997), Barb Grenemeier, of Lincoln, Nebraska, attaches self-adhesive paper to the plate back.

1. Press down on the paper so it comes in contact with the full plate surface; crimp at rims as needed.

2. When you break the plate, the pieces will stay intact for easy reconstruction.

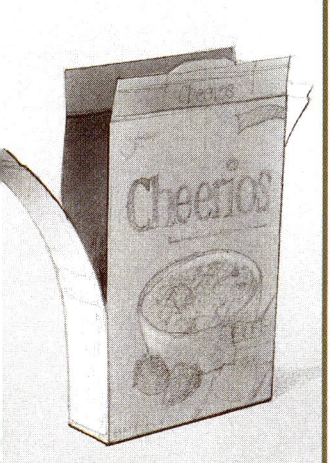 

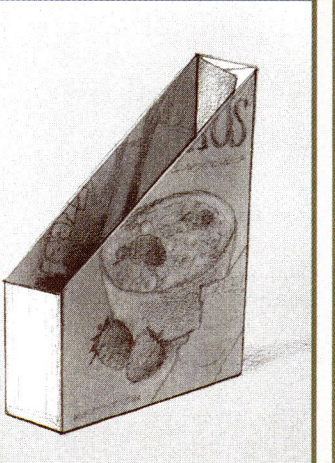 

STORING MAGAZINES

Here's how Fran Saraduke, of Aurora, Colorado, organizes her craft magazines. Start with a cereal box larger than the magazine.

1. Cut along the lengths of the side panels—just down to the height of the magazine on one side and about two-thirds of the way down on the other side.

2. Fold the cut sections to the inside and glue them down.

3. Fold the front and back panels diagonally and glue them down.

4. Cover the outside with contact paper or other durable paper and add a label.

CHOCOLATE CURLS

For quick chocolate curls, run a carrot peeler along the edge of a chocolate bar. The bar should be at room temperature.

STRINGING BIGGER BEADS

Corrugated cardboard channels can handle small beads (see Quick Tips, Fall 1997), but for larger beads, Leba Freed Pierce, of Albuquerque, New Mexico, uses plastic drinking straws as adjustable spacers between the rows. Tape or glue the straws to a piece of cardboard.

HANDMADE CARDS

Dawn Harris, of Jackson, Louisiana, uses light bulb packaging in her handcrafted holiday cards. The flexible ridged paper adds textural interest when glued behind cutout designs. For color contrast, spray-paint the pieces before gluing.

Quick Home Accents

Dress up your holiday table with this fast and easy crinkled organza table collar.

HOLIDAY WRAPS

Looking for a fast yet elegant way to transform your holiday table? This table collar, made from 24"-wide crinkled metallic organza, may be the answer.

To get started, measure the circumference or perimeter of the table. Consult the chart, right, for fabric requirements. You'll also need ⅝"-wide ribbon to match the tablecloth, 34-gauge spool wire, and a sewing machine with a pin-tuck foot.

Tear the organza on the crosswise grain into a series of 6½"-wide strips. Trim off the selvages and sew the strips end to end. Finger-press one long edge ⅜" to the wrong side. Using a pin-tuck foot, zigzag the 34-gauge wire in the fold (to create the crinkled edge shown above). Machine-baste the opposite long edge, gathering slightly. Topstitch a ⅝"-wide ribbon over the gathered edge. Seal the raw cut edges with fray preventer. Cover the table with a tablecloth, then use double-stick tape to attach the crinkled organza collar to the table edge. ◆

COLOR PHOTOGRAPHY:
Carl Tremblay

DESIGN:
Dawn Anderson

STYLING:
Ritch Holben

FABRIC YARDAGE CHART

Table Circumference or Perimeter	Required Yardage
72"	⅝ yard
96"	¾ yard
120"	1 yard

The Perfect Gift

These sweet and simple chocolate-dipped spoons are designed for flavoring coffee or other hot drinks.

CHOCOLATE-DIPPED SPOONS

Chocolate-dipped spoons make a fabulous last-minute gift. The supply list is short, the set up minimal, and the work time brief. And unlike many food gifts, these elegant spoons will last unprotected for at least 3 weeks.

To cover the spoons, we dipped each one in melted coating chocolate, which is available at candy-making and bakery supply stores, then added designs with melted white chocolate. It's important to use coating chocolate for covering the spoon, as baking chocolate contains cocoa butter, which requires careful heating and cooling to prevent hazy streaks in the finished product.

To melt the chocolate, hook the handles of two 1-cup Pyrex measuring cups over the rim of a large pot. (Anchor them with large binder clips if they are unstable.) Fill the pot with water until the measuring cups are halfway submerged; take care not to get any water inside the measuring cups.

Carefully place ten or twelve chocolate chunks into each cup, then heat the water, stirring the chocolate constantly, over low to medium heat. Once the chocolate is melted, turn the water down to a simmer to keep it liquefied. Follow the specific directions at the right to create the spoons shown above (left to right). ◆

■ Marbled Spoon

Dip bowl of spoon into white chocolate. Tap spoon handle against side of pot to even out coverage and dislodge excess chocolate. Dip thin edge of kitchen knife into dark chocolate and press against length of bowl of spoon to create thin, contrasting line. Zigzag clean, straight pin across bowl of spoon, through stripe from handle to tip, to create marbled effect. Stand spoon upright in teacup and refrigerate 10 minutes.

■ Star Spoon

Coat spoon with dark chocolate and refrigerate 5 minutes. Drop small amount white chocolate in center of spoon. Using clean straight pin, pull white chocolate from center outwards to make five points of star. Touch up any uncovered areas using pin dipped in white chocolate.

■ Two-Tone Drizzled Spoon

Coat spoon with dark chocolate, then wipe lower half of bowl clean with paper towel. Refrigerate 5 minutes, then dip tip of spoon into white chocolate. Refrigerate 5 minutes. Spoon melted chocolate into two small plastic bags. Using oven mitts, twist empty portion of bag to force chocolate into bottom corner. Snip tiny hole in each bag. Holding pastry bag steady, squeeze chocolate in steady stream; move spoon underneath bag to create delicate lines on contrasting half of spoon. Repeat with second bag, then refrigerate spoon 10 minutes.

COLOR PHOTOGRAPHY:
Carl Tremblay

DESIGN:
Rodney Sterbenz and Elizabeth Cameron

STYLING:
Ritch Holben

LOW-SEW

Elegant Sachets in 6 Easy Steps

Quick-sew these delicate pillows using silk and organza, then fill them with fragrant potpourri.

🌶 BY DAWN ANDERSON

Coordinate the sachet's fabric with its contents: orange-yellow silk with citrus peels and soft purple silk with dried lavender.

THESE ELEGANT SACHETS—filled with fragrant materials such as fir needles, dried roses, dried lavender, and citrus peels—are so beautiful you may not want to hide them in a drawer.

Each sachet is sewn from two types of fabric: silk dupioni for the outer flange edging, and gold metallic organza for the interior "window" portion. The delicate mesh of the organza window lets the scent of the sachet's contents escape. I coordinated the silk fabric color with the sachet's contents: moss green for fir needles, orange-yellow for dried citrus peels, soft purple for dried lavender, and magenta for dried rose petals.

Although most of the potpourri ingredients listed above are fairly fragrant on their own, you can enhance the scent with a fixative ingredient such as oak moss or cellulose fiber, and an essential or fragrance oil. The fixative retains the scent from the oils and keeps the potpourri fragrant for a longer period of time.

Dawn Anderson is a writer and designer living in Redmond, Washington.

COLOR PHOTOGRAPHY:
Carl Tremblay

ILLUSTRATION:
Mary Newell DePalma

STYLING:
Ritch Holben

MATERIALS
Yields 4 same-scent sachets

- 1 to 2 cups dried lavender, rose petals, balsam fir needles, or citrus peels
- ¼ cup oak moss or cellulose fiber
- Essential oil*
- ¼ yard 45"-wide silk dupioni*
- ⅛ yard gold metallic-colored organza
- Thread to match fabric

*match color of fabric to scent or color of dry material

You'll also need:
sewing machine; rotary cutter; quilter's acrylic cutting guide; self-healing cutting mat; iron and ironing board; fabric chalk pencil; sewing shears; hand-sewing needle; pins; point turner; measuring cups; and quart-size zipper-lock bag.

INSTRUCTIONS

1. *Mix potpourri.* If using oak moss, cut or tear it into ½" pieces. Place oak moss or cellulose fiber in zipper-lock bag, add 10 to 20 drops essential oil, seal bag, and shake well. Add dried material and shake until fully blended. To set scent, set sealed bag aside in dark place for 2 to 3 weeks.

2. *Cut fabric pieces.* Using rotary cutter, guide, and cutting mat, cut four 7⅞" x 9⅝" sachet covers and four 3⅝" x 5¼" pillow inserts from silk; longer edge should run along crosswise grain. Cut four 3⅝" x 5¼" organza inserts.

3. *Crease covers to mark flanges.* Using matching thread, stay-stitch silk sachet cover scant ¼" from edge all around. Lay cover flat, right side up. Using chalk pencil, draft line 1⅜" from each edge. Fold each edge on marked line and press toward wrong side to set crease. Lay cover flat, right side up, fold down each corner diagonally until creases match, and finger-press (see illustration A, next page). Repeat process for each cover.

4. *Sew flanges.* Press raw edges ¼" toward wrong side, just beyond stitching line. Lay cover right side up. Fold corner in half diagonally, aligning raw edges, and pin; it is OK to crease flange allowance, but do not crease body of

Sewing the Silk Sachet

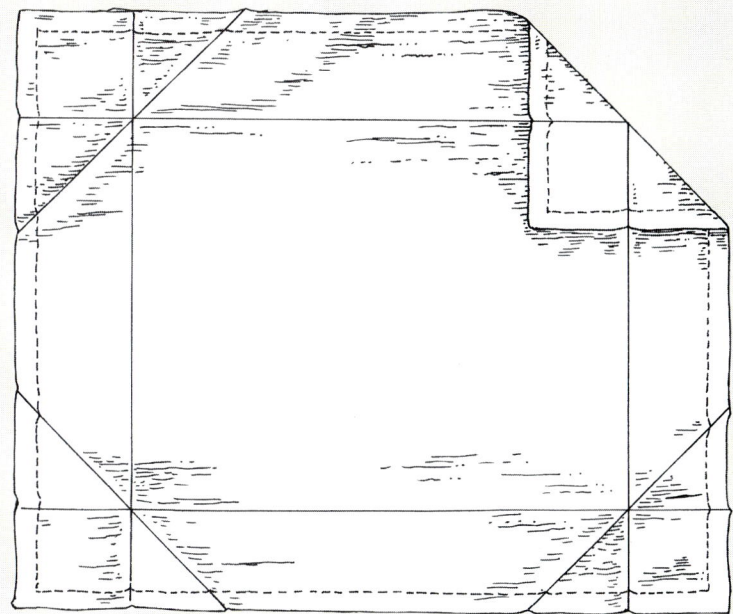

A. Crease a silk rectangle to mark the flange edge.

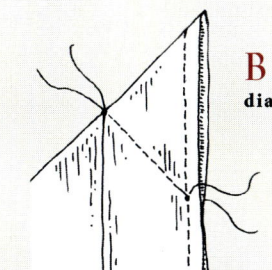

B. Sew each corner diagonally.

C. Press each corner to set the flange.

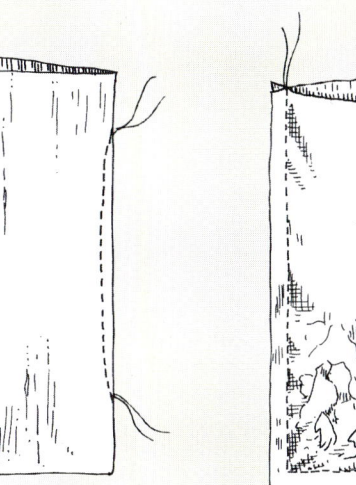

D. Fold the silk insert in half, then stitch a dart along the fold line.

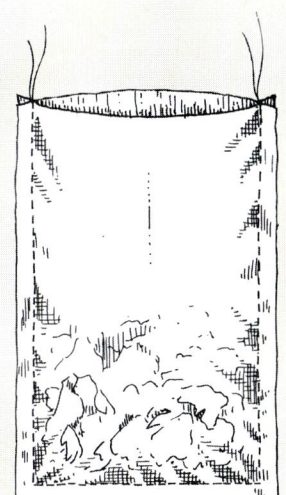

E. Set the organza on top and stitch it on three sides to make a pocket. Fill it with potpourri until about one-third full.

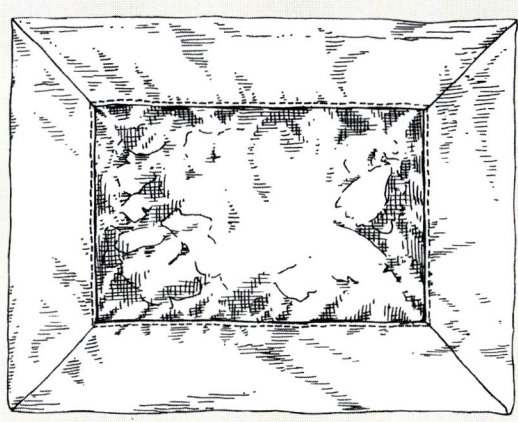

F. Trap the insert edges under the flange and topstitch the flange edge.

cover. Stitch from fold to stay-stitching, following diagonal crease set in step 3 and back-tacking at beginning and end (illustration B). Repeat to sew remaining corners. Trim excess fabric ¼" beyond stitching and press seam allowances open with tip of iron (illustration C). Turn cover right side out, push out corners with point turner, and tuck raw edges to inside. Press well. Repeat process for each cover.

5. *Sew and fill pillow inserts.* Fold silk insert in half lengthwise, right sides together. Starting and ending 1" from raw edge, stitch ⅛" dart along fold line (illustration D). Open flat, wrong side up, and press dart to one side. Lay insert flat, right side up. Set organza insert right side up on top, raw edges matching. Stitch on three sides scant ¼" from edge to make pocket. Transfer ¼ to ½ cup potpourri to pocket until about one-third full (illustration E). Pin open end, then test-fit pocket under flange; flange should fit snugly and conceal raw edges and stitching. Add or remove potpourri as necessary, then stitch pocket closed to make pillow. Repeat process for each insert.

6. *Assemble sachets.* Center pillow insert under flange, as in step 5, so organza side shows through opening created by flange. Manipulate potpourri away from stitching lines, then pin through all layers. Using short stitch length (about thirty stitches per inch), topstitch flange edge all around (illustration F). Press flange. Repeat process for each sachet. ◆

DESIGNER'S TIP

To dry your own citrus peels, tear fresh, thin peels into ¼" to ½" pieces, place on a foil-lined baking sheet, and bake them at 150 degrees for 2 hours or until thoroughly dry.

PAPER CRAFTS

Custom-Size Folded "Envelopes"

Make a beautiful paper enclosure for any gift, such as stamps, wine labels, or postcards.

🌿 BY NANCY OVERTON

Select your sleeve papers to suit the occasion: gold and white papers for formal invitations, such as weddings; earthy taupe and ivory papers for everyday gifts; or blue and silver papers for Hanukkah gifts.

COLOR PHOTOGRAPHY:
Carl Tremblay

ILLUSTRATION:
Mary Newell DePalma

STYLING:
Ritch Holben

THESE FOLDED PAPER SLEEVES ARE designed to house flat gifts such as theater tickets, gift certificates, or photographs. Not only are the sleeves fast and easy to make, but you can custom-fit them to the gift using a simple formula.

There are two basic versions of the sleeve: square and rectangular, which is basically a variation of the square. Both versions comprise two parallelograms, which you stack perpendicular to one another pinwheel-style. To open and close the card, the four pointed ends fold inward and overlap, much the way a box lid closes. While it's easy to custom-size the sleeve, I recommend mastering the technique for the square sleeve before trying the rectangular version, as the latter is slightly more complicated.

The type of paper you select for the sleeve depends, in part, on its size. For small gift enclosures or note cards, the weight of the paper will be immaterial, but for larger sleeves (i.e., more than 5" square) it should be thick enough to remain stiff and look substantial. I recommend art papers made for dry media such as conté crayons or pastels; these papers are also suitable for folding, another important consideration. Avoid watercolor papers, for example, which are not made to be creased, or heavy handmade papers that will not fold straight or that will crack when folded.

The sleeve design requires two different papers; I recommend using two papers of similar thickness but of contrasting color and/or texture. If you must use two different weights of paper, be sure to place the heavier paper outside the thinner one, so the flimsier paper does not become the back of the sleeve.

I like to line my paper sleeves with a third paper, but it is not absolutely necessary. My liner has an extra flap, which pulls back to reveal the lining's pattern, but there's no single right way to make the liner, and you can experiment as desired. Whatever you decide, the liner should be made from a lighter-weight paper than that used for the sleeve's exterior.

Nancy Overton, a craft designer and author, lives in Oakland, California.

DESIGNER'S TIP

Determining Paper Grain
Whenever two papers are glued together, it is important that the paper grains run in the same direction to prevent buckling and warping. The easiest way to determine paper grain is to examine the alignment of the paper's fibers in strong light. If you're still unsure, try one of these methods:

■ **Bend method**
Bend a sheet of paper in half (but do not crease it) to gauge the spring. Then turn the sheet 90 degrees and bring the other two edges together. The sheet will bend more easily along the line of the fibers, or with the grain.

■ **Fold method**
Paper folds more easily when creased with the grain. A crease made against the grain will produce a rough, broken edge at the fold.

■ **Tear method**
Paper will tear more cleanly with the grain than against it.

INSTRUCTIONS
Making a Square Sleeve
1. *Cut sleeve rectangles.* Measure size of gift item to be enclosed and then determine folded sleeve size, e.g., 5" square. Multiply one edge measurement by 3 to determine rectangle size, e.g., 5" x 15". Choose two contrasting art papers for sleeve exterior and a third slightly lighterweight paper for sleeve liner. Using grid ruler, X-Acto knife,

PAPER CRAFTS

and cutting mat, cut one 5" x 15" (or alternative size) rectangle from first paper, long edge parallel to paper grain (see Designer's Tip, previous page, for determining paper grain). Repeat to cut second rectangle from contrasting paper, long edge perpendicular to paper grain.

2. *Cut liner rectangle.* Subtract 1/8" all around from finished sleeve size, e.g., 4¾" square. To determine size of liner rectangle, multiply one edge measurement by 2½" and round up to nearest quarter inch, e.g., 4¾" x 2½" equals 12". Cut one liner rectangle measuring 4¾" x 12" (or alternative size) from liner paper; note grain direction.

3. *Cut and fold points.* Lay one sleeve rectangle flat on cutting mat. Using pencil and acrylic grid ruler, lightly divide each long edge into thirds. To make point, align ruler diagonally from corner to nearest mark on opposite long edge and cut with X-Acto knife (see illustration A, below). Repeat to make parallel cut at other end of paper. Fold each point onto middle section, outer edges even and diagonal edges butting, to form square (illustration B), then crease with bone folder. Repeat process to cut and fold second sleeve rectangle.

4. *Assemble sleeve.* Stack two sleeve rectangles, pencil marks aligned, to form pinwheel (illustration C); points should fold easily onto middle section without buckling. Join middle sections using glue stick.

5. *Fold and glue liner.* Lay liner rectangle flat. Fold one short edge toward middle (exact measure not required) and crease (illustration D). Turn liner face down. Fold other short edge under so area between folds forms a square that measures 1/8" smaller all around than finished sleeve size (illustration E). Turn over. Fold down longer end to make flap (illustration F). Lay sleeve flat with points opened; glue liner to center of sleeve, matching paper grain.

6. *Close sleeve.* Enclose gift within liner. To close sleeve, fold any point (#1) onto middle section (illustration G). Next, fold adjacent point (#2) onto middle section. Fold point #3 into place, then fold point #4 over #3 and insert it under #1 (illustration H).

7. *Trim sleeve.* To add elastic cord, thread tassel or button onto cord, wrap cord once or twice around sleeve, and knot ends in back so cord fits snugly without buckling paper (illustration I). For traditional seal, wrap paper strip around sleeve, notch one end to suggest ribbon, overlap and glue ends, and finish with wax seal.

Making a Rectangular Sleeve

Note: Master the technique for making a square sleeve before attempting the rectangular version.

1. *Cut sleeve rectangles.* Determine folded sleeve size, e.g., 3" x 6". Multiply shorter edge by 3 to determine first-cut sleeve size, e.g., 9" x 6". Multiply longer edge by 3 to determine second-cut sleeve size, e.g., 3" x 18". Proceed as for square sleeve, step 1, to cut two sleeves.

2. *Cut liner rectangle.* Subtract 1/8" all around from finished sleeve size, e.g., 2¾" x 5¾". To determine liner size, multiply shorter edge by 2½" and round up to nearest quarter inch, e.g., 7" x 5¾". Cut one liner from liner paper, long edge parallel to paper grain. Follow square sleeve instructions, steps 3 through 7, to complete assembly. ◆

MATERIALS

- Medium- to heavyweight art papers
- Metallic elastic cord and buttons or tassels or sealing wax and seal

You'll also need: glue-stick; bone folder or substitute; X-Acto knife; quilter's acrylic grid ruler; self-healing cutting mat; scissors; pencil; and blank piece of paper or calculator.

Making the Folded Envelopes

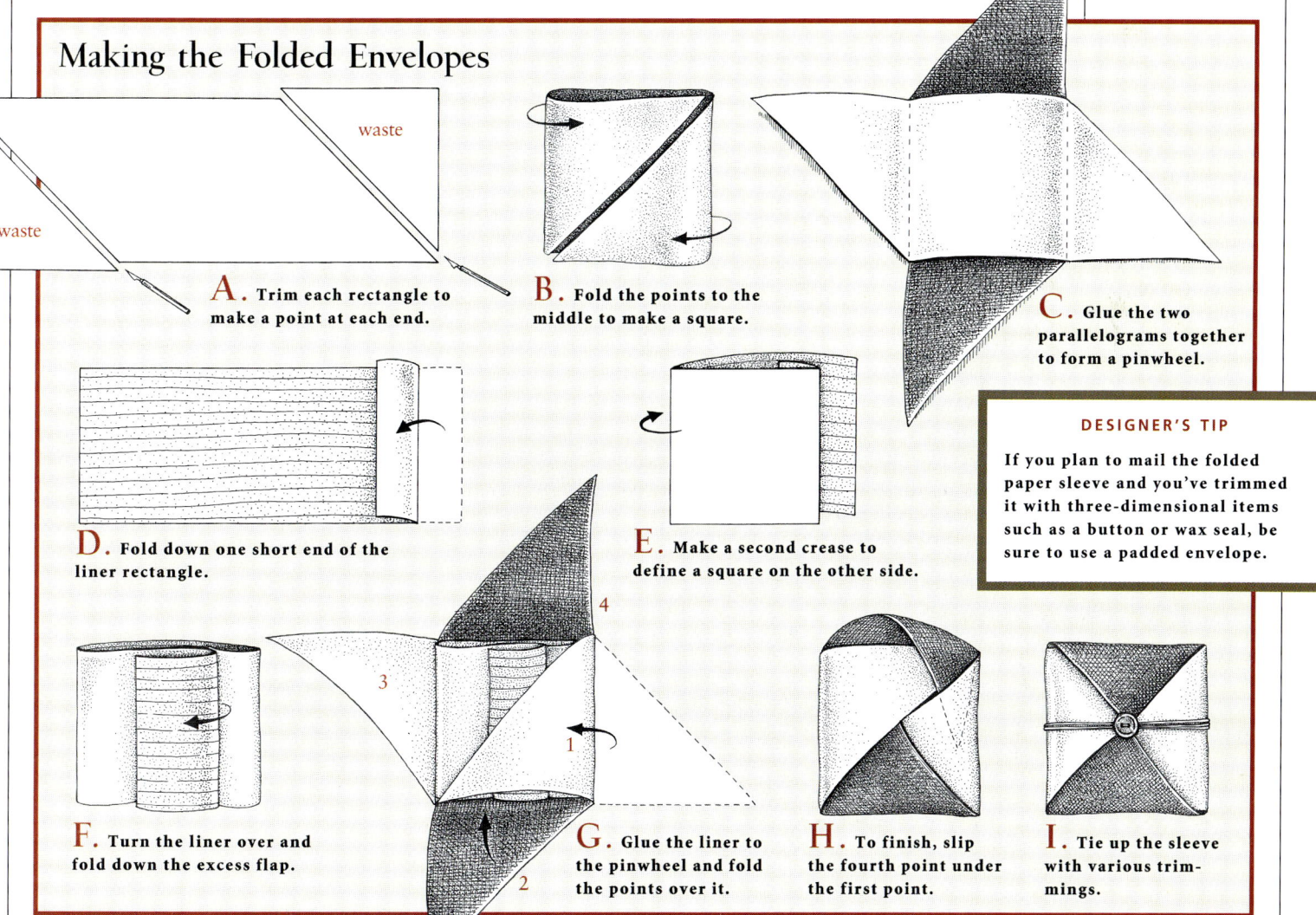

A. Trim each rectangle to make a point at each end.

B. Fold the points to the middle to make a square.

C. Glue the two parallelograms together to form a pinwheel.

D. Fold down one short end of the liner rectangle.

E. Make a second crease to define a square on the other side.

F. Turn the liner over and fold down the excess flap.

G. Glue the liner to the pinwheel and fold the points over it.

H. To finish, slip the fourth point under the first point.

I. Tie up the sleeve with various trimmings.

DESIGNER'S TIP

If you plan to mail the folded paper sleeve and you've trimmed it with three-dimensional items such as a button or wax seal, be sure to use a padded envelope.

HOLIDAY DECORATIONS

The Classic White Rose Wreath

Assemble this easy holiday wreath by weaving the stems of artificial roses through a wire wreath form.

BY CAROL ENDLER STERBENZ

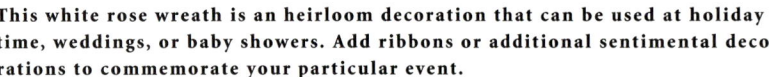
This white rose wreath is an heirloom decoration that can be used at holiday time, weddings, or baby showers. Add ribbons or additional sentimental decorations to commemorate your particular event.

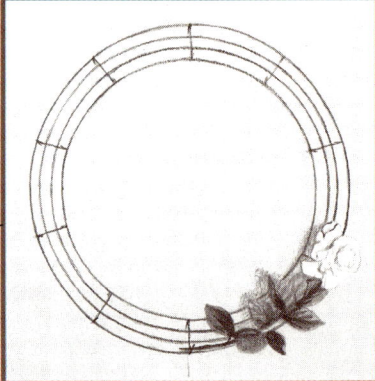

A. Weave a rose stem onto a wire wreath form.

B. Weave in new roses, covering the existing stems.

C. Accent the finished wreath with red berries.

MATERIALS

- 50 to 70 white artificial roses
- 10 to 15 sprigs small red holly berries
- 7 to 10 sprigs large burgundy berries
- 20" wire wreath form
- 30-gauge green florist wire

You'll also need: wire cutters; and ruler.

COLOR PHOTOGRAPHY:
Carl Tremblay

ILLUSTRATION:
Nenad Jakesevic

STYLING:
Ritch Holben

THIS BEAUTIFUL WHITE ROSE wreath comes together quickly and easily. The trick: Weave the stems of the roses through a wire base. The roses both affix and serve as the decoration.

To give the wreath a Christmas feel, I added red berries of two different sizes. By varying this addition, or the color of the roses, you can create a wreath for any season. Create a springtime decoration by mixing pink, yellow, and ecru roses together with crab apples.

INSTRUCTIONS

1. *Prepare roses.* Using wire cutters, trim each rose stem to 12".

2. *Join roses to wreath form.* Lay wire wreath form face up on flat surface. Weave one rose stem under one spoke and over adjacent spoke, pulling it through until rose lodges on top (*see* illustration A, above). Insert stem of new rose next to first rose and weave stem onto wreath form in same way. Continue adding new roses over existing stems. Weave all stems in same general direction, and work from side to side of wire base for full, even coverage (illustration B). Poke leaves through to underside of wreath base. Use remaining roses to fill out wreath where needed, weaving stems through existing stems instead of wire spokes if wreath base is obscured.

3. *Add berries to wreath.* Attach larger burgundy berries first, then small red holly berries to wreath. Arrange berry sprigs on front of wreath at random and anchor with florist wire from the back (illustration C). ◆

ORNAMENTS

Keepsake Silver Bird Ornament

Recreate the look of sterling silver for pennies.

BY NANCY OVERTON

COLOR PHOTOGRAPHY:
Carl Tremblay

ILLUSTRATIONS:
Nenad Jakesevic

STYLING:
Ritch Holben

THE IDEA BEHIND THIS CHRISTmas ornament is simple: transform an inexpensive Styrofoam bird into a faux silver-plated ornament using a leafing kit. The silver-plated bird is then glued to a wire perch, which is "weighted" with two beads at the other end.

Nancy Overton, a craft designer and author, lives in Oakland, California.

INSTRUCTIONS

1. *Apply sealer and base coat.* To make temporary handle for bird, uncoil and straighten wire "feet" or insert short length of 14-gauge wire into base. To free hands during work, insert feet or wire into florist foam brick so bird stands upright. Apply sealer over entire bird, working from bottom up. Let dry 1 hour. Repeat to apply gray basecoat. Let dry 1 hour.

2. *Apply adhesive.* Brush one coat adhesive onto bird; let dry until clear and tacky (up to 1 hour). To test for tackiness, press finger against bird; when surface is sticky like tape, adhesive is ready. Repeat brush on second coat.

3. *Apply silver foil.* Cut 2" x 6" strip of foil. Wrap strip shiny side out around bird, covering as much of surface as possible. Rub strip with fingers to transfer silver film to bird (see illustration A, below). Peel up foil. Repeat process with new foil to coat remaining blank areas; do not recoat previously covered areas. Let dry 1 hour.

4. *Burnish and antique surface.* Using soft brush, apply very light sealer coat to entire bird; let dry 20 minutes. Brush antiquing medium (or black paint) onto surface. Wrap index finger with soft cloth, then work medium into crevices and recessed areas (illustration B). Let dry 20 minutes. Apply final sealer coat and let medium dry 1 hour.

For variation on this design, substitute other small Styrofoam animals, or use gold leaf over a base coat of ochre acrylic paint.

5. *Make wire perch.* Cut 4¼" length of steel wire. Using needle-nose pliers, bend wire to match perch template 1 on page 45; for smooth curves, bend wire in short sections rather than all at once. Use round-nose pliers to shape open loops at each end, matching perch template 2. Remove temporary handle from bird. Using small scissors, carve 1"-long groove ¼" deep in bottom of bird. Test-fit hooked end of perch in groove, then hot-glue in place (illustration C).

6. *Attach counterweight.* Using round-nose pliers, bend small loop in one end of 20-gauge silver wire. Thread two silver beads on wire and push down to loop. Cut excess wire ½" beyond bead, loop this end, and join to lower perch loop so beads dangle freely. To hang ornament, balance perch on tree branch. ◆

MATERIALS

- 3"-long Styrofoam bird
- Two 1" hollow silver beads
- 5" 14-gauge galvanized steel wire
- 6" 20-gauge silver wire
- Delta Renaissance Foil kit, Burnished Silver

You'll also need:
perch templates (see page 45) round-nose pliers; needle-nose pliers; wire cutters; flat ¼" paintbrush; scissors; ruler; hot-glue gun; soft cloth; and florist foam brick.

MAKING THE SILVER BIRD ORNAMENT

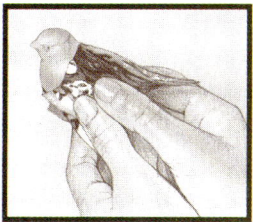

A. Apply the the sealer base coat and adhesive, then rub on the silver foil.

B. Work the antiquing medium into the crevices with a soft cloth.

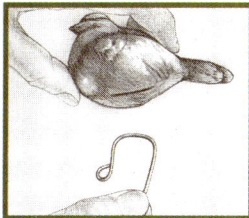

C. Hot-glue the perch onto the underside of the bird.

SCREENS

The Easiest Four-Panel Screen You'll Ever Make

Use one poster and four wooden plaques for a heavenly hinged mural.

🕊 BY ELIZABETH CAMERON

Although it looks like we used four separate posters for this screen, the secret to its flowing, mural-like effect is using one poster cut into four pieces.

COLOR PHOTOGRAPHY:
Carl Tremblay

ILLUSTRATION:
Mary Newell DePalma

DETAIL PHOTOGRAPHY:
Daniel van Ackere

STYLING:
Ritch Holben

MATERIALS

- Angel poster at least 15" tall x 30" wide
- Four 7¼" x 13" arched wood plaques
- Six 1¼"-long x 1½"-wide brass hinges with screws
- 2 ounces gold metallic acrylic paint
- Gold metallic felt-tip pen
- Decoupage medium (e.g., Mod Podge)

You'll also need:
1"-wide foam brush; 1"-wide stiff-bristled brush; X-Acto knife; self-healing cutting mat; screwdriver or hammer; 150-grit sandpaper; 24" x 36" sheet of newsprint (or tape smaller sheets together); paper towels; sponge; cotton balls or brayer; spray mister; ruler; and pencil.

L OOKING FOR A FAST AND EASY way to decorate your sideboard or mantel during the holidays? Consider this four-panel hinged screen, which you can assemble using five basic materials: a poster, four wood plaques, glue, decoupage medium, and hinges.

The construction technique is very simple. Start by cutting the poster into four individual pieces, then glue them to the wooden plaques. Seal the images and hinge the panels together.

I recommend selecting your wooden panels first, then shopping for the poster. This ensures that the poster you find will be large enough to cover all four wooden panels and the right scale for the panels. Of course, the project can also be done in reverse: If you find an image that you love, from a calendar or greeting card, for example, you can measure it and then search for wooden panels to fit. But because the number of usable images greatly outnumber the number of readily available wooden panels, choosing your panels first will probably make things easier.

Elizabeth Cameron is a freelance writer living in Brighton, Massachusetts.

INSTRUCTIONS

1. *Select images.* Lay four wooden plaques edge to edge on newsprint, and trace outer edge. Remove plaques. Using X-Acto knife and cutting mat, cut along marked line to make window in shape of plaques. Discard inner cutout portion. Lay angel poster face up on cutting mat. Lay cutout window on top and maneuver to frame desired portion of poster (*see* illustration A, next page).

2. *Cut out images.* Line up wooden plaques within window, beveled edges facing down. Remove window. To cut poster, hold X-Acto knife blade at a 45-degree angle and run along beveled edge of each plaque; to cut side edges, temporarily remove neighboring plaque (illustration B). As you complete each cutout, set it and its plaque aside.

3. *Sand and paint panels.* Using 150-grit sandpaper, lightly sand each plaque. Wipe off dust with lightly misted paper towel. Using foam brush, apply one coat metallic gold paint to all surfaces; let dry

Making the Four-Panel Screen

A. Use a newsprint window template to frame a portion of the poster.

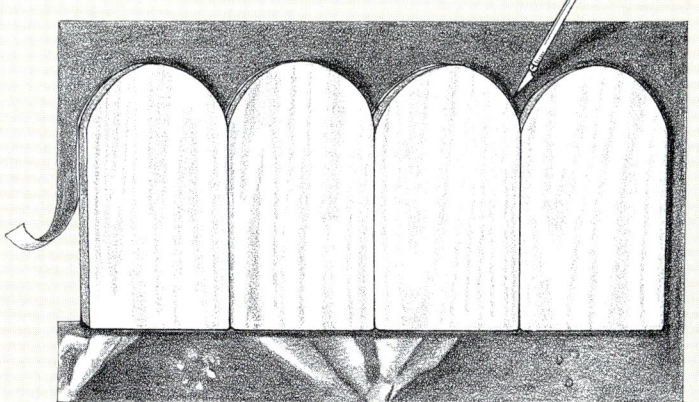

B. Use the plaques as templates to cut the poster panels.

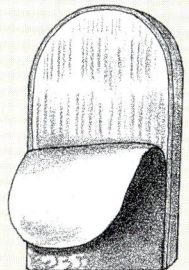

C. Glue each cut poster panel to its wooden plaque.

D. Hinge the plaques together to make a folding screen.

20 minutes. Apply second coat, then let dry at least 1 hour, but preferably overnight.

4. *Glue cutouts to panels.* Using stiff brush, spread glue thinly and evenly over front surface (beveled side) of one plaque. Position cutout on plaque and press down. Working from center out, rub cotton ball over surface in circular motion, or roll brayer over surface to press out air bubbles and ensure adhesion. Wipe oozing glue from edges with damp sponge. Repeat process to glue images to remaining plaques (illustration C). Let dry 1 hour. Examine edges carefully. If cutout extends beyond beveled edge, turn plaque face down on cutting mat and run X-Acto knife carefully along edge to trim.

5. *Add finishing details.* Run gold marker along white edges of cutout image. Using stiff-bristled brush, apply Mod Podge to images, brushing in different directions to simulate brush strokes of oil painting. Let dry overnight.

6. *Hinge plaques together.* Lay four plaques face up, side by side, in desired order. Turn second plaque face down on third plaque. Following hinge manufacturer's instructions, join left edges with two hinges placed 1½" and 7½" from bottom. Set first plaque on second plaque, wrong sides together, and hinge right edges in same way. Join third and fourth plaques wrong sides together to complete screen. Resulting screen will zigzag when standing up (illustration D) and fold flat for storage. ◆

DESIGNER'S TIP

Hinged screens can be assembled from any size wooden panel or board. To join the panels, choose a hinge flange size that spans the full width of the panel edge. The hinge pin should extend just beyond the edge to ensure that adjacent panels fold flat.

CREATING A CRACKLED FINISH

The poster I selected for the hinged screen shown on page 14 included cracks on the images. If your poster does not feature cracks, however, you can add them easily using a crackling medium. For the panel pictured above, I used Anita's Faux Easy Fragile Crackle. (Make sure your decoupage medium has dried completely before applying the crackle medium.) Unlike many crackling mediums, which only act when brushed over a base coat of paint, Fragile Crackle is transparent, meaning it won't obscure the image. After I created a grid of crackles on top of the print, I dipped a paper towel into burnt umber acrylic paint and rubbed it across the crackled surface. The paint settled into the cracks, making the pattern more evident. —E.C.

A New Use For Rubber Stamps

You can create finely detailed gilded designs on glass by coating your rubber stamp with size instead of ink or paint.

🌂 BY RITCH HOLBEN

To create a seasonal version of this charger, use a stamp with holly leaves and berries or combine stamps depicting nuts and berries.

COLOR PHOTOGRAPHY:
Carl Tremblay

ILLUSTRATION:
Michael Gellatly

STYLING:
Ritch Holben

MATERIALS
- Clear glass dinner charger (or other glassware)
- Copper leaf
- Transparent glass paint, cobalt blue
- Japan size

You'll also need:
rubber stamps with designs of varying size; ink pad; clean, soft-bristled brushes; glass cleaner; paper towels; poster board; metal straightedge or ruler; pencil; large sheet of plain white paper; compass; masking tape; soft, clean cloths; scissors; and mineral spirits.

Other items, if necessary:
razor blade (for correcting mistakes).

LOOKING FOR A NEW WAY TO USE your rubber stamps? Consider stamping gilded or leafed designs. The technique is simple and effective: Brush the rubber stamp with size, stamp the design, then apply metal leaf over the size and brush away the excess.

I used this technique to stamp and leaf a copper-colored design on the back of a clear glass charger. However, you can also apply this technique to other types of glassware, such as the back side of a large glass bowl or dessert plates, or on wood frames or boxes.

On the chargers, I back-painted the copper leaf design with cobalt blue glass paint, but you can vary this design easily to suit your tastes. You can change the color of paint or the color of the leaf or skip the back painting entirely and simply seal the design with a coat of transparent sealer.

I tested a variety of different rubber stamps and found the technique works well no matter what the detail of the stamp. Be aware, however, that size reaches a ready stage of tackiness much quicker on a fine-grained stamp (about 5 minutes with japan size) than on a more solid design (about 15 minutes, which is more typical with japan size). Be sure to adjust your work time accordingly and do a test stamp on a glass jar that you can discard. Note also that rubber stamps that have previously been used with ink should be cleaned thoroughly using mineral spirits before applying size.

Ritch Holben is a photo stylist, designer, and author living in Nahant, Massachusetts.

INSTRUCTIONS

1. *Make template.* Invert charger onto poster board, then trace and cut out outline. Find center of charger using illustrations A and B, next page, then divide circle into eighths, by eye or with straightedge and compass. Load rubber stamp with ink. Thinking of charger as clock face, rubber-stamp largest design on template at twelve, three, six, and nine o'clock positions. Stamp smaller designs in between large ones (illustration C). Clean rubber stamps thoroughly with mineral spirits.

2. *Stamp charger.* Clean charger using glass cleaner and paper towels. Protect work surface, then set charger face down on template, and tape down to prevent shifting. Brush thin, even coat size on face of rubber stamp; stamp once on

Finding the Center of the Charger

A. To find the center of the charger, place a corner of paper on the edge of the circular template. Mark points A and A_1 where the edges of the paper cross the circle, then connect these points using a pencil and a straightedge.

B. Rotate the paper and repeat the process. Connect points B and B_1 as before. The two resulting lines will intersect at the center of the circle. Use this point to divide the template into eighths.

Decorating the Glass Charger

C. Stamp the designs onto the template.

D. Lay the charger over the template, stamp it with size, then apply copper leaf to each image.

E. Back-paint the rim of the charger with glass paint.

plain white paper to shed excess. Stamp size over one template location, taking care not to let stamp slip or slide. To correct a mistake, clean plate with mineral spirits and soft, clean, cloth, let dry, and begin again. Stamp size at all locations, reloading stamp after three or four presses, and changing to small stamp as needed. Let size dry until tacky (5 to 15 minutes, depending on stamp detail).

3. *Apply copper leaf.* When size is tacky, tear sheet of copper leaf into small pieces. Apply one piece leaf over each sized stamp (illustration D). Tamp each design lightly with cloth, then gently buff away excess leaf until clean image appears. To correct a mistake, gently scrape leaf off with razor blade, clean plate with mineral spirits, and apply size with stamp as before. When complete, let dry overnight. Clean rubber stamps thoroughly with mineral spirits.

4. *Back-paint rim.* Brush cobalt blue glass paint on underside of charger rim, covering copper leaf (illustration E). Stop painting where bottom of charger begins. Let dry following manufacturer's instructions. Apply second coat if needed and let dry. Clean brush. ◆

LOW-SEW

Court Jester Stocking

This elegant Christmas stocking, which stands upright on its own, can be filled to overflowing.

🔔 BY DAWN ANDERSON

Use a series of coordinated stockings to decorate a sideboard or mantel, or use one stocking alone as the central focus of a holiday centerpiece.

COLOR PHOTOGRAPHY:
Carl Tremblay

ILLUSTRATION:
Mary Newell DePalma

STYLING:
Ritch Holben

INSTEAD OF HANGING FROM A mantel, this striking "Court Jester-style" Christmas stocking stands upright on its own. Sewn from dupioni silk, it makes a unique holiday decorating accent, used alone or in pairs.

The stocking's bootlike design relies on two tricks to keep it upright. First, the walls of the stocking use two layers of silk with fusible knit interfacing and lightweight batting in between, which gives the fabric extra body. Second, the stocking features a padded chipboard sole, to stabilize the bottom.

The stocking requires two or three different colors of fabric: one for the body of the stocking, one for the lining, and one for the cuff. In the design shown above, I sewed the stocking from red silk dupioni, and the lining and cuffs from gold silk dupioni, but you can substitute any other fine-weave fabric. For variation on this design, choose a third color for the lining. I sewed tiny charms in a pattern over the outside surface. If you select fabric with a pattern, you may opt to skip this step.

Dawn Anderson is a writer and designer living in Redmond, Washington.

MATERIALS

- 1/3 yard 45"-wide cranberry silk dupioni (for stocking body)
- 5/8 yard 45"-wide gold silk dupioni (for lining, cuff, and insole)
- 2/3 yard 60"-wide fusible nylon knit tricot interfacing
- 1/2 yard 36"-wide rayon fusible woven interfacing
- 1/3 yard 45"-wide lightweight batting
- Six 1/2"-diameter silver thread balls with self-loops
- Thread to match fabrics
- 8" x 10" 2-ply chipboard
- 20" Perle cotton (or similar cord)
- White craft glue
- Spray adhesive

You'll also need:
stocking, cuff, and insole patterns (see pages 48 and 49); sewing machine; iron and ironing board; small dressmaker's ham or tightly rolled hand towel; rotary cutter; acrylic grid ruler; self-healing cutting mat; sewing shears; beading needle; embroidery needle; hand-sewing needle; pins; point turner; waxed paper; a heavy book; X-Acto knife; and scissors.

Other items, if necessary:
approximately 110 brass charms (for decorating stocking body).

INSTRUCTIONS

1. *Prepare patterns and fabrics.* Prepare stocking, cuff, and insole patterns (pages 48 and 49), then cut out with scissors. Using rotary cutter, grid ruler, and cutting mat, rough-cut the following items: From red silk fabric, cut two 12" x 17" rectangles for stocking, longer edge along crosswise grain. From gold silk fabric, cut two 12" x 17" rectangles for lining, four 8½" x 10½" rectangles for cuff, and two 5" x 11" rectangles for insole; run longer edges along crosswise grain. From fusible knit interfacing, cut four 12" x 17" rectangles. From lightweight batting, cut two 12" x 17" rectangles and one 5" x 11" rectangle. From fusible woven interfacing, cut four 8½" x 10½" rectangles. Fuse knit interfacings to wrong side of same-size red and gold rectangles.

2. *Sew stocking.* On flat work surface, stack one large batting rectangle, one red silk rectangle right side up, one red silk rectangle right side down, and one batting rectangle. Align long edges at top, and pin through all four layers. Position stocking pattern on stack and pin to top batting only. Using pattern as a template, stitch curved edges all around; leave top straight edge open. To improve accuracy at toe, change to shorter stitch length. Unpin and remove pattern. Trim seam allowance 3/8" from stitching all around (see illustration

A, below), then trim batting layer only as close to stitching as possible on both sides. Clip curves, turn right side out, and press.

3. *Sew lining.* Place two gold rectangles right sides together and align long top edges. Pin stocking pattern to fabric as before. Stitch curved edges all around, leaving opening for turning between dots. To reinforce seam, stitch ⅛" inside previous stitching. Unpin and remove pattern. Trim off excess fabric (illustration B). Clip curves, turn right side out, and press lightly.

4. *Sew cuffs.* Cut four cuffs from woven fusible interfacing; separate into two pairs. Place one pair on wrong side of 8½" x 10½" gold rectangle, align top straight edges, and fuse following manufacturer's directions. Place this "cuff" rectangle and a plain gold rectangle right sides together and pin. Set machine to 25 stitches per inch. Using interfacing as a template, machine-stitch cuff points all around along edge of interfacing; leave top straight edge open. Trim seam allowance ½" from stitching all around (illustration C). Clip into allowance at inner points. Press back top seam allowance, trim full seam allowance ⅛" from stitching, and trim across lower points. Turn cuff right side out, push out points with point turner, and press. Repeat process for second cuff.

5. *Make insole.* On chipboard, mark one large and one small insole (*see pattern*); cut out both pieces with X-Acto knife. Following manufacturer's instructions, apply spray adhesive to larger insole. Set insole face down on 5" x 11" piece of batting, then press to adhere. Use scissors to trim excess even with insole edge. Lightly spray batting surface of insole, then press insole batting side down on wrong side of 5" x 11" gold silk rectangle. Trim fabric ¾" beyond insole edge all around; clip into allowance every ⅜" to make tabs. Apply thin bead white craft glue to edge of insole, fold tabbed allowance onto wet glue area, and press down. Set waxed paper on top, and weight with heavy book. Repeat process to cover smaller insole with remaining gold fabric, but omit batting. Let both pieces dry 30 minutes. Glue insoles back to back, weight with book, and let dry 1 hour.

6. *Gather sole.* Cut 10" length of cord. Turn stocking inside out, lay cord along sole seam allowance, and zigzag over cord between dots; leave ends loose (illustration D). Thread one end of cord into embroidery needle, then draw needle into seam allowance near dot, and knot end of cord. Draw up cord from other end, gathering sole to 5¾", knot end, and clip off excess. Turn stocking right side out. Insert small dressmaker's ham or tightly rolled hand towel into stocking, then press gathered sole from right side. Repeat process to gather sole of lining.

7. *Sew charms to stocking.* Thread beading needle with red thread. Beginning about 1" below top edge of stocking, sew row of five charms 1¾" to 2" apart. Stitch a second row of five charms 1" to 1⅛" below first row, staggering placement diagonally for subtle diamond pattern. Continue sewing charms in staggered rows, stopping 2" from bottom seam. Set insole into stocking, stand stocking upright, and check charm placement. Remove insole. Sew additional charms to toe, any bare areas, and other side.

8. *Assemble stocking.* Place cuff against right side of stocking, top edges together, then raise cuff ½" beyond stocking top edge to align cuff and stocking stitching lines (*see* patterns). Machine-baste 1" from cuff edge along stitching line (illustration E). Repeat process to baste second cuff to other side. Trim batting close to stitching, but do not trim fabric. Turn stocking wrong side out. Set lining into stocking, right sides together and side seams matching, align top edge ½" below cuff edge, and pin. Stitch 1" from upper edge of cuff, along machine basting; do not trim seam allowances (illustration F). Turn right side out through opening and slip stitch opening closed (illustration G). Press upper edge of stocking, then drop lining inside stocking. Hand-tack silver ball to each cuff point. Set insole into stocking (illustration H). ◆

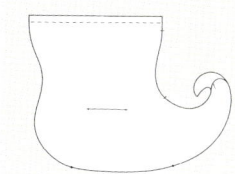

PATTERNS
See pages 48 and 49 for pattern pieces and enlargement instructions.

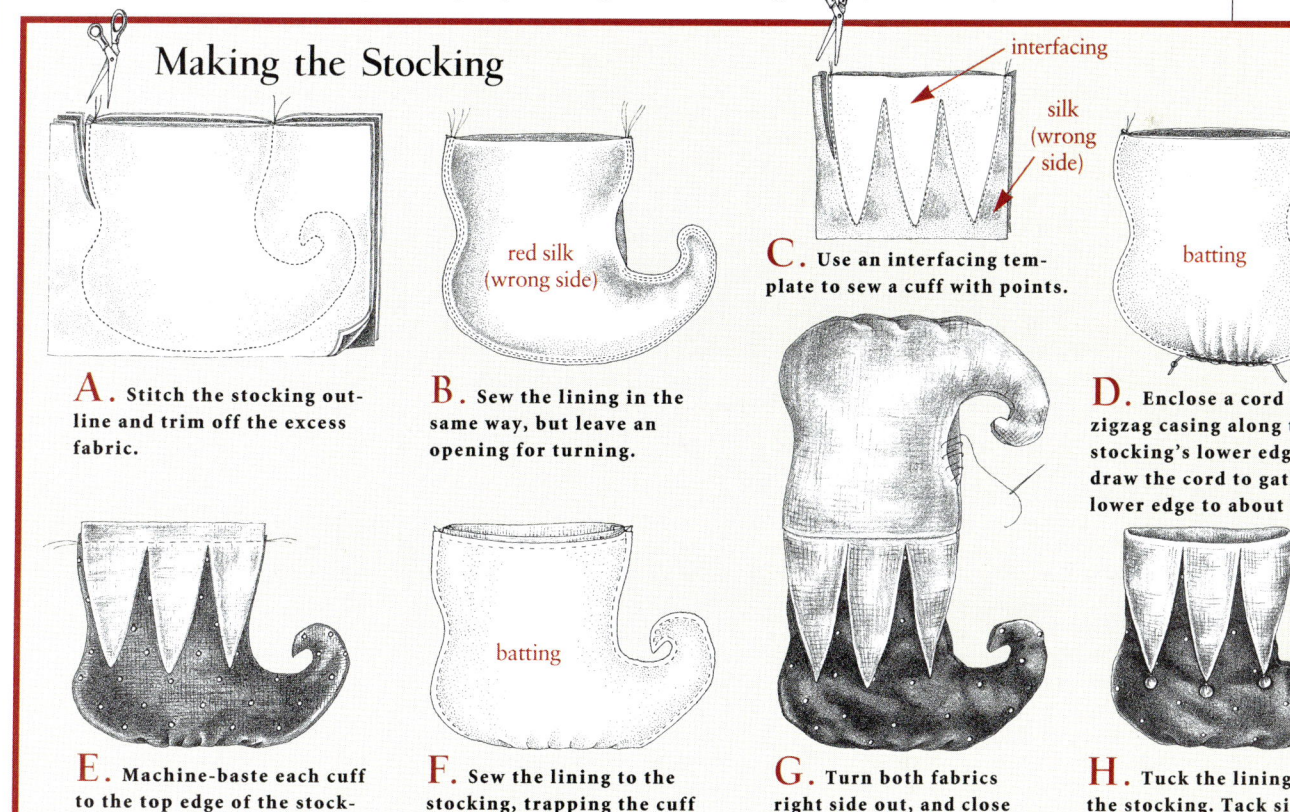

Making the Stocking

A. Stitch the stocking outline and trim off the excess fabric.

B. Sew the lining in the same way, but leave an opening for turning.

red silk (wrong side)

C. Use an interfacing template to sew a cuff with points.

interfacing
silk (wrong side)

D. Enclose a cord in a zigzag casing along the stocking's lower edge, then draw the cord to gather the lower edge to about 5¾".

batting

E. Machine-baste each cuff to the top edge of the stocking.

F. Sew the lining to the stocking, trapping the cuff in the seam.

batting

G. Turn both fabrics right side out, and close the opening.

H. Tuck the lining inside the stocking. Tack silver balls to each cuff.

HOLIDAY DECORATIONS

Secrets of Christmas Crackers

Your search for snaps is over. We've found two mail-order sources for both snaps and tubes.

🎄 BY DAWN ANDERSON

These holiday crackers can be filled with fortunes, charms, candy, confetti, or small pieces of jewelry.

DESIGNER'S TIP

You can substitute toilet tissue tubes for mailing tubes in this project. Simply cut the giftwrap about 6" longer than the length of the tube and 1" to 2" wider than the tube circumference.

COLOR PHOTOGRAPHY:
Carl Tremblay

ILLUSTRATION:
Judy Love

STYLING:
Ritch Holben

BRING A TOUCH OF GREAT BRITAIN to your home this holiday season with these quick and easy Christmas crackers, which snap open to reveal small candies, charms, or gifts. All you need to make these festive favors are mailing tubes, snaps, giftwrap, and double-stick tape.

I mail-ordered my snaps and tubes from Impress; see Sources & Resources, page 48. The snaps are paper strips about 11" long with a piece in the middle that pops when you pull both ends. To make the cracker, I rolled up the snap and a mailing tube in giftwrap. The ends of the paper snap stick out at each end of the rolled cracker. If you pull on the ends, the snap pulls apart with a pop, in turn tearing the giftwrap. The cracker can then be torn open and the candy, gifts, and so forth removed.

Dawn Anderson is a writer and designer living in Redmond, Washington.

INSTRUCTIONS

1. *Prepare mailing tubes.* Using handsaw, cut one mailing tube in half; set cut halves aside. Remove one end cap from remaining tube, fill tube with confetti, candy, or prizes and replace cap.

MATERIALS
Yields 1 cracker

- Two 1¼"-diameter x 4¾"-long mailing tubes
- Snap
- Holiday giftwrap
- ½"-wide ribbon
- Gold bullion
- Confetti, wrapped candy, small prizes, and so forth
- Double-stick tape

You'll also need:
X-Acto knife; self-healing cutting mat; acrylic cutting guide; small handsaw; cotton string; ruler; and pencil.

2. *Cover tube with paper.* Use illustration A, below, as reference for following step. Cut 5" x 12" rectangle from giftwrap. On wrong side, mark long edges 3½" in from each short edge. Apply strips of tape between marks. Align filled tube on one strip, parallel to long edge, and press to adhere. Lay snap on giftwrap parallel to tube. Position cut tube halves from step 1 at each end of filled tube, then roll all pieces across paper, trapping snap between layers. Press firmly to seal remaining taped edge.

3. *Shape and trim cracker.* Pull cut tube halves out about 1" at each end. Wind string once or twice around unsupported section of giftwrap and cinch tightly (illustration B). Remove string. Tie ribbon around each cinched end as if wrapping a package. Cut twelve 1½" lengths bullion (do not stretch). Stretch one length at midpoint, wrap once around cinched section, and twist ends together to secure. Repeat process to attach six lengths to each end of cracker. Remove cut tube halves (illustration C). ◆

Making the Crackers

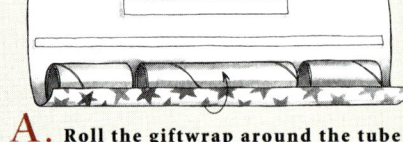

A. Roll the giftwrap around the tube and snap.

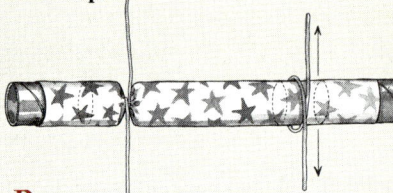

B. Cinch the ends with cotton string.

C. Decorate the ends with ribbon and gold bullion.

Jeweled Cage Ornaments

Make these cagework decorations using a simple wrap-and-trap technique.

BY ELIZABETH CAMERON

COLOR PHOTOGRAPHY:
Carl Tremblay

ILLUSTRATION:
Mary Newell DePalma

STYLING:
Ritch Holben

THESE CAGELIKE, BEADED ORNAments use a simple construction technique I call "wrap and trap." The beads are strung one by one onto a wire, then trapped in place by wrapping a second, thinner gauge of wire around the original wire and the bead. The resulting strands of beaded wire are then shaped into a sphere to create the finished ornament.

The design is fairly forgiving, as the spacing between the beads is up to you. However, I don't recommend spacing them any closer than ½" together; otherwise the beads can interfere with the wire intersections at the poles.

Elizabeth Cameron is a freelance writer living in Brighton, Massachusetts.

INSTRUCTIONS

1. *Sort beads.* Arrange beads on flannel cloth in desired order. Repeat sequence until all beads are set out.

2. *String beads.* Wrap 20-gauge wire five or six complete revolutions around soda can, add 1", and clip with wire cutters. Unwind 10 inches of 24-gauge wire from spool, but do not cut. Hold two wire ends together, and twist 24-gauge wire around 20-gauge wire two or three times, for spiral about ½" long. Slip first bead from lineup onto 20-gauge wire, and slide it down to spiraled section. Twist 24-gauge wire around 20-gauge wire two or three times, locking bead in place. Slip on second bead from lineup, and twist wire to trap bead (*see* illustration A, below). Repeat process, continuing until all beads are strung or you reach end of 20-gauge wire. To end off, spiral 24-gauge wire around 20-gauge wire for ½" and clip wire from spool.

3. *Shape first round of wire sphere.* Cut two 6" lengths of 28-gauge wire; set one aside. To establish circumference, wrap beaded wire once around can, as in step 2. Hold intersection securely, and slip circle off can. To anchor intersection, lodge beaded wire under spiraled wire, and bind once or twice with 28-gauge wire; do not cut wire end (illustration B).

4. *Shape successive rounds of sphere.* Slide one hand 8" to 10" down beaded wire and draw up into same-size circle formed in step 3. Bind together at established intersection, using existing wire; use reserved 28-gauge wire to bind intersection at opposite pole. Bend second circle slightly so it runs alongside first circle, forming segment on imaginary sphere. Continue shaping and lashing, segment by segment, until all wire is used (illustration C). To end off, bind securely and clip and crimp end (illustration D). ◆

For a variation on this design, intermix different size, color, or types of beads.

MATERIALS
- 50 to 75 red 6mm round faceted glass beads
- 20-gauge silver wire
- 24-gauge silver wire
- 28-gauge silver wire

You'll also need: needle-nose pliers; wire cutters; soda can; ruler; and flannel cloth.

Making the Ornament

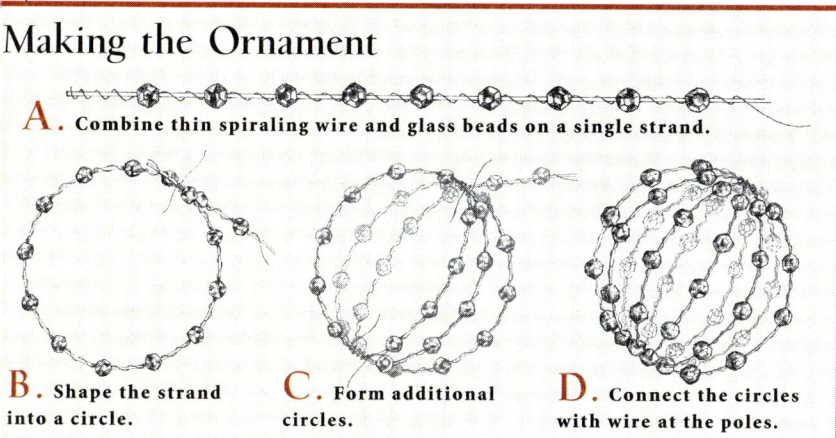

A. Combine thin spiraling wire and glass beads on a single strand.

B. Shape the strand into a circle.

C. Form additional circles.

D. Connect the circles with wire at the poles.

DECORATIVE FOOD

Gilded Gingerbread Cookies

Dress up your holiday gingerbread recipes with this trio of sparkling materials: lustrous powder, edible glitter, and gold dragées.

🍂 BY DAWN ANDERSON

For variation on this design, use the Luster Dust in dry form or change the color of the edible glitter.

MATERIALS
Yields twenty 6" star cookies

Cookie Dough
- 3 cups all-purpose flour, sifted, plus extra for baking sheets and patterns
- 1 teaspoon baking soda
- 1½ teaspoons ground ginger
- 1½ teaspoons ground cinnamon
- ½ teaspoon nutmeg
- ½ teaspoon ground cloves
- ½ cup butter
- ½ cup dark brown sugar, firmly packed
- 1 egg
- ½ cup unsulfured molasses
- 1 tablespoon lemon juice

Icing/Decorations
- Egg white of one large egg
- 1 cup confectioners' sugar
- ½ teaspoon vanilla extract
- ¼ teaspoon cream of tartar
- Lemon extract
- Gold Luster Dust
- Gold edible glitter
- Gold dragées
- Narrow gold cord

You'll also need:
star pattern (*see* page 45); two 2-ounce plastic squeeze bottles, each with coupler; cake decorating tips, sizes 1 and 2; electric mixer; sifter; large mixing bowl; medium-sized bowl; wet and dry measuring cups; measuring spoons; plastic wrap; waxed paper; tweezers; ruler; rolling pin; baking sheets; wire racks; paring knife; coffee mug; plate; ⅛"-diameter straws; thin cardboard; gluestick; scissors; custard cup or small glass jar; straw; and small, new paintbrush.

COLOR PHOTOGRAPHY:
Carl Tremblay

ILLUSTRATION:
Nenad Jakesevic

SILHOUETTE PHOTOGRAPHY:
Daniel van Ackere

STYLING:
Ritch Holben

LOOKING FOR A FAST AND EASY way to dress up your holiday gingerbread recipes? Consider this trio of metallic materials, borrowed from the cake-decorating world: Luster Dust, an edible metallic powder; edible glitter, made from gum arabic; and gold dragées.

Luster Dust, a nontoxic metallic powder, comes in gold, silver, or copper. You can use the dust dry to add a light dusting of color or moisten it with lemon extract and use it like watercolor paint. Edible glitter, made from the same material as that used on the back of envelopes, is available in a wide range of colors, from gold and silver to red, green, and rainbow. The third member of this metallic trio—dragées—is available in gold and silver in a range of sizes.

To create the cookie shown above, I started by painting the gingerbread with liquefied gold Luster Dust, then piped an outline and polka dots using white icing. Last, I positioned gold dragées on the cookie and finished off with a dusting of edible glitter.

Dawn Anderson is a writer and designer living in Redmond, Washington.

INSTRUCTIONS

1. *Make star template.* Prepare star pattern (*see* page 45). Trim pattern ½" beyond edges, then glue to cardboard. Cut along pattern outline.

2. *Mix cookie dough.* In medium-sized bowl, sift together flour, baking soda, ginger, cinnamon, nutmeg, and cloves; then set aside. In large bowl, beat butter and brown sugar with mixer until fluffy. Mix in egg, molasses, and lemon juice. Add one-half dry ingredients and mix well, then add remaining dry ingredients and mix on low speed until combined. Divide dough in half. Form each half into ball,

DECORATIVE FOOD

The cookie at far left features piped designs on plain gingerbread, while the cookie at far right uses silver Luster Dust.

flatten slightly, and wrap with plastic wrap. Refrigerate 2 hours.

3. *Cut and bake cookies.* Grease and lightly flour baking sheets. Place flattened dough balls on sheets, cover with wax paper, and roll to 1/8" thickness. Remove waxed paper. To cut cookies, dust cardboard template with flour, set on dough, and run paring knife along edge. If dough distorts, press knife blade straight down into dough instead of slicing through it, or rechill rolled dough 5 minutes to firm it up for cutting. Cut as many cookies as possible (*see* illustration A, below). Gather up scrap dough and refrigerate for reuse. To make hanging hole, pierce tip of star point with straw approximately 1/4" from edges. Refrigerate baking sheets with cut dough 15 minutes; preheat oven to 350 degrees. Bake cookies 8 to 10 minutes, taking care not to overbake. Transfer cookies to wire racks and let cool.

4. *Prepare icing.* Beat egg white, confectioners' sugar, vanilla, and cream of tartar until smooth and peaks begin to form. Transfer icing to two 2-ounce squeeze bottles and cap with size 1 and 2 tips. Set bottles upside down in mug.

5. *Apply Luster Dust.* Place 1/2 teaspoon lemon extract in custard cup or jar, add small amount gold Luster Dust, and stir with brush to consistency of watercolor paint. Brush mixture across surface of each cookie for opaque coverage. If mixture is too watery, add more Luster Dust; if mixture becomes dry, add more lemon extract (illustration B).

6. *Add icing and dragées.* To start icing flow, shake bottle down sharply once or twice; store upside down in mug when not in use. Referring to design on template (*see* pattern, page 45) and using size 2 tip for lines and size 1 tip for dots, pipe icing onto cookie surface. Hold squeeze bottle at 45-degree angle with tip 1/8" above surface (illustration C). To add dragées, pipe dot of icing onto cookie, then set dragée into position with tweezers while icing is still wet (illustration D). Let icing harden 20 minutes.

7. *Apply edible glitter and hanging cord.* Place cookie on waxed paper. Crush glitter between fingers, sprinkling it over entire cookie (illustration E). Shake cookie gently from side to side to distribute glitter, then turn cookie upside down to shed excess. Save for reuse. Repeat process for each cookie. To hang cookies, thread 8" length cord through hole and tie off (illustration F). Slide knot behind hole. ◆

DESIGNER'S TIPS

■ To prevent the distortion that comes when shapes are transferred, roll out the dough directly on the baking sheet. If your baking sheet has rims that will interfere with rolling, turn it over and use the other side.

■ After you've gathered up the scraps from the first batch of gingerbread dough, refrigerate them while you work with the remaining half. Continue alternating with each half until you've cut all the cookie designs.

■ For straight, even lines when piping the icing, move the squeeze bottle quickly and smoothly. Do not let the tip of the bottle touch the surface of the cookie.

MAKING THE GINGERBREAD ORNAMENTS

A. Cut the star-shaped cookies using a cardboard pattern.

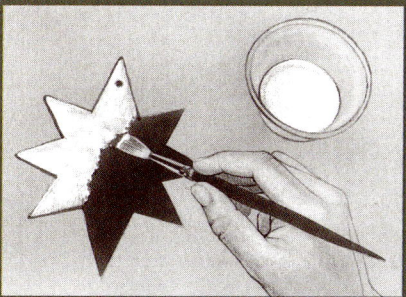
B. After baking, "gild" each cookie with liquefied Luster Dust.

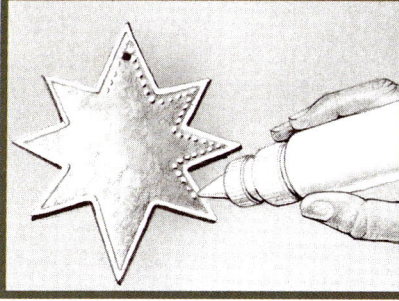
C. Pipe the icing, using a squeeze bottle for maximum control.

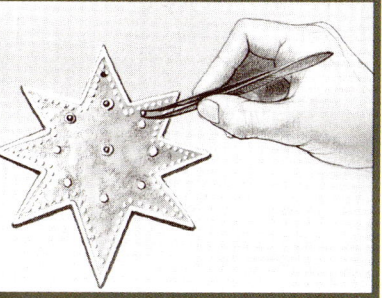
D. Use tweezers to set each gold dragée into position.

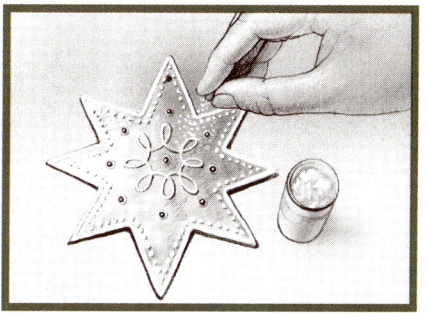
E. Sprinkle the cookie surface with edible glitter.

F. To hang the cookie, tie on a narrow gold cord.

PATTERN
See page 45 for pattern.

GIFTS

Terry Cloth Baby Animals

Sew your own soft-bodied bunny and piglet from scraps, then add character with a few quick stitches of floss.

🐾 BY MICHIO RYAN

Quick-sew six fabric pieces together for a charming gift.

COLOR PHOTOGRAPHY:
Carl Tremblay

ILLUSTRATION:
Judy Love

STYLING:
Ritch Holben

MATERIALS

Baby Bunny
- 12" x 12" white terry cloth
- 2" x 12" pink terry cloth
- Matching thread
- 1½" white pom-pom
- Two ¼" black pom-poms
- Brown embroidery floss
- White embroidery floss
- Plastic pellets
- Fiberfill
- Washable fabric glue

Piglet
- 12" x 12" pink terry cloth
- 2" x 12" cream terry cloth
- Matching thread
- Two ¼" black pom-poms
- Brown embroidery floss
- Pink embroidery floss
- Plastic pellets
- Fiberfill
- Washable fabric glue

You'll also need:
patterns (*see* pages 46 and 47); sewing machine; sewing shears; ball-head pins; long hand-sewing needle; embroidery needle; size 3 steel crochet hook; ruler; and fabric pen.

THESE TINY STUFFED ANIMALS, which make a wonderful holiday gift for children and adults alike, are fast and easy to assemble. Both versions require four primary supplies: a 12" piece of terry cloth, fiberfill, plastic pellets for stuffing, and embroidery floss for the facial details.

The two animals are variations on one pattern. I gave each animal a particular look by using different facial features and tails, and adding a snout and hooves to the piglet. I used terry cloth for both versions, but you can substitute any type of fabric with a roughed-up or looped texture, such as bouclé. You can also recycle old terry towels in good condition, or use fabrics with a slight stretch, such as stretch terry.

I used two different fillers for the animals: fiberfill in the head and arms, and plastic pellets for the body. The fiberfill keeps the head light, preventing it from toppling over; it also helps keep the embroidered features in place. The body, in contrast, needs a poseable, slouchy posture; this is best achieved by using plastic pellets. (I found a one-pound bag of plastic pellets, enough to fill four or five baby animals, for $3.50; *see* Sources & Resources, page 48, for details.) If you're making just one animal or can't find plastic pellets, you can substitute seed beads, but try to match the color of the bead to the fabric to prevent show-through. *Note:* These stuffed animals are designed for children age 3 and older.

INSTRUCTIONS
Note: Sew all pieces making scant ¼" seams.

Making the Baby Bunny
1. *Cut terry cloth pieces.* Prepare patterns on pages 46 and 47. From white terry cloth, cut one 2"-wide strip along lengthwise grain; set aside for ears. Using patterns, cut one body front, one body back, two arms, two head fronts, and two head backs.

2. *Make ears.* Stack pink and white terry cloth strips wrong sides together. Pin ear pattern to strips. Straight-stitch along pattern outline through both layers. Reposition pattern and repeat to stitch second ear. Cut out ears close to stitching. Place one ear on machine bed pink side up. Using pink thread in machine and white thread in bobbin, satin-stitch curved edge all around. Repeat to finish second ear.

3. *Stitch head.* Fold short edge of ear pink side in, and machine-baste to head front between marks. Pin front and back heads right sides together, then stitch seam, leaving neck edge open (*see* illustration A, next page). Join remaining head pieces in mirror image, then sew both halves together to complete head. Turn head right side out (illustration B).

4. *Stitch body.* Fold body back in half right sides together; stitch center back seam, leaving 1½" opening for turning.

Making the Baby Bunny

A. Sew the head pieces together, catching an ear in between.

B. Join the two head halves and turn right side out.

C. Join the front and back bodies, easing the seams to fit.

D. Sew the head and the body together, turn right side out, and stuff from the back.

E. Add facial features using pom-poms and embroidery floss.

Making the Piglet

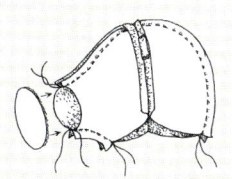
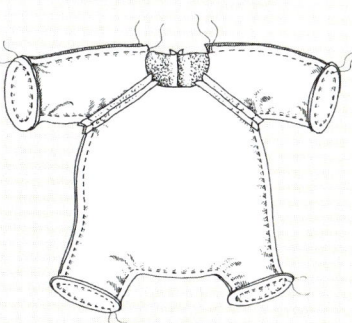

F. Sew the head like the bunny's, then ease in the snout circle.

G. Sew the body front and back together, and add the hoofs.

H. Assemble the body, add stuffing, and stitch facial features using embroidery floss.

DESIGNER'S TIP

If you can't find the right shade of terry cloth for this project, it's fairly simple to dye your own fabric. I recommend using fiber-reactive dye on white 100% terry cloth. Be sure to test the dye on a scrap before immersing the entire piece.

Stitch one arm to each side of body front, right sides together and making raglan-style seams. Sew body front to body back, easing fit all around; leave neck edge open (illustration C). Do not turn right side out.

5. *Join head to body and stuff.* Slip head inside body, right sides together and seams matching. Stitch neck seam all around. Turn body right side out through back opening. Stuff head firmly with fiberfill to fill out curves and muzzle. Pad chest and arms lightly with fiberfill. Fill tummy cavity and legs with approximately ½ cup plastic pellets. Slip-stitch opening closed (illustration D).

6. *Add tail and facial details.* Using white thread, hand-tack white pom-pom to back rump for tail. Insert two ball-head pins into head to fix position for eyes; mark with fabric pen and remove pins. Knot end of white thread. Insert needle into back neck and draw out at one eye mark; pull snug so knot lodges inside fiberfill. Reinsert needle into head at mark, draw out at back neck, and pull gently to indent eye socket. Repeat to make second eye socket, then end off.

Using six strands brown floss, embroider nose in satin stitch and muzzle in straight stitch. Using white floss, make two stitches at end of each limb to suggest paw pads. Glue two black pom-poms to eye sockets; let dry overnight (illustration E).

Making the Piglet

1. *Cut terry cloth pieces.* Prepare patterns on pages 46 and 47. From pink terry cloth, cut one 2"-wide x 6"-long strip along lengthwise grain; set aside for ears. Using patterns, cut one body front, one body back, two arms, two head fronts, and two head backs. From cream terry cloth strip, cut one 6"-long strip for ears and five snout/hoof circles.

2. *Make ears.* Same as Baby Bunny, step 2.

3. Stitch head. Place ear cream side down on head front between marks; machine-baste in place. Pin front and back heads right sides together. Stitch seam, leaving neck edge open. Join remaining head pieces in mirror image. Sew both halves together, leaving straight edge open for snout. Ease snout into opening, right sides together, and stitch by hand or machine (illustration F). Turn head right side out.

4. *Stitch body.* Using double thickness (12 strands) pink embroidery floss and size 3 steel crochet hook, chain 50. To create curly tail, single-crochet in every other chain back to starting point; end off. Fold body back in half right side in, sandwiching end of tail in center back seam. Stitch seam, leaving 1½" opening for turning. Stitch one arm to each side of body front, right sides together, making raglan-style seams. Sew body front to body back, easing fit all around; leave straight edges open. Ease hoof into each opening, right sides together, and stitch as for snout. Do not turn piglet right side out (illustration G).

5. *Join head to body and stuff.* Same as Baby Bunny, step 5.

6. *Add facial details.* Indent eye sockets as for Baby Bunny, step 6. Thread embroidery needle with six strands brown floss; embroider nostrils and mouth in straight stitch. Glue two black pom-poms to eye sockets; let dry overnight (illustration H). ◆

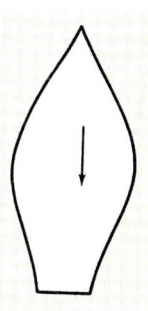

PATTERNS

See page 46 and 47 for pattern pieces and enlargement instructions.

MASTER PROJECT

Heirloom Angel Tree Topper

This elegant tree topper requires ordinary craft materials and practically no sewing.

BY MICHIO RYAN

The finished angel, which measures about 12" high, can also be used on a mantel or sideboard surrounded by fresh greens, or as a holiday centerpiece.

COLOR PHOTOGRAPHY:
Carl Tremblay

ILLUSTRATIONS:
Michael Gellatly

STYLING:
Ritch Holben

MATERIALS

- 3" porcelain doll's head and hand set
- 5/8 yard 45"-wide burgundy rayon velvet
- 1/4 yard 45"-wide cream crinkle moiré
- 1 yard 3/8"-wide purple grosgrain ribbon
- Burgundy sewing thread
- 17" x 17" posterboard
- 14" x 14" 1-ply chipboard
- Thin kraft paper (on roll)
- Three 12" chenille stems
- 24-gauge brass wire
- 2 cotton balls
- Masking tape
- Pale gold micro glitter
- 2-ounce container blue acrylic paint
- 2-ounce container dark gold metallic acrylic paint
- Fabric paint (any color) in applicator bottle (e.g., Tulip Colorpoint)
- Acrylic gesso
- Acrylic gel medium
- White craft glue (e.g., Sobo)
- Acrylic spray sealer, matte finish

Trims

- 6" square green-gold sheer fabric (cut on selvage)
- 7 1/2" square olive chiffon fabric
- 1/4 yard 1 1/2"-wide gold woven ribbon
- 2/3 yard 5/8"-wide brown wire-edged ribbon
- Five 1/2" pale pink ribbon roses
- 1/2 yard 4 mm plastic pearls
- 6 1/2"-long goldtone chain (e.g., cut from costume jewelry)
- Three 1" to 1 1/2" goldtone key and cross charms
- Three gold jump rings

You'll also need:
torso, wing, and coat patterns (see page 43); spray adhesive; X-Acto knife; acrylic cutting guide; self-healing cutting mat; large compass; protractor; soft (#1) pencil; metallic gold fine-tip marker; scissors; paper clamp; staple remover; stapler; chain nose pliers; wire cutters; hot-glue gun; emery board; sewing machine; pins; sewing shears; clean, large soft-bristled brush; 1" flat bristle brush; medium round brush; detail brush; spray mister; copier paper; newsprint; and tall, narrow-necked bottle.

THOUGH THIS BEAUTIFUL ANGEL tree topper resembles a doll, with its porcelain face and draped robes, the construction is actually much simpler. The angel's body consists of a chipboard torso, which is stapled to a cone formed from posterboard. The angel's clothing, fashioned from paper, fabric, and assorted trims, is simply hot-glued to the cone. Finishing details include wings cut from chipboard, a rose and pearl veil, and metal charms at the waistband.

I started with a ready-made porcelain doll's head and hand set, purchased for $4.99. I needed to anchor the ceramic head to a torso of some type, to which the other parts of the angel could be attached. To make the torso, I used a thin piece of chipboard folded over and stapled at one end; the folded end is then glued into the curved base of the head unit. To make the lower half of the angel's body, I formed a cone from posterboard, which I stapled to the torso. The open underside of the cone will fit on top of a Christmas tree, while the angel's clothing can be attached on the outside. The clothing includes a moiré lining, a paper dress, and a fabric tunic, all of which are bound in place by a finishing waistband.

To make this angel as realistic as possible, it needed wings. I couldn't find premade wings that fit the style of the tree topper, so I cut my own from cardboard, then used acrylic gesso and fabric paint to add dimension. Then, I painted the wings gold and covered them with glitter. To attach the wings to the angel, I designed them with a tab, which is tucked into the back of the waistband.

INSTRUCTIONS
Getting Started

1. *Cut chipboard pieces.* Photocopy torso, wing, and coat patterns (page 43); set coat pattern aside. Spray torso pattern with adhesive; affix pattern to 1-ply chipboard. Using X-Acto knife, cutting guide, and mat, cut along solid outline. To create smooth curve when torso is bent later on, score dash lines lightly. Set torso aside. Repeat process to cut wings, but do not score dash lines. Lift wing pattern from chipboard, reposition on new piece of chipboard, and cut separate blade for each wing. Lift off wing pattern and set aside.

2. *Cut fabric coat and dress pieces.* From burgundy velvet, cut one coat on fold, observing grain line. Open coat and lay flat to cut front opening at one end, as indicated on pattern; set cutout strip aside. From cream moiré, cut two 4"-square undersleeves, one 3"-square bodice, and one 7" x 10" skirt with crinkle grain running parallel to shorter edge.

3. *Cut paper gown pieces.* Cut 26" square of thin kraft paper. Mist both sides lightly until damp, gather softened paper into bundle, and twist gently to make "rope." Clamp ends together, and let dry overnight. Gently unfurl crimped rope, and lay flat until bone dry. Using acrylic grid ruler and pencil, draft one 10" x 24" skirt. Then draft two 5" x 8" arms with crinkle grain running parallel to shorter edge. Cut out pieces with scissors.

Making the Wings

Note: Insert wing tab into bottle to hold wings upright.

1. *Shape and seal wings.* Apply white craft glue to blades, position blades on front wings, and press to adhere; let dry 20 minutes. Lightly mist peaks and lower tips of wings on both sides. When chipboard is softened and pliable (1 to 2 minutes), carefully bend peaks forward and curve lower tips back (*see* illustration A, right). To set curves, brush heavy coat of acrylic gesso over entire wing surface; coat front and back of wings, but leave middle tab section plain; let dry 20 minutes. To soften and sculpt blade area, brush acrylic gel up against blade so it lodges against ridge. To round off top edge, scrape brush along edge to deposit bead of gel, then run brush lightly along bead to smooth it. When gel is dry (1 to 4 hours), sand and round off edges with emery board.

2. *Add feather details and glitter.* Lay wings face up on flat surface. Referring to pattern, sketch in feather details lightly with soft pencil. To give feathers dimension, go over all sketched lines with fabric paint applied directly through fine-tipped nozzle. Let dry 1 hour, or until paint forms firm skin. Paint front and back of wings with gold acrylic paint; let dry 20 minutes. Brush very thin coat white glue onto front and back of wings; do not coat middle tab section. Sprinkle pale gold micro glitter onto wings, catching excess on sheet of paper placed underneath (illustration B). Let dry 1 hour. Using clean, large soft-bristled brush, gently dust off loose glitter particles. Funnel excess glitter back into container. To prevent further shedding, spray wings with one or two light coats acrylic matte sealer.

3. *Prepare wings for joining to angel.* Rest wings face up. Carefully score two center lines, as indicated on pattern. Bend wings back slightly; final position can be adjusted after wings are attached to angel. Cut 3" length from reserved burgundy strip. Rest wings face down. Hot-glue strip to wing tab and center section; curl side edges under and fold excess at top onto wing front and glue down (illustration C). Set wings aside.

Making the Armature

1. *Join angel head to torso.* Bend torso into U shape, score lines on inside, and staple bottom straight edges together. Apply hot glue generously to top curved section of torso. Set angel head on torso.

2. *Join torso to cone base.* Using compass, draft 16" circle on posterboard. Using protractor and ruler, draft 110-degree segment of circle. Cut out segment with scissors. To make base, curl segment into cone, overlapping straight edges ½" at bottom and tapering toward tip. Mark outside edge of overlap with pencil. Hot-glue overlapped sections together, then reinforce seam with tape. Remove staples from torso. Press pointed end of cone flat, fit torso over it, and staple through all layers (illustration D).

3. *Add chenille arm piece to torso.* Using 24-gauge wire, bind three chenille stems together at one end. Braid stems together, then bind other end; braid will be 10" to 11" long. For arm padding, cut 8" x 9" rectangle from kraft paper. Make ¼" accordion folds parallel to 8" edge, then bundle crinkled paper around braided arm piece to soften folds; to hold in place, crimp at middle and secure with dab of hot glue. Center arm piece inside torso loop and hot-glue to upper shoulders. Hot-glue porcelain hand to each end (illustration E).

Adding the Clothes

1. *Make undersleeves.* Roll one 4"-square undersleeve wrong side out to form loose tube; run crinkle grain along length of tube. Slide tube onto forearm, gather and crimp end around forearm/braided arm join, and bind with wire; remainder of tube will flow forward, covering hands. To shape billowing undersleeves, draw tube back on itself, turning it right side out. Gather and crimp end over previous join and bind with wire. Repeat process to make second sleeve.

2. *Make bodice.* Lay cream bodice right side up, crinkle grain running vertically. Run bead of hot glue along lower edge. Quickly turn bodice face down and press glue edge against lower edge of porcelain bust; bodice will cover face. Place two cotton balls on torso (illustration F). Fold bodice down over

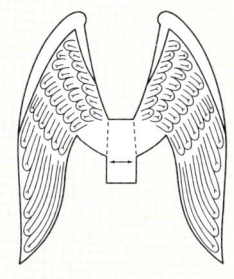

PATTERNS
See page 43 for pattern pieces and enlargement instructions.

DESIGNER'S TIP
Porcelain's inherent coolness causes hot glue to "freeze" quickly. To join porcelain pieces, apply hot glue to the nonporcelain component. To join the angel head, for example, apply the glue to the chipboard torso, not the porcelain head itself.

Making the Wings

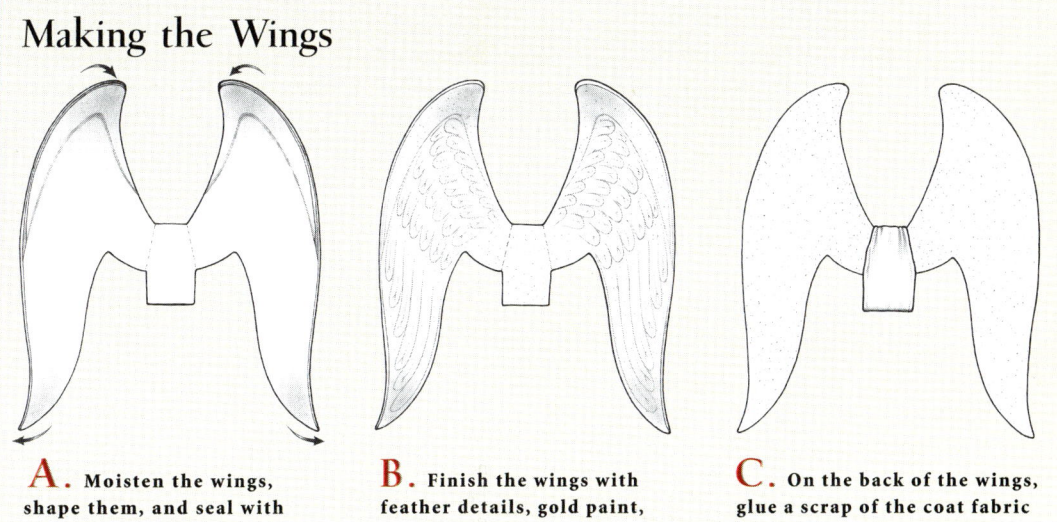

A. Moisten the wings, shape them, and seal with gesso.

B. Finish the wings with feather details, gold paint,

C. On the back of the wings, glue a scrap of the coat fabric to the tab section.

MASTER PROJECT

cotton balls and glue down side and bottom edges.

3. *Make underskirt.* Lay cream skirt face down on flat surface, with short edges at sides. Beginning at middle of top edge, shirr and crumple fabric with fingers. Set crumpled section against front lower edge of cone base, right side facing down, and secure with hot glue. Repeat process to glue fabric at each side (illustration G), swathing fabric around three-fourths of cone; leave back uncovered (it will be covered later). To cover cone, bring free edge up and gather and crimp around waist, forming full, loose folds. Bind at waist with wire (illustration H).

4. *Paint gown skirt and sleeves.* Lay 10" x 24" paper gown skirt and 5" x 8" arms flat. Fold up one long edge of each piece ½". Cut 24-gauge wire 2" longer than folded edge. Set wire into crease, then glue down fold with white craft glue, encasing wire inside. Let dry 30 minutes, then clip off wire ends. Lay pieces flat on newsprint, hemmed side face down. Using 1" brush, paint facing surface (right side) with blue acrylic paint; let dry 30 minutes. Using metallic gold fine-tip marker, draw cross-shaped stars interspersed with small dots in grid pattern across surface. Turn pieces over and paint reverse side dark metallic gold.

5. *Attach blue gown.* Gather blue skirt around torso waist, hemmed edge at bottom and overlapping edges at center front. If skirt is too long, trim waist edge with scissors. Bind skirt to waist with wire. Slip sleeves over arms and bind near bust/arm join; do not trim sleeves, as excess will be drawn up with ribbon garters. Secure all joins with hot glue. Part blue skirt in front to reveal cream skirt (illustration I).

6. *Make burgundy velvet coat.* Fold coat in half, right side in, and machine-stitch side seams from lower edge to dots on pattern; finger-press seams open. Hot-glue ⅜"-wide purple ribbon to raw edges, mitering corners as indicated on pattern. Place robe on angel so lapels are ¾" to 1" apart, exposing bodice (illustration J).

Assembling the Angel

1. *Add wings and girdle.* Bind waist with wire, cinching coat into soft folds. Insert wing tab under wires at center back, so feathered side of wings faces front; secure with hot glue (illustration K). Hot-glue one end of 6½" chain to front waist, other end to back waist, so chain arcs across side skirt. Join key and cross charms to chain with jump rings. For girdle, cut 7½" length of 1½"-wide dull gold ribbed ribbon and 7½" square of olive chiffon. Cinch chiffon to form loose rope, center rope on ribbon, and wrap both around waist; secure with hot glue at center back. Shape wire-edged hem of blue skirt into soft, billowing folds. Arrange coat over blue skirt and secure at several spots with hot glue (illustration L).

2. *Add armbands.* For each sleeve, cut 12" length of ⅝"-wide brown wire-edged ribbon. Tie ribbon snugly around sleeve above elbow, cinching concealed paper bundle; trim excess. Hot-glue strand of pearls to top of ribbon, trimming excess after coming full circle. Adjust paper sleeve to flare out over undersleeve, exposing gold lining (illustration L).

3. *Add veil.* Drape 6"-square of green-gold sheer fabric on head so selvage falls loosely across crown; hot-glue at center and at back; turn raw edges under, and tuck remainder between wings and coat back. Dot back of pink ribbon rose with hot glue and press onto front edge of veil; glue will bleed through veil and adhere to hair. Attach four more roses in same way, framing face. Cut 7" strand of pearls. Hot-glue ends to top center of crown to form circle; let remainder drape down back of veil (illustration L). ◆

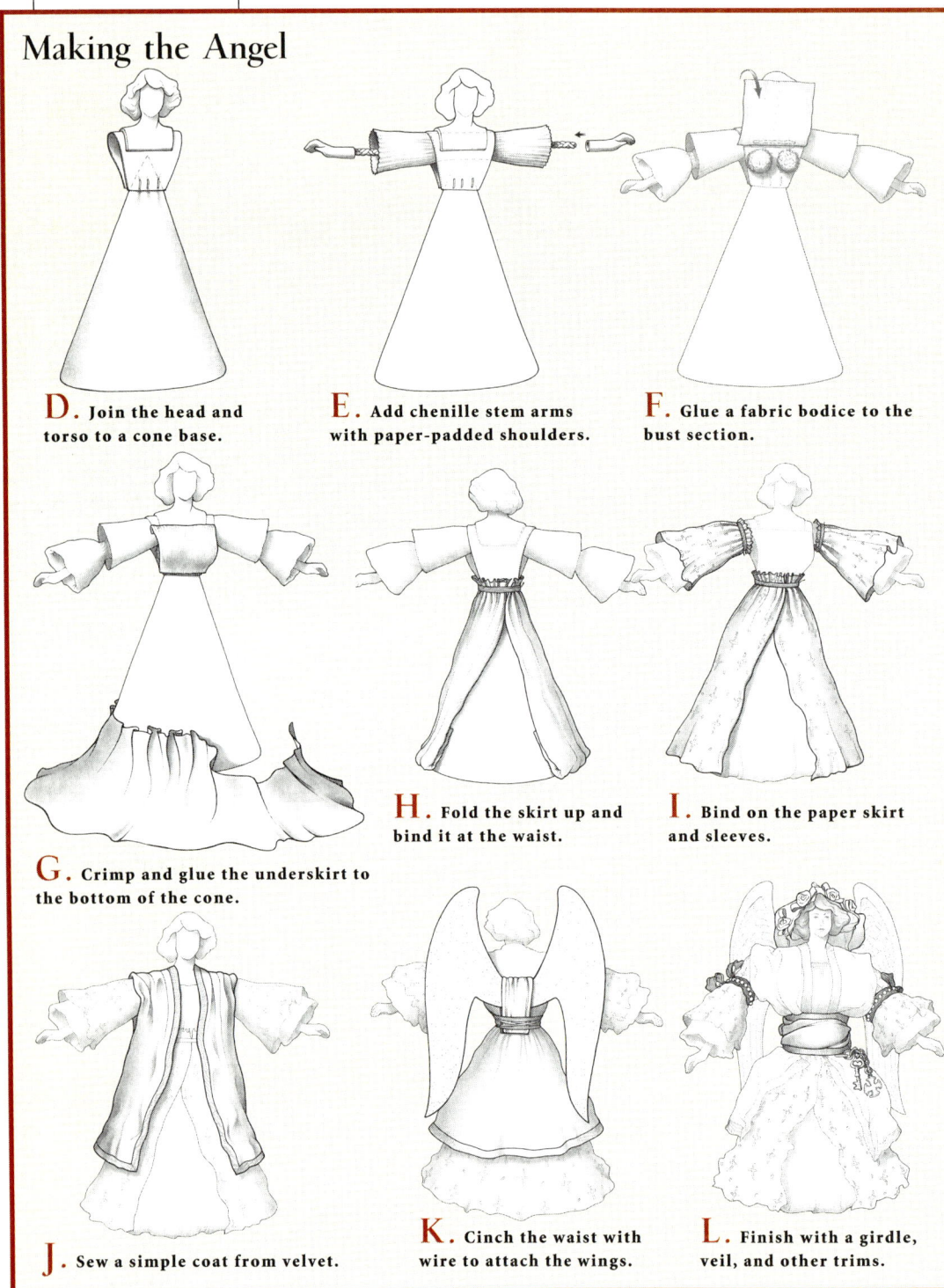

Making the Angel

D. Join the head and torso to a cone base.

E. Add chenille stem arms with paper-padded shoulders.

F. Glue a fabric bodice to the bust section.

G. Crimp and glue the underskirt to the bottom of the cone.

H. Fold the skirt up and bind it at the waist.

I. Bind on the paper skirt and sleeves.

J. Sew a simple coat from velvet.

K. Cinch the waist with wire to attach the wings.

L. Finish with a girdle, veil, and other trims.

Frosted Glitter Martini Glasses

Create a smooth, durable effect by combining epoxy with microfine glitter.

BY MICHIO RYAN

COLOR PHOTOGRAPHY:
Carl Tremblay

ILLUSTRATION:
Nenad Jakesevic

STYLING:
Ritch Holben

B Y COMBINING MICROFINE GLITTER and epoxy glue, I found a way to produce a sparkling surface that looks like it has been heat-fused to the glass. Add some etched frosting, and you can transform ordinary glassware into festive holiday accents.

Several kinds of adhesives will stick to glass, but not all are suitable for this project. Epoxies undergo a chemical reaction resulting in a hard, durable bond. The bits of glitter are so small, however, that they don't interfere with this bond, and after the epoxy has cured it will not come off the glass. Furthermore, because epoxy levels out, the finished effect is smooth and level.

INSTRUCTIONS

1. *Define etching area.* Clean glasses using cotton ball and alcohol. Wrap ½"-wide tape around rim of each glass; apply ¼" tape over crinkled edge to smooth line. Mask stripe on stem 1" below bowl. For tight seal, press down edges with credit card.

2. *Make square masks.* Turn each glass upside down on clean newsprint. Working freehand, use X-Acto knife to score random-sized squares, ¼" to 1¼" across, on self-adhesive labels; score smaller square inside each larger square. Remove solid and "doughnut" squares from backing and adhere at random to outside bowl of glass (*see illustration A, below*). Press all edges with credit card.

3. *Etch glassware.* Put on rubber gloves and goggles. Following manufacturer's instructions, apply etching cream to outside bowl between rim and stem masking tape. Repeat for each glass. Let cream set 3 to 5 minutes, then wash off cream and remove tape to reveal etched design (illustration B). Wash glasses in soapy water and dry thoroughly.

4. *Apply masks for glitter borders.* For each etched doughnut, cut self-adhesive square slightly smaller and press into place on each glass. Lay strip of ¼"-wide tape parallel to square edge, allowing ¹⁄₁₆" to ⅛" gap; fold end of strip back on itself to make tab. Place additional strips along remaining three sides to complete square border mask. Repeat process for each cutout square (illustration C).

5. *Apply ring masks to stem.* Wrap ¼" tape once around base of each glassware stem; fold end of strip back on itself to make tab. Wrap parallel strip ³⁄₁₆" away for glitter ring. Mask two more rings near bowl of glass in same way.

6. *Apply glitter to border and ring areas.* Put on canvas gloves. Following manufacturer's instructions and using toothpick, mix small amount epoxy on plastic lid. Stir in equal amount glitter. Using clean toothpick, spread thin layer glitter-epoxy mixture onto unmasked areas bordering squares and stem rings. Work quickly, mixing more glue and glitter as needed. As each glitter border is completed, remove tape. Set aside 1 hour to cure (illustration D). ◆

Although epoxy forms a very durable bond, these glasses should be washed by hand to protect the decorative effect.

MATERIALS

- Martini glasses
- Silver microfine glitter
- Armour Etch cream
- 5-minute epoxy

You'll also need: 2" x 4" self-adhesive labels; ¼"-wide quilter's masking tape; ½"-wide masking tape; rubber gloves; splash goggles; canvas gloves; rubbing alcohol; newsprint; cotton balls; X-Acto knife; flat toothpicks; disposable plastic lids; foam brush; and credit card.

DECORATING THE GLASSES

A. Mask a design using self-adhesive squares.

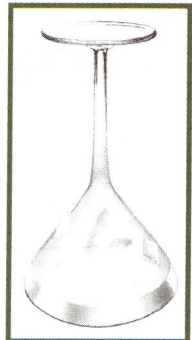

B. Etch the glass to make the design permanent.

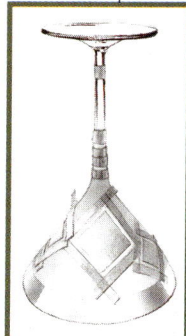

C. Mask the edges of each larger square...

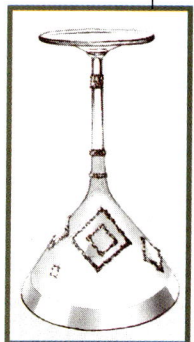

D. ...to add an epoxy and glitter border.

FRAMES

How to Create the Look of Brushed Steel
Gently scrub aluminum tooling foil with steel wool for a subtle, decorative pattern.

BY NANCY OVERTON

This aluminum frame features a swirling brushed effect. For variation, like wavy or straight lines, change the direction and movement of the steel wool.

MATERIALS
- Flat unfinished hardwood frame*
- 36-gauge 12"-wide aluminum tooling foil (on roll)
- Turquoise velveteen fabric remnant
- 1-ply chipboard
- Heavy-duty spray adhesive (e.g., Krylon)

*outer dimensions no larger than 8" x 10"

You'll also need: hardwood burnishing tool; #0000 (very fine) steel wool; utility knife; self-healing cutting mat; metal-edged ruler; grid ruler; scissors; pencil; newsprint; and masking tape.

COLOR PHOTOGRAPHY:
Carl Tremblay

ILLUSTRATION:
Mary Newell DePalma

STYLING:
Ritch Holben

YOU CAN MAKE THIS BRUSHED aluminum frame in about 2 hours. The trick: aluminum tooling foil, which is easy to cut and bend around a plain wood frame. Once you've attached the foil to the frame, you can create the effect of brushed steel using very fine steel wool.

Tooling foil is available for about $5 per 10-foot roll at art supply stores such as Pearl Paint. The foil comes in a roll measuring 12" wide, so you can use it to cover frames measuring up to 8" x 10". The foil is very soft, making it easy to work with, but it is also easily scratched or dented. For this reason, work on a clean, flat surface free of blemishes, and treat the foil carefully.

The foil should be attached to the frame using a heavy-duty workshop-quality spray adhesive such as Krylon. I tested Elmer's glue on my first frame, but the foil did not form a firm bond.

Nancy Overton, a craft designer and author, lives in Oakland, California.

INSTRUCTIONS
Note: Tooling foil becomes marred and dents easily. To prevent blemishes, use clean hands and work upon a clean, smooth, and dry surface.

1. *Cut foil rectangle.* Cover work surface with newsprint and tape down edges. Unroll about 2 feet of foil. Using grid ruler and pencil, mark rectangle 2" larger than frame all around. Cut out rectangle with scissors.

2. *Cut opening in foil rectangle.* Remove back, glass, and cardboard liner from frame and set aside. Center frame face down on foil rectangle. Holding pencil perpendicular to surface, lightly trace edge of frame opening. (Note that traced opening will be slightly smaller than actual opening because of pencil position.) Using metal-edged ruler, utility knife, and cutting mat, cut neatly and precisely along marked lines. Discard cutout section.

3. *Adhere foil strip to opening.* Measure depth and perimeter of frame opening, then add ⅛" to perimeter measurement. Mark strip of foil to these dimensions and cut out using metal-edged ruler, utility knife, and cutting mat. Following manufacturer's directions, apply spray adhesive to one side of foil strip. Stand frame on edge, perpendicular to work surface. Set end of strip even with inside corner, adhesive side down, and slowly press onto inside opening, even with wood edges (see illustration A, next page). When you reach adjacent corner, use burnishing tool to bend foil so it hugs corner angle. Turn frame 90 degrees and repeat process to adhere strip to adjacent edge. Continue all around. When you reach starting point, crimp foil to match angle, cut on crimp line with scissors, and press into place. Burnish entire strip to ensure good adhesion.

4. *Adhere foil to frame front.* Apply spray adhesive to one side of foil cut in step 2. Lay foil adhesive side up. Hold frame face down over foil, make sure openings are centered, and press gently into place. Turn frame foil side up. Press foil onto frame, from opening out to edges, all around. Using burnishing tool, bend foil overlap toward interior (illustration B). Burnish entire surface to flatten foil and ensure good adhesion.

5. *Adhere foil to frame edges and back.* Using fingers, bend foil around one edge of frame; burnish this edge from front to back. Repeat process on opposite edge. Trim excess foil even with corners (illustration C). Repeat process to adhere and burnish remaining two edges; cut edges should meet or overlap slightly at corners. Bend remaining foil onto back of frame; trim corners diagonally to miter them (illustration D). Examine frame and burnish entire surface again to make sure all areas are flat and secure. Proceed gently at corners and where edges meet, because they are easily bent.

6. *Cut chipboard mat.* Measure length and width of opening at back of frame. Draft rectangle to these dimensions on chipboard. For mat interior opening, draft lines 1" in from each edge all around; note that about ⅜" of 1" mat width will be hidden by rabbet overlap. Using utility knife, ruler, and mat, cut chipboard mat along marked lines.

7. *Laminate velveteen to chipboard mat.* From velveteen, cut rectangle ½" to 1" larger than mat all around. Apply spray adhesive to wrong side; also spray one side of chipboard mat. Lay mat adhesive side down on velveteen and press to adhere. Turn over and press from right side. Turn face down. Using scissors, cut an X in interior section. Fold each triangular section onto back of mat, press to adhere, and trim off excess all around (illustration E).

8. *Brush surface.* Using a light touch, rub steel wool in circular motion across surface of frame, including inner and outer edges. Insert glass, mat, picture, cardboard liner, and frame backing into frame from wrong side (illustration F). ◆

DESIGNER'S TIP

Use a hardwood frame for this project, rather than pine. Pine is soft, meaning it will scratch or dent more easily, which in turn can scratch or dent the tooling foil.

Making the Brushed Steel Frame

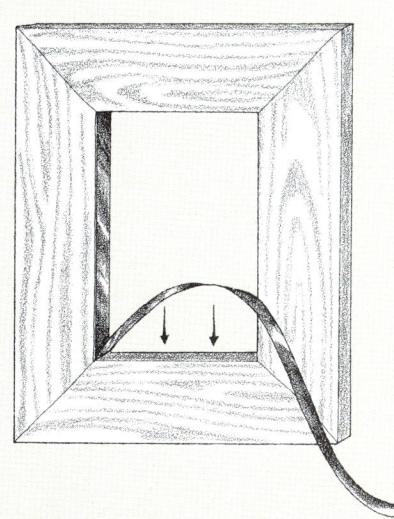

A. Adhere a foil strip to the inside edge of the frame.

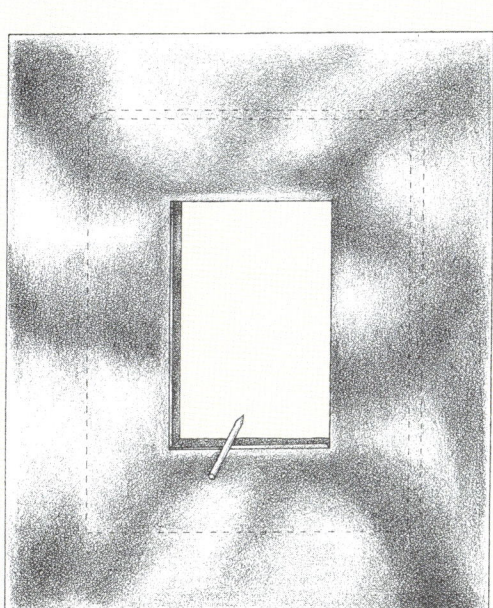

B. Adhere foil to the frame front and burnish down.

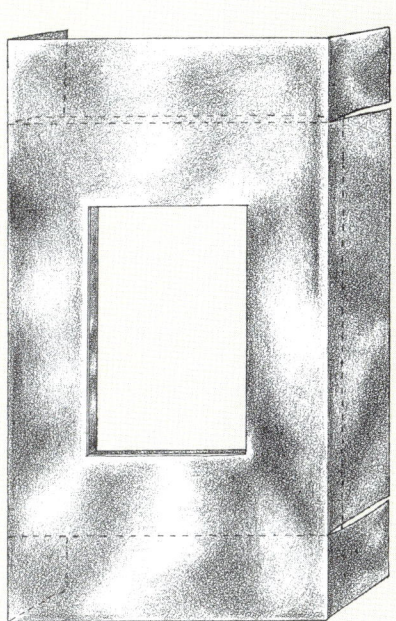

C. Bend the foil onto the frame sides, one pair at a time.

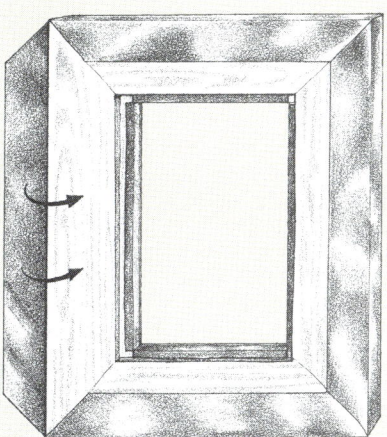

D. Bend and adhere the excess foil to the frame back.

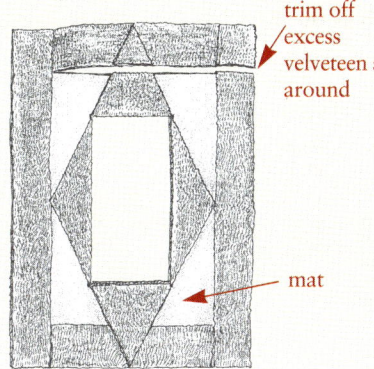

E. Cut a chipboard mat and cover it with velveteen.

F. For a brushed steel look, rub the foil with steel wool.

CANDLES

The Fastest Way to Decorate Candles with Sheet Wax

Use your blow-dryer to adhere designs made from honeycomb wax to a pillar candle.

BY NANCY OVERTON

MATERIALS

- Wax sheets (assorted colors)
- 3"-diameter pillar-style candles

You'll also need: small star-shaped cookie cutter; can of soup (unopened); blow-dryer; craft or X-Acto knife; newsprint; self-healing cutting mat; acrylic grid ruler; tape measure; graph paper; pencil; and scissors.

Using this one technique, you can create an endless number of design variations on your pillar candles.

COLOR PHOTOGRAPHY: **Carl Tremblay**
ILLUSTRATION: **Nenad Jakesevic**
STYLING: **Ritch Holben**

IF YOU'RE LOOKING FOR A SIMPLE way to dress up a solid-colored candle, this cut-and-press technique is for you. Each of the three candles shown above was decorated with designs cut from sheets of honeycomb wax. The cut wax images are heated slightly with a blow-dryer, then pressed in place.

Each candle shown varies in its level of difficulty. To create the beginner's version, the star candle shown at left, I cut out shapes using a cookie cutter. For the intermediate candle, which is decorated with diamonds, I measured and cut squares of wax using an X-Acto knife and grid ruler. For the plaid candle, which I consider to be the most time-consuming of the three, I cut the horizontal stripes from wax, then filled in the vertical stripes of the pattern with smaller pieces of wax.

Sheet wax comes in both smooth and honeycomb sheets, each about 1/8-inch thick. The wax cuts easily with a craft or X-Acto knife and ruler for geometric designs, scissors for freehand designs, or biscuit and/or cookie cutters for prefabricated designs. When working with the sheets of wax, keep your surface clean, as the soft wax picks up dirt and blemishes easily.

Nancy Overton, a craft designer and author, lives in Oakland, California.

INSTRUCTIONS
Making the Star Candle

1. *Cut stars.* Lay wax on sheet of newsprint. Set cookie cutter on wax, set can on top, and press down firmly to cut wax clear through (*see* illustration A, below). Gently poke wax star from cutter with fingertip or eraser end of pencil. Repeat process to cut additional stars.

2. *Affix stars to candle.* Using blow-dryer at low setting and holding dryer about 12" away from stars, heat stars 10 to 15 seconds or just enough to make them pliable. Heat candle in same way, rotating it to warm all sides. Briefly reheat stars. Position one star against

MAKING THE STAR CANDLE

A. To cut through the stiff wax, press on the cookie cutter with a soup can.

MAKING THE DIAMOND CANDLE

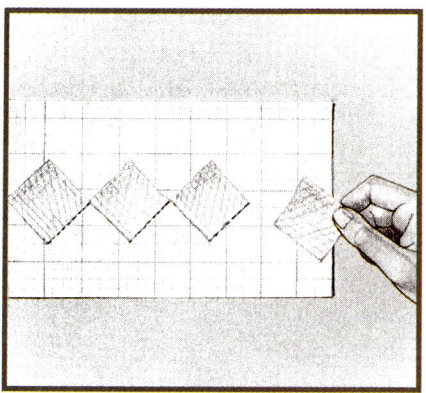

B. Arrange four wax diamonds across the template to check the fit.

C. Complete the diamond grid, trimming off the upper and lower edges.

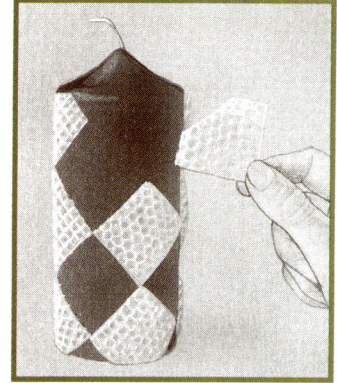

D. Heat the diamonds, then adhere them to the candle.

candle and press gently until adhered. Repeat process for remaining stars.

Making the Diamond Candle

1. *Determine wax area.* Measure candle height and circumference. Draft and cut out rectangle this size on graph paper for template.

2. *Cut diamonds.* Divide candle circumference by 4. On new sheet of graph paper, draft one line this length. Then draft second, perpendicular line, measuring the same length, bisecting the first line (makes a plus sign). Connect ends of lines to make a diamond. Lay wax on sheet of newsprint. Using grid ruler, X-Acto knife, and template drawn above, score four squares this size on wax; complete cuts with scissors. To test-fit squares, arrange them on point in horizontal row across middle of graph paper template from step 1 (illustration B). If points at each end extend beyond side edges of template, shave two adjacent sides to make diamond slightly smaller. Repeat to fill template. Trim overhang even with edges of template (illustration C).

3. *Affix diamonds to candle.* Using blow-dryer at low setting, heat diamonds 10 to 15 seconds, as with stars. Heat candle in same way, rotating as above. Position diamonds from one horizontal row on candle one at a time and press gently to adhere. Complete one horizontal row around circumference of candle. Continue until all pieces are adhered (illustration D).

Making the Plaid Candle

Note: Use a medium-tone 3"-diameter candle and light and dark honeycomb waxes for this design.

1. *Determine wax area.* Same as Diamond Candle, step 1.

2. *Cut horizontal stripes.* Lay dark wax on sheet of newsprint. Using grid ruler and X-Acto knife, score 1"-wide strip equal to candle circumference; complete cut with scissors. Repeat process to cut one strip for every 3" of candle height. Lay strip(s) horizontally on graph paper template equidistant from each other and from top and bottom edges. From light honeycomb wax, cut same number of 3/8"-wide strips, plus one extra. Lay light strip 1/4" above each dark strip; lay extra 1/4" above lower edge.

3. *Affix horizontal strips to candle.* Heat stripes and candle with blow-dryer as in Diamond Candle, step 3. Lay candle on side at middle of template. Lift wax stripes around candle, one at a time, from each side. As each stripe comes full circle, trim and butt ends (see illustration F).

4. *Cut and affix vertical stripes.* Score and cut 1"-wide strip (any length) from light honeycomb wax. From this strip, cut 1/4" segment to fit space from base of candle to lowest horizontal stripe. Heat briefly and press into place. Repeat process to adhere a total of four segments equally spaced around candle base. Next, cut four segments to fit space between lowest horizontal stripe and stripe above it; heat each segment, align with segment placed previously, and press into place. Continue filling gaps between horizontal stripes to build four vertical stripes from bottom up. To finish plaid, score and cut 3/8"-wide dark honeycomb strip. Starting at base of candle, cut segments to fit gaps and adhere them 3/8" to right of light vertical stripes (illustration G). ◆

MAKING THE PLAID CANDLE

E. Position the wide and narrow wax strips horizontally on the template.

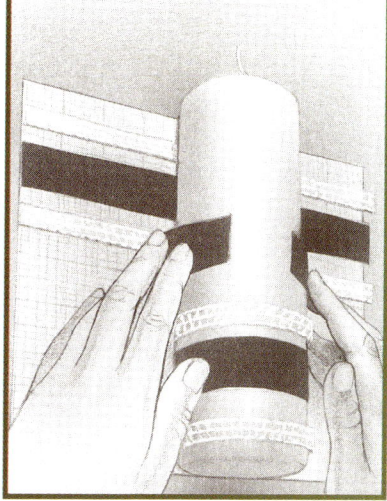

F. Lift each stripe and press it in place.

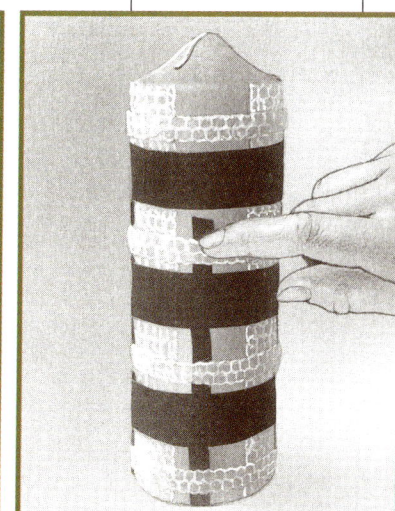

G. Add the vertical segments of the plaid design one by one.

ORNAMENTS

Elegant Ribbon Tassel
Substitute wood findings for a knotted top and rolled knitting tape for fringe.

BY DAWN ANDERSON

MATERIALS
- 9 5/8 yards 1/4"-wide variegated silk knitting tape
- 1 yard silk embroidery ribbon to match knitting tape
- Thread to match knitting tape
- 1 1/4" wood candlecup
- 5/8" wood candlecup
- 3/4"-diameter wooden disk
- 2-ounce acrylic paints in the following colors: buttermilk, crimson, light green, and black
- 1-ounce container gold acrylic enamel paint
- Clear acrylic spray sealer with gloss finish
- Wood glue

You'll also need:
3/4" flat brush; 1/8" and 1/4" flat shader brushes; small round brush; small, stiff brush; fine-line paint syringe; watercolor palette or disposable plastic lid; 220-grit sandpaper; 600-grit wet and dry sandpaper; paper towels; painter's tape; sewing machine; iron and ironing board; hand-sewing needle; thin-gauge wire; scissors; pencil; spray mister; ruler; and florist foam brick.

COLOR PHOTOGRAPHY:
Carl Tremblay

ILLUSTRATION:
Mary Newell DePalma

STYLING:
Ritch Holben

For variation on this design, substitute store-bought fringe for knitting tape.

TO MAKE THE HEAD OF THE TASsel, I glued together two candlecups with a small wooden disk in between. To make the ribbon "tassel strings," I created a fringe using silk knitting tape, then rolled the fringe into a tassel shape. Last, I glued the rolled fringe into the candlecup.

Dawn Anderson is a writer and designer living in Redmond, Washington.

INSTRUCTIONS
Making the Tassel Head

1. *Glue wood pieces.* Apply wood glue to open end of smaller candlecup and one side of disk. Press together and let set. Repeat to glue larger candlecup to disk (*see* illustration A, right). Let dry 1 hour. Sand with 220-grit sandpaper. Wipe dust with lightly misted paper towel.

2. *Paint base coat.* Using 3/4" flat brush, apply three coats buttermilk to wood surfaces; let dry 20 minutes after each coat and sand lightly with 600-grit sandpaper after third and fourth coats.

3. *Paint stripes and details.* Use the color photograph, above, as a reference for the painting steps. Use 1/4" and 1/8" flat shader and small, round brushes for larger areas; use syringe for stripes and dots. Let dry 1 hour and apply sealer following manufacturer's instructions.

Attaching the Ribbon Tassel

1. *Sew ribbon fringe.* Lower sewing machine needle to down position, measure 2 7/8" to right of needle, and lay strip of painter's tape on machine bed as guide. Measure and cut fifty 6 1/2" lengths of knitting tape. Set remaining piece (about 20" long) on machine bed to serve as base ribbon, and lower needle into one end. Fold one cut ribbon length in half on machine bed with fold on tape guide and loose ends crossing base ribbon in front of needle. Machine-stitch through all layers. Fold new cut ribbon, place adjacent to first ribbon, and continue stitching. Repeat process to sew all cut ribbons to base ribbon (illustration B).

2. *Roll fringe.* Using warm iron, press ribbon fringe, stopping 1/4" from folds. Measure 3" section of base ribbon. Roll 3" section snugly, with base ribbon on outside, and hand-tack. Continue rolling and tacking 3" segments. As you near end, trim excess ribbon 1" beyond fringe, wrap securely, and hand-tack.

3. *Make tassel cord.* Cut two 18" lengths silk embroidery ribbon, then cut twelve 18" lengths matching sewing thread. Hold all lengths of ribbon and thread together and knot one end. Hold knotted end steady and begin twisting other end. As soon as cord begins to kink and twist on itself, fold cord in half, hold ends together, and allow cords to spiral together. Tie knot 6" from folded end; trim excess close to knot.

4. *Assemble tassel.* Cut 8" length of wire, fold in half, and loop through unknotted end of tassel cord. Using wire, draw cord through small opening at top of tassel head until knot lodges inside, then remove wire. Apply wood glue inside tassel head and around top of ribbon tassel. Insert tassel into head (illustration C). If necessary, push stray ribbon ends up into tassel head using needle. Let glue dry overnight. ◆

Making the Tassel

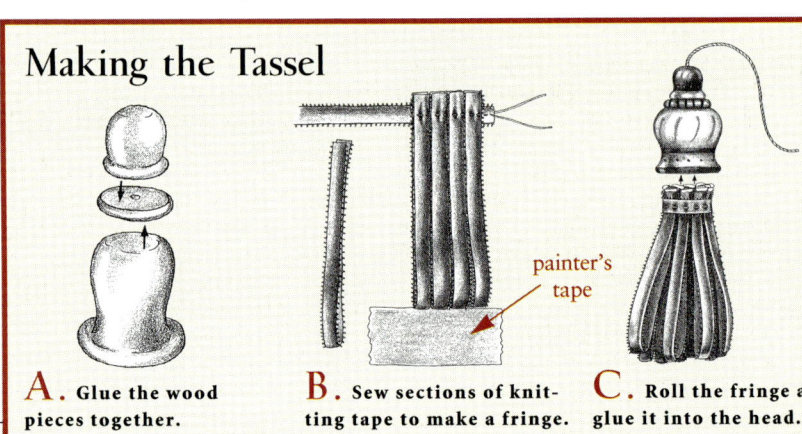

A. Glue the wood pieces together.

B. Sew sections of knitting tape to make a fringe.

C. Roll the fringe and glue it into the head.

DECORATIVE FOOD

Meringue Mushrooms

These delicate confections, piped from meringue, make a unique edible gift.

BY SUSAN LOGOZZO

THOUGH THESE REALISTIC MERingue mushrooms may look complicated, the hardest part about making them is getting the correct grip on a pastry bag.

To get started, you'll need to mix up a batch of meringue, which is made from egg whites, cream of tartar, and sugar.

You will pipe the mushrooms out of a large pastry bag. The mushrooms are made in two pieces: stems and caps. Pipe the stems first, as the meringue is firmer early on, and the stems need more stability to stand up straight. Don't make the stems too high or they will tip over; aim for about 1½" high. If they vary slightly in size and shape, they will look more realistic.

Bake the stems and caps in a 200-degree oven for 30 to 40 minutes, then leave them to dry in that same oven (with the heat turned off) overnight. Once dry, they can be assembled. This is done by carving a small hole on the cap underside, coating the cap with melted chocolate, and inserting the stem into the hole. As the chocolate hardens it will hold the stem in place.

Susan Logozzo is a food designer and writer living in Charlestown, Massachusetts.

Package these 2" mushrooms in a box lined with organdy.

MATERIALS

- 4 large fresh and cold egg whites (½ cup)
- ½ teaspoon cream of tartar
- 1 cup sugar
- 4 ounces semisweet chocolate chips

You'll also need: 2 large pastry bags or 1 large bag with coupler; ¼"- and ½"-diameter round pastry tips; 2 large baking sheets; electric mixer; very clean glass or stainless steel mixing bowl; measuring cup; measuring spoons; double boiler; spatula; butter knife; paring knife; plastic or tin container with cover; waxed paper; flour; and shortening.

DESIGNER'S TIP

If you want tan-colored mushrooms (I call them East Coast mushrooms), set the oven for 250 degrees and leave the stems and caps to bake for 45 to 50 minutes to take on some color. Then turn off the oven and leave them to dry overnight.

COLOR PHOTOGRAPHY:
Carl Tremblay

ILLUSTRATION:
Nenad Jakesevic

STYLING:
Ritch Holben

INSTRUCTIONS

Note: For the best results, bake the meringue on a clear, dry day.

1. Mix meringue. Lightly grease and flour baking sheets; set aside. Place egg whites in mixing bowl. Begin beating at low speed. As whites begin to foam (2 to 3 minutes), gradually increase speed and add cream of tartar. Continue beating until whites form soft peaks. Beat in sugar 1 tablespoon at a time, increase speed to high, then beat additional 5 to 8 minutes or until mixture is thick, firm, and has dull satin sheen.

2. Pipe mushroom stems. Preheat oven to 200 degrees. Fit pastry bag with ¼" tip. Transfer one-third meringue to bag, then fold down or twist open end closed. Hold bag perpendicular to surface, with tip about ¾" above baking sheet, and squeeze gently. When meringue measures about ¾" across, lift bag straight up to form cone shape 1½" high (*see* illustration A, below). Repeat process to pipe twenty-four stems total; allow ½" spacing between stems. Place baking sheet in oven.

3. Pipe mushroom caps. Fit same or new pastry bag with ½" tip; transfer remaining meringue to bag. Hold bag perpendicular to surface, with tip ¼" to ½" above baking sheet. Squeeze gently and raise bag slightly to form round, puffy "pillow" about ⅝" high and 1" to 1½" in diameter (illustration B). Repeat process to pipe twenty-four caps total; allow ½" spacing between caps. Smooth pointed peaks with butter knife in circular motion. Place baking sheet in oven with stems. Bake 30 to 40 minutes, or until firm. Turn oven off, leave both trays in oven with door closed, and let dry at least 2 hours but preferably overnight.

4. Assemble caps and stems. Melt chocolate chips in double boiler, stirring with spatula until smooth. Remove from heat. Using tip of paring knife, sculpt ¼"-deep hole in flat side of cap. Using butter knife, spread thin layer melted chocolate across flat side of cap. Gently press pointed end of one stem into hole (illustration C) and stand mushroom upright. Repeat to assemble remaining stems and caps. Let chocolate harden 1 hour.

5. Store mushrooms. To keep mushrooms fresh for several days, layer them between sheets of waxed paper in plastic or tin container, and cover tightly. For longer periods, store in tightly covered plastic container in freezer. ◆

MAKING THE MUSHROOMS

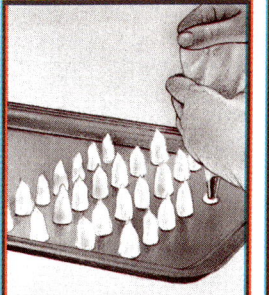

A. Pipe the meringue into stem shapes...

B. ...then pipe the mushroom caps.

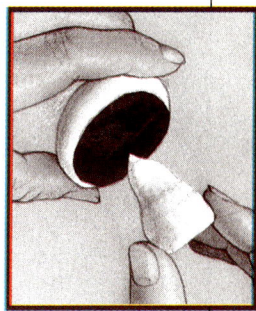

C. Join the cap and stem.

LOW-SEW

Luxurious Zip Cases from Fabric Scraps

Use a no-pattern technique to make a zippered bag: measure and cut the pieces to size using a cutting mat and a rotary cutter.

🌺 BY FRANCOISE HARDY

This no-pattern purse construction can be adjusted to make use of any size fabric scrap. Purchase a zipper to match the length of the new purse opening.

COLOR PHOTOGRAPHY:
Carl Tremblay

ILLUSTRATION:
Mary Newell DePalma

STYLING:
Ritch Holben

THESE ZIPPERED PURSES MAY look complicated, but are actually very simple to make. You won't need a pattern for either purse: The rectangular pieces can be measured and cut to size using a gridded cutting mat and a rotary cutter.

For a playful design I made the purses using a brightly colored suede, sateen coat lining, and a plastic zipper. You can change the materials or colors, however, to match an existing purse, to suit the time of year, or with a particular person in mind. Consider substituting such fabrics as Ultrasuede, lightweight vinyl, velveteen, wide-ribbed corduroy, or "fantasy" fabrics such as fake fur.

The zipper tabs on these purses work fine by themselves, but for added charm I attached a tiny bell to each zipper pull. You can substitute any attachable object that can stand up to wear and tear of pulling a zipper.

Francoise Hardy is a Boston-based artisan and craftsperson.

INSTRUCTIONS
Making the Large Purse

1. *Cut purse lining.* Use rotary cutter and cutting mat to cut 8" x 12" lining from quilted satin (or alternative fabric).

2. *Sew zipper to lining.* Lay lining right side up on flat surface. Lay zipper face up along short edge, with pull stop ¼" in from long edge. Using zipper foot, stitch 3⁄16" from edge (*see* illustration A, next page). Match free zipper tape to opposite edge of lining and stitch down in same way (illustration B).

3. *Sew zipper to suede.* Using rotary cutter and cutting mat, cut one 8½" x 12" rectangle from suede (or alternative fabric). Lay suede right side up on flat surface. Place zipper right side down along short edge. Using size 12 needle and thread to match suede, stitch through all layers 1⁄16" in from first stitching; begin and end stitching even with lining edge (illustration C). Repeat process to stitch zipper to opposite suede edge (illustration D).

4. *Sew purse sides.* Open zipper halfway. Lay piece flat, wrong side out,

MATERIALS
Large Purse
Finished size 6" x 8"

■ Fabric, at least 10" x 12"
■ Quilted satin lining fabric, at least 14" square
■ 9" large-toothed zipper
■ Thread to match fabric and satin
■ ¾"-diameter bell

Small Purse
Finished size 4" x 5"

■ Fabric, at least 7" x 10"
■ Satin lining fabric, at least 10" square
■ 8" x 10" batting
■ 7" large-toothed zipper
■ Thread to match fabric and satin
■ ½"-diameter bell

You'll also need:
sewing machine; size 8 machine needle; size 12 machine needle; rotary cutter; self-healing cutting mat; hand-sewing needle; and pins.

and pin suede and lining side edges together. Using appropriate needle and thread, machine-stitch side edges; run stitching on all sides as close to zipper tape as possible; leave 3" opening along one lining edge for turning (illustration E). Remove pins. Turn purse right side out and slip-stitch opening closed (illustration F). Slip lining down inside purse. Attach bell to zipper pull.

Making the Small Purse

For this smaller, unquilted version, cut one 5½" x 8½" rectangle from suede and one 5" x 8" rectangle each from satin lining fabric and batting. Pin the satin to the batting at the corners. Proceed as for the Large Purse, steps 2 through 4, to sew the pieces together. The excess zipper will lodge between the suede and the lining. ◆

> **DESIGNER'S TIP**
> This zippered bag design can be used in a larger version to make a soft portfolio. Substitute leather for the purse body and use a heavy brass zipper, or use brightly-colored suede and a large-toothed zipper. You'll also need a leather needle for your sewing machine and heavy-duty thread.

Making the Zipper Purses

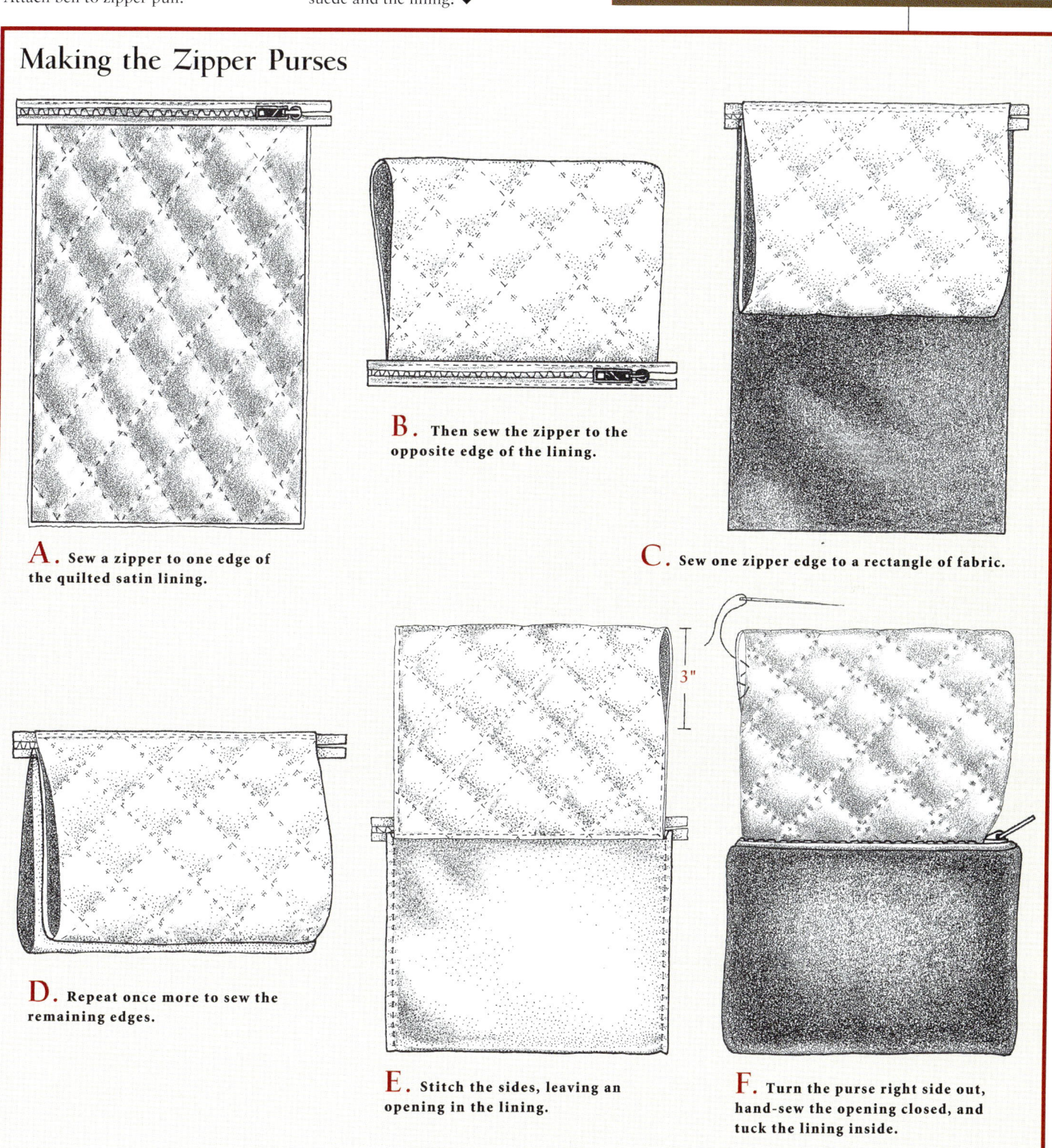

A. Sew a zipper to one edge of the quilted satin lining.

B. Then sew the zipper to the opposite edge of the lining.

C. Sew one zipper edge to a rectangle of fabric.

D. Repeat once more to sew the remaining edges.

E. Stitch the sides, leaving an opening in the lining.

F. Turn the purse right side out, hand-sew the opening closed, and tuck the lining inside.

BEADING

Beaded Votive Candle Holder

Build a simple framework from three thin brass rods, then wrap it with strings of glass seed beads.

BY DAWN ANDERSON

Once the beads have been strung, the construction of the votive goes fairly quickly. To build the sides, wrap the beads from spoke to spoke.

MATERIALS

- Standard glass votive candle (1⅞"-diameter x 2⅝" tall)
- Twenty 20" strands glass seed beads
- Two 36"-long x .045" brass rods
- 28-gauge brass spool wire
- 24-gauge brass spool wire

You'll also need: round-nose pliers; flat-nose pliers; chain-nose pliers; wire cutters; flexible tape measure; permanent marking pen; flannel cloth or corrugated cardboard, top ply removed; masking tape; and narrow-necked bottle.

COLOR PHOTOGRAPHY:
Carl Tremblay

ILLUSTRATION:
Michael Gellatly

STYLING:
Ritch Holben

THIS COLORFUL BEADED CANDLE holder, which holds a standard glass votive candle, makes a wonderful Christmas decoration virtually anywhere in the house. To make the holder, I bent three thin brass rods, then shaped the ends of the rods into spirals. These brass rods serve as the underlying structure to which you attach strings of glass seed beads.

To facilitate beading, be sure to buy seed beads that are prestrung on thread. You will need to transfer the beads to thin-gauge brass spool wire, an easy but somewhat time-consuming process. To transfer the beads without difficulty, lay each strand flat on a piece of flannel cloth to prevent the beads from rolling, or use a corrugated cardboard holder (*see* Quick Tips, Fall 1997, page 5).

Dawn Anderson is a writer and designer living in Redmond, Washington.

INSTRUCTIONS

1. *Bend brass rods.* Using wire cutters, cut 16" length of brass rod. Mark midpoint with permanent pen. Measure from midpoint 1" in each direction and make two additional marks. Using flat-nose pliers, grip rod at outer point and bend up at right angle; make bend at second outer point in same manner. Cut and bend two additional rods to match.

2. *Shape brass rods.* Grip rod between thumb and forefinger about 1" beyond bend. Using short, deliberate motions, bend rod into gentle outward curve. Using round-nose pliers, coil end into ½"-diameter loop. Grip loop with flat-nose pliers and continue curling to form spiral; for even spacing, move pliers along rod in ¼" increments, bending as you go. Repeat process to shape other side. Shape two remaining rods to match.

3. *Join brass rods.* Rest votive upside down on bottle neck. Lay one rod across votive base so coiled ends hang down sides. Using flat-nose pliers, bend two remaining rods at midpoint to make 60-degree angle. Set angled rods alongside first rod, midpoints touching, to form six-spoked design (*see* illustration A, next page). Bind rods together at midpoints with 24-gauge wire to form hub (illustration B). Measure and mark votive circumference into six equal segments using permanent marker and making tiny tick marks. Align each spoke with mark and tape to votive.

4. *Transfer beads to wire.* Set aside one 20" strand of seed beads. Lay remaining nineteen strands on flannel cloth or in corrugated cardboard channels. Carefully transfer beads from one strand to 28-gauge spool wire a few inches at a time. Continue until you have transferred five strands (100"). Clip wire to measure 30" total; coil each end to prevent beads from sliding off. Repeat process for remaining 18 strands.

5. *Bead base of votive.* Cut 26" length of 28-gauge wire. Twist end three times around a brass spoke at hub. String two beads from reserved strand on wire, slide beads snug against spoke, and twist wire once tightly around adjacent spoke. Repeat process to complete circle of beads around hub. For next round, string three beads between spokes. Make beads as snug as possible and allow a bead to sit on top of each spoke to conceal it (illustration C). Continue in this manner, increasing bead count between spokes on each round, until all reserved beads are used.

To end off, spiral wire along spoke between beads for several rounds, pulling snug with chain-nose pliers after each wrap; clip excess and crimp end against inside spoke.

6. *Complete beading.* Join in one strand of prestrung beads, twisting wire end tightly around spoke. Carry strand across frame to next spoke, separate beads to expose wire, then wrap wire once around spoke, pulling snug with chain-nose pliers. Strive for even tension; strand spanning spokes should be snug, but not tight, and should not sag. Join additional strands by twisting around spoke as before. After beading base and about ¼" of sides, remove tape and glass votive and stand project upright (illustration D). Continue beading up sides until you reach coiled spirals. ◆

HISTORICAL TIDBIT

Glass seed beads have been around since 200 B.C., as a favorite decorative tool for crafters and artisans alike. First popular in India, then, later, in Africa and South East Asia, seed beads were used to create jewelry designs and woven textiles that reflected the taste of each culture. Beads were also used to express social or marital status, political or religious affiliations, and personal tastes. Girls in Kenya, for instance, exchanged wooden bead necklaces for those made from colorful seed beads to signify they were of marrying age, while Indonesians believed costumes made of durable glass gave the wearer the power of strength.

As trade routes expanded beyond Europe and the Far East, the seed bead grew in popularity. In 1492, when Columbus discovered modern day America, glass seed beads were among the many items transported by his fleet. With their range of splendid colors and eye-catching ability to reflect light, these small, glass adornments soon replaced the porcupine quill American Indian tribes had used to decorate their traditional dress. During the 17th century, the beads became a prominent item on the international trade circuit, and were traded for such valuables as gold, slaves, African ivory, and American furs, according to *The History of Beads* **(Harry N. Abrams, Inc., 1987).**

—Melissa Nachatelo

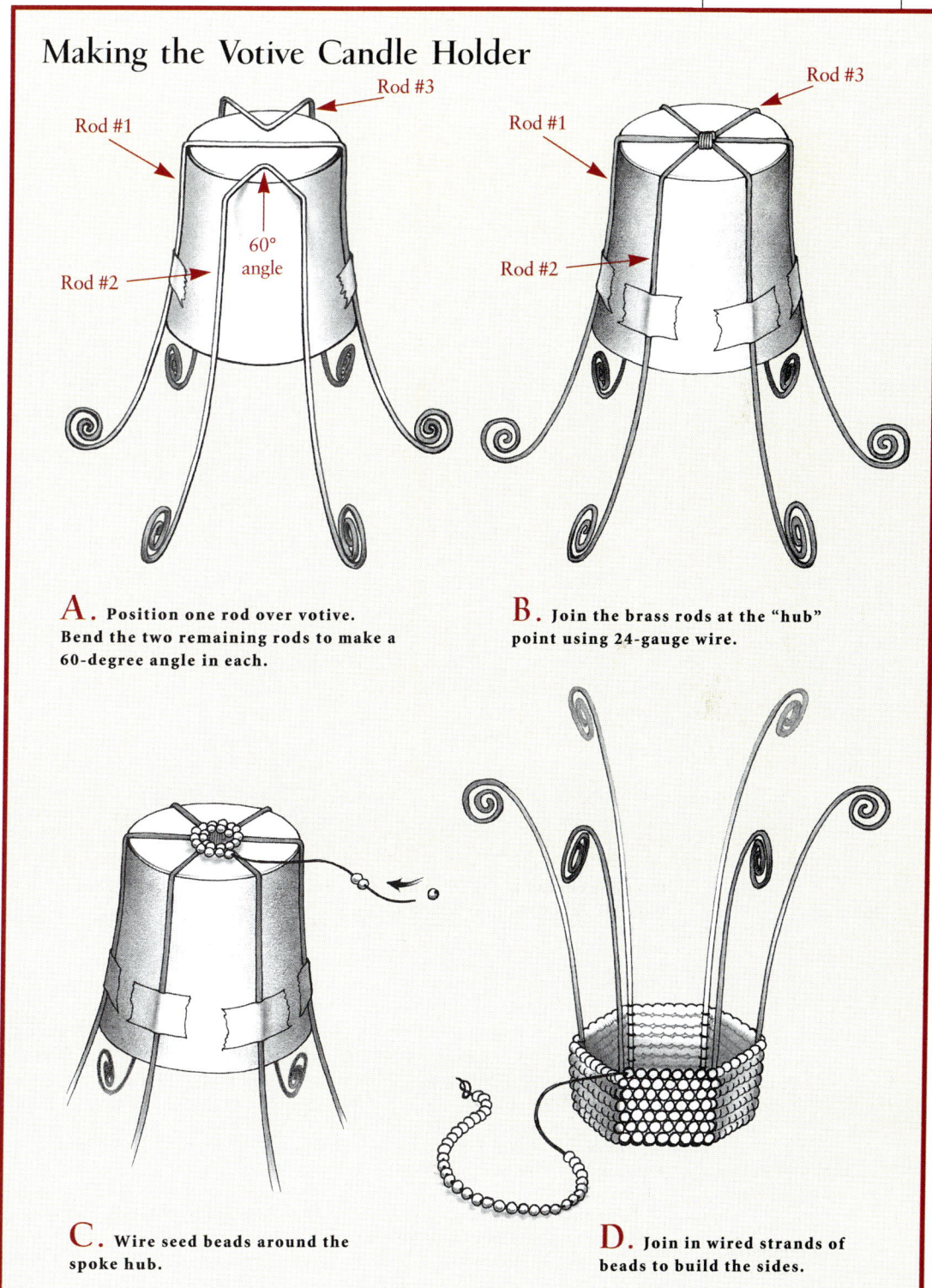

Making the Votive Candle Holder

A. Position one rod over votive. Bend the two remaining rods to make a 60-degree angle in each.

B. Join the brass rods at the "hub" point using 24-gauge wire.

C. Wire seed beads around the spoke hub.

D. Join in wired strands of beads to build the sides.

HOME DECORATING

The Best Way to Make 12-Point Glitter Stars

Connect three sets of chipboard triangles for the perfect star every time.

BY MICHIO RYAN

These sparkling, three-dimensional stars have a variety of holiday uses. Create a centerpiece with several different-sized stars, use one as a tree topper, or hang them as ornaments.

COLOR PHOTOGRAPHY:
Carl Tremblay

ILLUSTRATION:
Michael Gellatly

STYLING:
Ritch Holben

THIS 12-POINTED STAR SEEMED overwhelming to make—until I broke it down into its basic geometric components. Each star requires twelve equal-sized chipboard triangles, fabric-covered florist stems, and glue. To give the stars a festive look, I covered them with gold microfine glitter.

I started by cutting twelve triangles from the chipboard, then glued the base of the four triangles to a florist stem. Then I bent the stem into a square, which forms a four-pronged structure. When I glued three of these four-pronged structures together, the result was a three-dimensional star with an open center.

This open design greatly reduces the number of sides that need to be cut: a 12-sided star with a solid core would require 36 pieces. The tradeoff, however, is a weaker structure. To remedy this, I glued the star points and florist stem together with Beacon FabricTac glue, which sticks instantly but is neater than a hot-glue gun.

When selecting glitter, look for microfine-grade glitter. This is especially important if you plan to use the stars as a tabletop or mantel decoration because microfine glitter gives a more refined sparkle at close range than glitter with larger particles.

INSTRUCTIONS

1. *Cut out twelve star points.* Using pencil and steel ruler, draft one star-cutting diagram per star on 2-ply chipboard. Lay marked chipboard on cutting mat. Using X-Acto knife and steel ruler, cut on marked lines to make twelve star points. For use as tree ornament, use awl to pierce hole in tip of one point.

2. *Join star points to florist stems.* Cut 5" strip of masking tape for each small star, 9" strip for large star. Lay tape flat, sticky side up. Line up four star points along tape, ½" in from long edge; trim excess tape at each end. Using wire cutters, cut 6" florist stem for each small star, and 10" florist stem for large star. Lay stem on tape, butting it against short edge of points and allowing 1" of stem to extend at each end. Use chipboard spatula to apply Aleene's glue along length of stem. Fold tape up onto points, trapping stem inside (*see* illustration A, next page). Use X-Acto knife to trim out excess tape between points.

MATERIALS

Yields one 11" (large) and four 5½" (small) stars

- 0.65 ounces microfine glitter
- 2 ounces metallic acrylic craft paint (to match glitter)
- 9" x 13" piece 2-ply chipboard
- Six 18" fabric-covered florist stems
- 1"-wide masking tape
- Aleene's Thick Designer Tacky glue
- Beacon FabricTac glue
- White craft glue
- Button thread
- Spray sealer

You'll also need:
star-cutting diagrams (*see* page 46); X-Acto knife; self-healing cutting mat; steel ruler; scissors; wire cutters; tweezers; 1" flat soft-bristled brush; pencil; sheet of white copier paper; and newsprint.

Other items, if necessary:
awl, pin, and nylon or decorative cord (for using star as a hanging ornament).

Making the Glitter Stars

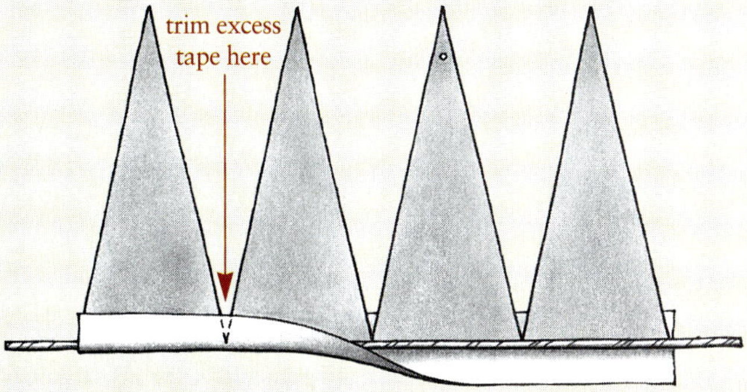

A. Tape and glue four star points to a florist stem. (trim excess tape here)

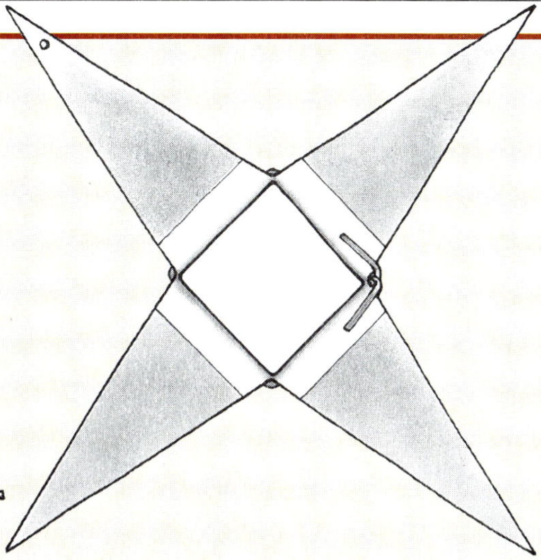

B. Bend the stem into a square to make a flattened, four-prong star.

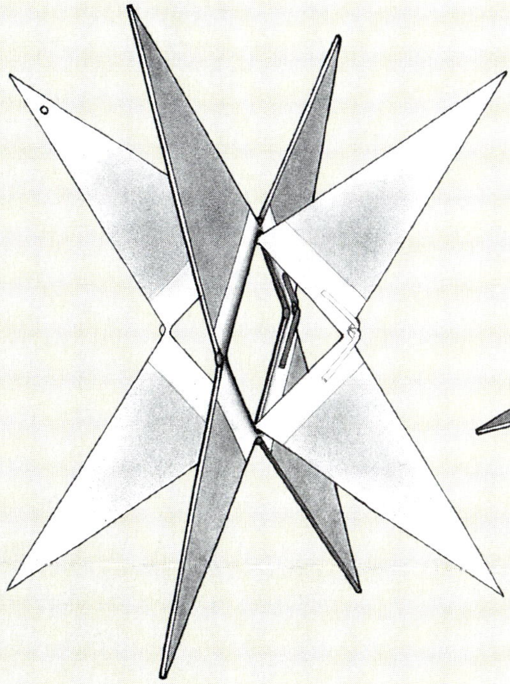

C. Join two of the flattened stars together...

D. ...then add a third and final flattened star to complete the design.

DESIGNER'S TIPS

- For a faceted effect, coat one side of each triangle with gold and the other side with silver. To create a new color of glitter, combine two colors. You can make pale lavender glitter, for instance, by mixing purple and silver glitter.

- For a more festive display, wind strings of miniature tree lights loosely around the stars. This will highlight their latticelike, open design.

Repeat process to make three four-point stems per star.

3. *Join stems to make star.* Bend stem to form simple star with square opening in middle (illustration B); twist and lap wire ends to secure. Bend second stem in same way, shape it around star, and twist wire ends together (illustration C). Repeat process to join third stem around first two; stagger twisted joins to avoid excess bulk at any one bend (illustration D). Trim, then tape over wire ends to conceal. Tie button thread around wobbly joins to stabilize them. Seal all joins with Beacon glue. Let dry overnight. Repeat process for remaining stars.

4. *Paint star and apply glitter.* Protect work surface with newsprint. Using soft-bristled brush, apply metallic paint to entire star surface, including edges. Let dry 20 minutes. Clean brush. Brush ordinary white glue over entire star surface. Hold star with tweezers over copier paper and sprinkle with glitter, turning star until all surfaces are covered. When through, crease white paper and funnel excess glitter back into container. Repeat process to paint and glue glitter to each star, cleaning brush in between painting and gluing steps as necessary. Let dry 1 hour. To discourage glitter from shedding, apply spray sealer following manufacturer's instructions. To use hanging hole, poke glitter from hole with pin and thread with nylon or decorative cord. ◆

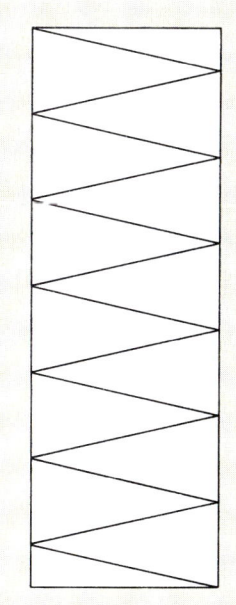

DIAGRAMS
See page 46 for pattern pieces and enlargement instructions.

GIFTS

Pleated Wire Mesh Night-Light
Fold wire mesh into accordion pleats, then accent one edge with faceted glass beads.

BY LILY FRANKLIN

MATERIALS
- Night-light with 4-watt bulb
- 1 square foot brass 60 x 60 grade wire mesh
- Faceted glass beads in the following colors and sizes:
  10 round 8mm amethyst
  10 round 6mm moss green
  5 oval 5mm red
  5 diamond 7mm pink
- Ten 2" brass head pins
- Ten 8mm brass jump rings

You'll also need: old scissors; needle-nose pliers with wire cutters; round-nose pliers; awl; tweezers; hardwood block; craft stick; grid ruler; and pencil.

COLOR PHOTOGRAPHY:
Carl Tremblay

ILLUSTRATION:
Michael Gellatly

STYLING:
Ritch Holben

For variation on this design, substitute silver-colored mesh, or brightly-colored translucent 4-watt Christmas tree bulbs.

INSTRUCTIONS

1. *Prefold brass mesh.* Using grid ruler and pencil, mark 3½" x 10½" rectangle on brass mesh. Cut out rectangle with scissors. Measuring from one short edge, draft ten parallel lines 1" apart across rectangle. Lightly fold mesh on marked lines, working on one side only (do not accordion-fold) and stopping ½" from long edges. Turn mesh over. To make accordion folds, bring adjacent folds together and crease lightly, again stopping ½" from edges.

2. *Complete folds and pierce holes.* Fold each long edge of brass mesh 3/16" toward one side (the inside), and crease firmly with craft stick. Recrease accordion folds firmly, this time going out to edges. Set mesh on wooden block. Using awl, pierce ten holes along top edge, one at each inside fold, through both layers of mesh (*see* illustration A, below) to create hanging holes for beads.

3. *Assemble shade.* Using scissors, trim scant 1/16" from each short end. Bring short ends together, drawing mesh into star-shaped tube (illustration B). To join two ends, open up folds at top and bottom of one end, overlap ends, then refold top and bottom edges, crimping firmly so star holds shape.

4. *Join beads to shade.* On each head pin, thread three beads. On remaining five pins, thread one green, one pink, and one amethyst bead. Clip pins ½" beyond amethyst bead. Using round-nose pliers, shape remaining part of pin into eyelet. Using tweezers and needle-nose pliers, open jump ring, slip ring through eyelet and pierced hole, and close jump ring. Join remaining bead drops to shade in same way, alternating colors (illustration C). Slip shade over bulb. ◆

IF YOU USE NIGHT-LIGHTS IN YOUR home, you know how plain and boring most hardware store varieties can be. This simple replacement shade, assembled from wire mesh and faceted beads, can transform your nighttime lighting in just minutes.

The technology involved is simple: I removed the light's plastic shade and replaced it with a pleated, springy sleeve that fits over the bulb. The sleeve is made from 60 x 60 grade wire mesh, which is stiff enough to hold the springiness in the folded pleats. I punched holes along the top edge using an awl, then decorated the edge with transparent glass beads.

There are several important considerations to keep in mind when selecting your night-light or examining existing lights for retrofitting. The shade should be easily removable so the project can be slipped over the bulb. After removing the shade, check the collar area to be certain that the bulb socket has no exposed metal rim, which could come in contact with the metal shade and pose the threat of shock. The bulb should also screw in far enough so that its metal contact is not exposed. Last but not least, consider the distance between the night-light and the electrical wall socket: 1" is ideal.

Lily Franklin is a designer living in Albuquerque, New Mexico.

Making the Night-Light Shade

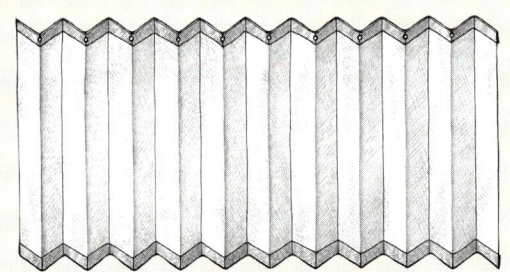

A. Make accordion folds in a rectangle of brass mesh, then pierce holes along the top edge.

B. Bring the short ends together to form a star-shaped cylinder.

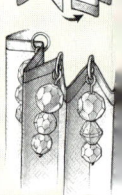

C. Add ten beaded drops around the top edge of the shade.

PATTERNS

Christmas 1997 Patterns

Heirloom Angel Tree Topper

(*see* article, page 26)

NOTE: PHOTOCOPY WINGS AND ROBE AT 200%.
PHOTOCOPY TORSO AT 100%.

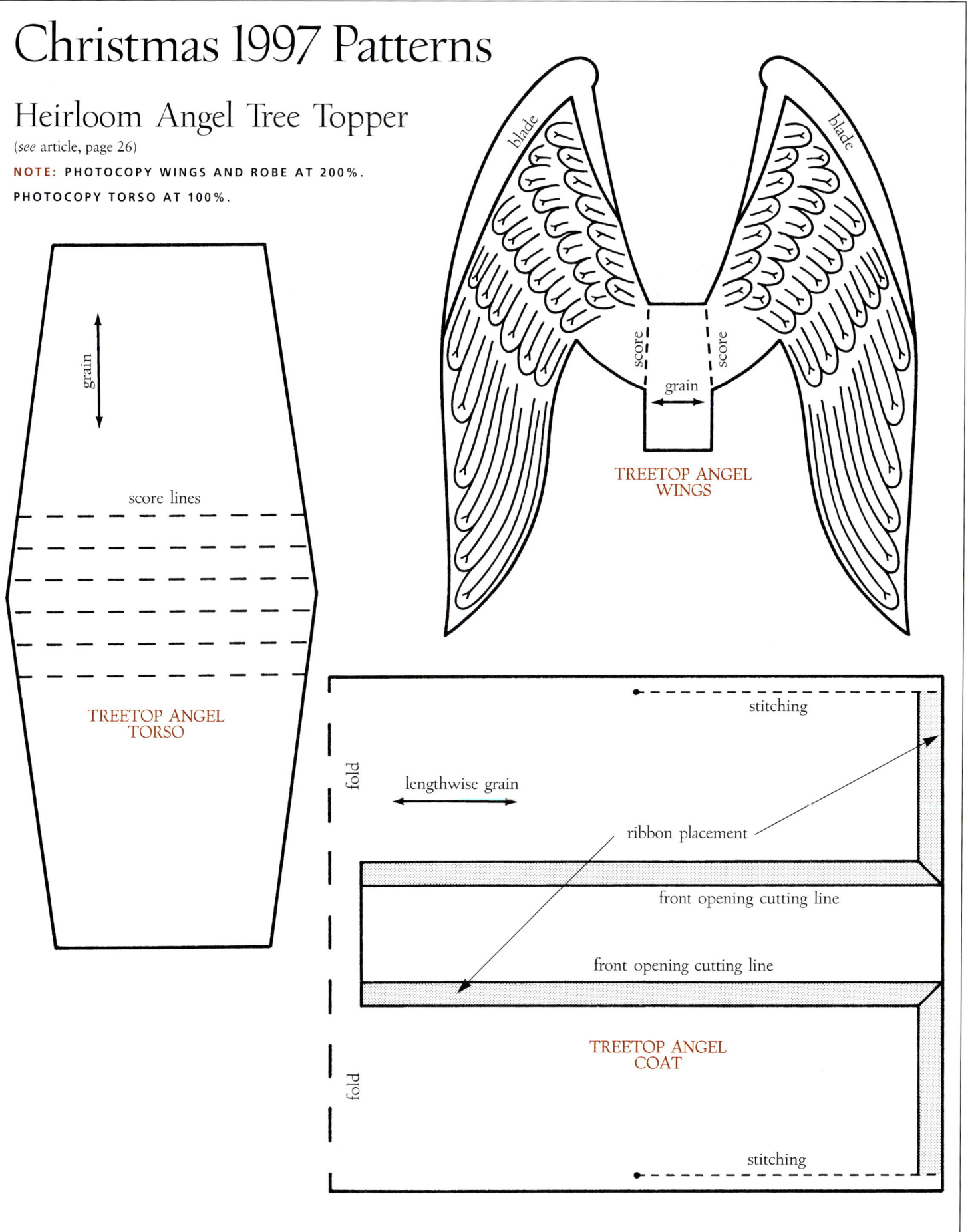

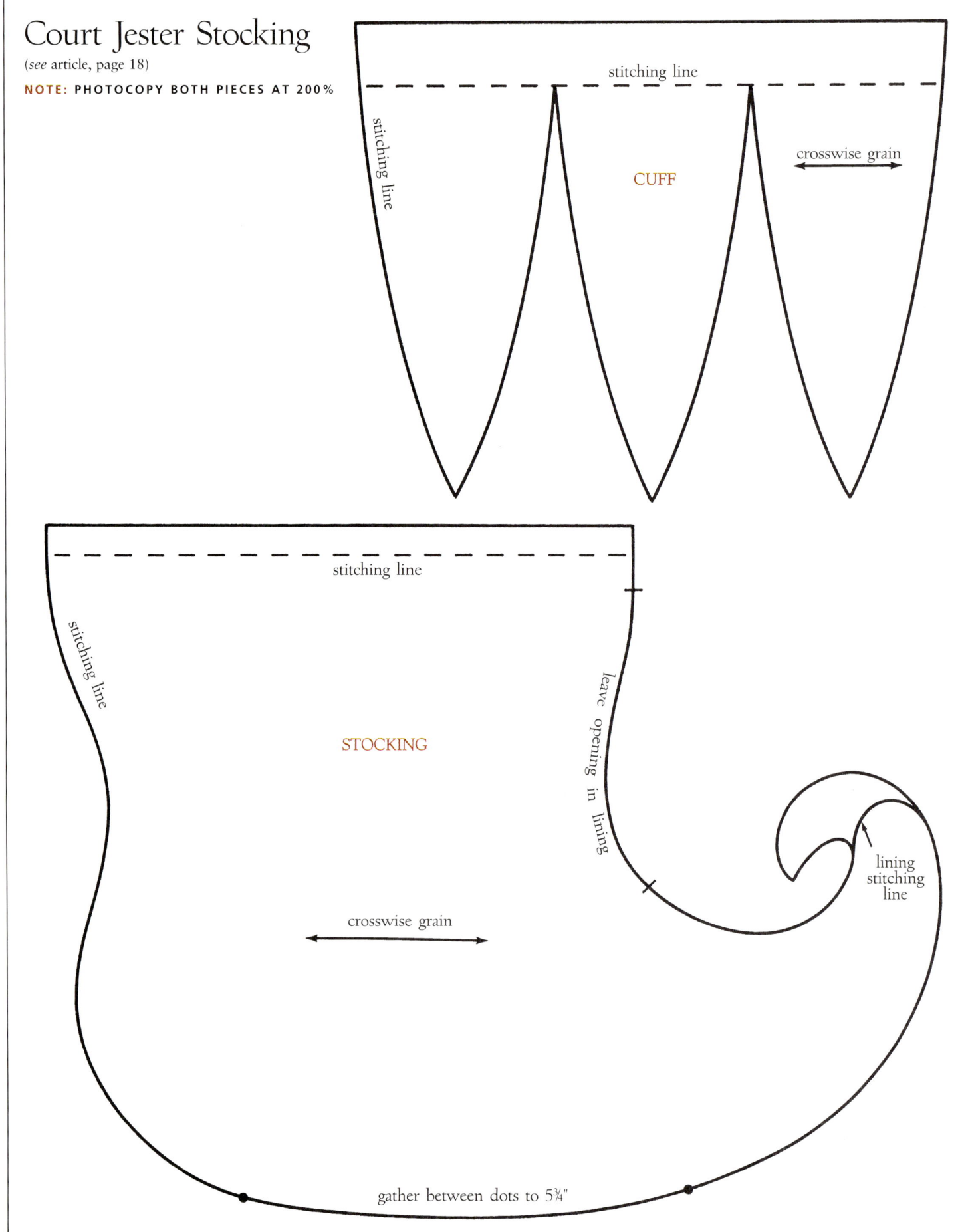

PATTERNS

Gilded Gingerbread Cookies
(*see* article, page 22)
NOTE: PHOTOCOPY TEMPLATE AT 100%

GINGERBREAD TEMPLATE

Keepsake Silver Bird Ornament
(*see* article, page 13)
NOTE: PHOTOCOPY BOTH PIECES AT 100%

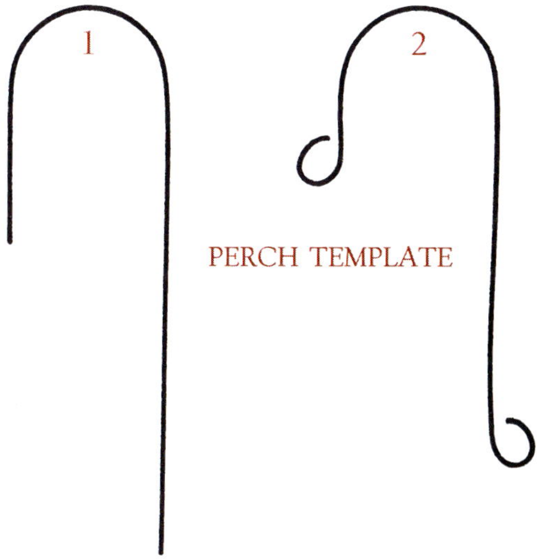

1   2

PERCH TEMPLATE

Court Jester Stocking
(*see* article, page 18)
NOTE: PHOTOCOPY INSOLE AT 200%

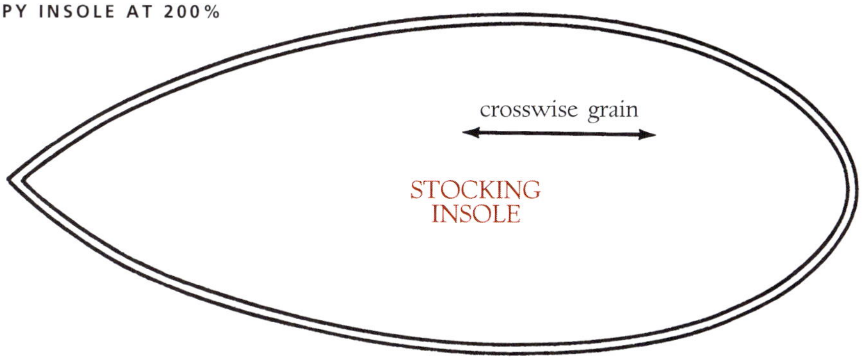

crosswise grain

STOCKING INSOLE

CHRISTMAS 1997 • HANDCRAFT ILLUSTRATED   45

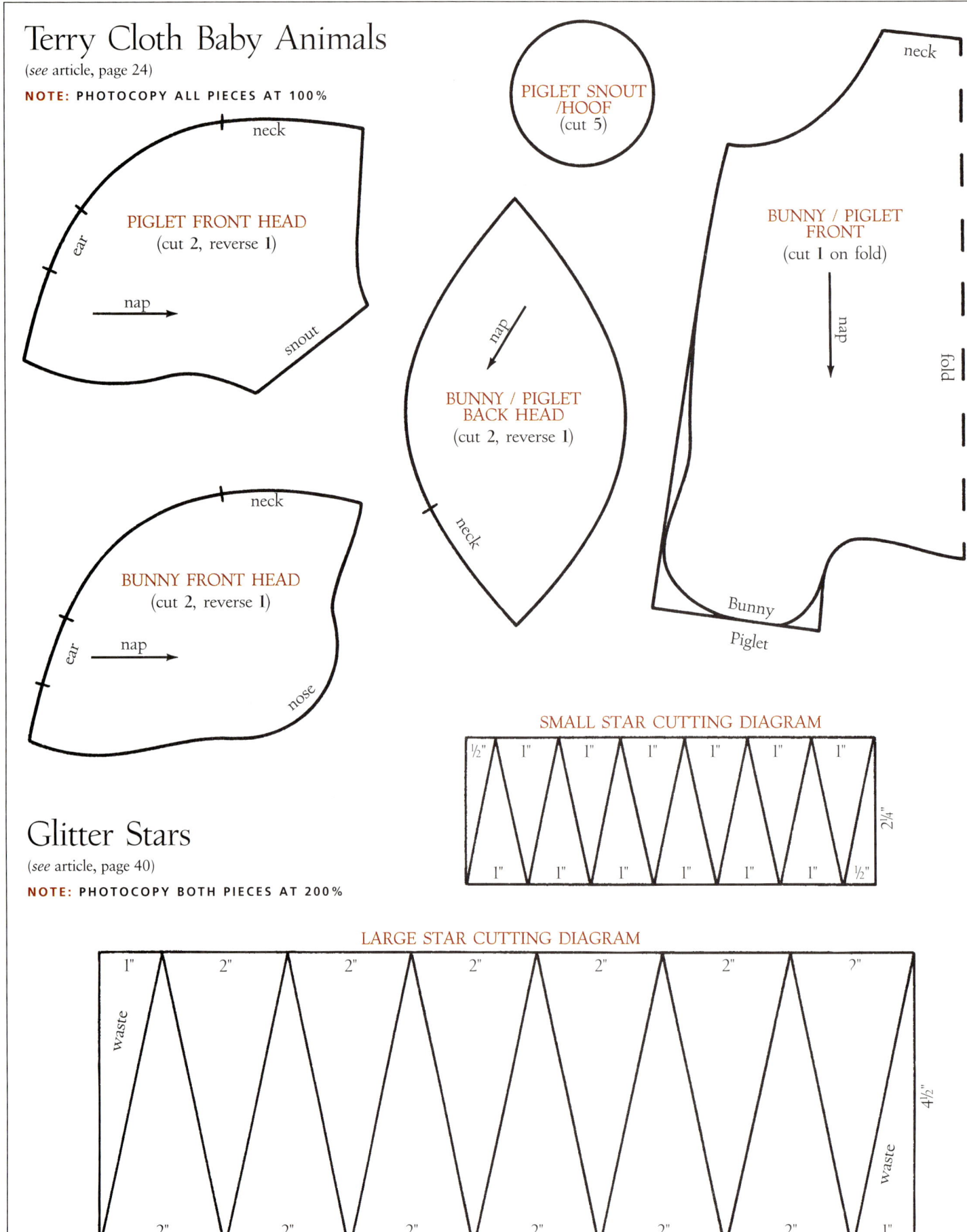

Terry Cloth Baby Animals

(see article, page 24)

NOTE: PHOTOCOPY ALL PIECES AT 100%

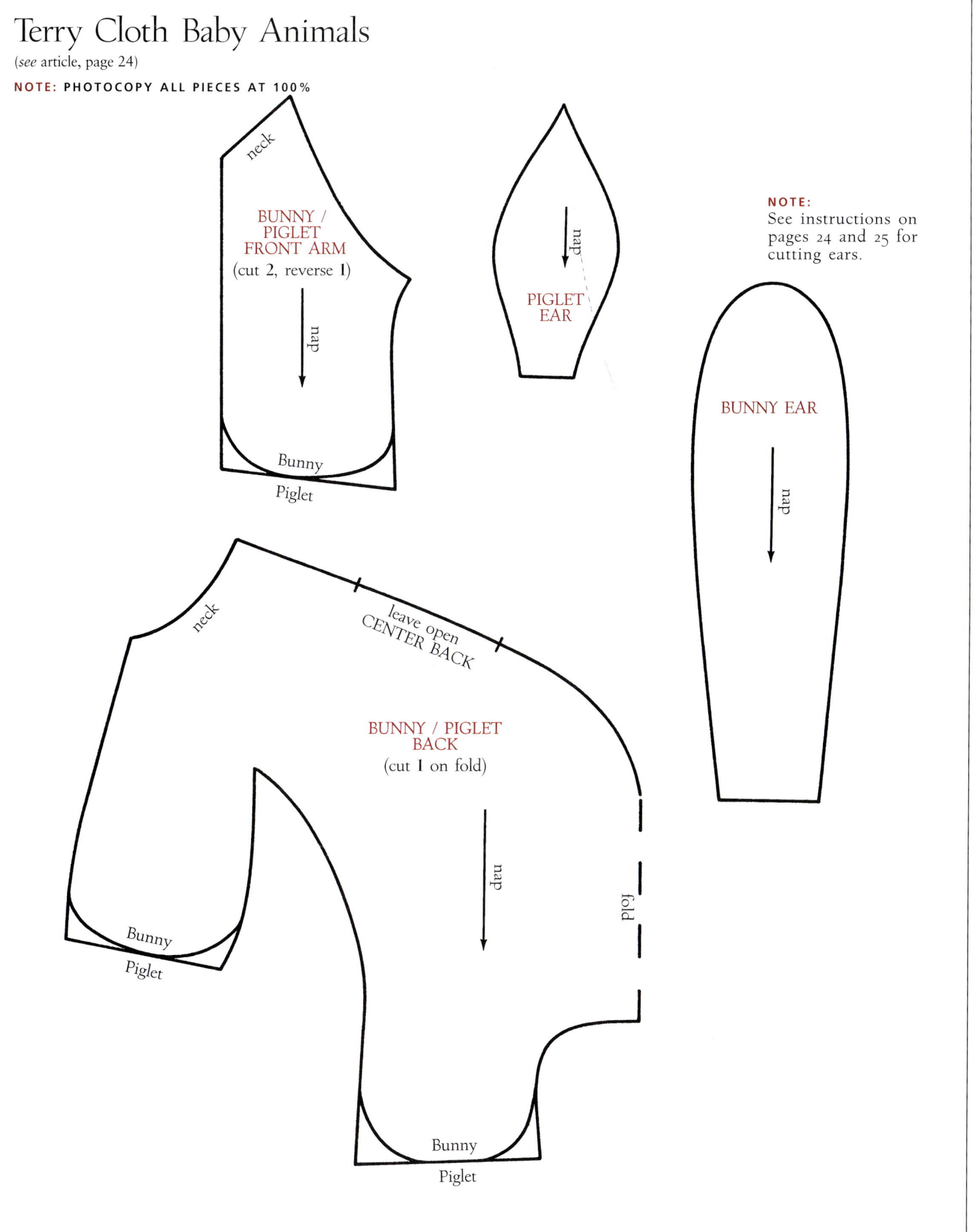

Sources & Resources

The following are specific mail-order sources for particular items, arranged by article.

Most of the materials used in this issue are available at your local craft supply store, florist, fabric shop, hardware store, or bead and jewelry supply. Generic craft supplies can be ordered from such catalogs as Craft King, Dick Blick Art Materials, Newark Dressmaker Supply, Pearl Paint Company, or Sunshine Discount Crafts. The following are specific sources for harder-to-find items, arranged by article. The suggested retail prices listed here were current at press time. Contact the suppliers directly to confirm prices and availability.

Perfect Gift, page 7
Coating chocolate starting at $2.99 per pound from Sweet Celebrations Inc.

Easy Sachets in Six Steps, page 8
Four-ounce units of lavender for $2, rose petals for $1.27, balsam fir needles for $1.42, and fragrance oils starting at $3 per ounce, all from San Francisco Herb Co. Lavender dupioni silk starting at $2.49 per ¼ yard and organza starting at $2.56 per ¼ yard from Super Silk, Inc. Rose dupioni silk from $14 per yard from G-Street Fabrics. Sage dupioni silk starting at $14.95 per yard from B&J Fabrics.

Folded Paper Sleeves, page 10
Medium to heavy-weight art paper starting at $2.50 per package from Sax Arts & Crafts.

Keepsake Silver Bird Ornament, page 13
Birds starting at $2.05 from Craft King. Delta Renaissance Foil kit (Burnished Silver) for $8.99 from Alpine Imports.

Four-Panel Screen, page 14
Four 7-x-13-inch wooden panels (# 20-9650) for $7.75 each from Viking Woodcraft.

A New Use For Rubber Stamps, page 16
Copper leaf for $9.19 per 25 sheets from Sax Arts & Crafts.

Freestanding Court Jester Stocking, page 18
Dark green dupioni silk for $9.95 per yard from Super Silk, Inc. Ultra-loft batting available through Fairfield Processing.

Christmas Crackers, page 20
Ten cracker snaps for $3 from Coffee Break Designs. Three mailing tubes with end caps for $3.25 and 10 snaps for $3.25 from Impress.

Jeweled Cage Ornament, page 21
Faceted glass beads starting at 15 cents from Beadworks.

Gilded Gingerbread Cookies, page 22
Luster Dust for $3.99 per 2-gram bottle, edible glitter for $2.25 per ¼-ounce bottle, gold dragées $3.95 per 2-ounce bag, and 2-ounce plastic squeeze bottles with couplers for $2.25, all from Home Cake Decorating Supply Co.

Terry Cloth Baby Animals, page 24
Two-pound bag of poly-pellets from Fairfield Processing.

Angel Tree Topper, page 26
Angel head and hands set starting at $2.85 from Craft King.

Frosted Glitter Martini Glasses, page 29
Armour Etch's "Glass Etching Cream" for $5.50 per 3-ounce bottle from Eastern Art Glass.

Brushed Steel Frame, page 30
Aluminum tooling foil starting at $6.35 per 10-foot-roll from Dick Blick.

Sheet Wax Candles, page 32
Flat wax or honeycomb sheets (8 x 16-inch) starting at $2.99 per sheet (12 sheet minimum) from The Barker Company.

Silk Ribbon Tassel, page 34
Five-eighth-inch wood candle cup for 8 cents, 1¼-inch candle cup for 16 cents, and ¾-inch wood wheel for 7 cents from Craft Catalog.

Zippered Purses, page 36
Seven-inch zipper for 45 cents and 9-inch zipper for 55 cents from Newark Dressmaker Supply.

Beaded Votive, page 38
Brass rod starting at 80 cents from Special Shapes Catalog Division.

Glitter Stars, page 42
Aleene's Thick Designer Tackyglue for $2.15 per 4-ounce jar from Craft King.

Mesh Night-Light, page 42
Brass mesh for $11 per sheet, 2-inch long capped-end wires for $1.25 per dozen, and 8mm faceted amethyst/aubergine beads for $3.50 per strand, all from Metalliferous. Gold-tone clip rings (¼-inch diameter) for $1 per bag and 7mm pink, diamond-shaped beads for 50 cents each from Toho Shoji.

Quick Projects, page 49
Red or green 18-gauge aluminum wire for $6.75 for 10 feet and gold metal bead for 50 cents from Metalliferous. Crinkled organza for $2.56 per ¼ yard from Super Silk, Inc.

The following companies are mentioned in the listing above. Contact each individually for a price list or catalog.

ALPINE IMPORTS
7104 N. Alpine Road, Rockford, IL 61111; 800-654-6114

B&J FABRICS
263 West 40th Street, New York, NY 10018: 212-354-8150

THE BARKER COMPANY
15106 10th Avenue S.W., Seattle, WA 98166; 800-543-0601

BEADWORKS, INC.
149 Water Street, Norwalk, CT 06854; 203-852-9108

COFFEE BREAK DESIGNS
P.O. Box 34281, Indianapolis, IN 46234; (317) 290-1542

CRAFT CATALOG
P.O. Box 1069, Reynoldsburg, Ohio 43068; 800-777-1442

DICK BLICK ART MATERIALS
P.O. Box 1267, Galesburg, IL 61402-1267; 800-933-2542

FAIRFIELD PROCESSING CORP.
Call 800-243-0989 for retail suppliers in your area.

G-STREET FABRICS
Mail-Order Service, 12240 Wilkins Avenue, Rockville, MD 20852; 800-333-9191

HOME CAKE DECORATING SUPPLY CO.
9514 Roosevelt Way N.E, Seattle, WA 98115; 206-522-4300

IMPRESS
120 Andover Park East, Tukwila, WA 98188; 206-901-9101

METALLIFEROUS
34 West 46th Street, New York, NY 10036; 888-944-0909

NEWARK DRESSMAKER SUPPLY
6473 Ruch Road, P.O. Box 20730, Lehigh Valley, PA 18002-0730; 610-837-7500

PEARL PAINT COMPANY, INC.
308 Canal Street, New York, NY 10003; 800-451-7327 (catalog) or 800-221-6845 x2297 (main store)

SAN FRANCISCO HERB CO.
250 14th Street, San Francisco, CA 94103; 800-227-4530

SAX ARTS & CRAFTS
P.O. Box 510710, New Berlin, WI 53151; 800-558-6696

SPECIAL SHAPES CATALOG DIVISION
P.O. Box 7487, Romeoville, IL 60446-0487; 800-517-4273

SUNSHINE DISCOUNT CRAFTS
P.O. Box 301, Largo, FL 34649-0301; 800-729-2878

SUPER SILK, INC.
P.O. Box 527596, Flushing, NY 11352; 800-432-7455

SWEET CELEBRATIONS INC.
P.O. Box 39426, Edina, MN 55439-0426; 800-328-6722

TOHO SHOJI
990 6th Avenue, New York, NY 10018; 212-868-7466

VIKING WOODCRAFTS, INC.
1317 8th Street S.E., Waseca, MN 56093; 800-328-0116 ◆

Quick Projects

Dress up your holiday gifts in just minutes using these contemporary decorations.

Package decorations shown clockwise from upper left: Looped bead, bowless ribbon, buttoned band, and spring wire.

DREAMING OF A WHITE PACKAGE

Out of wrapping paper? Never fear. You can "wrap" a plain box without using wrapping paper or ordinary bows. We substituted common craft materials such as buttons, elastic cord, and wire for a modern, upbeat look.

■ **Looped bead:** Cut a piece of elastic four times as long as box circumference. Loop one end of elastic four times through small gold doughnut, then tie closed and trim ends. Stretch loops out from gold doughnut until they all measure same length. Gather looped ends (opposite small gold doughnut) into point, and thread point through green bead and large gold disk. Push bead and disk up to small gold doughnut, then maneuver knot of elastic to hide it inside small gold doughnut. Slip elastic loops over box to hold it closed.

■ **Bowless ribbon:** Cut a 1¼"-diameter disk from lid of plastic food container. Punch four holes in square pattern on disk using hole puncher. Fold a 1-yard strip of 1¼"-wide ribbon 3" from end, roll fold into point, and thread it through one hole in disk. Rethread through same hole, leaving 2" loop of ribbon behind. Insert ribbon loop on underside, then rethread as before. Repeat process to form eight loops of ribbon (four on each side of disk). Pull underside set of loops around edge of disk, so all eight loops are pointing in same direction. Tie ¼"-wide gold elastic into two loops, then tie in secure knot. Position disk on box, then slip elastic over box to hold disk in place. Puff loops of ribbon to hide knot in elastic and plastic disk.

■ **Buttoned band:** Run ribbon around box, then tape in place on underside. Working at top of box, gather center of ribbon with knotted piece of thread. Secure button on top with hot-glue.

■ **Spring wire:** Cut one piece each of green and red aluminum wire that measure twice box circumference. Wrap wires around opposite sides of box, then join together at box top. Thread 1"-diameter metal bead onto wires and cinch it close to box top. To create coiling on wire ends, wrap each wire around a pencil six or seven times. ◆

COLOR PHOTOGRAPHY:
Carl Tremblay

DESIGN:
Michio Ryan

STYLING:
Ritch Holben

Pressed Tin Mirror Frame

Start with a 24" tin ceiling tile. Using tinsnips, cut an "X" in the middle of the tile, using the embossed pattern as a guide. To form the frame opening, bend the four triangular flaps to the wrong side and hammer them flat with a mallet. Clip diagonally into each outside corner to define the four outer corners of the frame, then hammer back the resulting triangular flaps. Hammer three of the edges over a 3/8"-thick piece of plywood to form a boxy channel. Hammer the fourth edge flat. Slide a 1/4"-thick mirror into the channels from the open end. Attach a cord to the open end for hanging.

COLOR PHOTOGRAPHY: **Carl Tremblay**   DESIGN AND STYLING: **Ritch Holben**